Informal Ambassadors

NEW STUDIES IN U.S. FOREIGN RELATIONS

Mary Ann Heiss, editor

Informal Ambassadors

American Women,
Transatlantic Marriages,
and
Anglo-American Relations, 1865–1945

❧

Dana Cooper

The Kent State University Press
Kent, Ohio

Library of Congress Catalog Card Number 2013049035
ISBN 978-1-60635-214-4
Manufactured in the United States of America

LIBRARY OF CONGRESS CATALOGING-IN-PUBLICATION DATA
Cooper, Dana, 1977–
Informal ambassadors : American women, transatlantic marriages, and
Anglo-American relations, 1865–1945 / Dana Cooper.
pages cm. — (New studies in U.S. foreign relations)
Includes bibliographical references and index.
ISBN 978-1-60635-214-4 (hardcover) ∞
1. United States—Foreign relations—Great Britain. 2. Great Britain—Foreign relations—
United States. 3. Politicians' spouses—Great Britain—History—19th century.
4. Politicians' spouses—Great Britain—History—20th century. 5. Women—Political
activity—Great Britain—History—20th century. 6. Women—Political activity—Great
Britain—History—20th century. 7. Aristocracy (Social class)—Great Britain—Biography.
8. Americans—Great Britain—Biography. I. Title.
E183.8.G7C78 2014
327.7304109'034—dc23
2013049035

18 17 16 15 14   5 4 3 2 1

for Noel

Once an Empire, now democratic,
Whose Emperors, always pragmatic,
Used political wedding
More than war for the spreading
Of Austria. (Most diplomatic.)
—Holger Martin

Let others wage war; you, happy Austria, marry!
—King Matthias Corvinus

Contents

Acknowledgments

Over a decade has passed since I first discovered transatlantic marriages as a master's student in the dusty plains of West Texas. Throughout the researching and writing process, I have been, and continue to be, rewarded with amazing life—first as a scholar, now as a wife, mother, and professor in the Piney Woods of East Texas. To say that I have acquired a few personal and professional debts along the way would be a tremendous understatement. I hope a few pages can come even close to expressing my gratitude for the opportunities that made this experience and book possible and adequately thank the faculty, friends, and family members who have made this road so incredible.

My love affair with history began at Angelo State University, whose dedicated history faculty introduced me to one beautiful story after another. There, John Wheeler talked me out of being a pediatrician, and Shirley Eoff made me love British history. I am indebted to both James Ward and James Siekmeier, who steered me toward diplomatic history. I can never thank these scholars enough for their commitment to their students and to me as a very young historian.

My years at Texas Tech University were brief but influential. To David Snead, I owe the genesis of this project. Paul Carlson, Alwyn Barr, Paul Deslandes, Aliza Wong, and Julie Willett offered critical instruction in what it meant to be a historian. Likewise, the inspirational faculty at Texas Christian University raised the bar even higher and helped me reach goals I sometimes thought impossible. Claire Sanders, Rebecca Sharpless, Sara Sohmer, Ken Stevens, and Steven Woodworth challenged me and served as tremendous role models. I especially thank Mark Gilderhus, who took me under his wing, showed me early on the importance of balancing family and work, and never failed to provide clarity on a personal and professional basis. His belief in me and in this project helped bring it to fruition.

Good colleagues and excellent friends abound at Stephen F. Austin State University, and I am most fortunate to be here. On a daily basis, I enjoy an energetic department, am surrounded by a terrific college, and work with truly amazing professors across the university. I am most thankful to my department chairs, Troy Davis and Mark Barringer, for their guidance and assistance and to early career mentors Randi Cox and Phil Catton, who taught me so much. Dean Brian Murphy, of the College of Liberal and Applied Arts, offered me countless opportunities, and Provost Ric Berry has provided tremendous professional support.

Special friends offered much needed encouragement: Perky Beisel, Kathleen Belanger, Lesa Beverly, Jill Carrington, Leslie Cecil, Karol Chandler-Ezell, Ken Collier, Ray Darville, Dianne Dentice, Karen Embry-Jenlink, Piero Fenci, Tracey Hasbun, Erika Hoagland, Joyce Johnston, Linda Levitt, Mike Martin, Christine McDermott, Darrel McDonald, John Moore, Jannah Nerren, Emmerentie Oliphant, Heather Olson-Beal, Jeana Paul-Urena, Amanda Rudolph, Paul Sandul, Tom Segady, Scott Sosebee, Louise Stoehr, Bob Szafran, Janet Tareilo, Mike Tkacik, Gail Weatherly, and Kimberly Welsh have made SFA a special place to live and work.

I am grateful, too, to dear friends and colleagues outside my home university. Kim Kato, James Hindman, and Megan Weatherly have offered great friendship and professional guidance for many years. Paul Boller, Frank Costigliola, Jessica Gienow-Hecht, and Kyle Longley each played a critical role in the early development of this project and offered much needed perspective. Early opportunities to publish with some notable historians and test the significance of transatlantic marriages marked important turning points for this book. I express great thanks to Charlotte Wallin, Daniel Silander, Kimberly Jensen, and Erika Kuhlam for their willingness and patience to afford me such chances. Catherine Allgor offered generous encouragement and remarkable advice to me when she did not need to or stand to benefit in any way; rarely do junior scholars experience such kindness. Her thoughts made this book a much better product. A special thanks goes to Claire Phelan for being an extraordinary historian, amazing colleague, and treasured friend through the best and worst of times. I shudder to think how different the past decade would have been without her and how much this project would have suffered had it not been for her candor in asking the hard questions, demanding the very best, and never doubting that this project would reach its conclusion.

My education and professional development have been inundated with good friends and great opportunities. None of it would have happened without the generous financial support of many institutions, organizations, and foundations. Early opportunities to present nationally and internationally were generously supported by the TCU AddRan College of Liberal Arts in addition to a host of research grants including the TCU graduate dean's travel grant, the Boller travel grant, the Boller/Worcester research grant, the Graduate Student Senate research grant, and a Nokia, Inc., research award. Key research trips were made possible by a research travel grant to the Herbert Hoover Presidential Library, a summer faculty research grant from SFA, and the Ruth R. & Alyson R. Miller Fellowship at the Massachusetts Historical Society. An added bonus of researching at the MHS was a wonderful friendship with Conrad Wright. Finally, a much-needed semester of leave provided by SFA allowed for an extended period of writing and reflection that benefitted this book immensely.

The Kent State University Press, including Susan Cash, Carol Heller, and Will Underwood, has been terrific to work with. Joyce Harrison was a consummate professional and kept me on task. I thank Erin Holman for her keen eye, kind support, and generous encouragement. I am so thankful to Ann Heiss; I cannot say enough about how eagerly she championed this project at a very early stage. She saw its potential and had the patience to help a rookie transform a dissertation into a book.

And I save my greatest thanks and appreciation for my family. Brenda Cooper, I thank you for willingness to move—literally and figuratively—into this crazy world we call academia and support this family every step of the way. Without her childcare and moral support, this book would have taken far longer to write. More important, my children are better people because of her time and love. Amory and Christian have never known a time that mommy wasn't talking about her London ladies, and they love me anyway. It's only fitting that I found my daughter's name (the old English version of *amore,* French for love) in old letters in an archive in Boston. And the scariest and best moments before my darling son was born occurred as I wrote the last version of the manuscript. Their entire lives have been intertwined with this book. What will they do without their "other" sibling?

But this book is dedicated the dearest man I have ever known and am so unbelievably lucky to call my husband. As I reflect on the circumstances that have brought Noel and me to this point, it comes as no surprise that our married life started almost exactly when I stumbled upon this project. We became engaged within days of my first reading that transatlantic marriages had doubtless influence upon transatlantic relations. As we planned our wedding, I was researching the nuptials and marriages of the women in this book. He married me anyway and embarked wholeheartedly on this adventure. I have had many doubts, but he never did. When I feared graduate school would never happen, he promised me he would make it happen, if necessary. Never I have I ever felt anything but absolute and unconditional love, support, and friendship from him. And he has never failed to make me laugh. He deserves much more credit and recognition than I could ever express here. But this book is as much his as it is mine. Without him, none of this may have ever happened. I would not have wanted to make this journey without him by my side.

Chronology

1836 Birth of Joseph Chamberlain, the son of a manufacturer, in Camberwell, London,

1837–1901 Victorian era, the reign of Queen Victoria

1849 Birth of Lord Randolph Henry-Spencer Churchill in Blenheim Palace, Oxfordshire, England

1854 Birth of Jennie Jerome, the eldest daughter of financier Leonard Jerome and his wife, Clara Hall, in Brooklyn, New York

1855 United States passes the Nationality Act, which states that American citizenship was based on a husband's nationality, not a wife's

1859 Birth of George Nathaniel Curzon in Kedleston Hall, Derbyshire, England

1861–65 American Civil War

1864 Birth of Mary Crowninshield Endicott, the daughter of William Crowninshield Endicott Sr., in Salem, Massachusetts

1870 Birth of Mary Victoria Leiter, the daughter of Levi Z. Leiter, in Chicago, Illinois

1871 Birth of Charles Richard John Spencer-Churchill, the 9th Duke of Marlborough

1874 Marriage of Jennie Jerome to Lord Randolph Churchill, son of the 7th Duke of Marlborough, making her Lady Randolph Churchill

   Lady Churchill gives birth to her first son, future British prime minister Winston Churchill

1877   Birth of Consuelo Vanderbilt the only daughter of William Kissam
        Vanderbilt and Alva Smith Vanderbilt, and the granddaughter of the
        shipping and railroad mogul, Cornelius Vanderbilt, in New York City

1879   Birth of Nancy Witcher Langhorne, daughter of Chiswell Dabney
        Langhorne and Nancy Witcher Keene, in Danville, Virginia

        Birth of William Waldorf Astor, the son of the extremely wealthy
        William Waldorf Astor and Mary Dahlgren Paul, in New York City

1880   Lady Churchill gives birth to her second son, John Strange Spencer-
        Churchill

1885–89 President Grover Cleveland appoints William Endicott, Mary's father,
        secretary of war

1887   British-American Fisheries Conference held in Washington, D.C.,
        attended by Joseph Chamberlain, chief plenipotentiary

1888   Secret engagement of Joseph Chamberlain and Mary Endicott in the
        spring

        Marriage of Mary Endicott to Joseph Chamberlain

1895–99 Venezuelan Boundary Dispute

1895   Marriage of Mary Victoria Leiter to George Nathaniel Curzon, the
        1st Marquess Curzon of Kedleston

        Marriage of Consuelo Vanderbilt to Charles Richard John Spencer-
        Churchill, the 9th Duke of Marlborough, making her the Duchess of
        Marlborough and Winston Churchill's cousin by marriage

        Death of Lord Randolph Churchill

1896   Mary Curzon gives birth to her first daughter, Mary Irene Curzon

1897   Marriage of Nancy Langhorne to Bostonian Robert Gould Shaw

1898   Curzon is appointed viceroy of India and created Baron Curzon of
        Kedleston; Mary becomes Baroness Curzon and vicereine of India

        Mary Curzon gives birth to her second daughter, Cynthia Blanche
        Curzon

        Nancy Langhorne Shaw gives birth to her first son, Robert Gould
        Shaw III

1898   Spanish-American War

1899–1902   Boer War (South Africa)

1899–1905   Lady Churchill founds and edits the *Anglo-Saxon Review*

1899   In response to the Boer War, Lady Churchill organizes the American
            Amazons

1900   Marriage of Lady Churchill to George Cornwallis-West

1901–10   Edwardian era, the reign of King Edward VII

1903   Divorce of Nancy Langhorne and Robert Gould Shaw

1904   Vicereine Curzon gives birth to her youngest daughter, Alexandra
            Naldera (Baba) Curzon

1905   Curzon resigns as viceroy of India

1906   Marriage of Nancy Langhorne to Waldorf Astor, making her Lady
            Waldorf Astor

            Following her death in London, Mary Curzon is buried the Curzon
            home at Kedleston.

            Separation of Consuelo and the Duke of Marlborough

1907   The United States passes the Expatriation Act: any American woman
            marrying a foreigner must assume the nationality of her husband
            and relinquish her American citizenship

            Lady Astor gives birth to her first child with Lord Astor, William Wal-
            dorf Astor, the 3rd Viscount Astor

1909   Lord Astor makes an unsuccessful bid for election to the House of
            Commons as a Conservative from a Plymouth constituency

            Lady Astor gives birth to her only daughter, Nancy Phyllis Louise Astor

1910–36   Georgian era, the reign of King George V

1910   Lord Astor wins a seat in the House of Commons.

1912   Separation of Lady Churchill and Cornwallis-West

            Lady Astor gives birth to Francis David Langhorne Astor

1914–18   World War I

1914   Divorce of Lady Churchill and Cornwallis-West

            Death of Joseph Chamberlain in London

1916   Lady Astor gives birth to Michael Langhorne Astor

        Marriage of Mary Endicott Chamberlain and Reverend William Hartley Carnegie

1917   Marriage of George Curzon and Grace Hinds, daughter of the U.S. minister to Brazil

1918   Marriage of Lady Churchill and Montague Phippen Porch, a member of the British Civil Service in Nigeria.

        Lady Astor gives birth to her youngest child, John Jacob Astor

1919   Lord Astor serves in the House of Commons until his father's death, when he becomes a Lord and thus a member of the House of Lords

        Lady Astor runs for and is elected to the seat Waldorf vacated

1920   With the Nineteenth Amendment, American women attain suffrage

1921   Divorce of Consuelo and the Duke of Marlborough

        Marriage of Consuelo and French lieutenant colonel Jacques Balsan

        Death of Lady Churchill; and burial in the Churchill plot at St. Martin's Churchyard, Bladon, Oxfordshire, England

1922   Lady Astor's seven-week speaking tour of the U.S., Canada, and England

        The United States passes the Cable Act, which states, "Any woman marrying an alien ineligible for citizenship shall cease to be an American citizen."

1924   Austen Chamberlain, Mary Endicott's stepson, becomes British foreign secretary

1925   Death of George Curzon in London

1926   Annulment of the Vanderbilt-Marlborough marriage

1928   Suffrage granted to all British women over twenty-one years of age through the Representation of the People Act

1931   The United States amends the Cable Act to allow American women to retain their citizenship after marrying aliens ineligible for American citizenship

1936   Death of Reverend William Carnegie

1937   Neville Chamberlain, Mary Endicott's stepson, becomes prime minister

1945   Lady Astor leaves Parliament at her husband's urging

        The United States' War Brides Act is passed

1952   Death of Lord Astor, after which Lady Astor largely withdraws from public life

1953   *The Glitter and the Gold,* Consuelo Balsan's insightful but not entirely candid autobiography, ghostwritten by Stuart Preston, is published

1956   Death of Jacques Balsan

1957   Death of Mary Endicott Chamberlain Carnegie at Lennox Gardens, London, England, and burial in Westminster Abbey

1964   Death of Lady Astor at Grimsthorpe, in Lincolnshire, England, and burial at Cliveden

        Death of Consuelo Balsan in Southampton, Long Island, New York, and burial in Saint Martin's Churchyard, Bladon, Oxfordshire

Introduction

An Extraordinary Galaxy of American Women

> Let's simply recognize that anyone following [Secretary of State Hillary] Clinton will have very big pumps to fill.
>
> —ANNE-MARIE SLAUGHTER

The position of women within the field of diplomacy has changed significantly in recent years. Three recent U.S. secretaries of state—Madeleine Albright, Condoleezza Rice, and Hillary Rodham Clinton—have been women. As evidence of the last's worldwide influence, the so-called Hillary effect has been cited as opening doors for women as diplomats, at home and abroad, as more women serve as representatives to and for the United States than ever before. In 2010, some twenty-five female ambassadors—an all-time high—were posted in Washington, D.C. While women remain a conspicuous minority of the nearly two hundred accredited ambassadors in the nation's capital, the five-fold increase of female ambassadors to the United States since the late 1990s is remarkable. Furthermore, more than forty women currently represent the United States to other nations. The sudden increase has been described as its own diplomatic coup.[1]

The world has remarked repeatedly upon the impressive trio of American women who have recently served as secretaries of state. Their individual and collective power in advancing American interests and championing women's rights has not gone unnoticed at home or overseas, by men or women, young or old. One American teenager recently asked his reporter mother, "You mean a *man* can be secretary of state?" Barely a decade after Madeleine Albright became the first female U.S. secretary of state, the position was described as "the women's spot—a safe expected place for women to be." Anne-Marie Slaughter, professor of politics and international affairs at Princeton University and former director of policy planning for the State Department, argues that "women are particularly well-suited to nurturing relationships, marshaling cooperation and conducting tough negotiations," thus, making them ideal for diplomatic endeavors. "Given that women are far less likely to be able to use coercive power than men are," observes Slaughter, "we have been skilled for centuries at getting others to want what we want."[2] Thus, if we pursue the premise that truly adept diplomats are masters of the so-called art of letting you have my way, then the majority of, if not all, diplomats should be women.

And yet, that Secretaries Albright, Rice, and Clinton are women still garnered considerable attention, highlighting a latent underpinning of diplomacy, to wit, that while women might be ideally suited for diplomatic *work,* their fitness as diplomatic *leaders* remains dubious. "Women's traditional, unpaid work," Katherine Hughes maintains, "was and is necessary to the practice of diplomacy abroad and because of this that work was coopted by the institution."[3] Until 1972, the Foreign Service forced female officers to resign their posts following matrimony; at the same time, it encouraged men to marry. Not only did marriage ostensibly make a man a more stable, dependable employee, his wife became an unofficial asset to his career.[4] A woman's work inside the home—tending to details in the alleged private sphere—made it possible for her husband to pursue the official side of diplomacy outside of the home.[5] Thus, because diplomatic wives were busy performing such important, but "informal," tasks as organizing dinners, supervising the staff and/or servants, calling on the wives of other leaders, and socializing on an unofficial level with local acquaintances, male diplomats could devote their full attentions to the formal aspect—mediation and negotiating—of their job as international liaisons. The conceptions of man/woman, public/private, and formal/informal diplomacy as opposites remained fixtures of the collective mind at the State Department well into the twentieth century.

Such conceptions about the suitability of men's *abilities* and women's *activities* have long gone unquestioned within the diplomatic world. As Joan Scott asserts, "gender becomes a way of denoting 'cultural constructions'—the entirely social creation of ideas about appropriate roles for women and men . . . [and] is a way of referring to the exclusively social origins of the subjective identities of men and women."[6] Thus, sex differences determined what role a man or woman could assume within the diplomatic world; consequently, a gendered categorization determined their respective poli-social tasks.[7]

Rarely have wives played such intimate roles as they have in diplomacy and foreign affairs, and yet remained so overlooked.[8] Historian Catherine Allgor argues, "The diplomat's work is more like the classic stereotype of women's work—subtle, diffuse, contingent, dependent on the intuitive reading of character. . . . Such realities of diplomatic life make the study of gender in this context particularly profitable."[9] This perspective may help explain why historians seldom consider the informal side of diplomacy in general, and wives in particular, which stems from the reality that entertaining and related efforts are exceedingly difficult to discern or quantify.[10] Rarely does archival information reveal the efforts of diplomatic wives behind the scenes (after all, they are working behind the scenes), though diplomats occasionally remarked that their spouses could be "exceedingly useful on the social end."[11] But such an investigation can challenge scholars' assumptions about diplomacy, marriage, and women overall. Utilizing such an approach and questioning the supposed line separating public and private spheres—a line that Linda Kerber and other scholars have seen as limiting our understanding of women in history— appears hazy at best.[12] Under this microscope, the personal becomes political, thus infusing a host of relationships once viewed as "private or merely social," as Cynthia Enloe puts it, "with power, usually unequal power backed up by public authority."[13]

Although women have without question been integral to the functionality of diplomacy since its inception, female faces in diplomatic circles have rarely been brought to the forefront, as historians have seldom considered what they "have seen out of the corner of their eye, if they saw it at all."[14] But what if historians simply refocused the lens through which they traditionally view diplomacy by following Emily Rosenberg's call to analyze "power systems from various perspectives situated on the periphery"? As diplomatic wives have played such a critical role in diplomatic operations, and diplomacy revolves around the relationships between countries, then the wives of international marriages between powerful nations obviously take on new meaning for historians. Thus, such a shift in perspective is not as drastic as some historians might initially presume; as Rosenberg suggests, "A peripheral view comes less from where we stand than from the critical questions we frame."[15] In that vein, this book regards the wives in Anglo-American marriages as critical figures in Anglo-American diplomatic history, in a manner of speaking, moving them from the periphery, to the center.

American-Born, British-Wed Wives

In reviewing one of the most vital relationships in American diplomacy, that between the United States and the United Kingdom, historians find a significant cohort of women to evaluate as crucial to that alliance. While the special relationship goes almost unquestioned in the twenty-first century, such a rapport would have been difficult, if not impossible, for either Americans or Britons to imagine in the early nineteenth century. While diplomatic historians have emphasized a variety of events in explaining the Anglo-American rapprochement, they only occasionally mention the numerous transatlantic marriages that bound these two countries during the late nineteenth and early twentieth centuries.[16] Despite the many books and articles that have mentioned the topic of transatlantic marriages, the subject typically receives perfunctory consideration, a side issue within the larger and (traditionally defined) more significant issues at hand. Nonetheless, these marriages united wealthy American heiresses and British aristocrats in significant numbers between 1865 and 1920.[17] Howard Temperley notes that no fewer than sixty peers married American women between 1870 and 1914.[18] According to Charles S. Campbell, "more than seventy Americans had married titled Britons by 1903; more than a hundred and thirty by 1914."[19] Bradford Perkins's numbers also support Campbell's. In writing this book, I have documented 588 marriages between American heiresses and members of the British peerage, barons, and landed gentry between the American Civil War and World War I. Whatever the precise number one settles on, it is indisputable that a significant number of transatlantic marriages pledged British and American families to one another at the turn of the twentieth century.

If the exact number of these marriages is in dispute, so is their influence on Anglo-American relations. Campbell argues that they created "an extraordinary galaxy of American women married to British governmental leaders. One might almost stop with that in explaining the rise of friendly feelings between America and Britain."[20] In a later work, he went even further, asserting that "such trans-Atlantic unions doubtless had wide influence on policy."[21] But not all diplomatic historians agree. Perkins argues that while these marriages advanced contact between elite American and British social circles, "the political importance of these marriages was not great, for in very few cases . . . did the husband gain a leading position."[22]

A historical debate thus exists as to the influence of transatlantic marriages on Anglo-American relations. Historians will be hard-pressed to present irrefutable evidence demonstrating that these marriages helped to transform policy or relations; however, they can examine the activities of American-born, British-wed women, their subsequent lives in Great Britain, and public perceptions of them and their nuptials on both sides of the Atlantic that influenced Anglo-American relations, at a key moment in history. More fully exploring the lives of women allows for a consideration of not only the shift in international public opinion regarding them and their marriages but also their informal international impact. In considering their personal activities, public associations, political affiliations, and decision making, this work erases the line between the alleged public space and private life of both men and women as it concerns Anglo-American relations during the period at hand.

Specifically, it considers five particular marriages that span the period from the end of the Civil War through World War II. Beyond simply presenting the compelling narratives of these unions, this book also does for transatlantic marriages what Kati Marton has done for presidential ones in considering "husbands and wives at the precarious intersection of power, love, and marriage."[23] The five marriages profiled here present the varied ways American women dealt with their British husbands and new families; an unfamiliar culture and people; success or failure of their marriages; adaptation or resistance to English life; and personal decisions to discard, maintain, and intermittently negotiate their individual and collective American identities in Britain. While each of the marriages ended differently, it is notable that all five women chose to be buried in Great Britain.

Jennie Jerome's vows to Lord Randolph Churchill in 1874 marked the beginning of the "age of trans-Atlantic marriages in high places."[24] Through her marriage, her husband's political career, her personal relationships with influential Britons, and her son Winston's political career, Lady Churchill used her position in England to advance British-American unity and worked steadfastly to improve Anglo-American relations. In her private and public life, Lady Churchill found a way to retain her American heritage while taking a leading role in London's poli-social circles.

Just as Lady Churchill molded her son and husband's political careers for Anglo-American interests, so did the second American-born, British-wed woman considered here. When Mary Endicott married Joseph Chamberlain in 1888, few Americans or Britons could have anticipated the level of personal or professional influence she would have on him. Following their wedding, Joseph's political speeches took on a decidedly pro–Anglo-Saxon tone, largely as a result of his nuptial treaty with Mary. As a reserved but incredibly kind woman, Mary stepped smoothly into her new roles as political wife, stepmother, and international social secretary for her American and British families. In her nearly seventy years in England, through her vast transatlantic correspondence, she sought to lessen the distance between Boston (her birthplace) and Birmingham (her adult home) and bring her Anglo-American families closer together. As a drawing-room diplomat, she proved that private hostessing could have significant public ramifications.

Though not a political activist like Lady Churchill or a social butterfly like Mary Chamberlain, Mary Victoria Leiter found her own way to influence British attitudes toward Americans. As the compliant political wife of George Nathaniel Curzon, she represented the soft power side of America and American women not only to England but to India as well. Following a five-year secret engagement, the couple married in 1895. Four years later, Lord Curzon became Viceroy of India. For the next six years, Lady Curzon frequently traveled alone between India and England, acting as George's personal ambassador and political emissary, relaying his plans for India to his fellow Members of Parliament and keeping George abreast of political developments in London. Her subservient demeanor was a feminine facade that masked a keen political mind and fiery temperament. Her loyalty to George knew no bounds—even when it cost him his career and her life.

Shortly after the love match between George and Mary Curzon, another American woman entered into a transatlantic marriage, but not by choice. Consuelo

Vanderbilt, the great-granddaughter of Cornelius "Commodore" Vanderbilt, married the 9th Duke of Marlborough in November 1896. The marriage epitomized the socioeconomic exchange of dollars for dukes so common in these marriages. Until this point, most transatlantic marriages met with fanfare on both sides of the Atlantic. Shortly after this miserable union between two people who never loved one another, Anglo-American public opinion turned decidedly against such ties. Consuelo's marriage may have ended in divorce, but her life in Britain afterward demonstrates the power American women held as envoys in influencing transatlantic ideals.

Finally, the most famous, and in some circles infamous, American woman to enter an Anglo-American marriage was Nancy Langhorne Shaw. Her 1906 marriage to William Waldorf Astor coincided with the steady decline in transatlantic marriages, even as she became the most candid consul and famous American woman in British history. As the first woman to take a seat in the British Parliament, in 1919, she used her political connections—public and private—with leading men and women in the United States and Britain. More than any other woman on either side of the Atlantic before her, Lady Astor challenged discrimination toward women in politics, confronted head-on stereotypes about Americans, and—for better and for worse—influenced Anglo-American relations during a crucial time in the nations' shared history.

A close examination of Anglo-American marriages reveals a broad spectrum of pursuits and possibilities. As a British wife, Lady Randolph did all she could under the guise of traditional women's work—hosting dinners and instigating dialogue between critical individuals—both in her home and through her attendance of Parliament meetings to promote positive perceptions amongst Britons. Over the course of her life abroad, she slowly united other American-born, British-wed wives as a collective legion of women who promoted a united Anglo-Saxon identity and ameliorated Anglo-American relations. Mary Endicott Chamberlain continued these efforts as a member of the American Amazons and in her own right by pursuing professional meetings and important dinners with American ambassadors to Britain. The extensive correspondence of both Mary Endicott Chamberlain and Mary Leiter Curzon established an elite Anglo-American network of leaders on both sides of the Atlantic. But all of these women's activities remained chiefly behind the scenes and were thereby shielded from public criticism, as their labors were conventional, voluntary, and deemed appropriate under the facade of elite women's work, which mimicked the traditional duties and expectations of diplomats. While Lady Consuelo Marlborough's initial impact as an American-born, British-wed wife began in this protected category, like Lady Churchill and Mary Chamberlain, she exhibited her greatest influences after her marriage had ended, as she pursued more overtly political opportunities, much like Lady Nancy Astor, as the two gradually dedicated their endeavors to improving the lives of women. Their individual and collective activities abroad shaped the perspectives of Anglo-Americans on both sides of the Atlantic while cracking a glass ceiling of sorts by redefining who could act and how one could serve as an informal ambassador.

Poli-Social Marriages

While historians may disagree as to the importance of transatlantic marriages, both Britons and Americans commented frequently on the participants. In the beginning decades of this marital trend, most Americans were "pleased when [they heard] that another American girl had entered the exclusive circle of the British aristocracy."[25] American heiresses were often very rich, exceptionally beautiful, and exceedingly well trained in elite social behaviors. In the words of one Briton at the turn of the century, "It must be very hard . . . for a bachelor from the other side, whatever prejudices and affections he brings across, to keep from trying to marry an American girl."[26] For example, after her marriage to Joseph Chamberlain in 1888, Mary Endicott Chamberlain attended a Town Hall meeting with her husband in his home constituency of Birmingham. Following the meeting, Mary exited the building to shouts of "Three cheers for our American cousin!"[27] In many cases, Britons responded approvingly regarding intermarriage with their "American cousins."[28]

As one analyzes British political leaders and the women they married, a significant difference from American government leaders becomes apparent: British leaders relied on their wives throughout their careers, an alliance they candidly reflected upon in personal letters and diaries. Before Lord Salisbury became prime minister in 1885, he openly acknowledged the importance a wife would play in his political life. In one journal entry, he wrote: "I have come to the conclusion that I shall probably do Parliament well if I marry, and that I shall certainly [make] nothing of it if I do not." Georgina Alderson, whom he married in 1857, proved quite an asset to his political career. She organized her calendar around his activities and responsibilities, monitored his exercise and sleep schedule closely, and entertained guests in their home while he worked at the House of Commons. She often sat in the Ladies' Gallery, waiting for her husband to finish his tasks, a commitment that often resulted in their walks home together at dawn.[29] Such a hands-on, involved, and visible partnership was quite the exception in American political circles in the same period; hence, a transatlantic marriage opened doors for conspicuous women such as Jennie Jerome, who reveled in her front-and-center, poli-social status in England, a position unlikely for her had she married an American. But in the context of transatlantic marriages, in which American women played much more decisive roles in their husbands' careers, and in diplomatic circles, in which women's work was necessary and pivotal to international relations, an unprecedented combination of opportunities provided American-born, British-wed women the chance to successfully shape Anglo-American perceptions and relations.

Clearly, British politicians considered successful marriage with the right women key to prominent governmental careers. Selecting a woman intimately familiar with the game of politics could significantly aid a leading official, as in the case of Viscount Henry Palmerston, who married Emily Lamb. Having grown up in political circles, much like Mary Endicott Chamberlain, Emily became Palmerston's confidante; he often shared with her private details of the political wrangling of the House of Commons. Utilizing the practice of the salon, a significant social weapon both Liberal and Conservative political wives in Britain employed through the nineteenth and early twentieth centuries, Emily entertained men and women in her drawing room. Acting as her husband's unofficial political manager, Emily (like Mary Curzon) held as much inside knowledge and as many valuable personal contacts as any other politician of the period. Henry Asquith, prime minister from 1908 to 1916, described Emily as "an active and most efficient co-partner in Palmerston's fortunes."[30] While ambassador to Paris in the 1930s, Lord Tyrell observed of leading wives, "A woman with the right personal gifts who married a diplomat . . . [is] invaluable to the public service and one can think of many Ambassadors and Ministers in the past, who have owed a great part . . . of the success of their best work to their wives."[31] Thus, the women in this study prove they were both the diplomats and the wives, the very people whose implicit social activities repeatedly open international political doors.

British politicians have long recognized the power of a talented and witty hostess-wife. But in the same manner that she could aid her husband, a British political wife could also act as a detriment to his career. If she lacked familiarity with political intrigue, if she chose not to entertain frequently, or if she took no pleasure socializing with other politicians and their wives, her husband's career reflected her perceived reluctance. When future prime minister Arthur Balfour considered marriage to Margot Tennant, Queen Victoria expressed her disappointment with her home secretary's choice, pronouncing Margot "unfit for a Cabinet Minister's wife."[32] While she did not outline her objections to Margot and did not provide Balfour any suggestions, Victoria clearly deemed a certain type of woman as the ideal politician's wife. The selection of a wife, as something of a nongovernmental official, has long been an important decision for British government officials.

The wives of British politicians in general and of prime ministers specifically "played a part which was very much an extension of the social role they would have fulfilled in England."[33] Exhibiting this, Lady Jennie Churchill maintained that "Englishwomen have a much greater opportunity than their American sisters to engage in public and political affairs," a realization that may have surprised more than one American-born, British-wed wife. According to Lady Churchill, an "Eng-lishwoman occupies nearly all her working hours with meetings and functions of various kinds, many of them of a semi-public nature." Based on her upbring-ing in the United States and adult life in Britain, Lady Churchill argued that Eng-lishwomen directly influenced politics, "whereas [such influence was] so limited among American women as to be inappreciable."[34] Despite the rigidities of the British class system, more opportunities existed for women to exert political and social influence than in the ostensibly egalitarian United States.

Accordingly, British political marriages hold great significance for our examina-tion of American diplomatic history. Unlike their sisters across the Atlantic, the wives of American politicians had few opportunities to exert influence on their hus-bands' careers. An American wife married to a British politician at the turn of the twentieth century, however, enjoyed tremendous opportunities for international influence, which proved especially true for both Lady Churchill and Lady Curzon, as they represented the United States not only to England but also to their particu-lar outposts (Ireland and India) as a result of their husbands' political assignments. Consequently, the consideration of Anglo-American marriages, and specifically the activities and contacts an American woman gained through her marriage to a British politician, opened the door for these women to serve as informal ambas-sadors—entertaining in the same manner as American diplomats, and specifically their wives, while making valuable personal and professional contacts, similar to British political wives.

Unfortunately for the participants in transatlantic marriages, the public often viewed these unions as simple exchanges of money for titles—loveless transactions of capital for class—epitomized in 1896 by the garish wedding and disastrous mar-riage of Consuelo Vanderbilt to the 9th Duke of Marlborough.[35] In the years follow-ing the Civil War, a number of American men, such as Consuelo's father, made siz-able fortunes well in excess of hundreds of millions of dollars.[36] While these families had the wealth to earn elite status on an economic level, old-money families resisted the intrusion of the nouveau riche into their tightly knit circle. Consequently, many of the newly wealthy left the United States for London in pursuit of social accep-tance, seeking, and in many cases buying, marriages for their daughters to noble-men of Britain in a near desperate attempt to, as Greg King has described, "prove they were both respectful of and equal to their European models."[37]

Not surprisingly, these young women's decisions to renounce their American democratic heritage and republican virtues for the title of "lady" left a sour taste in the patriotic mouths of many American citizens. As historian Milton Plesur asked, "Was not Europe the home of monarchies, despotisms, colonialism, and destitute dukes searching for American heiresses—in short, everything that the United States abhorred?"[38] To earn social acceptance in elite American circles via the stamp of British aristocratic approval was anathema for the majority of Americans. From the democratic perspective of the United States, a titled American was not an American at all.

This same period witnessed great economic growth in the United States while the landed wealth of the British aristocracy endured a quick and significant decline. Not surprisingly, British aristocrats believed Americans literally buying their way into London's high society threatened centuries of Britain's landed wealth and political dominance.[39] There remained a tendency in British society to regard the big spenders from the United States as uncouth.[40] Given these circumstances, it is little wonder that the public perception of Anglo-American marriages shifted over time from approval to aversion.

Women's Work, Man's Job

Just as Anglo-American marriages resulted from an array of motivations on both sides of the Atlantic, a serious study of transatlantic marriages and their influence on Anglo-American relations reflects an abundance of recent developments in diplomatic history. Chiefly, it intersects with women's history as a cross-fertilization of social and cultural history, as Thomas Zeiler has urged historians to reconsider "transnational (essentially, nonstate) interactions across borders."[41] Just as Allgor argues that the "the marriage of women's history to the mainstream political narrative has revealed that gender is a primary category of historical analysis," the same can be said of women's history and diplomatic narrative.[42] Undoubtedly, the process of diplomacy has long revolved around dinners, drinks, and discussion. Women, and wives specifically, have held claim to traditional duties related to domesticity and hospitality regardless of country or historic period. Hence, the procedure of diplomacy falls under the category of women's work, but history has long regarded the process as a man's job.

Thus, a central question of this book is that of who was considered eligible as a diplomat in the late nineteenth century and what type of background, education, and training such a position required beyond the proverbial pale, male, and from Yale criterion. Attachés were expected to be well educated and well versed in the behavior and language of diplomacy. Their children often dined with the politically influential, knew the proper utensils for any course of a lengthy meal, were fluent in other languages (most often French), spoke intelligently and congenially, and exhibited flawless deportment with ease. Notably, elite Americans provided this exact training for their sons *and* daughters, but for very different reasons. While elite Americans taught their children such lessons eventually to fulfill different expectations—sons to *do*; daughters to *marry*—the outcome was the same. As our American-born, British-wed women received the guidance and preparation suitable for future diplomats, they were at least as savvy and adept in high poli-social circles as their American brothers and British husbands. Though they did not hold the title "diplomat," they had received the same instruction and demonstrated the same traits and conduct required of ambassadors.

This gendered perspective of diplomatic representation, broadly defined, and Anglo-American relations, specifically, opens the door to analyzing women's wider influence within diplomatic history. Scott's challenge for scholars to reconsider "the history of politics and the politics of history" remains especially relevant for diplomatic historians and historians of women to rethink "war, diplomacy, and high politics" where it applies to international relations.[43] But such investigation cannot be performed with a traditional approach, as Rosenberg has pointed out, by searching for women in diplomatic history, as there are very few "exceptional women" who have served in official diplomatic capacities. Rather, she urged historians to examine situations in which women pressed "the possibilities of the socially constructed women's spheres to the limit, all the while helping redefine their boundaries" and revisit the idea from a gendered perspective.[44] But this book makes it be possible to merge Rosenberg's two ideas—the exceptional woman, as well as women doing women's work—and reevaluate one of the longest and most complicated relationships in U.S. history. By considering the politically complex, economically motivated, and diplomatically charged marriages of truly exceptional American women who married into the highest levels of British poli-social circles and then acted just as elite/diplomatic wives would, should, and could in the midst of an evolving Anglo-American relationship, we are able to do just that.

New and Old Views of Diplomatic History

Such an analysis of women's work as it pertains to diplomatic history dovetails with the emerging focus on cultural diplomacy to emphasize the cultural commonalities between various societies. Cultural diplomacy analyzes the differences in cultures and how these differences can help or hinder relations between countries and serves as a powerful lens through which to examine such aspects of diplomatic relations as "social affinities, comparative analysis, cultural conceptions, psychological influences, local traditions, and unspoken assumptions." Thus, as Jessica C. E. Gienow-Hecht argues, "culture affects nations and global systems as much as, if not more than, power and economic interests."[45] This approach to diplomatic history is particularly valuable in assessing the idea of a special cultural connection between the United States and Great Britain as well as challenging stereotypes of typical American and British traits and behavior.

Informal diplomacy, an academic cousin to cultural diplomacy, also plays an important role in this particular study of Anglo-American marriages. Catherine Forslund defines informal diplomacy as "any exchange between citizens or groups of citizens from two or more nations outside the boundaries of the official governmental institutional apparatus (ambassadors, ministers, secretaries, et al.)."[46] The leading persons representing the United States to Great Britain in any period are the diplomats and ambassadors dispatched to London. But in an increasingly globalized world, where people of all countries frequently come into contact with one another, these informal interactions help shape conceptions of other nations and peoples. Hundreds of American women married British aristocrats, political leaders, and military officers during this period. Many of these women were the only Americans some Britons ever personally met. As a result, these women served as informal ambassadors for the United States, living their lives abroad and acting as personal advertisements for what Americans believed and what the United States represented. Whether American women made a negative or positive impression, Britons formed personal opinions and implemented public decisions toward the United States in this period largely based on these American women. Clearly, this role carried immense influence for those willing to embrace such a position.

Closely related to the idea of informal diplomacy is the significance of unofficial ambassadors. Recent works, such as Donna Alvah's *Unofficial Ambassadors: American Military Families Overseas and the Cold War, 1946–1965* (2007) and Zeiler's *Ambassadors in Pinstripes: The Spalding World Baseball Tour and the Birth of the American Empire* (2006), enforce the idea of nongovernmental actors as potential and influential representatives for the United States overseas. As Alvah argues, the military encouraged families "to act as 'unofficial ambassadors' in their everyday activities among local people in foreign countries . . . [as they] could help foster good relations with residents of foreign countries."[47] Likewise, Zeiler contends that in an era of a new world economy and "the constant pressure of Anglo-American globalization and the 'soft power' of U.S. business and other transnational contacts," such as Anglo-American marriages, "held the promise of imperial rewards."[48] As recent diplomatic scholarship suggests, a host of players outside the employ of the U.S. Department of State were now eligible to influence overseas perceptions of Americans and America. While the notion of unofficial ambassadors is a slippery slope, and by no means does one international trip accredit an individual as an informal diplomat, the proposition that untrained, uneducated, unstaffed individuals could—and often did—potentially influence foreign relations has gained significant ground among historians of foreign relations.[49]

In assessing informal and unofficial means of international influence, the individual and collective opinion of a people and populace is critical. By shaping individual personal opinions, American-born, British-wed women helped mold a wider body of public opinion. Public opinion has long been important in studying

diplomatic relations between two countries. According to Thomas A. Bailey, public opinion has long shaped basic foreign policy; thus, "sprouting from the fertile
soil of experience, they represent the needs, interests, and hopes of people."[50] In
this period, Americans held a variety of opinions about the British. On the one
hand, many Americans proudly considered themselves Anglophobes, detesting the
former mother country and everything that it represented. On the other, many described themselves as Anglophiles, people who cherished a shared heritage with
Great Britain and valued the "special relationship" that Americans had with their
British cousins. While several historians have characterized the late nineteenth century as an era of either extreme Anglophilia or Anglophobia, these two sentiments
existed side by side, albeit generally among different groups of Americans.[51] For
the most part, lower- to middle-class workers, immigrants, and specifically Irish
and German Americans held anti-British attitudes while upper-middle-class to
wealthy Americans of British descent held pro-British opinions. These public sentiments influenced American politics: the Anglophobes generally voted Democratic
(largely due to Irish- and German-American constituents) while Anglophiles typically voted Republican. Still, no openly pro-British politician in the United States
could have been elected in the nineteenth century.[52] This reality is best evidenced by
an executive decision to keep Mary Endicott's engagement to Joseph Chamberlain a
secret, lest President Cleveland lose his 1888 reelection bid, as Mary's father served
as Cleveland's secretary of war, a position that facilitated his daughter's meeting
with Chamberlain. Even during this period, public opinion on international issues strongly influenced American domestic politics and foreign relations. Consequently, as important as what these women did with their Anglo-American unions
was what people on both sides of the Atlantic perceived they did through their
transatlantic marriages.

While this study uses a variety of subfields of diplomatic history, readers should
note that this project examines foreign relations—not foreign policy. The difference,
while subtle, is important. To study foreign relations means to examine the specific
associations, contacts, connections, and interactions between two or more countries. By contrast, foreign policy focuses more exclusively on the strategies, principles, and procedures involved in pursuing a course of action with one or more nations. Clearly, these two elements of diplomacy influence one another. As Thomas
G. Paterson explains, "historians of *American* foreign relations try to study the combination of factors that has produced an *American* foreign policy, an *American* participation in the world."[53] In analyzing transatlantic marriages, this study examines
relations between Great Britain and the United States within a given period and
how these women, acting as informal ambassadors for the United States, changed,
altered, or affected the way Britons and Americans saw one another. Consequently
foreign policy, in terms of tracking specific lines of dialogue between formal British
and American diplomats, functions as a limited consideration here.

Overall, this study pursues the concept of hard versus soft power. Hard power, which Joseph S. Nye defined as "co-optive behavioral power—getting others to want what you want," has long been the ultimate purpose of diplomacy.[54] Just as Slaughter acknowledges women's preference of persuasion over pressure, Nye argues for the superior yet gentle prowess of "soft power resources—cultural attraction, ideology, and international institutions," hardly new concepts for diplomatic historians.[55] This seemingly simple categorization of diplomatic acts through "attraction rather than coercion or payments" unifies some of the latest trends in diplomatic scholarship—transatlantic, gender, cultural, and informal considerations—to examine one of the oldest and most complex relationships in history.

In many ways, transatlantic marriages constitute a very old method, perhaps the oldest, of diplomacy. For centuries before Anglo-American marriages became the nuptial trend of choice in the late nineteenth century, feuding kingdoms had practiced international marriages for the benefit of their territories. Numerous kings and queens from rival nations married their sons and daughters to one another to achieve cease-fires, as acts of good faith in treaties, to gain more territory, or protect their own kingdom from invasion, which supports Enloe's claim that that "empires rose and fell according to which marriage schemes succeeded and which failed."[56] The union of Ferdinand to Isabella marks one of the earliest strategic European nuptials, just like the marriages of Queen Victoria's children, all of whom married, not of their own accord, the daughters and sons of necessary European allies. While Victoria and Albert enjoyed a marriage based on true love, they did not allow their children to do the same, instead utilizing the unions for the benefit of the British Empire.[57]

The Anglo-American marriages examined in this book illustrate the oldest form of diplomacy unfolding in the modern world. These marriages held great potential for British-American relations at the turn of the twentieth century. Thus, Germany, France, Italy, and even Ireland watched them closely. Clearly, many European nations worried that Anglo-American marriages, amid a "potent imperial ideology [based on] the racial affinities of Anglo-Saxonism and the Anglo-American 'special relationship,'" might alter the delicate power balance between England and continental Europe.[58] In the United States, immigrants such as Irish and German Americans issued critical statements about these unions as their own dislike for Britain brought concern that their new country had grown too close to the evil British Empire. Potentially closer relations between the United States and Great Britain could eventually spell disaster for immigrants' home countries and for immigrants themselves in the United States, who could do little but stand by and wonder what such a large number of marriages between wealthy American women and powerful British policymakers might mean for the transatlantic world.

Just as many scholars have noted but given little serious consideration to the practice of transatlantic marriages, so did many people on both sides of the Atlantic during the period under review. One newspaper, for example, wrote dismissively of one of these unions: "Her waist, 20 inches; her inheritance, $20 million."[59] For the majority of publications critiquing these marriages, the American heiresses were nothing more than a nineteenth-century version of Paris Hilton—a silly little rich girl famous for simply being rich—and who had discarded her American identity for nothing more than a bankrupt duke who was much more interested in courting her father, his lawyer, and his personal banker than her exclusively. But a serious investigation of Anglo-American marriages reveals that there is much more to the story; this is the sort of investigation that this book undertakes.

After a discussion of the major factors that transpired following the American Civil War that made transatlantic marriages popular and desirable for American women, British men, and Anglo-American families on both sides of the Atlantic Ocean, this book explores five distinct case studies that represent the overall pattern for American women who married British men in this period. While these specific American-born, British-wed women are closely analyzed regarding their activities and efforts on behalf of Anglo-American relations, they are representative of more than five hundred women of the same birth and nuptial category who lived abroad as informal ambassadors for their homeland and whose every word and deed held significant ramifications for the emerging special relationship based on their own personal and professional relationships.

The final chapter and the conclusion consider the myriad factors that lead to the decline and ultimate legacy of Anglo-American marriages. Chapter 7 analyzes the perceived "American invasion" of Great Britain and the various reasons that public opinion turned against Anglo-American relations at the turn of the century. Both Britons and Americans expressed strong attitudes condemning these marriages, each for their own reasons. While Anglo-American marriages still occurred after 1900, as did Lady Astor's, the number declined significantly in the wake of intense scorn. The last chapter presents all final conclusions concerning Anglo-American marriages.

These women surprised their families, both British and American, as they exhibited an extraordinary degree of agency in a period that clearly placed women outside the boundaries of politics and diplomacy. Without the formal title of "diplomat" or membership in Parliament, they exerted an incredible amount of influence in the male-dominated arena of foreign affairs and international politics. They served as informal ambassadors who worked to improve relations at the turn of the twentieth century and played important roles in terms of influencing foreign relations. Furthermore, they demonstrated keen abilities to demasculinize the traditionally male world of diplomacy as on a daily basis they acted as ambassadors posted to a foreign country. Their positions as the wives of leading members of the British aristocracy provided them with unprecedented access to the eyes and ears of individuals at the highest level in Great Britain, the very decision-makers who formulated and implemented foreign policy with their home country. During the period under consideration, the United States and Great Britain began to view one another less as adversaries and more as allies. Consequently, these women deserve recognition for the crucial roles they played at a critical time of international relations and certainly give new meaning to the phrase "foreign affairs." In a period that did not afford women the right to vote, through their transatlantic marriages, they skillfully and successfully blurred the lines of public politics and private lives. Without formal education in politics or foreign policy or the title or staff provided to a diplomat or ambassador, these women created a unprecedented degree of agency within a world that would have undeniably recoiled at the idea of a female diplomat or politician. Both collectively and individually, they functioned as pseudo-diplomats between their country by birth and country by marriage.

Based on the connections established between diplomatic and women's history, our examination turns to the overall trend of transatlantic marriages and five specific women involved in such unions. These women had all the tools for success as both diplomats and diplomatic wives: elite background, extreme wealth, social connections, superb beauty, exquisite etiquette, knowledge of a foreign language, and congenial personalities. Based on the demands and duties placed on diplomats and their wives since the nineteenth century, historians can clearly view Anglo-American marriages as having created a transatlantic and transnational network of politically charged and diplomatically significant unions. Utilizing a biographical approach, as Molly Wood has done, this method "gives historians a tool by which to challenge some of the common assumptions about women's behavior, motivations, and activities" while also answering Zeiler's call to observe "non-state and public actors on the international stage."[60] These women walked the fine line between their American and British loyalties. Like so many diplomats and wives before them, they lived under an international spotlight. People on both sides of the Atlantic monitored their every action, association, and friendship. As a result, scholars can examine these women as informal ambassadors as part of the larger picture of Anglo-American history.

By overlapping and fusing diplomatic history with gender and women's studies and finding the intersections among these disciplines, this book demonstrates that not only could women act as ambassadors, even during a period in which they could not apply for State Department employment, but they influenced Anglo-American relations to a degree never before considered by historians. As Rosenberg has surmised, this work "linger[s] at the intersections, walking the borders to analyze from the outside in" to authenticate the roles, efforts, and activities of American women who married into the highest social and political circles of Britain, where they lived their lives abroad as informal ambassadors.[61]

CHAPTER ONE

Courting Transatlantic Marriages

Before the century is out, these clever and pretty women from New York will pull the strings in half the chanceries in Europe.

—BRITISH PRIME MINISTER LORD PALMERSTON

Before American women began marrying into the highest poli-social circles in Britain in the latter nineteenth century, a host of factors laid the groundwork to make such unions desirable for both parties; thus, the courtship of such marriages is rooted in historical events neither country could have ever predicted. Although many people and numerous books would have readers believe the trend of Anglo-American marriages simply sprang up overnight and later died out as quickly as it began, such is not the case. A number of factors within the United States and Great Britain during the mid- to late nineteenth century allowed an Anglo-American marital market to flourish. Many Britons viewed these American women as nothing more than socially hungry "Dollar Princesses," as their mothers pursued British titles and social acceptance at any cost. From an American perspective, bankrupt dukes stole American girls from their democratic republic to restore British estates and castles financially with no concern for their tender, feminine American hearts. In either case, love allegedly played a limited role. Arriving in New York for her son's wedding to May Goelet, the Dowager Duchess of Roxburghe explained: "Why, money isn't everything to an Englishman. There are other considerations when he marries, for instance, fondness for the girl."[1] Such perspectives exaggerate the motivations of the participating parties. Certainly economic incentives existed for both British and American persons involved in these marriages, but reducing the complexities of Anglo-American marriages down to mere dollar (or pound) signs causes one to overlook the many layers of historical dynamics at work.

Rather than analyzing Anglo-American marriages from a strictly British or American viewpoint, one must see transatlantic marriages as the interaction of several countries—including France—although Great Britain and the United States remain the central players. Until recently, scholars of American history had resisted placing the United States in a multinational context or viewing it as one nation among many. As professor of international history Jessica Gienow-Hecht has suggested, "the history of American culture—including high culture—must be resituated in the context of diplomatic history, transatlantic exchange, and international relations."[2] Just as the United States searched for its own unique culture and social identity during this period, many affluent Americans found themselves torn between and Anglophobic and Anglophilic views of European high culture. Although proud of their democratic country, many wealthy Americans found it difficult to avoid replicating a European, or even British, cultural identity on American soil in expressing an appreciation for art, music, architecture, fashion, and etiquette. Consequently, the cultural interactions, and sometimes collisions, of the United States and Great Britain played a central role in Anglo-American marriages.

Dollar Diplomacy? Economics and Anglo-American Marriages

While culture functioned as a means both to divide and unite British aristocrats and American heiresses in their marriages, economics served as the principal factor in courtship. Significant changes in the economies of the United States and Great Britain allowed for previously mentioned economic incentives. By the mid-nineteenth century, Great Britain had entered a period of acute economic decline, which had serious implications for not only the country's landed elite and aristocratic classes but also its political leadership. This relative collapse of the British economy coincided with the U.S. economy's substantial expansion.[3] Thus, each country looked to the other in the wake of a slow but steady changing of the economic guard on the world stage.

By 1860, two major developments acted as catalysts in changing the U.S. economy. First, the growing industrial economy quickly replaced the agrarian one. Second, the American Civil War, as Walter LaFeber asserts, "marked the transference of power from planters to industrialists and financiers."[4] Four years of warfare on American soil allowed the relocation of political leadership and economic power from the South to the North, specifically to New York. A corresponding shift occurred in Congress. With the secession of thirteen southern states, many congressmen opposed to the governmental aid of corporate business no longer prevented Republican centralization from replacing Jacksonian democracy.[5]

The era of a close alliance between big business and government assistance began in earnest after the Civil War. In 1860, the United States had only 30,000 miles of railroad; by 1913, more than 259,000 miles of railroads connected people and markets across the country. In 1866, Standard Oil produced 1 million barrels of oil, and in the succeeding three decades it increased its production twentyfold. U.S. steel production jumped from 1.1 million tons in 1880 to 4.3 million in 1890. Textile exports to China rose 120 percent between 1887 and 1897.[6] The gross national product tripled between 1865 and 1898. The recovering South also participated in this economic growth: Between 1870 and 1891, cotton production in the South doubled from 4.3 million to 9 million bales. In its first six months of production in 1871, one Birmingham, Alabama, plant produced more than 300,000 tons of steel.

In the two decades preceding the twentieth century, the population of the United States more than doubled, and the available labor force mirrored this growth. As a result, most company profits averaged more than 20 percent. During this same period, American imports decreased from 14 percent in 1869 to 5.9 percent in 1909. American exports began consistently exceeding imports by the end of the nineteenth century. Between 1860 and 1897, exports tripled to more than $1 billion, thus ending three hundred years of an American trade deficit. More important, agricultural goods comprised only two-thirds of all exports by 1900, down from nearly 85 percent in 1880. On the eve of the First World War, the United States contributed one-third of the world's industrial production; not only had it made the transition from an agrarian society to an urban, industrial country, it had also replaced Great Britain as the "workshop of the world."[7]

While technology and a large workforce played key roles in the Second Industrial Revolution (1871–1914), foreign investment was the critical factor in American economic expansion in this period. Between 1865 and 1914, private investment in American entrepreneurship exploded to reach between 18 and 20 percent, double the same measurement from the 1850s. In the 1880s, foreign investment totaled more than $3 billion, with British investment alone at $1.5 billion.[8] In 1895, a State Department official concluded, based on "business reasons alone, we ought to cultivate friendly relations with Great Britain."[9] It is ironic, then, that many of the American men who made millions of dollars largely based on British investment later turned to British social circles when looking for suitable husbands for their daughters.

Such an incredible explosion for the U.S. economy resulted in great personal wealth for a number of individual Americans. By 1865, Philip Armour had benefited from an annual income of $2 million from meat processing. Other major businessmen included Andrew Carnegie, Cyrus McCormick, J. P. Morgan, and E. H. Harriman, all "architects of the Second Industrial Revolution." In the 1840s, fewer than twenty Americans held net worths of $1 million; by the 1860s, several hundred people could lay claim to millionaire status, and several were multimillionaires.[10] So many individuals had earned such incredible fortunes during the Gilded Age that the title "millionaire" was not as impressive in 1890 as it had been in 1860. Commenting on the increase in American millionaires, in the 1870s society leader Ward McAllister proclaimed, "A fortune of only a million is respectable poverty."[11]

As a growing number of men became captains of industry, a large portion of their income made its way to Great Britain through transatlantic marriages and dowry contracts. Depending on the socioeconomic class and status of a family, and especially the father, dowries varied greatly. In Anglo-American marriages, they were generally quite significant, hence the stereotype of bankrupt British dukes pursuing American heiresses based on their fathers' wealth. These "fortune-hunters viewed daughters and granddaughters of robber barons, not unlike the way great capitalists looked upon their own enterprises," as Frederic Copel Jaher argues, "as investment of time, energy and skill that would, if properly handled, yield maximum profits."[12] Gustavus Myers estimated in 1909 that approximately five hundred American women had married titled foreigners and that the dowries attached to these transatlantic marriages resulted in a net loss of an estimated $220 million to the U.S. economy.[13]

For all the fortunes flowing into Great Britain from the United States, the nation's economy did not improve; rather, it entered a period of significant decline related to economic instability across Europe and the increasing U.S. industrial power. Until the 1870s, land ownership in Britain equated to political, economic, and social power. As David Cannadine explains, "Land was wealth. . . . [L]and was status. . . . [A]nd land was power: over the locality, the country, and the nation."[14] Until the last quarter of the nineteenth century, land value continued to increase consistently as the quantity of landowners increased slightly. The "great depression" in Great Britain between 1873 and 1896 marked a drastic change in the incomes of aristocratic landowners across the country. General deflation resulted in a dramatic decrease in agricultural production and the overall value of land.[15] As an example, the annual revenue from the Duke of Manchester's estates plummeted from £95,000 to a deficit of £2,000.[16] At the beginning of the nineteenth century, agriculture accounted for approximately one-third of the national income of Britain. Over the next century, while agricultural production increased in absolute terms, it decreased on a proportional level. By 1900, only 10 percent of the national economy derived from agriculture.[17]

Part of this downturn stemmed from an increase in American economic rivalries and the production of competitively priced foodstuffs, but it also came from the "massive influx of cheap foreign goods from North and South America" combined with the growing significance of the "highly concentrated industrial economy."[18] Wheat prices in England decreased by 50 percent between 1870 and 1895, and the total acreage of grain production dwindled by two-thirds in the same period. As agricultural prices plummeted, peasants revolted not only in Britain but in con-

tinental Europe. Rent rolls, the fees paid by tenants to farm land owned by aristocrats, plunged by an astounding 30 to 50 percent.[19] Landownership was no longer
the safest or most secure means of wealth; therefore, the fundamental source and
definition of European aristocratic political power no longer existed. As Charles
George Milnes Gaskell surmised, "economically and politically, the patricians were
no longer the lords of the earth." Some aristocrats found their financial situation so
unstable that many sold their property or rented out their estates.[20] The most valuable assets many British aristocrats had to sell were their titles—and more than a
few Americans in this period were interested in purchasing such assets.

The British economic downturn resulted in radical changes in personal wealth
and the country's political control. Of the British millionaires who died between
1858 and 1879, four-fifths had been landowners. Among the same class, between
1880 and 1899 only a third of the deceased had owned land, and the number continued to drop after 1900. Before 1895, aristocrats held the majority of British cabinet
positions, but after 1895, aristocrats rarely served as cabinet officials. Fearing that the
British aristocracy might die out, the British Parliament created a number of new
peerages; between 1901 and 1920, 159 were created. A new type of peer emerged.
Of the new peerages, businessmen accounted for sixty-six. Roughly half described
themselves as industrialists, and thirty-four worked as professionals (mostly law-
yers), while only twenty-two peerages went to men of landed background.[21] Before
1885, only 10 percent of the peerage had connections to commerce and industry,
whereas after 1885 that number increased threefold.[22] The traditional profile of a
British peer had forever changed.

These radical changes meant that the profile of British political leadership underwent an equally thorough transformation. Although political families, family
connections, and powerful family names still helped individual peers enter local
and national politics, new faces and new backgrounds entered the House of Commons for the first time.[23] Such changes allowed people like Joseph Chamberlain,
a manufacturer and mayor of Birmingham, to enter the House of Commons as a
Liberal statesman. Although his entry into once closed circles marked a significant turning point in British politics, Chamberlain's commoner standing often
prevented his full immersion into elite aristocratic circles. Commenting to Lady
Mary Elcho, Arthur Balfour remarked, "Joe, though we all love him dearly, somehow does not absolutely or completely mix, does not form a chemical combination with us."[24] Nonetheless, Chamberlain's presence opened the doors for others
without aristocratic backgrounds to penetrate the halls of Parliament and set the
stage for Nancy Astor, one significant American woman who entered British politics as a result of her transatlantic marriage.

American and British Societies Converge

The incredible growth in American industry and the economy overall resulted in a new generation of American wealth, as New York City became the home of new money.[25] These nouveau riche families—the Vanderbilts serve as a prime example—in the United States held the wealth to earn elite status economically but not socially, as "old money" families—the Astors, the DuPonts, the Rothschilds—resisted the intrusion into their tight-knit circle. The biggest difference between old money families and the nouveau riche was that people like the Vanderbilts had worked for their fortunes. Old money families enjoyed their position as members of the leisure class, as their wealth stemmed from real estate or some other means of revenue that did not require their daily labors. Thus, the old money families resented the apparent assumption of newly rich Americans that such fortunes automatically bought their way into the established social circles of Boston, Charleston, Philadelphia, and especially New York City. The upper classes of these cities functioned regionally, while the elite social circles of New York City dictated the standards of houses, wealth, and entertainment for all socially affluent Americans. Succinctly stated, "What happened in New York mattered."[26]

The flood of new American fortunes tested the exclusivity of society as it existed in New York City under the leadership of two individuals, Ward McAllister and Caroline Astor, the latter better known as *the* Mrs. Astor. Originally from Savannah, Georgia, McAllister worked as an attorney in California before traveling widely across Europe. Upon his return to the United States, he married a wealthy American woman named Sarah Gibbons. Combining his social connections with his wife's fortune, he became a member of New York society. Caroline Schmerhorn married William Backhouse Astor Jr., in 1853, and she went by "Mrs. Astor" for the rest of her life. Together McAllister and Mrs. Astor set out to draw a clear line around the old money and socially acceptable residents of New York City in an effort to differentiate themselves from the nouveau riche. Establishing an elite association they called the "Four Hundred," allegedly based on the number of people who could fit into Mrs. Astor's ballroom, the duo identified those New Yorkers considered socially fit to represent an American aristocracy.[27] "There are only about four hundred people in fashionable New York society. If you go outside that number," McAllister reasoned, "you strike people who are either not at ease in a ballroom or else make other people not at ease."[28] The "Four Hundred" attended fashionable dinners and exclusive balls to which nouveau riche could only aspire. "The first object to be aimed at is to make your dinners so charming and agreeable that invitations to them are eagerly sought for," McAllister once explained, "and to let all feel that it is a great privilege to dine at your house, where they are sure there will be only those whom they wish to meet."[29] Society thus functioned on lines of acceptance, connections, and exclusivity. Their "nouveau riche" label kept newcomers on the outside of the highest social circles. While families such as the Vanderbilts had the money to earn elite categorizations based strictly on economics, "old money" families such as the Astors resisted any new-comers into their "Four Hundred" club out of fear that additional members would diminish their elite status.[30]

While entry into elite social circles clearly relied on the fortunes of established families, a division separated men and women's prescribed duties. While men at-tended to the business decisions regarding their wealth and income, women han-dled the day-to-day dealings of maintaining social standing with other affluent women. The planning of lengthy dinners, the arranging of annual balls, and the distributing of calling cards all relied on the efforts and attention of women. Part of their job involved playing hostess at these massive society functions. Their knowl-edge of etiquette, notably a European or British definition of protocol, served as a means of evaluation by their societal peers. A woman's performance and the suc-cess of various social engagements determined her standing in American society and reflected on her husband's standing as well. Notably, this peer evaluation pro-cess of society follows closely the method of marriage and assessment in diplomatic service overseas.

Through her activities in society, a woman held an official job both inside and outside the home. A proper woman only appeared in public newspapers three times in her life: her birth announcement, her wedding announcement, and her death announcement; otherwise, she tended all but anonymously to her duties as a wife and mother with the assistance of various servants and nannies. But through her social role, a woman exerted a tremendous amount of influence under the guise of maintaining her husband's good name and her family's social standing. Years after Alva Vanderbilt had fought her way into New York society, she reflected, "I know of no profession, art or trade, that women are working at today . . . as taxing on mental resources as being a leader of society."[31] Recognizing women's necessary role in society, the "Four Hundred" identified single women as individual members of society. Of the couples and people listed as members of the "Four Hundred," over sixty women's names appeared independently. While this may seem insignificant at first glance, the identification of women as members of society recognized their pseudo-occupation within the demanding and complex world of society.[32]

One behavior practiced by members of the American social elite, old money and new, was that of conspicuous consumption. Building massive houses in fash-ionable neighborhoods in New York and immense estates in Newport, Rhode Is-land, the new summer vacationing location for elite Americans, allowed wealthy persons to present their affluence for public screening. To work their way into elite circles, nouveau riche families purchased expensive paintings and sculptures, not simply to decorate their elaborate homes but also to demonstrate that they appreciated fine art and understood the value of such objects just like the old money families of New York. To at least act as though they frequented the same places, many nouveau riche persons also attended the theater and operas typically patronized by old money families. Several also spent their summers in Newport, to locate themselves in proximity to those members of the "Four Hundred." As Ward McAllister once explained, "If you want to be fashionable, be always in the company of fashionable people."[33] The practices of conspicuous consumption and conspicuous leisure offered nouveau riche families some hope that they could eventually feign or buy their way into the tight-knit circles of New York City.[34]

Wealthy Americans also visited other leisure destinations. An increasing number of elite and aspiring elite from the United States traveled throughout Europe, and especially Great Britain. The social circles of Europe offered some level of social currency when one returned to United States, and the advent of accessible transportation to Europe made such journeys safe and feasible. Beginning in the 1870s, consistent annual improvements in steamship service allowed a steadily increasing number of Americans to visit Europe for pleasure and to test their abilities to navigate the socially complex world of elite European circles. Vessels typically used to ship industrial products, such as those of the Cunard Line, expanded their passenger capacities, due to the increasing demand by Americans to travel abroad. Other companies—such as the English White Star Line, the French Line, the Hamburg American Line, and the Holland American Line—followed suit, thereby providing Americans with several choices in transatlantic travel. Competition between the companies decreased prices significantly: in 1860, the price of a first-class passage between the United States and Great Britain was roughly £17 ($76.50) but had dropped to £9 in 1883, a little over $40. Prices rose slightly in the 1890s, but one could still purchase a round-trip ticket for around $63—the same price as a bicycle in the same period. For those interested in traveling in steerage, the price was generally one-half of the first-class ticket. For everyone, the trip lasted a short ten days.[35] According to the Hon. Maud Paucefote, "year by year America creeps nearer and nearer to England by means of the accelerated speed of steamers."[36]

Such advancements in transatlantic travel allowed socially ambitious Americans shunned by Mrs. Astor and the "Four Hundred" to try their hand in European social circles. Not only did a voyage to England provide an opportunity to recover from American ostracism, but it also gave the chance to participate in dinners and balls in European cities, such as Paris and London. If a family, or, more typically, mothers and daughters, could gain valuable invitations to parties given in major cities, such success abroad might result in social acceptance at home. A number of Americans found that while their status at home prevented them from entering the elite social circles, quite the opposite proved true abroad.

At first, most Americans spent weeks and even months in Paris, long considered *the* ultimate European city in which to enjoy fine food and elaborate parties. But with the onset of the Franco-Prussian War in 1870, London became the European city of American choice. As the *London Times* concluded, "when an American has made a fortune he finds it almost impossible to live quietly in his own country. The chief attraction is England."[37]

When Americans began spending their leisure time in London, they found themselves awed by the time-honored tradition of the London Season. This period lasted ten weeks, corresponding with the schedule of Parliament; hence, the cemented connection between politics and society. Depending on the hunting season, some families began moving from their country estates into the city as early as January, but May 1 marked the official beginning of the London Season. Gentlemen and ladies participated in nearly endless dances, concerts, court balls, dinners, private balls, breakfasts, public parties, and sporting events.

The London Season originated at the turn of the seventeenth century and functioned primarily as a marriage market for Great Britain's aristocratic families. Brought up separately from girls by nannies and nursemaids, boys then received formal education at boarding schools while girls learned from in-house tutors. Rarely did boys and girls interact with one another until after their presentation at Court. No acceptable young lady could spend even half an hour with a young man absent of supervision without seriously damaging her reputation, and thus her chances at a successful marriage. Proper young *ladies*—to refer to one as a *woman* suggested she was experienced sexually—were accompanied by their maids during the day and by chaperones in the evening. The annual Season provided the first opportunity for gentlemen and ladies to mingle under permissible circumstances and evaluate acceptable and available individuals as potential spouses. It was the venue for families to introduce their daughters for marriage through formal entertaining.[38]

A young woman's presentation at the Royal Court marked the first step in her formally participating in the London Season. Her presentation to the monarch and to society as well required the acquisition of an impressive wardrobe. One Season typically required an inventory exceeding three hundred items—an investment that could cost more than $20,000.[39] A young lady needed approximately fifty gowns (anywhere from $800 to $2,500 each), several cloaks, fans, jeweled combs and hairnets, in addition to jewels including diamonds and pearls. And her training for the proper deportment and learning to curtsy often took months. A young lady's presentation required sponsorship by a female relation who had previously survived the same exercise. Alternatively, women from foreign countries, explains Anne De Courcy, and "British women married to foreign nationals could be presented only through the diplomatic representative of the country concerned."[40] Consequently, the introduction of American women to British society required the literal and figurative stamp of approval of the diplomatic corps; hence, the connection between Anglo-American marriages and Anglo-American relations is clear, as the vetting and approval of American ladies for presentation overseas mimicked the official presentation of papers of consuls abroad.

All eyes fixed on the young lady during her moment of public evaluation by royalty and by all of London society. This event marked her official entrance into the adult world; it symbolized her passage from the schoolroom to the ballroom. Needless to say, being presented at court held the potential for great success or a terrible failure.[41] Furthermore, an American woman's success or failure abroad determined much in terms of Anglo-American perceptions and relations.

Generally speaking, a young lady officially entered society via Court presentation at the age of eighteen, while gentlemen officially participated in the Season after finishing their education at Oxford or Cambridge. Bachelors active in the London Season might be older than the ladies by anywhere from four to ten years. For the gentlemen and ladies involved, a typical day started with a horseback ride through Hyde Park. A lady trained from an early age to ride gracefully through Rotten Row or the Ladies' Mile, shaking hands with friends and dismounting with ease, thereby demonstrating not only that her family had a country estate but also that she had received ample equestrian lessons. Breakfast followed the morning ride, after which women tended to household errands or called on very close friends, reserving the afternoons for formal calls on necessary acquaintances. After lunch, men spent the afternoon at Parliament or at men's clubs. Everyone dined together in the evening at six or seven o'clock, with an opera or other activity afterward; at no time from the beginning to the end of the performance did a gentleman leave his lady alone. Balls and dances started at ten in the evening and could last until three in the morning. A ball generally began with a waltz, followed by a quadrille, and then one or two other styles of dances; thus, all participants had to be well versed in the art of dancing. A mutual acquaintance could introduce a gentleman to a lady for a single dance, but that gentleman could not presume to pursue a lady afterward. Servants assisted guests in their respective dressing rooms, and the hostess supplied a full set of toiletries for any emergencies.[42]

Following her presentation at court, a young lady would likely attend some twenty-five breakfasts, thirty dinners, fifty balls, and sixty parties in a single London Season. In addition to these various engagements, each month of the Season included one major event. The Derby, a horserace for the masses, occurred in May or June, with Ascot following as the Season's climax. The Henley Regatta took place in July, along with the cricket contests between rivals such as Eton and Harrow or Oxford and Cambridge. Parliament adjourned on August 12, which coincided with the beginning of grouse season and a return to the country. Mid-August's mass exodus from London in came as suddenly as the influx of wives, carriages, footmen, and servants had earlier, "because everyone knows: better dead than seen alive in London in August."[43]

A young lady had two or three Seasons to marry—or have high society consider her a failure. London elites regarded any woman who reached the age of thirty unmarried as a hopeless spinster. But one nearly foolproof way to enjoy a triumphant Season was to catch the eye of the Prince of Wales, Edward VII, better known as Bertie. American women practiced this particular method of social entry, as the prince considered American ladies with a special regard. If a young American could strike his fancy with an especially lovely dress or through a charming conversation, he might ask her to dance. A single dance with the Prince of Wales earned an American lady passage into London society, which gave her invitations to the best dances and dinners and allowed her to meet all the best people in London. When Edward gave an American heiress his royal seal of approval, she became fashionable and was deemed successful in London society.[44]

While Edward would one day become King of England, he did little to prove his seriousness or dedication to the job prior to formally accepting his crown. His parents, Queen Victoria and Prince Albert, had set a royal tone of sobriety, simplicity, and stoicism, and Bertie found his parents' attitude toward the London Season and social life in general boring. The royal couple took their roles as dutiful monarchs so seriously that they found it difficult to delegate any royal duties to their son. Reacting to this air of solemnity; the absence of responsibility; and a wide availability of wine, women, and song, the crown prince earned a reputation in Britain as a playboy. He loved to socialize, dance, and enjoy fine food and the company of beautiful and charming women. When enchanting American ladies began appearing in London after 1870, he developed a genuine admiration for them. "American girls are livelier, better educated, and less hampered by etiquette. They are not as squeamish as their English sisters," he explained, "and they are better able to take care of themselves."[45] In many ways, Bertie deemed Americans more desirable than their female British cousins as wives and leaders of poli-social circles.

Adding to Edward's fun-loving personality was his loyalty to those he took into his circle. Few men of Bertie's standing remained faithful to friends the way Edward did. Once he deemed a gentleman or a lady worthy of his time and affection, they remained close henceforth. While his parents rarely attended such Season affairs such as Ascot, Edward did so regularly, becoming acquainted with the members of the aristocracy, House of Commons, House of Lords, and their wives. He met a number of American ladies at such engagements and remained on close terms with them; among these women were Lady Randolph Churchill and Lady Mary Curzon. However, he maintained a small inner circle of intimate associates; this tight circle of friends earned the nickname "Marlborough House Set," because they so often spent time at the Prince's London residence. His enthusiastic acceptance of American heiresses into his private circle resulted in wide recognition of American heiresses as suitable for London's highest poli-social circles.[46]

American Women, British Men, and Marital Expectations

So who were these grandes dames who charmed Edward's heart, stimulated his wit, and gained admission into the most elite and privileged circles in the world— "women that could tell a good story" and, according to the prince "were born card players"?[47] American heiresses arrived in Great Britain in three waves. The "Buccaneers" were first group of American women who married into (or raided, depending on one's perspective) the British aristocracy, which includes the pioneering marital efforts of Jennie Jerome, roughly dating from 1860 to 1880. Their success proved that these women could more easily participate in the social elite overseas, and London specifically, than penetrate Mrs. Astor's cold heart in New York; there was "no need to flail again at the cliffs of New York indifference or slink home to remain a big fish in a small Midwestern pond." Next, between 1880 and 1900, "self-made girls" such as Mary Endicott, Mary Leiter, and Conseulo Vanderbilt entered London, succeeding by relying on "their own doings, built by each on her own charms, her own merits, her own unceasing efforts . . . transform[ing] herself from American nobody to English aristocrat." While their fathers worked constantly at increasing their fortunes, the daughters worked constantly at improving their minds, wardrobes, and standings in society. "Being American," they believed "anything could be accomplished by an act of will and plenty of effort." The final phase of American women in Britain, the American aristocrats, Nancy Langhorne Shaw, for example began around 1900 and continued until World War I. This type of American woman "would marry a nobleman not on a whim, not because she needed the social boost, but because it was her *right*."[48] By this point, the United States, behind the leadership of people like Mrs. Astor and Ward McAllister, had created an American version of the British nobility. The daughters of this new generation of American heiresses arrived in England confident in their own identity, culture, and wealth, and determined to enter the British aristocracy not to boost their family status at home but rather as equals of the men they married. Without a doubt, Nancy Astor demonstrates this newfound level of equality between American women and their British husbands.

Most young heiresses hailed from New York City or another significant metropolitan area in the Northeast, but many of them came from as far away as Florida, Texas, and California. Approximately half of the women who married European titles lived in New York City, underscoring the fact that the financial capital of the United States had found its place on Wall Street. Roughly 10 percent of transatlantic wives came from Boston and Philadelphia, while a small number were from the South. Thus, the basis of wealth remained secure in places like Boston or Chicago, in the cases of Mary Endicott and Mary Leiter, in their patrician inheritance, while the "newly risen rich" found their fortunes in New York City, as did Jennie Jerome and Conseulo Vanderbilt. "Parvenu elites . . . depended on publicity and costly display to elevate themselves," Frederic Copel Jaher contends, "upon imported or imitated European titles, artifacts and styles to substitute for their own lack of rooted credentials and conventions."[49] A number of American ladies from Louisiana participated in transatlantic marriages, but, based on the cultural connection they shared as French descendants in Louisiana, they were more likely to marry French nobles. Many young ladies from wealthy Louisiana families also spoke French fluently and could integrate into elite circles in France with relative ease. While many of the nouveau riche families in New England held an Anglophilic longing for Old England, many leading families in Louisiana held a similar passion for France.

Many of the American heiresses who married British aristocrats came from nouveau riche families who sought the approval and acceptance of the United States' old money families. The new generation of American money imitated what it saw as the behavior, leisure, and family traditions of the Rothschilds and the DuPonts. This meant hiring the very best nannies, tutors, and cultural educators for their daughters. Affluent parents shaped, trained, and molded their daughters almost from the cradle to represent the family as equivalents, if not the superiors, of the daughters of old American money in sophistication. Many newly rich Americans hired German or French tutors so their daughters could learn foreign languages from native speakers. These families also frequently hired former professors and dons from the best schools in England as their daughters' private tutors. For cultural training, they hired accomplished European musicians for private lessons suitable for an aspiring classical pianist. These families spared no expense in providing the very best in education and personal growth for their daughters. The goal was not to raise daughters to become scientists, professors, or accomplished musicians, however. It was to produce young ladies who could win over the social elite in America and travel to Europe, specifically England, to prove to the United States and the world that American ladies lacked for nothing and was all for which a husband could hope. Again, such an intense approach to education and deportment resulted in American women who were at ease in the highest circles of international intrigue and foreign affairs.

Years of educational and musical training paid off for the cohort of American ladies entering British circles. In 1888, one English periodical asserted, "It is a well-established fact, that there is no more fascinating creature to be found anywhere than a thoroughly well-born and well-bred American lady."[50] Another journal in 1896 described American women as "the most finished product of the democratic principle."[51] But for all their preparation and proper upbringing, American women did not become robotic personae of sophistication and culture. Instead, they retained a liveliness in personality and an ability to charm anyone—men and women—with their frankness and candor. "Compared to the European women," Richard Rapson explains, "the Americans were freer . . . more self-reliant."[52] In many ways, American ladies seemed completely different from their British sisters and offered European, and specifically British, men something fresh in their presence at dinners, at dances, and eventually, in marriage. According to financier Chauncey M. Depew, "The American girl comes along, prettier than her English sister, full of dash, and snap and go, and she is a revelation to the Englishman."[53] Comparing American heiresses to English and French women, Rudyard Kipling insisted, "The girls of America are above and beyond them all. They are clever; they can talk. Yea, it is said that they can think."[54] And as wives and informal ambassadors, they reigned supreme. Reported the *New York Times*, "What the American girl has 'put over' the British Empire is truly wonderful. . . . The American wife in England is a phenomenon that stands alone."[55] While a number of American influences began appearing during this period, with American products and trade expanding with great speed, journalist William T. Stead responded by writing that "among the influences which are Americanizing the world, the American girl is one of the most conspicuous, and the most charming."[56]

For all that American ladies had to offer in terms of their impressive intellects and sophisticated social graces, public opinion continued to fix on the monetary factor in Anglo-American marriages. When the *New York Times* announced the engagement of Miss May Goelet to the Duke of Roxburghe in 1903, the article stressed, "The present fortune of Miss Goelet is estimated at about $20,000,000."[57] While newspapers on both sides of the Atlantic hunted for even the most minute details of these young women's lives—from their shoe sizes to the shapes of their noses—Americans and Britons remained obsessed with the amount of money transferred as a result of such unions. Clearly, both sides stood to gain, since they typically functioned as informal contractual agreements that addressed the needs and desires of both parties: "high status and low income on the one side; high income and low status on the other."[58] Most often, the fathers of American heiresses hoped that their daughters' marriages would bring increased connections in England and result in increases in business. The mothers of American heiresses sought increased social standing in the United States.[59] But some confusion remains as to whether the actual women who married British aristocrats viewed themselves as pawns in complex exchanges of money for title or believed they decided for themselves on Anglo-American marriages. From a British perspective, the American woman "is set on getting the best she can for her money, or her father's money."[60] In either case, an American heiress would not receive any of her father's fortune if she did not marry. Therefore, her decision to marry resulted in access to wealth and international influence; she might as well marry someone with a title and enjoy the benefits provided to a British lady rather than an untitled American man. By embarking on her own international life, she began her journey as a lifelong emissary abroad.

Because of the allure of titles and influence, these American women left their homes, families, and homeland behind to live in another country. While New York City received immigrants, many New York heiresses left the United States never to return. Historians often discuss immigration in the sense of Europeans leaving their homes to journey to the United States. In marrying members of the British aristocracy, American women underwent reverse immigration, which proceeded along two courses: first, the process of cultural assimilation, the outward signs of the immigrant's adaptation to the dominant culture; and second, that of cultural identity, or the immigrant's views of her own fluid and changing ethnicity.[61] The failure or success of the American heiress's cultural transition, and very likely the failure or success of her transatlantic marriage, depended on the experience of the specific woman in the context of her union. The more successfully she adapted to British high culture, the more the British accepted her—because of or in spite of her American heritage. In many cases, Britons expected the American woman to take on a completely new identity. Following her marriage, she was always addressed as "Duchess Grosvenor" or "Lady Baring," as formal society in London did not permit the use of first names. If an American woman's activities appeared in British papers, the articles sometimes referred to her as "Lady Whitaker, formerly Miss Fitzgerald," highlighting the fact that with her transatlantic marriage, she left behind her family, her country, and her previous identity.

The list of American heiresses who married British titles during this period reads like a who's who of American political circles. Some of the more prominent political marriages included those of the daughter of President Ulysses S. Grant; the daughter of Grant's secretary of state, Hamilton Fish; and the daughter of Vice President Theodore Frelinghuysen.[62] Both of the daughters of United States ambassador to England John Lothrop Motley married Britons.[63] Additionally, William Whitney, Cleveland's secretary of the navy, supported both of his daughters' marriages to Britons.[64] After Mary Leiter Curzon's death in 1906, George Nathaniel Curzon, the former viceroy of India, married Grace Hinds, daughter of J. Monroe Hinds, the former U.S. Consul General in Rio de Janeiro.[65]

In 1876, Sir William Harcourt, the leader of the Liberal Party, married Elizabeth Motley, daughter of an American historian. Caroline Starr Balestier married the author Rudyard Kipling in 1892. Sir Michael Herbert, ambassador to the United States from 1902 to 1903, married Leila Wilson, the daughter of yet another American millionaire, Richard Thornton Wilson. This union also made Herbert the brother-in-law of Mrs. Cornelius Vanderbilt and a close social contact of John Jacob Astor. Leila's youngest sister, Grace, married Cornelius Vanderbilt III in 1896. Such a number of prominent Anglo-American marriages ultimately created an elite network of leading families on both sides of the Atlantic. Many Britons believed, "So close has the union between ourselves and the United States become that Americans are hardly looked upon as foreigners at all, so many people having American relatives."[66] Thus, the idea of Anglo-American marriages influencing foreign relations had become one of maintaining the family business.

As an American heiress arrived in Great Britain as the wife of a leading British man, her new countrymen and -women constantly scrutinized her behavior, speech, and mannerisms as a reflection of her American nationality. Some American-born, British-wed women considered their national identity as both negotiable and malleable, given the circumstances at any given moment, by rejecting or affirming their American or British identities in everyday interactions by contesting various cultural practices. Other transatlantic wives felt that their marriages required the complete metamorphosis of becoming traditional British wives, thus shedding all aspects of their personalities that identified them as American. These women did not consider maintaining both identities simultaneously a wise course of action or even a possibility.[67] In fact, many of them became highly sensitive and aware of their American identity and nationality only after they had left the United States. American heiresses could never assume to assimilate fully themselves into British culture and circles, always being identified as the American wife of . . . or the American mother of . . . even decades after having left the United States permanently. They would have benefited from the advice George I gave his sons: "Never forget that you are foreigners . . . and never let them remember it."[68] Some of our American-born, British-wed envoys were more successful in this endeavor, Conseulo Vanderbilt, for example, than others, such as Nancy Astor.

In efforts to integrate themselves as Britons and adapt to their new surroundings, American heiresses became high-profile hostesses in British political and social circles. As part of their duties as wives, specifically as the wives of British dukes, lords, or Members of Parliament, American ladies played important roles as foreign relation mediators while acknowledging their subordinate status. "But in this historical moment, a small group of Anglo-American women . . . learned how to create and manage a domestic environment in which the business of influencing others was the major occupation," Susan Harris explains, as her "public image was rooted in her domestic, and secondary, relations, suddenly became the woman who could control other lives and public values." Her wealth provided the time and means for her to devote her days and energy to hosting the day's leading men and women at parties and dinners, thus making her a leading woman as well. A successful hostess, much like a clever diplomatic wife, made people feel comfortable in her home, spoke with her guests, listened to visitors, acted as a confidante. Not altering opinions directly but rather creating the situation and atmosphere for conversation and personal exchange of ideas and concerns, the physical space of a hostess's home functioned as an important element of her power. The hostess herself influenced those around her by "putting other people in contact with each other and so directed the conversation," Harris continues. "In this, her power lay not in her direction to any particular individual but rather in her ability to bring people together so that they could enact the agenda that she set."[69] For the American-born, British-wed women now living permanently in Great Britain, the agenda evolved over time to focus on the amelioration of Anglo-American relations.

In efforts to bring about a close relationship between the United States and Great Britain, many wives acted not only as drawing-room diplomats but as philanthropic activists, using their volunteer efforts for Anglo-American causes. Now formally ladies in British aristocratic circles, American women played the role of Lady Bountiful—known for her charity, generosity, and volunteerism—frequently volunteering in the communities in which they lived, but the causes of their volunteer activities often focused on Anglo-American relations in some capacity. Through her volunteer efforts, a woman could exercise some degree of power within the traditionally masculine worlds of diplomacy and government while still utilizing the shield of women's charitable work. Thus, as K. D. Reynolds maintains, volunteerism in aristocratic political society actually reverses the notion of "separate spheres," as women actively led family estates, community interests, and national (and in this case, international) politics in a nongovernmental partnership with other women. As she argues, "a working aristocracy required women as well as men to function fully, and not simply for the hereditary dimension."[70] These American-born, British-wed women created public roles for themselves, both individually and collectively, through the subtle and skillful manipulation of soft power as they placed Anglo-American relations, and the need for the United States and Great Britain to see each other as allies instead of adversaries, at the forefront of public consciousness on both sides of the Atlantic.[71]

In becoming the ideal British wife, an American woman needed to have a great deal of wealth, serve as a talented hostess, and use her leisure time for volunteer work—all in an effort to endear herself not only to her husband and his family but to all Britons. But who were these men who chose to look outside their country when selecting a wife? Much like their future spouses, aristocratic men in Britain enjoyed privileged upbringings and the best in educational experiences. These men grew up in fine country homes where they received their primary education from private tutors before they obtained their secondary education at places like Eton, Harrow, Rugby, and Winchester—elite boarding schools largely reserved for the sons of leading British families. These young men generally pursued their university educations at Oxford or Cambridge, the two oldest schools of higher education in United Kingdom, thus becoming "Oxbridge Men." The significance of their educational experiences rests on the fact that from the age of thirteen, elite British men matured personally and intellectually in the absence of their families, individuals outside their socioeconomic class, and women. While family could visit them on approved weekends and during various events like the annual boat races, these boys became men with the guidance of dons and professors. This personal and proximal distance from their families resulted in what Americans considered distant relationships among basically all members of elite British families. The British government informally charged Oxford and Cambridge with the production of socially and academically acceptable men to perform the duties of the British professional elite. "Part of this education consisted of the formation of an elite *esprit de corps*," Paul Deslandes maintains, "that encouraged a sense not only of a masculine community but of superiority."[72] Finally, their formative years occurred in the absence of women, thereby enforcing the "separate sphere" conviction that men and women pursued their various educational transformations to prepare British men for the halls of Parliament and women the halls of their London homes or country estates. But a closer inspection of such a separation proves that the supposed delineation is arbitrary at best. Overt actions, direct or indirect, on the part of American women to violate this separation of public and private domains met with immediate and harsh rebuke from not only their husbands but from Britons in general, as Mary Leiter learned very early from her very traditionally minded husband. British men saw such behavior as *women* not knowing their place in society while British women viewed it as indicative of an *American* identity. Nevertheless, British husbands desired their American wives to do their professional biddings, and this was deemed part of the wives' spousal identity and the couples' shared personal and professional success.

Once such a man completed his education, he embarked on a career as a member of the British professional elite. Predictably, he joined the government as a local or national politician, civil servant, colonial bureaucrat, lawyer, or perhaps as a military officer. But such an occupation frequently existed in addition to a hereditary title and an annual allowance based on his family's income from the landed estate, although British estates produced significantly decreasing agricultural profits for the sons of British aristocracy in this period. By elite British living standards, a bachelor who earned £500 a year had an adequate salary, while his peers deemed an income exceeding £1,000 annually as that of a wealthy man.[73] But such earnings would not allow him to marry, maintain a city and country home, employ servants, and start a family. A first-born son, thanks to the practice of primogeniture, could depend on one day inheriting his father's title, the family estate, and land, thus guaranteeing him a relatively secure income. But younger sons and, especially, daughters could anticipate little, if any, financial support from their families, which created a fair amount of sibling rivalry.[74] When rumors began to circulate that Jennie Jerome would marry Randolph Churchill, her sister Leonie confided in her diary: "Last night at the circus, someone told me that Jennie would marry the second son of the Duke of Marlborough—a Good Thing tho' he *is* a younger son."[75] Hence, if a wife brought her own fortune, or at least a stable income, into the marriage, she appeared a financially attractive spouse for a member of the British peerage. Since the agricultural decline across Europe affected the sons *and* daughters of British aristocrats, young British ladies could in no way bring a significant amount of money into a marriage. Once again, Anglo-American marriages seemed to address a number of issues for eligible bachelors and bachelorettes in Great Britain and the United States.

But not all British men married for money alone. George Nathaniel Curzon, the future Viceroy of India, contemplated his need for financial stability and desire for love for many years before marrying an American girl. In 1889, during a long visit with family friends Henry and Margaret White, Curzon spoke candidly to the latter about his apparent conflicting wishes. She wrote in her diary, "George Curzon came & spent the night—long talk about his marrying—says he must have money and won't marry unless he loves." She candidly observed, "Difficult combination—"[76] Curzon married Mary Leiter in 1895, a true Anglo-American love match, but this union was a distinct exception. More often than not, members of the British elite proved successful in their marital quest "for money if not necessarily for happiness."[77]

Another consideration for American heiresses in seeking out British aristocrats as husbands was the man's rank within the peerage. A duke ranked the highest among the British peers; only twenty-seven of these existed at any one time. As a New York newspaper explained in 1886, "Dukes are the loftiest kind of nobleman in England. . . . Of these there are only two available for matrimonial purposes. These are the Dukes of Manchester and Roxburghe. The Duke of Hamilton is already spoken for, the Duke of Norfolk is an old widower, and the Duke of Leinster only eleven years old."[78] If a woman managed to wed a duke, she earned the title of duchess and both of them were addressed formally as "Your Grace." But the complexity of titles and following proper etiquette in addressing a member of the nobility could produce entertaining exchanges. When hosting a luncheon on one occasion, Consuelo Vanderbilt, then Lady Marlborough, invited a member of the clergy. Prior to eating, she addressed her husband by inquiring, "May I say grace, Your Grace?"[79] This exchange proved far more entertaining to the American wife than her British husband.

A marquess fell far below a duke within the British hierarchy, who was always addressed as "Lord," while his wife received the title of "Lady." Following in descending order of the peerage were earls, viscounts, and barons; all of their wives were ladies. For all of these peers, the titles passed on to their children. Even farther below these men were baronets and knights, who were called "Sir" and their wives "Lady." Their children received no titles. While a great gap existed between a duke and a knight, all of these people were members of the British nobility. Nevertheless, American heiresses (and often their mothers) wanted to receive the most notoriety and rank out of their marriages; hence, dukes were the British husband of choice.[80]

In many cases, the courting practices between an American heiress and any member of the British peerage amounted to little more than newspaper advertisements and the negotiations with her father, his lawyer, and his personal banker. One 1901 advertisement in the *Daily World* disclosed the ultimate goal of securing marriage to an heiress, though "her age and looks are immaterial, . . . her character must be irreproachable."[81] In the same year, this call for a prospective wife appeared in the *Daily Telegraph*: "An English peer of very old title is desirous of marrying at once a very wealthy lady. . . . If among your clients you know such a lady, who is willing to purchase the rank of a peeress for £65,000 sterling, paid in cash to her future husband, and who has sufficient wealth besides to keep up the rank of a peeress, I should be pleased if you would communicate with me."[82] Both Americans and Britons, men and women, placed such advertisements. Another advertisement introduced a "refined young woman of 19 [who] wishes to meet [a] well bred man who can appreciate and afford the luxury of a well groomed companion; object, matrimony." Several advertisements placed by men and women in this period expressed an explicit goal by ending their personal ads, "object, matrimony." While the notices generally offered specific information regarding money, residence, and weight, they failed to mention details concerning "personal attraction and human compatibility."[83]

The wedding of an American heiress and a British aristocrat quite often served as an indication of how much money the young woman would bring to England and an opportunity for her family to advertise their wealth at home. After the Civil War, the traditional practice of a young couple being married in the parlor of the bride's family home fell out of style. With the growth of numerous fortunes in the United States, particularly in New York, lavish church weddings became fashionable. By the end of the nineteenth century, "house weddings came to be regarded as the shabby expedients of Baptists and Methodists, who had neither altar nor liturgy."[84] Many of these new weddings took place with ten or more bridesmaids (who, in some cases, had been selected by the mother of the bride and not the bride herself, for aesthetic purposes) in front of some two thousand or more guests, followed by an extravagant reception in which a full orchestra entertained the guests. At the wedding reception of Cornelia Sherman Martin to the Fourth Earl of Craven in

1893, the orchestra fittingly played "a popular Negro song, 'If You Haint Got No Money You Needn't Come 'Round.'" Such sacred occasions deteriorated into events for nouveau riche families to exhibit conspicuous consumption.

Problems for these young newlyweds derived from serious differences of marital expectations, not only in the purposes of their marriages but also in the roles the spouses would assume. Very often, a British aristocrat anticipated little more from his marriage than a woman who behaved as a proper British lady and fulfilled her duty in continuing the family line by producing at least one son, but preferably two—the proverbial "heir and the spare." Love and companionship rarely figured into it. This may be explained by the fact that men held very and functional conceptions of marriage, or perhaps it stemmed from how Britons approached marriage from very realistic and practical perspectives. Elite married couples in Britain often took sexual partners outside the marriage and treated adultery in a very matter-of-fact way. As John Gillis explains, "sex, like everything else, was seen in highly impersonal terms, as a duty or a right that transcended personal sentiment." Accordingly, the stability of a marriage in Britain "was dependent on how well a husband and wife performed their respective duties," Gillis clarifies, "not on how well they got along as a couple."[85]

For their part, American heiresses entered these unions with very different expectations. Young, and often naïve, they anticipated their married lives in Britain would replicate their thrilling London Season experiences. This romantic expectation could stem from a female viewpoint of marriage or a conception of marriage as it functioned in the United States. Much to their dismay, the courting ended the moment the bridge and groom exchanged vows. Overwhelming waves of homesickness flooded the hearts of American ladies in Britain and quickly resulted in very unhappy marriages indeed. Following Mary Leiter's marriage to George Curzon in 1895, she wrote home to her family, "Just tell the dear [American] girls once a month so they won't forget it *never never never* to marry away from home unless they find a George as it is always a sorrow to be an alien—and 50 years in a new country never alters your nationality and I shall never be an Englishwoman in feeling or character. And *oh!* the unhappiness I see around me here in England amongst American women."[86] Mary's family added to her homesickness, as they only infrequently visited to England. Her father missed Mary so much and saw her so little that he bitterly wrote in a letter, "Mary might as well be dead."[87]

With few exceptions, British men did not want to hear about their wives' unhappiness. After all, hundreds of British women would gladly take her place. For the most part, American women found their husbands' extramarital activities reprehensible. Very often, Anglo-American marriages ended in a transfer of wealth and an eventual signing of divorce papers.[88]

Anglo-Saxon Identity and the "American Colony" in London

Despite the individual success or failure of Anglo-American marriages, contemporary ideals concerning race told Americans and Britons that such marriages represented the overall union between the United States and Great Britain. Very different ideas about "race," "blood," and "civilization" existed in the late nineteenth century. Blood equated to race, and the two concepts included elements today considered cultural attributes and did not differentiate between social or biological traits. Many people thought of race as "a community of sentiments, modes of thought, an unconscious inheritance from their ancestors," thereby functioning as an "integrated physical, linguistic, and cultural totality."[89] The construction of an Anglo-Saxon identity blurred the line between blood and culture as many people began using phrases such as "Anglo-Saxonism," "English-speaking peoples," and the "Anglo-Saxon race." As Benjamin Disraeli once proclaimed, "All is race; there is no other truth."[90] This was a day and age in which "Americans in all parts of the world," Akira Iriye argues, "had come to take the superiority of the white race for granted."[91]

While scientific ideas about the alleged superiority of certain races emerged in the mid-nineteenth century, social Darwinism took hold in the United States in the late nineteenth century far more than elsewhere.[92] Political leaders, such as Theodore Roosevelt, and public orators, such as Josiah Strong, spoke of the inherent connection between the United States and Great Britain based on their shared language, heritage, legal system, and history. More and more leaders on both sides of the Atlantic verbalized the need for Anglo-Americans to come together to lead and civilize the world. The bleeding of Anglo-Saxonist ideas into foreign policy occurred within the same period that Rudyard Kipling's famous poem "White Man's Burden" was published.[93] Popular belief in both the United States and Great Britain dictated that only through a strong alliance between the two countries could they achieve something greater than themselves. As Walter LaFeber explains, "Salvation lay in the fulfillment of the Anglo-Saxon mission to reshape the world in the mold of western civilization."[94]

For many people on both sides of the Atlantic, transatlantic marriages seemed to foreshadow the "promising joint imperial ventures [between the United States and Great Britain] as they were happily united in the permanent ties of a race alliance."[95] Many apparently found satisfaction in what they envisioned as proof of the alleged Anglo-Saxon race coming full circle. According to a contemporary magazine, "the marriages of American girls with Englishmen far exceeds those with men of any other nationality, and the ties of a common language, blood and affinity make this but natural."[96] In view of this trend, Anglo-American marriages served as a "racial exceptionalist bridge between the United States and the British Empire." [97] What better way to fully illustrate the kinship and familial ties between

Britons and Americans? Thus, the union of an American woman and British man symbolized the marriage of interests of Great Britain and the United States. In this manner, transatlantic marriages represented racial alliances as a means to ease diplomatic relations, most often commented on by Mary Endicott Chamberlain, rather than simply a means of achieving economic ambitions. Upon the news of yet another Anglo-American marriage, the Marquess of Lorne gushed, "How the American alliance is getting on!"[98]

As a result of their marriages into the British aristocracy, American wives used their wealth and position to place Anglo-American relations at the forefront of a public transatlantic exchange of ideals. So many American women had married titled Europeans that an annual periodical that traced their numbers was launched. *Titled Americans: A List of American Ladies Who Have Married Foreigners of Rank* first appeared in 1890, and while it dealt with all American women who had married European nobility, the large majority of the unions were between Americans and Britons, evidenced by a section with the heading, "A Carefully Compiled List of Peers Who Are Supposed to be Eager to Lay Their Coronets, and Incidentally Their Hearts, at the Feet of the All-Conquering American Girl." As the *Titled American* insisted, "English titles enjoy greater consideration, both at home and abroad, than those conferred by any other State."[99] The *New York Times* echoed such sentiments when it branded this cohort as "American woman who have given their hearts and money to foreigners."[100]

Another Americans-in-London pamphlet appeared in 1902. The *Directory of Americans Resident in London & Great Britain, Americans Firms and Agencies* provided listings of American businesses in London, British-American merchants, American banks and bankers, and titled Americans; a classified business directory; a shopping guide; a residential directory; and a guide to American business enterprises in Great Britain. The directory identified those belonging to the American Society in London, and the Society of American Women in London, in addition to their meeting days and times. The directory also advertised "The Anglo-American Press" as the "only newspaper published in the United Kingdom specifically devoted to American interests."[101]

These publications, in addition to the hundreds of American-born, British-wed spouses, acted in concert to establish an unofficial American colony in London. A growing number of Americans lived in London or traveled regularly to Great Britain, to the point that organizations such as the Anglo-American League, formed in 1898, boasted a membership number exceeding five hundred.[102] In 1902, journalist William T. Stead estimated that some fifteen thousand Americans lived in London.[103] The American colony in London enjoyed a general acceptance by British society. In the words of one periodical, "All society is strife, but the storm centre of London society is unquestionably the American colony."[104] In quantity and quality,

American women residing in Britain exerted an extraordinary degree of influence as a result of their marriages to British aristocrats and their own efforts, activities, and relationships in Britain. Given these developments, Stead anticipated "a day when a considerable proportion of the head men in England will be sons of American mothers," arguably illustrated by the political careers of Jennie Jerome Churchill's son Winston and Mary Endicott Chamberlain's stepson Neville, both of whom served as prime minister and whose Anglo-American affinities served as an international priority throughout their respective political careers.[105]

A number of factors came together in the nineteenth century to bring about the trend of transatlantic marriages in general and Anglo-American marriages specifically. Changes in national economies, improvements in transatlantic travel, redefinition of societal elites, the approval of American women by Edward VII, the power of the London Season, and ideas concerning Anglo-Saxons all coincided, thereby courting transatlantic marriages. These unions resulted in the relocations of hundreds of American women to Great Britain with varying results. Some marriages succeeded, others faltered, and still others existed in name only. In every case, the ability or inability of an American woman to adjust and adapt to her new country, husband, family, and surroundings influenced British ideas about American women and the United States as a whole. By virtue of their marriages to leading British men, their lives unfolded under the watchful eye of London society, elite political circles, and public opinions of all Anglo-Americans. Just as her father worked to earn money, the American heiress worked "to make America respectable. . . . Because she was young and rich and pretty, and because her father and brothers were too busy making money to take on the job, the American heiress was the New World's ambassador to the old."[106]

But even as attachés, these women had much more to offer than simply their youth, money, and looks. People on both sides of the Atlantic observed American-born, British-wed women—their marriages, associations, friendships, influence—for reasons far more complicated and imperative than their tiny waists and huge dowries. While "the private lives of public men and women . . . have always been the subject of natural curiosity," this proved especially true for the women who through their marriages joined the ranks of the British aristocracy but, in their own ways, forever remained American.[107] Now we turn to examine five individual women who each approached their lives, marriages, and stations as liaisons in Britain differently, who created their own opportunities abroad, and who made the most of their unique international positions as ambassadors.

CHAPTER TWO

Amazon Attaché

Jennie Jerome Churchill

A girl born, and bred in the backwoods of some Western State, will adopt the manners and customs of her husband's country to such an extent that, after a few years, she might pass as of his nationality.

—LADY RANDOLPH CHURCHILL

The large majority of American women who married British aristocrats in this period hailed from New York City; in fact, the woman who often receives credit for serving as the pioneer in the Anglo-American marital market called Brooklyn home.[1] Born on January 9, 1854, Jennie Jerome was the second daughter of Leonard and Clara Hall Jerome. The Jerome family experienced both extremes—great successes and great failures—of the post–Civil War business boom and epitomized the rise of the nouveau riche. While Mr. Jerome worked in New York, making and losing multiple fortunes, the Jerome women conquered Europe, starting in Paris and moving to London, cutting a path for hundreds of American mothers and daughters to follow.

Leonard Jerome, a graduate of Princeton College, began his adult life in Rochester, New York.[2] After she married Jerome in 1849, Clara Hall bore four daughters. The first was born on April 15, 1851, and Leonard and Clara named her Clarita, in honor of her mother. The family enjoyed prominence in Rochester before Leonard moved his family to Brooklyn to chase even greater affluence in New York City. Jerome built two houses in Madison Square, one as his home and one that became the Manhattan Club House; he understood the importance of social capital as well as financial capital.[3]

While Jerome of course loved business, he also had cultural interests. He especially enjoyed the opera, almost as much as the opera singers, with whom he often

Lady Randolph
Churchill. HU023790.
© Hulton-Deutsch
Collection/CORBIS.

had affairs. He financed the careers of many singers, provided they were young and pretty, but his favorite was Jenny Lind. Hence, when his wife gave birth to a second daughter, in 1854, he suggested they name her Jenny. By the time Clara realized that her husband had named his daughter after one of his many talented mistresses, several months had passed. So Clara simply altered the spelling from Jenny to Jennie. Later, Clara insisted that "Jeanette" serve as the girl's formal christening name, thus further distancing her from the singer. The births of two more daughters followed: Camille in 1855 and Leonie in 1859.

Camille died suddenly in 1863 of a fever. Her death stunned the family but bonded the three remaining sisters—ages twelve, nine, and five—in a relationship they enjoyed throughout their lives. Each of the three, rarely seen apart, earned a nickname: "the Good" (Clarita), "the Beautiful" (Jennie), and "the Witty" (Leonie).All three married British aristocrats.[4] When his third, and youngest, daughter married an Englishman, Jerome protested, "Why couldn't she have married a normal American and lived in my Country!"[5]

While his wife and daughters occupied themselves in their impressive house in Madison Square, Jerome kept himself busy throughout the city. He had served as the American Consul at Trieste for three years, resulting in his daughters becoming bilingual at an early age, but he expressed little interest in politics after he returned to the United States. Instead, he embarked on a number of financial adventures, from newspaper ownership to real estate to Wall Street. He worked as an art collector, an attorney, a newspaper editor, and part owner of the *New York Times*. His ability to make and lose millions of dollars gave him the nickname "The King of Wall Street."[6]

As was the case for many other nouveau riche Americans, Jerome held sufficient wealth to belong to the New York elite, but for a number of reasons his family remained on the outside. Although the family's new money status was likely the reason, Clara blamed her husband's extramarital affairs for their family's social exclusion. Many wealthy men took mistresses, and they did so with great discretion. Jerome, however, made little effort to hide his adulterous relations, behavior elite society found repugnant. After years of enjoying great wealth, living in Madison Square, spending summer vacations in Newport, Rhode Island, and working to obtain success in New York social circles, Mrs. Jerome reached her limit. Her pride did not allow her to continue to seek Mrs. Astor's favor, but neither did it allow her to surrender her social ambitions. In 1867, she announced that her health required her to live abroad—in Paris. She had no known health problems, but nevertheless the family sailed for Europe so "she might consult the celebrated American physician Dr. Sims in Paris."[7] Mrs. Jerome later regained her health but notably did not return to the United States. She likely had grown tired of her husband's behavior and realized that it would likely prevent her daughters from marrying well. Overseas, however, his money afforded his family a home in Paris and a chance to enjoy the elite social circles that had eluded them at home.

The women of the Jerome family enjoyed all Paris had to offer. Their knowledge of Italian allowed them to learn French easily, and they quickly became *les belles Américaines*. Clarita especially enjoyed the Paris Season, making her debut at one of the Tuileries balls. Unfortunately, their joyous time in Paris came to an end in 1870. The beginning of the Franco-Prussian War drove hundreds of people, American and European, toward London. Mr. Jerome rushed to Paris to assist his wife and daughters in moving, but he returned to New York after they had moved to London permanently. Not wishing to return to the United States, the Jerome women remained in London for several months, returning only once to Paris, to find their beloved city of lights in ruins. They grudgingly returned to London, not yet known for its social life. But the city quickly became the social destination for affluent Americans; the war helped to make London, specifically during the London Season, the new destination for wealthy socialites.[8]

After settling into their new home, the Jerome women began testing the British social scene. In the summer of 1871, Jennie and her sisters paid their first visit to Cowes, a weeklong regatta that was part of the London Season. Jennie was presented to the Prince and Princess of Wales the next year at the Royal Yacht Squadron Ball, where she immediately caught Prince Edward's eye, thus assuring her success in London. Jennie never lacked for dancing partners that night; one British guest described her delight at the ball as clearly "American."[9]

Jennie's social triumphs in London, especially with Edward, meant that her sisters enjoyed great success as well. They received invitations to all the London Season events and to the best dinners and country estates. The following Season, however, brought Jennie's mother the transatlantic victory for which she had long hoped. In 1873, Jennie met Lord Randolph Churchill at Cowes. Taken with her immediately, Randolph told a friend he "meant, if he could, to make the dark one his wife."[10] Three days after their first meeting, Randolph asked Jennie to marry him. Ecstatic, Jennie expected her mother to share in her excitement. But Mrs. Jerome responded with anything but approval; in the subsequent weeks and months, she worked ceaselessly to end the engagement. Foreshadowing later title-hunting American mothers, she aspired for only the best match for her daughter. Anything less than a first-born future duke would not suffice.

Born in 1849, Lord Randolph Henry Spencer Churchill was the third son of Sir John Winston Spencer-Churchill, the 7th Duke of Marlborough, and Lady Frances Anne Emily Vane, Duchess of Marlborough, a commanding woman. (Jennie later recalled that "at the rustle of [the Duchess's] silk dress, the household trembled."[11]) Educated at Eton and Merton College, Oxford, Randolph exemplified the typical transatlantic groom. Despite his exceptional education, he took little interest in politics or any other profession, for that matter. Instead, he spent most of his time traveling across various countries in Europe and seemed interested in little beyond "comparative idleness" and "leisurely fashion." So his sudden announcement that he planned to marry an American girl he met at a party received a frosty response from his parents. He admitted to them that he knew little about Jennie or her family. To his father, he wrote, "Mr Jerome is a gentleman who is obliged to live in New York to look after his business. I do not know what it is."[12]

Understandably distressed, both sets of parents found this sudden engagement disconcerting. The Jeromes were upset by their daughter's impulsiveness. Likewise, the Marlboroughs considered their son's rash behavior disturbing. Although Anglo-American marriages became quite fashionable by the late nineteenth century, in 1873, most of British society regarded such unions "as experimental as mating with Martians."[13] Both sides thought the hasty romance would end as quickly as it began, and Mrs. Jerome's attempt to end the engagement included moving her daughters back to Paris temporarily. But the letters between the young couple continued, and Randolph even visited Jennie in France.

Though Jennie later admitted, "We had arrived at our momentous decision without much delay," both families eventually realized that this was more than a flighty romance.[14] Rather than concede the situation entirely, however, the Marlboroughs saw an opportunity to test their son's devotion to his fiancée and secure his future. They consented to their son's engagement if he would stand for Woodstock, the family borough, and run for Parliament. He attacked his campaign with passion and, in typical British political style, encouraged Jennie to share his new interest. In one of the many letters he wrote during their engagement, he asked her to read one of Prime Minister Benjamin Disraeli's speeches, printed in the *London Times*. From the beginning, Randolph invited and welcomed his future wife as a full partner in his political career. As a future wife of a British politician, Jennie was expected to participate "in the family business—in this case, however, the family business was politics."[15] Determined to match her fiancé's political intellect, Jennie read the speech in addition to everything she could find concerning British politics.[16] She understood that as the wife of Lord Randolph Churchill she would need ample political knowledge. Her future husband ran for and won a seat in the House of Commons, and a wedding date was set for the spring.[17]

Before the two could marry, a number of financial details required settlement. Under normal circumstances, a woman's dowry passed directly from her father's hands to her husband's, leaving her at the mercy of her spouse. But Mr. Jerome saw little reason to follow protocol with his precious Jennie. When he explained to Randolph and the Duke of Marlborough that he planned to provide Jennie with her own "pin money," a settlement separate from her husband's—and a decision decidedly abnormal in this period—he nearly ended the engagement. With his father's urging, Randolph told his future father-in-law that unless the dowry in its entirety came to him directly, "all business between us was perfectly impossible and he could do what he liked with his beastly money." Eventually, the three compromised and agreed on a settlement that yielded £50,000 in capital through government and railway stocks, a mortgage worth some $300,000. Jerome also provided £2,000 in annual income for the couple and £1,000 for his daughter's personal use.[18]

The night before the wedding, Jennie wrote in her diary, "This is the last time I shall wind the clock. . . . This is the last time I shall look in this old mirror. Soon nothing will be the same for me anymore: Miss Jennie Jerome with be gone forever."[19] Her words could not have been more accurate. The next morning, April 15, 1874, with the Prince of Wales's secretary, Sir Francis Knollys, serving as Randolph's best man, a clear sign of Edward's approval of the union, the happy couple married, though not in the United States or Britain.[20] Instead, they wed at the British embassy in Paris, symbolic of the Jeromes' ties to France and Randolph's British heritage.

When the time arrived for Jennie to leave with her new husband, her mother began to cry. To comfort her, Jennie responded soothingly, "Why, Mama, don't cry, life is going to be perfect . . . always."[21] Little did Jennie know what joys and sorrows life in Britain would bring. When the newlyweds arrived in May at Blenheim Palace, the Marlborough family estate, the new Member of Parliament from Woodstock and his beautiful American wife received an "enthusiastic reception" from cheering tenants and constituents as the first of the Anglo-American unions began with great fanfare and a welcoming reception. Leaving behind her American country, family, and identity, she began a new life in Britain as Lady Randolph Churchill.[22]

Early Marriage, Motherhood, and Ireland

Many Anglo-American unions began with an exciting courtship during the London Season, followed by an impressive church wedding, and quickly settled into a dull and monotonous marriage that included only an occasional dinner party or ball. But Lady Churchill had no intention of settling into anything of the sort. Her beauty and vitality demanded that her life function as a constant "whirl of gaieties and excitement." Of the few first months following her marriage she wrote, "I settled in London to enjoy my first season with all the vigor and unjaded appetite of youth."[23] Unlike some of her fellow Anglo-American brides, Lady Churchill pursued an eventful poli-social life.

At the many country-house parties and pigeon-shooting excursions Lady Churchill attended as a newlywed, she was often the lone American-born, British-wed bride. While the number of American women increased dramatically in the next three decades, in the 1870s Lady Churchill was the solo informal ambassador for all American women; thus, her actions took place on an international stage. Writing in her memoirs, she explained, "In England, as on the Continent, the American woman was looked upon as a strange and abnormal creature, with habits and manners something between a Red Indian and a Gaiety Girl." Writing of British expectations for American behavior, Lady Churchill remembered that "anything of an outlandish nature might be expected of her. If she talked, dressed, and conducted herself as any well-bred woman would, much astonishment was invariably envinced, and she was usually saluted with the tactful remark, 'I should never have thought *you* were an American,' which was intended as a compliment." Overall, Lady Churchill often thought her new fellow countrymen and women considered her "as a disagreeable and even dangerous person, to be viewed with suspicion, if not avoided altogether. Her dollars were her only recommendation . . . ; otherwise what was her *raison d'être?*"[24] British men and women monitored her every move and analyzed her every action. Lady Churchill's informal ambassador status began from day one in England; for better or worse, her demeanor now represented all Americans. But with this intense pressure came great power.

Part of Lady Churchill's initial aggravation stemmed from the fact that Britons could not detect the regional differences among Americans; they made "no distinction . . . among Americans; they were all supposed to be of one uniform type." Lady Churchill found it frustrating that "the cultured, refined and retiring Bostonian; the aristocratic Virginian, as full of tradition and family pride as a Percy of Northumberland . . . the cosmopolitan and up-to-date New Yorker . . . were grouped in the same category, all were considered tarred with the same brush." Of course, Britons were proud of the significant differences among people from York, Suffolk, and Cornwall but saw little reason to consider the possibility of the same existing among Americans from various parts of the United States. From a British standpoint, all Americans dressed in an exaggerated fashion and spoke with a nasal twang.[25] For better and for worse, British men and women viewed all American women as ambassadors living in Britain as a result of transatlantic marriages through the same lens.

Eventually, Lady Churchill turned this seemingly impossible situation to her advantage. On the one hand, if she, by British standards, represented all Americans regardless of any socioeconomic or regional differences, then any mistakes she made by British etiquette definitions would cast her individually and Americans as a whole negatively. On the other hand, like those of so many diplomats before her, her every deed could potentially reflect well on the United States as a whole. If Lady Churchill's life in Britain were destined to transpire under a magnifying glass, then she chose to make it exhibit all the positive characteristics of American women specifically and all Americans in general.

Upon realizing the possibilities for her marriage and her lifelong presence in London, Lady Churchill embarked upon a fabulously successful social life. Although her social life in London, attending the best parties and balls, differed little from that which she had enjoyed as a single person, she now acted as a hostess for the best parties and dinners, thus making her a leader of London society rather than simply a participant. Her social success as an American in London permitted Britons to entertain positive opinions of Americans in general. Her marriage to a leading aristocrat and Member of Parliament clearly helped establish her position in society. When Randolph gave his maiden speech—often an indicator of a member's future political success and career—in the House of Commons on May 22, 1874, his presentation received little notice. Randolph, often described as cold and unsociable, held his seat in Parliament because of his family's status in Britain, not because of his interest in politics or career ambitions. While her marriage provided the platform, Lady Churchill's own social charm and personal warmth prompted London society to see her as "the most beautiful woman anyone had set eyes on." Little time had passed before London society considered Lord and Lady Churchill as "the most sought-after young couple in England. . . . Every party that included the young Churchills proved a success."[26] By the end of their first Season as a married couple, they found all doors of society open to them—a nearly endless stream of ballets, balls, concerts, garden parties, horse races, hunting parties, operas, plays—and nearly endless opportunities to advance their distinct but intertwined poli-social careers.[27]

By attending and hosting notable events, Lord and Lady Churchill increased their individual and collective political and social capital. Lord Churchill gave his wife access to the most important individuals in England, while Lady Churchill gave her husband a sense of resilience and confidence he did not possess before his marriage. Britons also noted Lady Churchill's influence on her husband's career. At one party hosted by the Churchills, the Prince of Wales observed a long conversation between the prime minister and Lady Churchill. Afterward, he inquired of her, "Tell me, my dear, what office did you get for Randolph?"[28] Together, Lord and Lady Churchill interacted on a regular basis with the most influential people of their time, thereby securing his position in the House of Commons and her position as well. Much like a husband-wife diplomat team, they pursued their respective duties of politics and society. But in Anglo-American marriages, only the wife served as a representative ambassador from her home country.

At the same time, Lady Churchill embarked on another profession entirely—motherhood. On November 30, 1874, while at a shooting party at Blenheim Palace, she went into labor. Leaving the hunt, she gave birth to her first son, Winston Leonard Spencer-Churchill, named after his American and English grandfathers. His official birth announcement in the London Times noted that his mother had given birth, "prematurely, of a son."[29] Historians have frequently commented on the future prime minister's entry into the world, only seven months after his parents' marriage.[30] Healthy and robust, the newborn certainly appeared a full-term baby. However, his younger brother, born four years later, was also premature. If Lady Churchill had been pregnant prior to her marriage, everyone involved stood to lose much if such news became public. American and British societies would have shunned the couple and to their families, and their children would have grown up in shame. Any political careers, by father or son, could never have occurred. Thus, all parties repeatedly asserted the premature birth.[31]

For Lady Churchill, motherhood proved a delicate and constant negotiation of American and Victorian ideals of the proper care and raising of children. A number of private nurses and nannies tended to the daily needs of the children of British aristocrats and acted as a "physical barrier between children and parents."[32] Lady Churchill spent far more time with her children than was typical of her social class, but she remained aware that her every move, even her style of mothering, would be viewed as indicative of all Americans.

Like almost everyone who met Lady Churchill, Winston adored his mother. In his biography, he wrote, "My mother always seemed to me a fairy princess; a radiant being possessed of limitless riches and power." He continued, reflecting, "She shone for me like the Evening Star. I loved her dearly—but at a distance."[33] His birth and eventual leadership of Britain held great importance as the product of a transatlantic marriage. Christopher Hitchens has argued, "In many ways, Winston Churchill was the human bridge across which this transition was made."[34] Hence, not only the marriages of Anglo-Americans held great significance but potentially their offspring did as well.

These charmed early days of Lady Churchill's life in Britain came to an end in 1876, when Lord Randolph's older brother, the Marquess of Blandford, had an affair with Lady Edith Aylesford. While the Earl of Aylesford toured India with the Prince of Wales, he received a letter from his wife saying that she and Blandford planned to elope shortly. Humiliated, the Earl returned home immediately to begin divorce proceedings, and Lord Randolph stepped in on behalf of his brother. He asked the prince to influence Aylesford not to divorce his wife. When the prince refused, Lord Randolph encouraged his brother not to elope. During this time, Lord Randolph also came into the possession of some very intimate letters between the Prince of Wales and Lady Aylesford, which he shared with the Prince's wife. Lord Randolph bragged that he held the Crown of England in his pocket, as the letters could have prohibited Edward VII from becoming King.[35] The prince challenged Lord Randolph to a duel, which the latter could never accept, and the contest never took place. The prince announced that he would never frequent any event or house that continued to include the Churchills; he barred Lord and Lady Churchill from his social circle, and almost all members of his set followed suit. Randolph and the prince never completely mended the rift, though the Churchills returned to society a decade later.[36]

The young couple escaped their social ostracism temporarily by spending a few short months in 1876 in the United States with Lady Churchill's family, but they returned to England following a new development. At Prime Minister Disraeli's request, the Duke of Marlborough had accepted an appointment as viceroy to Ireland and offered Lord Churchill a position as his private secretary. Ireland seemed to solve all the problems at hand. "Not being in favor with the Court, from which London society took the lead," Lady Churchill wrote, "we were nothing loath to go."[37] Lord Churchill served as his father's assistant while his wife naturally assisted the duchess at all formal events.[38] This journey allowed Lord and Lady Churchill to escape their social banishment, and Lady Churchill now served as an ambassador from the United States to Ireland as well as to England.

Arriving in Ireland in December 1876, Lord and Lady Churchill found social life thrilling. Upon seeing Lady Churchill for the first time in Ireland, Lord Edgar Vincent D'Abernon wrote:

It was at the Viceregal Lodge at Dublin. She stood on one side, to the left of the entrance. The Viceroy was on a dais at the further end of the room surrounded by a brilliant staff, but all eyes were not turned on him or his consort, but on a dark, lithe figure, standing somewhat apart and appearing to be of another texture to those around her, radiant, translucent, intense. A diamond star in her hair, her favorite ornament—its luster dimmed by the flashing glory of her eyes. More of the panther than of the woman in her look, but with a cultivated intelligence unknown to the jungle. Her courage not less great than her husband. . . . [S]he was universally popular. Her desire to please, her delight in life and the genuine wish that all should share her joyous faith in it, made her the center of a devoted circle.[39]

But Lady Churchill offered the people of Ireland more than simply her beauty and charm. Famine returned to the country in 1877, and aid from England did little to alleviate the hunger and panic. The Duchess of Marlborough started the Irish Relief Fund, with the purpose of supplying basic goods to Irish families. Raising some £135,000 ($675,000), she collected more than 150,000 pounds of food, fuel, and clothing.[40] Lady Churchill supported her mother-in-law's efforts and quickly began traveling across Ireland to disperse provisions. Shocked by the peasants' profound poverty and living conditions, she was permanently affected by the experience. As she remembered, "In our walks, we had many opportunities of seeing the heart-rending poverty of the peasantry who lived . . . more like animals than human beings. Appalled by the one-room huts with little more than straw and blankets and diets that consisted of potatoes and salt with meat twice a year, she never forgot what she saw, nor would she ever allow Lord Churchill to forget.[41] Similar to American Mary Leiter Curzon's reign as British vicereine in India, Lady Churchill used her time abroad to represent Americans to Britain and Ireland. Both women tested the ambassadorial waters through charity endeavors, as these were deemed safe and socially accepted as women's work. As in diplomacy, women's work bore a striking resemblance to men's jobs.

Lord and Lady Churchill returned to England in 1879 with a new perspective on the Irish Question and on politics in general. Having spent three years among the Irish people, they were some of the very few Britons who had traveled or spent any significant time in Ireland at all. Following his political apprenticeship, Lord Churchill and his wife became even more interested in shaping British politics.[42] They now possessed a clear sense that their joint efforts could bring lasting change to not only Ireland but the disaffected throughout Great Britain. Lady Churchill's participation in a formal representative role, especially, influenced the rest of her life in London.

Return to London, Return to Parliament

Upon their return from Ireland, Lord and Lady Churchill moved into their new home. Lord Churchill returned immediately to Woodstock to stand for the general election in 1880. Despite his family name and a previously secure seat in the House of Commons, he was in political danger along with the other the Conservatives. Lord Churchill won his seat back by a mere sixty votes. The next few years in office proved critical for him to regain his constituents' trust.[43] During this time, Lady Churchill became the "power behind Randolph's every move"; many asserted that she was the most "significant woman in English politics apart from the Queen."[44] Given her dual status as both American and Briton, wife and ambassador, she also had a significant position on the international stage as a leading Anglo-American.

Their time in Ireland had brought Lord and Lady Churchill together, and they found they shared a love for politics. Lady Churchill began attending speeches at the House of Commons and sat for several hours each day in the Ladies' Gallery, where wives of the members could listen, or the Speakers' Gallery, where one could listen to speeches if invited. While it slowly became fashionable for politicians' wives to pay attention to the goings on in Parliament, a physical barrier separated men and women in the House of Commons. Regardless of the division, Lady Churchill spent near countless hours listening to speeches, following British politics, and conversing with the other politicians and their wives; the Ladies' and Speaker's Galleries became key spaces for political and social intrigues.[45]

During the early years of his return to the House, Lord Churchill began working with Sir Henry Wolff, John Gorst, and Arthur Balfour in creating a Fourth Party, an addition to the three political parties then existing: Conservative, Liberal, and Tory. The Fourth Party criticized the weakness of the Liberal government in power and the fumbling opposition of the Conservative Party. Between 1880 and 1884, these men met at Lady Churchill's home on a regular basis as her "house became the rendezvous of all shades of politicians." Lady Churchill watched as, she recalled, "Many were the plots and plans which were hatched in my presence by the Fourth Party, who, notwithstanding the seriousness of their endeavours, found time to laugh heartily and often at their own frustrated machinations."[46] For the most part, these men simply found a way to voice their dissatisfaction with all of the political parties presently engaged in the House. But more important for Lady Churchill, the meetings gave her an opportunity to better understand the complexity of private meeting rooms in politics, demonstrating, as historian Catherine Allgor has observed about American political wives in the Early Republic, "that a smoke-filled backroom and a lady's parlor are both political spaces."[47] The party also provided her an opportunity to slowly begin reentering British social circles.[48]

Lady Churchill also began testing the political waters somewhat independently of her husband. Sir Henry Drummond Wolff, another Conservative politician, approached Lord Churchill in 1883 about creating a new political society that could cut across all socioeconomic classes. They called the organization the "Primrose League," reflecting former prime minister Disraeli's favorite flower. Primrose members stated that their purpose was to "embrace all classes and all creeds except atheists and enemies of the British Empire."[49] The Duchess of Marlborough served as president of the Ladies' Council, and Lady Churchill became a dame in the organization. Lady Churchill traveled widely with her mother-in-law, organizing sing-alongs and presentations in an effort to win converts to the Conservative Party. While the Tories and Liberals mocked the new organization, the Primrose League spread across England. For once, the Conservatives beat the other two parties at their own game: crossing class barriers as they used attractive women to mingle with the working classes to win votes. Twenty years after its inception, the Primrose League boasted membership surpassing 1 million people, a fact that helped keep the Conservatives in power.[50] The Primrose League also afforded Lady Churchill the opportunity to find her own American voice in British politics and discover that, while she feared public speaking, she delivered speeches with ease and charisma. As an American woman, she discovered a wealth of opportunities, political and social, a byproduct of her Anglo-American marriage. She also realized that she possessed a great talent with the written word, a gift that later helped her husband in his own political career.[51]

By this time, the Churchill marriage functioned as more of a political "alliance than a love affair."[52] Early in their marriage, Lord Churchill contracted syphilis as a result of an extramarital affair. Since his wife never contracted the disease, and syphilis is highly infectious for the first two years, he likely told his wife, and they never again engaged in sexual relations.[53] Lord Churchill likely acquired syphilis in 1875, and the disease affected him the rest of his life. Rather than divorcing, Lord and Lady Churchill spent weeks and even months apart, which fueled gossip about their faltering marriage and adultery committed by both parties. Even though the conventional and romantic aspects of the couple's marriage ended, Lady Churchill remained loyal to her husband and his political career and frequent elections. To divorce him, unheard of in this era, would have been to reject the chance to serve as an informal ambassador in a country that afforded women a surprising degree of independence and influence with the very governmental leaders who pursued foreign relations with her homeland.

Lady Churchill became her husband's informal campaign manager beginning in the 1880s. Supervising and directing his political career, she became the face and voice of "The Wasp from Woodstock."[54] Notably, British and American campaigns functioned very differently. British politicians often printed and passed out flyers for election bids, while Americans seeking office took a much more assertive, to the point of aggressive, approach. Despite that British wives enjoyed more interaction and involvement on poli-social levels as byproducts of their husband's careers, Britons viewed Lady Churchill's candid campaign style as decidedly American as she traveled across Woodstock, going door to door and factory to factory, seeking votes for her husband. Accompanied by her mother-in-law, Lady Churchill trotted through the countryside behind horses decorated with pink and brown ribbons—Lord Randolph's racing colors. Undoubtedly, her in-laws took pleasure in Jennie's dedication to her husband's profession, as they called on approximately one thousand wives in Woodstock and visited various factories where their husbands worked. When she approached voters, Lady Churchill simply stated, "Please vote for my husband; I shall be so unhappy if you don't."[55] Accompanied by her winning smile, her charm and candor won many votes. Even her home country followed her efforts. Writing to his wife, Leonard Jerome bragged, "You have no idea how universally Jennie is talked about and how proud the Americans are of her."[56]

During one of Lord Churchill's elections, his wife and mother often heard various "jingling rhymes" discussing the American approach Lady Churchill had taking in securing her husband's reelection:

But just as I was talking,
    With Neighbour Brown and walking,
To take a mug of beer at the Unicorn and Lion
    (For there's somehow a connection),
Who should come but Lady Churchill,
    With a turnout that was fine.
And before me stopped her horses
    As she marshaled all her forces,
And before I knew what happened I had promised her my vote;
. . . .
Bless my soul! that Yankee Lady,
    Whether day was bright or shady,
Dashed about the district like an oriflamme of war.
    When the voters saw her bonnet,
With the bright pink roses on it,
    They followed as the soldiers did the Helmet of Navarre.[57]

Not everyone received Lady Churchill's efforts with approval or amusement. Her perceived American approach to campaigns and to the voters especially offended many British constituents. Lady Churchill's arrival at a factory one day was met with utter silence. When she inquired why workers would not speak to her, a man responded, "We don't like being asked for our votes." Lady Churchill replied, "But you have something I want. How am I to get it, if I don't ask for it?" This retort raised a laugh from the gentlemen, but Lady Churchill's method did not always melt the hearts of the voters. When Lady Churchill asked to speak to one Woodstock woman's husband, the woman called to him in the cellar, "Lady Churchill wants to see you." He responded, "Oh, does she? Well, tell Mrs. Churchill to go to——," at which point Lady Churchill "beat a hasty retreat."[58]

Although Lady Churchill sometimes found meeting with constituents trying, she always enjoyed the excitement of elections. Writing her memoirs, she remembered, "Reveling in the hustle and bustle of the Committee rooms, marshaling our forces, and hearing the hourly reports of how the campaign was progressing, I felt like a general holding a council-of-war with his staff in the heat of battle."[59] In a letter he wrote to her congratulating her success, Sir Henry James, the attorney general, noted Lady Churchill's influence on the elections: "You must let me very sincerely and heartily congratulate you on the results of the election, especially as that result proceeded so very much from your personal exertions. Everybody is praising you very much."[60] Realizing his American wife's value to his political career, Lord Churchill once wrote to her, "If I win, you will have all the glory."[61]

With Jennie at the political helm, Churchill won all of his reelection bids, and his wife did receive great accolades for her efforts, not only from her husband but also her mother-in-law and the British public as a whole. Called the "greatest electioneering helpmeet since the famous Duchess of Devonshire," Lady Churchill received credit for her husband's triumphant return to Parliament.[62] Through these elections, she slowly endeared herself to the British public. She also found the Queen's favor, as Victoria conferred on her the Order of the Crown of India in 1885. A royal recognition of this magnitude was quite an accomplishment for any American; the Queen originally found Anglo-American marriages distasteful.[63] Winning over the British monarchy one member at a time resulted in a trickle-down effect over entire the country.

Lady Churchill and Queen Victoria enjoyed an exceptionally close relationship until the Queen's death in 1901, upon which Lady Churchill was asked to offer her reminiscences of the monarch, a particular indication of improved relations between the British monarchy and Americans. Lady Churchill asserted that it was "no exaggeration to say that the American people have placed Queen Victoria on as high a pedestal of virtue as their imagination can build." Pushing Anglo-American relations publicly, she continued, "High and low, rich and poor, the whole English-speaking race realize that they have lost in Queen Victoria the greatest of their sovereigns and the best of friends."[64]

Lady Churchill's efforts at every level of the British government resulted in success. In 1886, the Conservatives took back the House of Commons and Lord

Salisbury became prime minister. As a result, Lord Churchill moved from the position of secretary of state for India, to which he was named in 1885, to leader of the House of Commons and the chancellor of the Exchequer, all at the young age of thirty-six.[65] But his tenure at these posts was short-lived. Syphilis began to take over his mind and body, and Lord Churchill became increasingly antagonistic and combative to even his closest friends and political allies. Six months after taking these posts, Lord Churchill picked a fight with the prime minister over the budget and resigned on December 20, 1886, with absolutely no warning to the Queen, his party, or his wife. The following morning, Lady Churchill read the announcement in the *London Times*. When she came downstairs for breakfast with the newspaper in her hand, her husband smiled and simply said, "Quite a surprise for you."[66] They never discussed it further; Lord Churchill's mind had left him, and there was little reason to engage him in any sort of rational argument. One newspaper wrote, "We are sorry Randy [Lord Randolph] is in the muck less for his own account that for that of the gallant American girl he had the luck to marry. She had worked so hard to popularize him and forward his ends."[67] Even the *London Times* noted that Lady Churchill's grace and charm greatly aided him in his political career during the brilliant days of his rapid rise to fame and power.[68] He owed much of his professional success to her and she in turn owed much of her increasing influence to his family name and position. His self-destruction, personally and professionally, must have been a bitter pill for her to swallow.

Nevertheless, Lady Churchill tended to her husband over the next decade as he began a slow decline in body and mind. When the chance for any recovery had gone, Lord and Lady Churchill took a final trip around the world, starting in June 1894. They visited the United States, Canada, and the Far East. Originally, they planned to spend several months in India, but Lord Randolph's health failed, and they returned quickly to England. On January 23, 1895, he slipped into a coma and died early the next morning, the cause of death listed as "General Paralysis of the Insane."[69] Some weeks later, when a parliamentary representative came to retrieve Lord Churchill's robes of office, Lady Churchill refused to surrender them, boldly declaring, "I am saving them for my son."[70] Though her term as a British political wife had ended, she had no intention of relinquishing her hard-won position as an American ambassador abroad.

While she had not been able to make her husband prime minister, Lady Churchill refocused her efforts on her son's political career. For twenty years, her ambitions had been intertwined with her husband's. She now placed the same drive and determination into Winston's career, becoming his unofficial political agent. He later described her as "an ardent ally, furthering my plan and guarding my interests with all her influence and boundless energy."[71] But in looking at her own life, Lady Churchill felt overcome with despair. Widowed at forty, what would she do now without her husband? While her Anglo-American union had ended, her tenure as an informal ambassador had just begun.[72] Like Consuelo Vanderbilt Marlborough would some twenty years later, Lady Churchill owed her position in London to her transatlantic marriage; and she found her purpose as an Anglo-American ambassador once her marriage ended.

The Venezuelan Boundary Dispute

Shortly after her husband's death, several events transpired in 1895 that forced Lady Churchill to reconsider her life in Britain. First, her son Winston spent several months in the United States. Writing to his mother about his time in her home country, he exclaimed, "What an extraordinary people the Americans are! Their hospitality is a revelation to me and they make you feel at home and at ease in a way that I have never before experienced." Because the United States was his mother's country, people, and heritage, they were a part of him as well, a fact he relayed in numerous letters to his family in Britain. As he wrote in one letter, "I am a child of both worlds," as was his mother.[73] Lady Churchill had spent the first twenty years of her life in the United States and the next twenty in Britain; thus, she identified as part of both countries. Rather than feel divided by two loyalties, she felt deep attachments to both. These connections only intensified as a result of an Anglo-American crisis in 1895 over a boundary in South America, in which she found her first overt role as an informal ambassador.

Representatives from the United States and Great Britain had bickered about the boundary between Venezuela and British Guiana for decades, but not until the fall of 1895, when President Grover Cleveland demanded that Great Britain submit to arbitration over the border, did the issue fully develop into a crisis. Invoking the rarely enforced Monroe Doctrine of 1823, Cleveland threatened war with Great Britain, if necessary. Justifiably astounded, the British government marveled at why the Americans suddenly found this decades-old situation so monumental. Relations between the United States and Great Britain became so tense that many in Washington, D.C., and in London found themselves in a very uncomfortable situation. Fearful of what the coming months might bring, many Americans withdrew to continental Europe or returned to the United States for an indefinite period.

But Lady Churchill had no intention of abandoning her informal diplomatic post. Instead, having learned from two decades at the center of London's political and social circles, she quietly began hosting small but frequent dinner gatherings for the most influential parties at the heart of this crisis, drawing upon her years of friendships with the most socially and politically influential persons in London and the British Parliament. Behind closed doors, she assured governmental leaders and influential newspaper editors that extreme political propagandists had created false war talk. In this manner, she operated as an informal ambassador and used social events (as any envoy would) and the alleged private sphere to establish an unofficial dialogue between her two countries.[74] Working in a non-governmental capacity, she told friends and acquaintances that such sensationalism would soon disappear. After spending time in England, one U.S. general reported to the American press that Lady Churchill led "ten daughters of the United States, who are working quietly and mightily to prevent war between the two countries that are looking at each other in a sinister way. For these women, the war means a thousand times as much as it does to other Americans; and they have untold power of international arbitration. . . . These particular ten are so situated that they are in the midst of the greatest powers that rule England today. Their influence, thrown upon the scales, would turn it whichever way they bent themselves."[75]

Lady Churchill wisely kept her dinners private, so as not to draw attention to her subtle transnational campaign or ruffle any political feathers on either side of the Atlantic. But her "soft power" efforts had an undeniable and significant calming effect on the situation, which both of her countries observed. British and American newspapers noted her diplomatic position as the American leader of Anglo-American brides living in Great Britain. One Boston newspaper ran an article with the headline, "Lady Churchill Was U.S. Best Ambassador [sic]."[76] A British correspondent wrote in the New York Journal, "It is difficult to estimate the power Lady Randolph Churchill would have in preventing a conflict between the two countries. . . . Cousins, friends, dear relatives and fortune over there! Home, children and immediate interests here!"[77] One British journalist asserted that "if there should come hard war talk, Lady Randolph Churchill would set out lecturing, as she did when she elected her husband a few years ago. And her talks would put things straight in a short time. . . . And she would be convincing."[78] Clearly, her husband's political career provided her the training and opportunity to learn political strategies. At this point, she utilized those experiences—the formal lessons learned on the campaign trail and as an informal member of and dinner hostess to the Fourth Party—on an international level as both the United States and Great Britain regarded their Anglo-American women as transnational intermediaries. Their efforts, performing women's work—dinner, drinks, and dialogue—were the very same as a formal emissary's, in diffusing war by any means. In part due to Lady Churchill's transnational efforts, as well as the efforts of the mysterious ten daughters of America, the United States and Great Britain avoided war over Venezuela. As a result, 1895 marked a year when Lady Churchill began to view her position as an American in Great Britain as an asset and increasingly served as an ambassador between her two countries.

The Anglo-Saxon Review

Lady Churchill continued hosting and attending dinner parties, but a specific dinner party in 1898 marked a new chapter in her life. When George Nathaniel Curzon, the husband of fellow Anglo-American bride Lady Mary Leiter Curzon, was named viceroy of India, Lady Churchill attended a going-away dinner party for the couple. She had a long conversation with the newly appointed representative, during which they discussed her position in society and her widowhood. Lady Churchill confided to Lord Curzon of her personal unhappiness and "bemoaned the empty life [she] was leading at that moment." Curzon attempted to comfort her by explaining that a "woman alone was a godsend to society, and that [she] might look forward to a long vista of country-house parties, dinners, and balls."[79] In the days after the dinner, Lady Churchill pondered Curzon's words to her and "found [herself] wondering if this indeed was all that the remainder of [her]life held."[80]

Instead of waiting for the next dinner invitation, Lady Churchill decided to start a literary review focusing on the relationship between the United States and Great Britain and her unique diplomatic position. In the years since she married and moved to Great Britain, Lady Churchill had endeared herself to her husband's exceedingly well connected family, members of Parliament, and the British monarchy. She had conquered the London social scene and fine-tuned her political management skills for her husband. Why not try her hand at a literary publication? Although such an endeavor seemed reasonable, given her American and British connections, a female editor was notably unusual in the Victorian period. While such would have been unheard of for a woman in the United States, in Britain, it was possible, though unusual. Lady Churchill, of course, was neither wholly American nor British; instead, she maintained a foothold in both countries, endearing herself to two influential audiences, making such an enterprise eminently feasible. With this project, she created yet another opportunity to unite her two countries, though she could not forget that such a publication was a business venture. Acting as a literary liaison, she had to identify an audience, retain readers, and generate a product people wanted to consume.[81]

Lady Churchill first named her magazine the *Anglo-American Review* but later changed it to the *Anglo-Saxon Review,* as the original title belonged to another journal.[82] While Great Britain and the United States considered the superiority of the Anglo-Saxon race a foregone conclusion, Winston cringed at the title of the periodical, as he viewed an Anglo-American alliance as a "wild impossibility."[83] His mother very much thought otherwise. As she saw it, the "interests of the United States were inextricably linked with those of Britain"; the "English-speaking peoples of the old and the new worlds had much more than history and a language in common."[84] Working closely with her friend Pearl Craigie, another American woman who had married into elite British circles, Lady Churchill became increasingly focused on her identity as a leader of the Anglo-Saxon world. More than ever, she believed her presence as an American in England and the production of a transnational publication could bring about improved relations and a better understanding among her Anglo-American kinsmen and -women.

Lady Churchill continued to develop her journal. Upon Winston's advice, she asked publisher John Lane to work with her. She began the project with considerable faith in Lane and his ability to promote her journal. But the pair quickly began quarreling about money, and the publication suffered.[85] The *Anglo-Saxon Review*, which Lady Churchill published "to render the United States and Great Britain more intelligible to each other," first appeared in June 1899.[86] Lady Churchill approached notable individuals from both countries to write articles on a number of subjects, including history, science, art, and current events as well as original printings of plays and poems. In 1900, the *New York Times* reported, "The literary contents are skillfully varied between history, fiction, 'actuality,' and criticism."[87] Contributors included the Honorable Whitelaw Reid, future American ambassador to the United Kingdom, 1905–12; author Henry James; playwright George Bernard Shaw; various members of the aristocracy; and even Lady Churchill herself. From the subjects published in the journal, which included George Washington and Her Majesty the Queen, to the writers themselves, the quarterly provided a literary and ideological connection between elite Anglo-Americans. It served as an intellectual reminder that an influential, transnational network existed between the United States and Great Britain.[88]

But because Lady Churchill hoped to foster a conversation among elites on both sides of the Atlantic, she failed to market her publication to a wide audience. The price of the publication, a guinea per issue (approximately £70 or $113 in 2009 values) automatically limited the number of potential subscribers, and thus circulation. One poem, penned by the English writer E.V. Lucas, playfully remarked,

> Have you heard of the wonderful magazine
> Lady Randolph's to edit with help from the queen
> It's a guinea a number, too little by half
> For the crowned heads of Europe are all on the staff.[89]

The journal's steep price stemmed from Lady Churchill's wish to separate it from the "miles of newspapers, tons of magazine articles, mountains of periodicals [that] are distributed daily between sunrise and sunset. They are printed; they are read; they are forgotten." She hoped its price alone would make her readers value the publication more than other sources of information and collect the quarterly as one of "the best products of an age."[90] Further, she intended her publication to connect the peoples of her two countries as she identified them—the *authentic* British aristocracy and the *manufactured* American aristocracy; this racial and classist motivation cost her financially.

Lady Churchill also identified her subscribers as members of an elite Anglo-American network and sought to forge a transatlantic bond through her publication. One of the ten volumes of the *Anglo-Saxon Review* includes a list of subscribers. The March 1900 issue (volume 6) presented an index of subscribers, thereby publicly identifying an elite and active transatlantic network of governmental leaders on both sides of the Atlantic. Much like the record of marriages between American heiresses and British aristocrats, the record reads as a political and social who's who of elite Anglo-Americans: Edward VII (the Prince of Wales), the Honorable Arthur Balfour (future prime minister, 1902–05), O. H. P. Belmont (the Duchess of Manchester's stepfather), Mrs. Joseph Chamberlain (fellow Anglo-American bride Mary Endicott), J. M. Choate (the U.S. ambassador to the United Kingdom, 1899–1905) George Cornwallis-West (Lady Churchill's future second husband), Lady Curzon of Kedleston (Mary Curzon, the vicereine of India), the U.S. Department of State, numerous members of the aristocracy, and various public libraries, including the Athenaeum Library in Minneapolis, Carnegie Library in Alleghany and Pittsburgh, Iowa State Library, Leeds Library, Manchester Free Library, and New York Public Library. The publication of subscribers explicitly identified a growing network of Anglo-American elites interested in and willing to support stronger Anglo-American relations, an audience Lady Churchill called upon repeatedly.

The journal reached an affluent readership in Great Britain and the United States with private subscriptions, and its audience was even wider when one includes those who read it in various public libraries. But the high price remained a point of criticism. On July 2, 1899, the *New York Times* announced, "Lady Randolph has planned her quarterly with daring and originality and has carried it out with remarkable success"; ten days later, it criticized the publication's price: "a guinea a number in London, or six dollars in New York, must seem a trifle 'steep' for a magazine."[91] Another New York paper reasoned, "You pay five dollars for this magazine. It may be good, but you can buy *The World* for a cent."[92]

After Lady Churchill published ten volumes, her transatlantic literary project ended. The publication had failed to produce a profit, and the strained business relationship between her and her publisher prevented them from working together to find a publishing alternative or a broader market. Lane believed Lady Churchill was too controlling over the quarterly and would not listen to his suggestions. Likewise disenchanted, Lady Churchill thought he never cared about her publication, was constantly out of the country, was unavailable for discussions, and was only interested in the volumes if they turned a profit. They ended the venture on a sour note.[93] The *Anglo-Saxon Review* finally ended because of money, a topic that, as long as she could maintain her lifestyle and social engagements, never interested Lady Churchill. Despondent over the journal's end, she confided to one of her sisters, "I no longer even want to understand money. . . . There is never enough of it however hard one tries. Better to put it from one's mind and trust in fate."[94]

While the *Anglo-Saxon Review* came to a disappointing end, the venture solidified Lady Churchill's position as a leading and credible authority regarding Anglo-American *relations,* which were subtly but importantly different from *policy,* both formal and informal. Her identity as an American-born, British-wed woman at the turn of the twentieth century provided her the opportunity to lead her two countries toward improved relations. Although her periodical was not connected to a military conflict, the publication experience provided Lady Churchill a bridge between her behind-the-scenes work during the Venezuelan boundary dispute and another burgeoning conflict far from either Britain or the United States.

Her next transatlantic project drew on the lessons learned from her failed publishing venture—it would include a formal business plan, strict financial management, and meticulous bi-national marketing. Determined not to repeat past mistakes, Lady Churchill built upon her growing organizational knowledge and increasing dual identity in future endeavors between her two countries. Using the elite Anglo-American network that she had helped to create and publicly identify through her publication, she expanded her international goals and called on her ambassadorial sisters to assist her in once again uniting Anglo-Americans.

The American Amazons

In the fall of 1899, the Boer War began in South Africa, marking an imperial struggle between British forces and African rebels. A similar conflict among Americans, Cubans, and Filipinos had occurred a year earlier in the Spanish-American War. Many Anglo-Americans drew similarities between the two encounters and concluded that the United States and Great Britain fought similar colonial wars as a consequence of their overseas empires, an international development that brought the two colonial powers closer together at the turn of the twentieth century.[95] Approaching the war from her unique ambassadorial status, Lady Churchill entertained the idea of organizing an American hospital ship to take to South Africa to tend to the wounded soldiers. She shared the idea with a friend, Sir William Garstin, a famous Egyptologist and something of an expert on South Africa. He encouraged her to follow through with the proposal: "Believe me, you will be making history."[96] Learning from Venezuelan boundary dispute and *Anglo-Saxon Review,* Lady Churchill thought this transnational pursuit would likely be fruitful. A truly

transatlantic charity that could share the organizational burdens as well as the potential achievements might be possible. After conferring with a number of American-born, British-wed women, including her two sisters, Lady Churchill decided
to go forward with the project.[97] She "galvanised American women in England at a
time when they did not yet see themselves as an identifiable group."[98]

On October 25, 1899, Lady Churchill hosted the first committee meeting in her
home to organize the American Hospital Ship Fund. The committee selected Mrs.
A. A. Blow as honorary secretary; Fanny Ronalds, treasurer; and Mrs. Cornelia
Adair, vice-chairman. Not surprisingly, it selected Lady Churchill as chair. Additional executive committee members included Lady Essex, Mrs. Arthur Paget,
and Mrs. Joseph Chamberlain, all Anglo-American brides. But members of the
committee may have also had more than charitable interests in mind. For example, Mrs. Blow's husband was secretary of the Great Shiba Mine and was also the
manager of one of South Africa's richest mining companies. Mrs. Paget's husband
commanded the First Scots Guards in South Africa, and Lady Essex's husband,
the seventh Earl of Essex, served in the Imperial Yeomanry in South Africa; thus,
their interests in South Africa were philanthropic, economic, personal, and due
to their shared Anglo-Saxon identification, racially motivated. While the committee members hoped to bring their countries closer together, they also held common
contemporary views regarding the superiority of the Anglo-Saxon race. Voicing the
collective hopes and desires of the executive committee, Mary Chamberlain, wife of
Colonial Secretary Joseph Chamberlain and daughter of former President Grover
Cleveland's secretary of war, reflected, "The control of the tropics devolves more
and more on the Anglo-Saxon race, and carries with it the responsibility for the civilization and welfare of the vast populations which turn to English-speaking people
for protection and good government."[99] These women saw their transnational work
as a service to their countries as well to their perceived racial obligation as Anglo-
Saxons. In other words, they saw themselves as neither wholly American nor British
but rather as Anglo-Saxon, and as a result, informal ambassadors of their race.

In their early meetings, the committee members decided that the funds col-
lected to purchase a British hospital ship would come strictly from American
donations, and they agreed that for this undertaking to truly reflect its transatlantic origins, a combination of American and British doctors and seamen would
constitute the ship's staff. The women began immediately organizing fund-raising
activities such as concerts, teas, and public entertainments. They also petitioned
donations from wealthy Americans. Just two days after their first meeting, on
October 27, 1899, a solicitation appeared in the *New York Times*:

> Whereas, Great Britain is now involved in a war affecting the rights and liberty of
> the Anglo-Saxon people in South Africa. . . . The people of Great Britain, by their

sympathy and moral support, materially aided the people of the United States in the war over Cuba and the Philippines; It is resolved that the American women in Great Britain, while deploring the necessity for war, shall endeavor to raise among their compatriots here and in America a fund for the relief of sick and wounded soldiers and refugees in South Africa. It is proposed to dispatch immediately a suitable hospital ship, fully equipped, with medical stores and provisions, to accommodate 200 patients for three months, with a staff of four doctors, five nurses, and forty noncommissioned officers and orderlies. To carry the foregoing resolution into effect the sum of £30,000 ($150,000) will be required which will have to be raised within a fortnight. Your sympathy and cooperation are earnestly desired.[100]

The American Amazons, as they named themselves, met daily during October and November. The women and their project received great approval in Great Britain and the United States. The *New York Times* regularly published all donations made to the transnational mission. Notably, many of the same people who subscribed to the *Anglo-Saxon Review* contributed to the American Amazons. The *St. James's Gazette* praised the women: "Few more graceful examples could be imagined of the courteous spirit of American sympathy with this country. . . . The widespread and generous responses to its appeals from both sides of the Atlantic show how warmly the merciful idea is accepted by the citizens in both countries."[101] One British paper commended "our American cousins," and another noted, "They have formed a strong committee, with Lady Randolph Churchill at its head. It is to be supposed, therefore, that the result will be a great success."[102]

The organization and strategic implementation of the American Amazons' transatlantic mission met with rapid success. Within two months, the group had raised over £45,000, more than enough to purchase a ship, hire a full staff, and sail to South Africa.[103] They purchased a former cattle boat from Bernard Nagel Baker, American owner of the Atlantic Transport Company. Baker generously agreed to transform the vessel into a hospital ship and maintain the ship and a crew—including surgeons, nurses, officers, and orderlies—all at his expense. Coincidentally, the ship's name was the *Maine,* the same as the ship that played a central role in the Spanish-American War.[104] The Amazonian ambassadors' efforts united the two countries at diplomatic, financial, and military levels.

Baker's offer to support the crew of the *Maine* largely addressed the American Amazons' financial concerns, but the selection of the crew proved a difficult task. Numerous nurses and doctors from the United States volunteered their services, but such generosity was denied, as, according to the *London Times,* "War Office rules forbid the employment of any medical men and nurses except those possessing British Diplomas."[105] In typical fashion, Lady Churchill used her personal connections with the British government to work around this; she sought and received permission for American medical professionals to join the *Maine*'s crew under "unusual privileges." As historian Richard Kahn explains, Lady Churchill's "social position and personal appeal, as well as the British-American politics of the situation, allowed her to exercise a degree of authority not usually tolerated by the military." Her close friend, Elizabeth Mills (Mrs. Whitelaw) Reid, the wife of the future U.S. ambassador to Great Britain, selected doctors, nurses, and orderlies as she had for the Spanish-American War a year earlier. Nevertheless, the ship remained under British control and leadership, as Col. H. F. Hensman, a retired British surgeon, served as the chief medical officer in command. Maj. Julian M. Cabell, retired United States Army surgeon, served as the *Maine*'s senior surgeon. Lady Churchill and her "lady benefactors," as the press dubbed them, selected nurses and orderlies from both countries to complete the crew. Thus, the American Amazons, "a group of influential and capable American women [, were] in control of a British military hospital ship in wartime, surely a highly unusual circumstance."[106]

Under a British flag, presented by the Duke of Connaught on behalf of Queen Victoria, and an American flag, yet another indication of monarchial approval and support of these informal ambassadors, the *Maine* set sail for Cape Town, South Africa, on December 23, 1899. Noting the special occasion, the Duke commented, "Never before has a ship sailed under the combined flags of the Union Jack and the Stars and Stripes." Anticipating potential personality conflicts, Lady Churchill decided to accompany the ship, to mediate any minor disagreements between the British and American staffs. These disagreements stemmed in part from transnational competition and a desire to prove the chain of command aboard the vessel. Other disagreements derived from hostilities between male and female nurses and perceptions of gender inferiority. While nurses on both sides of the Atlantic were traditionally female, this was a military vessel. Many aboard the *Maine* thought a female nurse caring for male soldiers was an inappropriate challenge of the military's masculine status quo. Not surprising to Lady Churchill, tensions arose between the American and British crews on their way to South Africa, and given her superb diplomatic skills, she smoothed things over. Major Cabell went so far as to give Lady Churchill credit for the ease of the transatlantic journey: "It was owing to her tact that several little threatened annoyances were avoided."[107] But upon arrival in South Africa, the crew quickly began caring for the sick and wounded soldiers, regardless of nationality.

Having no medical training, Lady Churchill helped the doctors and nurses when she could but spent most of her time writing letters home for the wounded soldiers. After four months of service in South Africa, British soldiers named the new 4.7 gun the "Lady Randolph Churchill" in honor of her work, a remarkable gesture of thanks to an American woman. Just before the ship returned to Great Britain, Lady Churchill received a letter of thanks from a group of soldiers: "It is impossible to express in a few words adequate thanks for all the comforts we have received on board. . . . We hope the next voyage of the ship will be as pleasant to you as this one has been to all of us." She also received letters of thanks from Elihu Root (United States Secretary of War, 1899–1904), the Lords of Commissioners of the Admiralty, Vice Admiral E. H. Seymour, and the U.S. War Department. Lady Churchill later described her work as "one of the most thrilling experiences of my life, certainly the most important public work I have ever tried to do."[108]

After four months in South Africa, Lady Churchill returned to London. But the American hospital ship *Maine* remained in service for a total of fifteen months. At the conclusion of the Boer War, the ship and all the equipment aboard were given to the British government. Now a permanent hospital ship, the *Maine* was assigned to the Mediterranean Squadron. In 1914, it ran aground and was abandoned near Scotland. Another British ship, the *Mediator,* was renamed the *Maine* in tribute to "the women of America."[109]

Lady Churchill's activism in the Boer War placed her as a leader of the Anglo-American world in the midst of military actions largely based on the assumed racial superiority of Anglo-Saxons and their alleged obligations as dutiful imperialists. Her actions as an American in London and the greater British Empire coincided with the Spanish-American War, another military engagement largely based on contemporary racial beliefs and the responsibilities of Anglo-Saxons around the world. Given the strong connections the United States and Great Britain made between race and imperialism at the end of the nineteenth century, one may draw an analogy between these Anglo-Saxon wars and, to borrow from Rudyard Kipling, describe Lady Churchill's transnational activism as a part of the Anglo-American world as the "white woman's burden," as much of the informal ambassadors' motivation for unity between their two countries rests on a shared racial identity.

In 1900, after her return to Britain, Lady Churchill married Captain George Cornwallis-West, a man twenty years her junior and an officer of the Scots Guards.[110] They divorced in 1913 but always remained fond of one another.[111] In 1918, Lady Churchill married a much younger man, colonial administrator Montague Phippen Porch.[112] In 1912, the *London Daily Mail* described her as "the busiest woman in London. . . . She has always been energetic. It is in her American blood."[113] But when World War I began in 1914, Lady Churchill (as she remained known throughout her life, despite her husband's death and her subsequent marriages) did not lead the American women's efforts in Britain. The transatlantic leadership torch had passed to the next generation of informal ambassadors.

Nonetheless, Lady Churchill remained a notable woman in Britain and the United States until her death on June 29, 1921, at the age of sixty-seven. In the summer of 1921, she suffered a fall that resulted in a broken ankle, followed by gangrene, which eventually resulted in an amputation. Though the surgery was initially successful, she died from a hemorrhage in the main artery of the leg.[114] An inquest followed, but the coroner rendered the death accidental.[115] She was buried at the churchyard at the Marlborough family estate, Blenheim Palace, next to Lord Churchill.[116]

In 1952, a plaque was placed at Lady Churchill's Brooklyn birthplace. Both American and British flags hung outside the home as diplomatic and consular representatives from both countries participated in the ceremony, an official appreciation for her informal ambassadorial efforts. Her elder son, Prime Minister Winston Churchill, expressed his "warm thanks" for such an "expression of friendship and good will."[117] Noting his mother's efforts on behalf of Anglo-American amity, he described the ceremony as "more than a family affair" but rather a "transatlantic one which concerns the unity of our two peoples" that symbolized "that often hidden feeling of affinity between us."[118]

Once described as "one of the greatest political and social powers of Great Britain," Lady Churchill lived her life to the fullest until its end.[119] Daisy Warwick, an old friend, once wrote to her, "Do you remember all the fun we had together in the old days, dear Jennie? But I never *regret* anything, do you? We have both *lived* our lives."[120] Her first marriage marked the beginning of hundreds of such transatlantic unions and the opening chapter of American-born, British-wed women working as informal ambassadors.[121] Her marriage was noted as "the first of those brilliant unions between American 'first families' and the British nobility which have done so much to knit together the social fabric of the two nations."[122]

During her exciting life abroad, through her success in the political and social circles in London and her philanthropic activities in Ireland, she represented the United States to Great Britain during a critical time in Anglo-American relations—"the first American woman to influence British history both in and out of parliament."[123] Her distinctly American approach to her husband's political campaigns and her own interests in politics made "the Conservative party more democratic [and enlarged] the sphere of women's activities" in Britain while advancing both of their respective careers in Britain.[124] Her assertive and unique projects aimed at bolstering Anglo-American relations met with both success and failure. Nonetheless, she placed herself squarely between her two countries by serving as an informal ambassador as the nineteenth century came to a close. Lady Churchill reached legendary status during her lifetime: one magazine called her "the most influential Anglo-Saxon woman in the world."[125]

Young Jennie Jerome's zest for life caught the eye of a young Lord Randolph Churchill and endeared her to the British public over the span of her life. Fellow Anglo-American bride Mary Leiter Curzon once wrote to her, "You are the only person who lives on the crest of the wave and is always full of vitality and suc-

cess."[126] For nearly five decades, Lady Churchill acted as political, social, and charitable leader of the Anglo-American ambassadorial community in London. She
and her fellow American-born, British-wed brides carved out a niche for themselves in Great Britain as informal diplomatists, military philanthropists, racially
motivated imperialists, and transnational activists. Although she received no formal training from the U.S. government, the nation could not have selected a more
charming, well-bred, beautiful, or talented hostess to represent it at a time when
Anglo-American relations could have either improved or worsened significantly.
Margot Asquith, wife of Prime Minister Herbert Asquith, once proclaimed that
Lady Churchill "could have governed the world."[127] Lady Churchill took on the duties of the traditional diplomat's wife—hostessing and establishing important contacts with influential people—while acting as a diplomat in her own right—taking
on a public role and influencing public opinion between her two countries. In so
doing, she shaped Britons' opinions of Americans, serving as an informal ambassador for the United States.

CHAPTER THREE

Drawing-Room Diplomat

Mary Endicott Chamberlain Carnegie

I feel that if [my two countries] were to come into conflict it would be a crime against the civilized world.

—MARY ENDICOTT CHAMBERLAIN TO ELLEN PEABODY ENDICOTT, DECEMBER 21, 1895

In the fall of 1933, Mary Endicott Chamberlain Carnegie informed her "beloved Miss May" that she had recently returned home and "during that week saw all my *families*."[1] Such a simple statement fails to reveal the sheer magnitude of the word "families" within the context of Mary's remarkable Anglo-American life. Following her marriage to Joseph Chamberlain in 1888, she left her biological American family for her marital British one. Having joined the ranks of Lady Churchill and the Dollar Princesses, Mary seemingly became just another of the hundreds of American heiresses who married into the British poli-social elite during the late nineteenth and early twentieth centuries. But as Lady Churchill's marriage and life in Britain demonstrate, to dismiss her marriage to Joseph Chamberlain as just another transatlantic union would be to miss an opportunity to examine the significant but subtle activities of one American-born, British-wed woman who wielded considerable soft power as a drawing-room diplomat.

As the American bride of Joseph Chamberlain, an outspoken Anglo-American advocate, Mary assumed a high-profile position. Her marital status granted her consistent personal access to leaders at the highest levels of British government. But she began winning over the British public, just as Lady Churchill had before her, at her new home. Following her marriage, she accompanied her husband to a public meeting in his hometown of Birmingham, the crowd welcoming her with shouts of "Three cheers for our American cousin!"[2] Though she was met warmly

Mary Endicott Chamberlain Carnegie. Photograph by Lafayette. London, 1920. Colonial Society Photograph Collection. Photograph number 53.1. Massachusetts Historical Society, Boston.

on this occasion, Mary soon discovered that her American identity would be both an asset and a detriment in her interactions with members of leading poli-social circles in England, something many Anglo-American brides learned through their public and private lives. Endicott's marriage, however, differed slightly from other Anglo-American marriages, as her husband was a member of neither the British aristocracy nor the Conservative Party.[3]

As the wife of the British colonial secretary and the stepmother of Prime Minister Neville Chamberlain and Foreign Secretary Austen Chamberlain, Mary exerted her own style of authority and influenced British perceptions of Americans until her death in London in 1957. Through an extensive transatlantic correspondence that spanned decades and growing familial relations that stretched across the Atlantic, Mary created an Anglo-American network on both a personal and a professional level. Furthermore, she made for herself a quiet and latent role as an informal ambassador by facilitating cordial relations among leaders of both of her beloved countries at a critical time in the history of U.S.-U.K. relations. Compared with other high-profile transatlantic brides, Mary has received very little attention by scholars, as evidenced by a sole biography published in 1965.

The Endicott family traced its roots to the colonial period, an auspicious genealogy that served Mary particularly well following her marriage and permanent relocation to England. Her father, William Crowninshield Endicott Sr. (1826–1900), descended from John Endecott (1588–1665), a soldier, surgeon, and agent for the Massachusetts Bay Company, which brought him to the colony in 1629. He held a variety of positions in the settlement—colonial assistant, deputy governor, governor, chief military official—until his death. Mary's father graduated from Harvard College in 1847, continued his legal studies at the same institution, and joined the Massachusetts Bar Association in 1850.[4] In 1859, he married a cousin, Ellen Peabody (1833–1927), daughter of renowned philanthropist George Peabody (1803–1892); thus, Mary came from "Puritan stock that . . . [could not] be excelled."[5] Mary's parents hailed from two of the oldest and wealthiest families in Salem, Massachusetts, and they enjoyed great political and social successes both individually and as a couple. They began their own family in 1860, with a son, William Crowninshield Endicott Jr., and in 1864 they had a daughter, Mary Crowninshield, named for her paternal grandmother.[6]

Mary's early years shaped her political, social, and religious perspectives in a manner distinct to affluent New England. Her parents and grandparents impressed upon her what it meant to be "a lady." She attended a select girls' school, though she never excelled there.

During the summers, Mary spent much happier days, with various family members at the farm in New Hampshire or at ancestral property in Nahant. Though it was somewhat unusual for American women of this period, she enjoyed a great deal of exposure to the discussion of current events. Conversations at the family dinner table easily shifted from local affairs to the Franco-Prussian War, which prepared Mary to contribute to later discussions with political leaders on both sides of the Atlantic.[7]

Mary's family promoted a strong Anglo-American awareness in their children from early ages. In 1876, when she was just twelve, Mary received a scrapbook her mother had started for her some years before. Instead of photographs, it contained a variety of poems, prayers, song lyrics, Bible verses, and newspaper articles from the United States and England. Some of the materials, initially chosen by her mother and to which Mary added, included "The Star-Spangled Banner"; selections from *A Child's History of England;* several poems by Alfred, Lord Tennyson; "The Battle-Hymn of the Republic"; and an article promoting Boston's centennial preceded by a prayer poem titled, "The Marriage at Windsor Chapel." Words from a sermon given at Westminster and a memorial poem concerning the death of Benjamin Disraeli were carefully arranged next to "God Save the President," printed by *Harper's*

Weekly. From an 1880 sermon given in Westminster Abbey by Dr. Phillips Brooks, the rector of Trinity Church in Boston, Mary learned that a Christian definition of Anglo-Americanism defied the distance of the Atlantic Ocean. Numerous articles and poems from the United States and England concerning the death of President James Garfield in 1881 also appeared in the scrapbook. *Punch* published a poem titled "England to America" that included the line "Columbia's sorrow; 'tis our own."[8] The scrapbook clearly reveals that she was raised by a religious mother who was also an American patriot; before Mary reached her teen years, her family imparted to her serious degrees of religious devotion, American nationalism, and Anglo-Saxon consciousness.

Mary was also privy to frequent dialogue concerning current events in Massachusetts and beyond. Though her brother attended Harvard between 1879 and 1883, she had not yet made her debut on the Boston social stage and thus could not enjoy the expanding circle of eligible bachelors made possible through his contacts. Instead, she spent most evenings reading in her father's vast library and listening to passionate legal and political debates among his colleagues. Such activities served Mary well later, when she proved herself a "delightful and informed companion" on both sides of the Atlantic.[9] Such exposure to fervent political discussions was due largely to her father's frequent and mostly unsuccessful campaigns at the state and national levels. He eventually became a judge on the Massachusetts Supreme Judicial Court, where he served from 1873 until 1882, but his dedication to the bench took a toll on his health. Upon his doctors' advice and further pressing from his wife, he agreed to embark on a tour of Europe, a common prescription for the affluent and overworked professional of this period. Thus, Mary made her first transatlantic journey.

Initially, she was devastated by her parents' pronouncement that she would join them for several months in Europe. Their desire to guard her place in society, and the unfortunate timing of her father's retirement, meant she would not enjoy formal entrance into Boston society with her friends. Instead, she spent her time as her parents' official travel coordinator and errand runner. She was visibly unhappy upon their departure from New York, and her uncle teasingly encouraged her, "Keep a stiff upper lip, Miserable!"[10]

Clearly dismayed to "miss all the parties, pretty dresses, and new excursions to Boston and Cambridge," Mary soon experienced a new world beyond the shores of Massachusetts. Following a ten-day journey aboard the R.M.S. *Republic,* the Endicotts stopped in Liverpool for a mere six hours before spending most of June in London. They visited Piccadilly, Hyde Park, Buckingham Palace, the Houses of Parliament, and other city sights. Overwhelmed by the experience, Mary wrote in her diary that she "could hardly believe my eyes that I was really seeing the places I had always heard & read of. As to talking that was impossible. I had all *I could* to look with my eyes [which] felt twice their size." Other cities throughout England and Europe all paled in comparison to London. Berlin, Paris, Monte Carlo, Milan, and San Remo failed to impress Mary as much as London had. Upon returning to London in the spring, she wrote, "Our long journey has gone off well & here we are comfortably established in our old quarters. . . . It seemed quite like a home coming."[11] Her Anglo-American heart had found its home.

Twelve months into their European vacation, Mary recorded in her diary, "A year ago to-day we left our native land. How little we then thought so long a time would pass before our return!" The Endicotts enjoyed another summer abroad, spending most of their remaining time in London. While there, they attended the opera, and Mary expressed her enjoyment and "wondered if I shall ever hear it again in Covent Garden." The family prepared to return home in the fall, and Mary took a last walk through Piccadilly and sorrowfully mused, "This is the last night I shall pass in this beloved London, and for how long? That is the question."[12] They returned to Nahant, Massachusetts, in September 1883 in the same vessel that had brought them across the Atlantic more than a year before. Though happy to see Salem again, she expressed great sadness at leaving Europe, London in particular. Unbeknownst to her, this would not be the last time she saw her beloved city.

Life in Washington, D.C.

Following their extensive tour of Europe, the Endicotts returned to business as usual. Mary resumed the activities expected of a young lady of her class and upbringing, which included French lessons, dancing lessons, and tea at Delmonico's. Meanwhile, her father returned to his public and political life in 1884, running unsuccessfully for governor of Massachusetts. The following year he was appointed secretary of war in President Grover Cleveland's first cabinet, a position he held until 1889. His acceptance of the offer had consequences for the entire family. His wife made arrangements to set up house in Washington, D.C., and make the social migration from Massachusetts to the nation's capital. This was no small feat, as she also had to navigate her daughter's reception by Washington society, since her coming out would now take place there instead of Boston. After an initial trip to Washington, the family leased a Gothic mansion near another cabinet official, Secretary of the Navy William C. Whitney.[13] Together, Mary and her mother adjusted to the demands of Washington and were well received by the city's elite. Upon her first formal appearance at a presidential reception, the press reported, "Miss Endicott . . . was quite the belle of the Blue Parlor. . . . Men of distinction seek her side and are fascinated by her conversations."[14]

Though the Washington press frequently commented on her beauty and charms, Mary possessed an intellectual strength that she reserved for her most intimate circle. While the rest of the family attended President Cleveland's inauguration, she chose to stay "behind and [have] time to think over what it meant to have Papa the Secretary of War."[15] She recognized that the initial excitement of the appointment was most exhilarating and that she "did not know whether I was on my head or on my heels."[16] But even as someone who was already accustomed to "being brushed, combed, unhooked, and laced in and out of one tiny-waisted dress after another," Mary candidly acknowledged "with an occasional sigh at [this] being the last of the old life."[17] She clearly recognized that her father's new political position signified the end of one life but also that it marked the beginning of a new life.

A British-American Fisheries Conference was arranged for the fall of 1887, the second year of Mr. Endicott's tenure as secretary of war. Tensions between the United States and Newfoundland threatened to wreck the unstable relationship between the United States and Great Britain throughout the late nineteenth century. Invited by Prime Minister Lord Salisbury to serve as the head of the British delegation to the conference, Joseph Chamberlain came to the United States as chief plenipotentiary. The hope on both sides of the Atlantic was that the conference would strengthen Anglo-American relations. But Chamberlain, whose many nicknames—Good Old Joe, Brummagem Lion, Pushful Joe, Orchid Joe, Old Man Eloquent—implied numerous conflicting personality traits, struck many as an odd choice by the prime minister.[18] Having voted against Irish Home Rule, Chamberlain found himself a man without a country as the Radical-turned-Liberal now split with his own party. According to many fellow politicians and constituents, he had betrayed Irish nationalism and wrecked Liberals' hopes with a single vote. It was at this moment that Lord Salisbury, recognizing Chamberlain's talents for business and his own desire for an alliance between the Liberal Unionist and Conservative Parties, sent Chamberlain overseas.[19]

The British delegation arrived in New York on November 7, and the Canadians followed ten days later. Chamberlain first met Secretary Endicott on November 20 at a dinner that preceded the first official meeting the next day. A week later, a reception was held at the British Legation. Although the Endicotts had traveled home to Salem for Thanksgiving, Mary's brother returned to Washington to accompany her to the party where she met her future husband for the first time. Clearly, something special existed between the two, as one witness observed: "He froze to her an hour ago, and hasn't left her yet."[20] Shortly after this initial meeting, the Endicotts hosted a dinner in their home with Mr. Chamberlain as the guest of honor, as formal dinners often invited informal opportunities for nongovernmental discourse and exchange among all guests. Following the event, Chamberlain wrote that the secretary of war was "of the bluest New England blood. . . . Mrs. Endicott is a very pleasant woman and their daughter one of the brightest and most intelligent girls I have yet met."[21] The Fisheries Conference ended its winter session on December 10, and Chamberlain held a dinner that night. He personally selected the flowers and had menus printed with American and British flags crossed, along with the motto, "Blood is thicker than water."[22] This message appears to have been intended as much for Mary as it was for the American fisheries delegation. Given his comments about Anglo-Saxons and Anglo-Americanism, in something of a predecessor of the "special relationship," Chamberlain pursued both profession diplomatic and personal goals simultaneously. He sent Mary a basket of roses and a poem three days later, a day she described as "glorious," which were followed by a book on Christmas Day.[23] Making his intentions clear, he called on her at her home several days later.

When Chamberlain left for New York after the holidays, he spoke to the press about his reactions to the United States rather than mentioning anything specific about the Fisheries Conference. In a statement that may have been meant as much for Mary as the newspapers, he declared that he had "been made to feel at home quite as much so as in England. I brought with me strong feelings of sympathy and goodwill for the American people. They have been made stronger by personal acquaintances with them. But what has struck me the most is the resemblance between us and the Americans. I don't feel like a stranger here; I feel at home."[24]

Given Chamberlain's personal history, his pursuit of Mary may seem questionable. At fifty-one, he was twenty-eight years her senior, a greater age gap even than that between President Cleveland and his young bride, Francis Folsom. Chamberlain was a two-time widower, both of his wives having died in childbirth.[25] One might have assumed that after a failed relationship with children's author Beatrix Potter in 1882, Chamberlain may have given up on finding love at this relatively late period. Many of his children were grown, so he did not need a wife to raise his them.[26] His eldest daughter, Beatrice, managed his house and numerous servants, which allowed Chamberlain to focus on his political career. Consequently, he had no practical domestic need to pursue a third wife. Like the Churchill, Curzon, and Astor transatlantic marriages, Chamberlain's relentless pursuit was, indeed, motivated by love and admiration for a remarkable woman, an American belle and English beauty.[27]

Chamberlain increased his letters to and calls upon Mary and, to see more of her, accepted all invitations that Washington presented. Chamberlain's anxiety and melancholy, visible since the death of his second wife, Florence, apparently lifted during his weeks in the United States. He had refused to dance since her death, but he changed his mind to be closer to Mary.[28] Unfamiliar with the American custom of "cutting in," he was infuriated when a competitive suitor stole he away; thereafter, he asked for "another turn" whenever he saw another man approach her.[29] He candidly wrote to Mary he "knew that you were the only girl for me."[30] At a dinner, he held her plate while she ate from it, declaring that neither his dignity nor anything else [would] stand in the way of my determined purpose to make the Puritan maiden my wife if that were humanly possible."[31]

At first the twenty-three-year-old Mary responded kindly but coolly to Chamberlain's advances. At this point in history, Mary's age hardly helped her marital prospects, but she was determined to marry well *and* to someone in public life. Shortly before Chamberlain's arrival in the United States, she admitted she had come "to the conclusion that my chances were against rather than for my marrying."[32] She did not reveal these sentiments immediately to Chamberlain but rather charmed him with her reserved hospitality and intelligent conversation. Her suitor saw her as neither "superior" nor "silly"; rather, he had "lighted on the exact medium . . . [of] perfection."[33] In contrast, for her part, even a month before their engagement, she wrote to a friend that she felt "like a safety match warranted not to go off—till struck on the right box. . . . I am in a very cool frame of mind."[34] Such calm exterior and grace under pressure would serve Mary well in her future emissary role in Britain.

Engagement to Chamberlain

When diplomatic talks resumed in the spring of 1888, Chamberlain intensified his concentration on domestic pursuits. While he focused on the Fisheries Conference, his attention to Mary demonstrated that "the negotiation of a treaty of love was a matter of a good deal more importance and interest than the discussion of dry details relating to bait and seines."[35] Chamberlain's use of the words "negotiation" and "treaty" was significant in his courtship. Not only did he see their connection as something to be negotiated and mediated, he recognized the diplomatic implications of such a "special relationship." In February, he wrote to Mary, "The time has come . . . when . . . I . . . pray you to end all uncertainty. . . . My work here is rapidly drawing to a close & my public duty will constrain me to return to England." But with this slight degree of pressure, he also offered his love and promises to assure her happiness as his wife. Finally, he wrote, "Now therefore decide. If you are not afraid & will trust me with your happiness, believe me, I will know how to guard it against the world."[36]

Mary had decided to accept Chamberlain and received his formal proposal at breakfast the next morning. But she kept her "great man" waiting until their meeting later that day when she finally informed him, "My Conqueror has won the victory."[37] Her acceptance of his proposal gave him incredible happiness: he suddenly found, "All women were beautiful—all the men were witty—and I was in the seventh heaven because I had all the while a vision of a little bit of old English looking through a doorway with her lips parted in pleasant expectation."[38] Clearly, the negotiated treaty was a successful agreement for both parties.

Unfortunately, her family's reaction to the news of Mary's engagement was anything but pleasant. Her brother balked at the idea of his sister marrying someone with a working-class background, regardless of his present position in British politics. Concerned with the engagement's political ramifications, Mary's father focused on the risks of such a pairing and feared that his daughter easily could be lost amid Chamberlain's vast ambitions.[39] Mary's mother, while sympathetic to her daughter's emotions, was hardly pleased at the notion of her living across the Atlantic. In an effort to challenge or perhaps outlast the engagement, the Endicotts delayed announcing it, for numerous practical reasons. First, the engagement between the secretary of war's daughter and the chief British commissioner could endanger the months of diplomatic work regarding the fisheries dispute. Furthermore, and infinitely more critical to Secretary Endicott's cabinet position, such an announcement would jeopardize President Cleveland's reelection campaign later that year—it would undoubtedly cost Cleveland the Irish-American vote. Thus, at the insistence of Mary's family, the engagement was kept secret for nine months.[40] Chamberlain saw very little of his fiancée until their wedding. At her parents' urging, the two rarely corresponded until after the 1888 presidential election.[41]

While transatlantic marriages were hardly uncommon, Mary's nuptials set something of a precedent. Typically, the American girls hailed from rich and aspiring families while the English husbands were poor but noble. But the Endicotts represented the old and established family and Chamberlain the nouveau riche, having risen from a modest background through manufacturing-based Manchester and making a name for himself in British politics. The Endicotts fiercely protected their public name and private life and worried that their daughter would find the abrupt transition from Boston to Birmingham more than she could handle. But her father's concerns may have been more about his personal feelings than any practical or political concerns. Upon visiting his daughter in England, he candidly told a journalist, "Nobody knows a thing about these marriages except the parents. It's the fathers that have to suffer! Yet, after all, our daughters leave us. . . . They [say] good-bye . . . for life . . . never expected to see them again this side of the grave."[42]

Nevertheless, the nuptials were set for the fall of 1888, just after the presidential election. Shortly after their secret engagement, the Fisheries Conference settled on its own treaty, and the requisite dinners and talk of Anglo-American amity followed. The treaty's success allowed Chamberlain to return home with new political verve. Defying Mary's father's wishes, he wrote to her that with "feet on my native heath," he felt revived, as "the fighting spirit is coming out."[43] This refreshed spirit was due to more than just the treaty. In a letter to Mary later that summer, he recalled his disposition a year before as "much harder . . . striving to steel myself & to play the game of life till . . . the cards [fall] from my hands, & caring little how soon that time comes." But with Mary as his fiancée, he wrote, all the "artificial insensibility is broken down. My youth has come back to me & I am as eager & as sensitive as ever I was."[44]

Though he pledged to keep his engagement secret and severely restrict any communication with Mary, Chamberlain gave his fellow Englishmen frequent indications of his new enthusiasm for closer Anglo-American relations. Upon his return to England, he gave a speech to the Devonshire Club in which he discussed relations with the United States and the colonies. He spoke to and for his countrymen when he declared that "every good Englishman who is worthy of the name sympathises with the objects of my recent mission . . . [and desires to] remove all causes of difference between the United States and ourselves." He attempted to assuage his colleagues' fears concerning "the introduction of American institutions into this country," which, given the increasing number of Anglo-American marriages, was a carefully crafted sentence with multiple meanings. He went on to affirm England's "appreciation of American institutions, and of the American people, which, perhaps, did not exist a generation ago." He further discussed the "universal feeling of goodwill and admiration . . . and a cordial desire for a hearty and for a durable friendship" with the United States, highlighting the "common blood, and common origin, and common traditions of the Anglo-Saxon race." He candidly announced his identity as a "sentimentalist" who would "never willingly admit . . . any policy that [would] weaken the ties between the different branches of the Anglo-Saxon race." He concluded by emphasizing the affection toward "our . . . fellow-kinsmen who are proud of the glorious tradition of our country, who share with us our history, [and] our origin."[45] Clearly, his looming marital treaty was influencing his international diplomacy.

Chamberlain's desire to remain in politics, and at an international level, was well known, and such words hinted at his ambition to become colonial secretary. But reviewing such a speech, given that he was at this moment engaged to an American woman, gives his rhetoric another meaning. In his political life, Chamberlain boasted publicly of his success regarding the fisheries treaty. Using international diplomatic opportunities and rhetoric, he simultaneously prepared his colleagues and constituents for the eventual announcement of his marriage to a woman from across the Atlantic. Such a powerful and open push for a renewed Anglo-Saxon identity cannot be separated from his private decision to enter a transatlantic marriage. He reiterated upon the celebration of his twenty-fifth wedding anniversary with Mary, "I have done all that is in my power to promote a union between this country and America."[46] Such transatlantic marriages clearly underscore the adage that the personal is political.

The remaining months until the presidential election passed slowly for Chamberlain and Mary. Rumors of "a real treaty" swelled on both sides of the Atlantic, speculating that "Mr. Chamberlain had concluded a separate and private treaty—one which, happily, requires no ratification by a political body—a treaty of marriage."[47] The *Boston Daily Globe* surmised, "While the treaty was rejected, the suitor was accepted."[48] Notably, the engagement was announced in the United States the day after the November election and Cleveland's defeat. Having endured a long separation from her future husband, Mary soon would be permanently separated from her family and entire way of life. Chamberlain traveled to the United States to claim his bride, and the frequently referred to "treaty concluded" when the "charming bride [and] happy groom" were married on November 15, 1888, at St. John's Episcopal Church in the capital.[49] The president, the Supreme Court justices, and members of the cabinet attended the wedding for the fair Puritan and English commoner, and President Cleveland offered a toast at the reception. Such attendance by persons at the highest levels of the American government serves as public proof that a growing number of Americans, and leading politicians in particular, sought improved Anglo-American relations and the byproducts of transatlantic marriages. Despite their initial reluctance, Mary's family eventually accepted Chamberlain into the fold, largely because of Mary's apparent happiness. As her grandmother wrote shortly before the wedding, "The most eventful moment of your life, my darling, is near at hand. . . . We have gained so much in your perfect happiness, far more precious to us than personal considerations could be."[50]

While Mary's life prepared her for a strong marriage, she was entirely unprepared to become a mother. But her stepchildren quickly put her anxieties to rest. Austen joyfully greeted his new American stepmother: "You will be to him all that we could not be and make him far happier than we have been able to do." Chamberlain had shown Austen a picture of his soon-to-be bride, and the latter wrote, "[I] began to feel as if we knew each other. I hope it won't be long before we have you here. . . . This letter won't tell you how glad I am for I can't write what I feel."[51] A letter from Beatrice, Austen's older sister, followed soon after, with an even greater message of delight at Mary's imminent arrival. Beatrice began her missive wishing "many times . . . that there was no Atlantic between us. . . . I find it very difficult to express on paper the warm welcome that I am longing to give you." Noting that some women would regard Chamberlain's children as "a heavy drawback," Beatrice beseeched Mary to "soon think of your family on this side of the water as belonging no less nearly to you than your family on that."[52] Letters from the other children followed in short order. Neville, Chamberlain's oldest son from his second marriage, wrote that he "look[ed] forward to this great change not only for father's sake but also for our own. With such good feelings on both sides beforehand how can we help being friends?"[53] With such a warm reception by so many eager family members, Mary had every reason to look forward to her marriage and relocation to England. Though she "never forgot the land of her birth," she "thoroughly identified herself with the land of her adoption."[54]

From Boston to Birmingham

As Mary prepared to embark on her new life as an American-born, English-wed woman, she received countless cards and letters of congratulations and encouragement before leaving for her honeymoon and new home in England. One particular letter from a cousin wished her "much love and many good wishes for the future. Your health and happiness. I shall be ready with a joyful greeting when you come to town." This cousin expressed the caution, however, that many of Mary's friends and family likely harbored based on her transatlantic marriage: "Being an American . . . so long living here . . . my thoughts recount to New England as my home and country. But Englishmen will welcome you in their land and be proud of you. Believe me."[55] Such observations and expression of pride at the success of American women abroad exist throughout an analysis of this cohort. Clearly, a sentiment of proving oneself on the international stage and winning over the other side, as in a diplomatic setting, remained constant through transatlantic marriages.

When "the little Puritan maid" and "flower of American aristocracy" landed in England, she and her new husband were met with the melodies "Hail, Columbia" and "Yankee Doodle," a recognition of Mary's heritage and warm welcome to her new home.[56] Chamberlain's constituents in Birmingham showered Mary with jewelry, including pearls, diamonds, and brooches made within the city, and her husband had a rose-house built as a wedding present. Upon her arrival as the new mistress of Highbury, the Chamberlain estate, she found three roses in bloom, which pleased her greatly. Her proud brother, who never fully accepted Mary's life in England, inquired often as to "how the roses have turned out. I hope well, for I should like to have you show those Britishers how much finer our roses are than theirs."[57] Even in matters of flora, William never lost his fiercely competitive Anglo-American streak.

Such competitiveness existed on the English side as well. In her formal presentation to the people of Birmingham, the crowd boasted, unprompted, "Joe can make love even more successfully than he makes laws!" followed by the proud claim, "Our Joey's a match for any Yankee!"[58] When Chamberlain addressed the people, he described his wife's journey to her new home in biblical terms. He boastfully declared that his "little maid from Massachusetts" was fully "prepared to take up her life amongst us, in the country to which she has come, in all its fullness and that she will say, with Ruth of old, 'Thy people shall be my people,'" which was met with thunderous applause.[59] In a simple statement, Chamberlain called on a shared Anglo-Saxon religious perspective while confirming Mary's identity as wholly British. He concluded by harkening back to comments of his diplomatic treaty with Mary and expressed thanks that the "American Senate had nothing to say about his private negotiations, which his hearers had just ratified by their presence."[60] Her introduction to Birmingham was deemed a success.

Life in England

Mary's formal presentation to the Queen and British political leaders followed shortly after her introduction to Birmingham. Both Queen Victoria and Prime Minister Lord Salisbury found immediate favor with Mary. As dinner invitations continued to arrive by the dozens, Mary handled an overwhelming social schedule with impressive ease. She even managed to win over Lady Dorothy Nevill, who controlled a social circle in London. The lady's earlier announcement to Chamberlain proclaimed that she could stand neither America's girls nor its tinned lobster, which did not bode well for Mary. But, once again, her nuanced diplomatic skills charmed even the most reluctant of Britons, which continued to amaze her husband. Mary's grandmother remarked on this, reminding her she had "always had a good deal of equanimity and self-possession, and it is evident that you will need it all, to acquit yourself of your part of the duties involved."[61] While most members of British society regarded American girls as ostentatious, Mary's quiet charm and reserved nature provided a distinct contrast of what America could offer individually and collectively.

Mary's days were spent running Highbury and responding to the needs of her husband and his children. Soon after her arrival, she began helping the two youngest girls make their way into English society. She focused the majority of her time, however, on Chamberlain's political schedule. She almost always traveled with him, but she never spoke publicly. She sat nearby as he crafted speeches, and she offered her support when asked. Along with Lady Churchill, Mary attended Parliament and sat in the Ladies' Gallery with the other "ultra-political" ladies, as Jennie described them.[62] The political knowledge she had gained as the daughter of a lawyer, judge, and cabinet member enabled her to follow the situation in London. As it became more popular for political wives, and especially American wives, to attend parliamentary proceedings, Mary's time and visibility there increased as well.

News of her transatlantic popularity traveled quickly. She received a letter from a family friend who boasted, "My Boston heart swells with pride at the thought of your great success among the Britishers, which, of course, I anticipated from the first."[63] Even the wife of the American ambassador commented that Mary's arrival had had sparked great excitement.[64] Mary's letters home confirmed her ease in her new homeland. Chamberlain confirmed Mary's acceptance by his fellow Britons in letters to her family as well. Intent on easing any remaining concerns Mary's parents may have had, Chamberlain assured her mother, "Your daughter is already as completely one of this family as she is of the other across the water."[65]

Mary dedicated a great deal of her time to her two families throughout her life in England and retained close relations with all of Chamberlain's children, especially Austen, as the two were so close in age. He expressed his fondness for Mary to her mother in more than one letter after meeting her family during a three-month visit to the United States in 1890. Upon his return home, he thanked her for "all your kindness during my long visit. I cannot tell you how much I enjoyed it, nor what a pleasure it was to be with Mary in her old home and learn to know all her family." Thankful for her presence in their lives, he continued, "She plays such a big part in our lives now, interesting herself so much in all we do and helping us so much in everything." He reiterated the great "happiness she has brought to us all and . . . sympathy and kindness in all that concerns us." He recalled his reaction to his father's engagement some years before, that it was "the best news [he] could have brought home . . . and the best of good news it has certainly proved to be."[66] Due to Lady Churchill's successful venture abroad and the particulars of the situation into which she married, Mary's triumph was secured early on.

While Mary indeed focused on her extended family, she also cultivated an influential circle of Anglo-Americans in England. Her visiting lists throughout the 1890s included elites from both sides of the Atlantic—Mr. and Mrs. Whitelaw Reid, the American ambassador to Great Britain; Senator and Mrs. Henry Cabot Lodge; Mr. and Mrs. William Kissam Vanderbilt, the parents of Consuelo Vanderbilt, who wed the 9th Duke of Manchester; Mr. John Hay, the American secretary of state; Lord and Lady Randolph Churchill; and Mr. and Mrs. Joseph Choate, another American attaché to Great Britain.[67] Unfortunately, no transcripts of these dinners exist, but Mary clearly became an informal ambassador herself by maintaining a demanding political and social schedule that rivaled that of any formal diplomat of the period.

Domestic Diplomacy

Mary's efforts to maintain her Anglo-American identity and connections as a "drawing-room diplomat" proved most helpful in the mid-1890s, less than a decade after her marriage, as diplomatic relations between the United States and Britain began to deteriorate.[68] Negotiators from both countries had bickered about the boundary between Venezuela and British Guiana for decades, but it was not until the fall of 1895, when President Grover Cleveland demanded that Great Britain submit to arbitration over the border, that the issue fully developed into an Anglo-American crisis.[69] Invoking the rarely enforced Monroe Doctrine of 1823, Cleveland, who again occupied the White House, threatened to go to war with Great Britain, if necessary. In a special message to Congress in December 1895, he argued that the doctrine was "essential to the integrity of our free institutions and . . . maintenance of our distinctive form of government." In a warning tone, Cleveland maintained that Britain's continued action regarding the boundary dispute would appear to the United States "as a willful aggression upon its rights and interests."[70]

While Lady Churchill hosted private dinners and made light of war talk, Mary was infuriated by Cleveland's declarations and fired off a letter to her mother: "What has come over the President? It seems to me almost inconceivable that he should have been in his right mind when he sent that message to Congress." From her decidedly Anglo-American perspective, the Venezuela boundary dispute did not fall under the purview of the Monroe Doctrine and certainly did not apply to an area that the English had controlled for years. She believed the acquisition of new territory was out of the question and voiced the ultimate fear so many felt on both sides of the Atlantic. "Think of how terrible it would be for America and England to go to war over a boundary line in Venezuela! And yet how can England be dictated to . . . The position has been made almost intolerable for her. . . . I feel that if [my two countries] were to come into conflict it would be a crime against the civilized world."[71] Given Mary's perspective as a woman of both worlds, hers was a position of authority, even as it maintained her nongovernmental status. She utilized her confirmed diplomatic skills to help avert a war during an uneasy time.

Justifiably astounded, the British government marveled at why the American government suddenly found this decades-old conflict so monumental.[72] The Panic of 1893 had weakened the American economy so significantly that many political and business leaders took a new and intense interest in Latin America as an area that could buoy the domestic economy.[73] Relations between the United States and Great Britain became so tense that American-born, British-wed wives in London found themselves in an uncomfortable situation. Fearful of what the coming months might bring, many Americans withdrew to continental Europe or returned to the United States for an indefinite period. In contrast, fear of war between their two beloved countries motivated women like Lady Churchill and Mary Chamberlain to take action.

Based on her prominence as a political wife and her husband's new position as colonial secretary, Mary did not have the luxury of retreating to the United States, nor would she have entertained such a thought. During her time in England she had clearly demonstrated her devotion to her husband, his career, and his family in a manner very similar to that of Lady Churchill. Coincidentally, Lord Salisbury, who had sent Chamberlain to the United States in 1887, thereby leading to his meeting Mary and eventually marrying her, was now prime minister and again turned to Chamberlain as colonial secretary to settle the dispute with the United States. That Chamberlain's wife was an American enhanced his ability to know, understand, and work with the Americans to find an acceptable diplomatic compromise. Chamberlain had met Secretary of State Richard Olney, a Bostonian, while visiting Mary's family two years earlier. Furthermore, thanks to her father's cabinet position, Mary personally knew President Cleveland. In this dicey foreign affairs situation, the personal and political cannot be divided.

Following the lead of Lady Churchill, Mary also utilized her position at the center of London's poli-social circles by hosting quiet but frequent dinner parties for the most socially influential persons in London and the British Parliament. In 1895 alone, the colonial secretary and Mary dined with Secretary and Mrs. Agnes Olney, another Boston native, more than half a dozen times while Mary lunched with Mrs. Olney on several occasions.[74] After observing the ongoing efforts in England, one U.S. general reported to the American press, "Ten daughters of the United States, who are working quietly and mightily to prevent war between the two countries that are looking at each other in a sinister way. For these women, the war means a thousand times as much as it does to other Americans; and they have untold power of international arbitration. . . . These particular ten are so situated that they are in the midst of the greatest powers that rule England today. Their influence, thrown upon the scales, would turn it whichever way they bent themselves."[75] Their labors did not go unrewarded. For the first time, Mary recognized the undeniable influence of her Anglo-American marriage and validated in strength of the "unofficial sphere [to] introduce issues, minimize risk, and bring life and emotion to the formation of public policy."[76] Once again, an American woman's degree of acceptable involvement and influence on British politics and foreign relations by virtue of her Anglo-American marriage proved vital to British-American relations. Chamberlain attributed the final settlement to his personal discussions with Olney, but Mary's gentle prodding for an Anglo-American accord influenced her husband as well.[77] Her efforts had an undeniable and significant calming effect on the situation, which both of her countries noticed. As one of the ten ambassadorial daughters of America, Mary had helped ensure that the United States and Great Britain avoided war over Venezuela.[78]

And even as one crisis was resolved, another quickly took its place. When the Spanish-American War erupted in 1898, Mary kept her finger on the pulse of both her countries. Horrified at the idea of American men fighting in Cuba, Mary's American family assured her that "we never dreamed another war would come, and everyone is outraged at it. The people do not want it. It is Congress that has *insisted* on it!"[79] Though Spain requested support from England, a letter from the colonial secretary assured the United States that no such help would occur. Taking the opportunity to promote his constant agenda of Anglo-American co-operation, Chamberlain announced that as "terrible as war may be, even war itself would be cheaply purchased if in a great and noble cause the Stars and Stripes and the Union Jack should wave together over an Anglo-Saxon alliance."[80]

The press wasted no time in attributing Chamberlain's words to the influence of his American wife, applying descriptions unheard of for a political wife in the United States. "A woman is the power that has stirred [Chamberlain] to come out so boldly. It is a little Boston girl . . . who has succeeded in upheaving all the power of Europe." Declaring Mary the "most talked about woman in England today," the press credited Chamberlain's political success to "the Puritan girl," as the devoted wife who made it possible. Confirming her power over her husband—and implying the considerable level of diplomatic influence American-born, British-wed women had over their husbands—the press argued that Mary's "husband would do what she wanted. She went to him. A word from him would swing millions. English money, English commerce, English interests of all kinds were with the United States."[81]

As Chamberlain's "admirable helpmate," Mary was constantly noted in England for her diplomatic influence successes.[82] She found great favor with Queen Victoria, who attributed her "*savoir faire* and self possession [as having] been acquired while acting as one of the cabinet ladies at Washington during her father's term" as secretary of state, which "has had the effect of considerably altering the ideas of Her Majesty with regard to the etiquette and social ethics that prevail at the White House."[83] So impressed was Queen Victoria that she presented Mary with the golden jubilee medal in 1895, a recognition generally reserved for reigning house members and, in a diplomatic context, foreign service families. As "a particular favorite" of Queen Victoria, Mary was one of the very few "non-royal" individuals to receive a gold rather than a silver medal.[84]

Consequently, Mary's fellow Americans felt "a certain degree of pride in the fact that a Salem woman stands so high in court circles."[85] But it was Queen Victoria's son, King Edward VII, who in 1904 bestowed upon Mary the title of Viscountess of Highbury, which made this American woman a member of the British peerage and confirmed her acceptance in Britain. Chamberlain refused any equivalent title for himself but noted her command of British political life and her worthiness of such an honor.[86] He fully acknowledged that his wife's "kindness, sympathy and interest made friends where I might have failed." Noting that Mary was unlike many other Anglo-American wives, the press relished the fact that she became a peeress in her own right unlike the "scores of 'princesses,' 'duchesses,' 'countesses,' and 'marquises.' . . . [T]hese American girls wear their title only by the courtesy of heraldry. They gain them because they were the rich daughters of rich fathers." Mary, in contrast, was described as "no social upstart" and the "real power behind the throne. [She understands] the affairs of world-wide importance in which her husband is one of the leading figures [and has] an intelligent grasp of the political situation in Europe."[87] Her heritage as an "American aristocrat" and her "quiet dignity" immediately challenged the "dollar princesses" stereotype. Her English compatriots saw her, rather, not as a "tuft hunting American girl [or] a flaunting daughter of the *nouveau riche*" but as "a young woman who felt as deep a pride in her ancestry as did the princesses of the blood royal, and who bore herself on all occasion with a modesty, a reserve, and yet a hauteur that made a good many of the English nobility feel a little cheap in her presence."[88] Thus, Mary's one-on-one interactions with Britons resulted in positive commentary on her as neither American nor British but wholly Anglo-American.

Mary continued in her constant companionship with Chamberlain and was his unofficial principal political secretary. As he was advancing in age, his family begged him to slow down and monitor his health more closely. In typical Chamberlain fashion, he responded, "I must either do my utmost or stop altogether and though I know the risks I prefer to take them."[89] His devotion to British politics and an imperial England resulted in a stroke in the summer of 1906, which left him an invalid until his death eight years later.[90] In politically savvy fashion, Mary withheld the news of the stroke from everyone but her immediate English family and canceled all of Chamberlain's commitments by explaining that *she* was ill.[91] Not even her American family knew of Chamberlain's true condition. A later diagnosis of gout was announced, which provided some time for Chamberlain to recover. Writing to Mary, her brother, William, inquired about Chamberlain's well-being and, not knowing the seriousness of his condition, playfully suggested that Chamberlain's son Neville, who was still a bachelor, should visit the United States. "We'll send him home with an American wife that will suit Ma and Pa. He apparently needs a smart American girl who will let him know as only an American girl can . . . that she thinks him wonderful."[92] Wisely, Mary never revealed her husband's declining health to her own family through correspondence, lest such information officially end an impressive governmental career.

Chamberlain's decline was slow and painful. He had resigned his cabinet post shortly before the stroke, and in 1914 he decided not to stand for reelection from Birmingham. Six months later, he suffered a heart attack. Mary rarely left his side, and she read all the political news to him, in the hope that he would recover. When she recounted the assassination of Franz Ferdinand, knowing the end result of such an event, Chamberlain stopped her from finishing the article. Later that day, he suffered a final heart attack. Writing in her diary, Mary simply stated, "At 10.15 my darling died quite peacefully in my arms."[93] Noting the calm and serenity that Mary provided to her husband and his children, Austen reflected, "To have seen her at my father's bedside and since is to have known faith so beautiful and courage so serene, that, once known, they can never be forgotten. I have never imagined any so holy."[94] Similarly to Lady Churchill and Lady Marlborough's experiences, Mary's experience as an Anglo-American envoy reached new heights following the end of her transatlantic marriage. Her position as Chamberlain's wife provided her an opportunity to advance Anglo-American relations through her husband's career, but it was her initiative as a drawing-room diplomat that established her as an informal ambassador.

Life after Chamberlain

Following Chamberlain's memorial service on July 6, 1914, Mary felt more detached from politics, even as war clouds gathered over Europe. A smattering of letters flowed across the Atlantic expressing great sadness at Chamberlain's death. Writing to one of Mary's dear friends in Boston, Austen summarized the close relationships forged by his father's Anglo-American marriage more than twenty years before based on "all we have in common of past memories on both sides of the Atlantic, and of present interests and affections. Nothing that affects Mary can be strange or without interests . . . to us." Thus, what happened to Mary, the American, concerned her entire British family. Thankful for what she meant to the entire Chamberlain family, he continued, "If it were not for Mary and all that she has brought into my life, I do not think I could go on."[95] Just as Lady Churchill had united Anglo-Americans through her *Anglo-Saxon Review,* Mary did the same through her vast communications and connections of her families on both sides of the Atlantic.

Mary's correspondence during this period focused on the rising tensions in Europe. Just months after she became a widow, her uncle feared the "whole future of England hangs in the balance."[96] A friend described all Americans and "this country [living] in suspense."[97] A cousin asserted that "the loyalty of the colonies, shown in the contributions of ships and money and men, is due in large measure to the inspirations of your husband."[98] The press seemed to speak to Mary's American family almost specifically when it declared that the "Allies should be more grateful than ever for the clear-sighted sympathy of the American public."[99]

In the midst of war, Mary found love again, coincidentally with the man who had conducted her husband's memorial service. Reverend William Hartley Carnegie and the former Mrs. Chamberlain married on August 3, 1916. Mary had her English family's blessing and was given away by Austen, who was so pleased with the union that he telegraphed her sister-in law, "Mary married in bright sunshine to light her new happiness."[100] Adding Carnegie's five daughters to Chamberlain's six children, Mary's family expanded once again, thus further extending her Anglo-American influence.

Her new union certainly brought her happiness, and she quickly resumed her informal poli-social activities. She and her second husband were summoned to Windsor to dine with King George and Queen Mary, who were most interested in hearing more about the United States and the perspective of its citizens. As Mary recalled in a letter, they wanted to know about "the Americans now here, and wanted to be told all I could about them and their point of view." The King confided to her that "one of the dreams of his life was accomplished in seeing the [United States and England] side by side, fighting the greatest causes in the name of liberty and justice and humanity."[101] The two nations would indeed fight side by side soon enough. Supporting the King's desire for stronger U.S.-U.K. relations and his wife's position as an intermediary of Anglo-American relations, Reverend Carnegie maintained, "It is a truism to say that the world's progress depends mainly on the extent to which America and the British Empire cooperate with each other on terms of mutual confidence and cordiality," a goal the cohort of informal ambassadors worked toward nearly constantly.[102]

As evidence of their wishes for positive Anglo-American relations, following the United States' entry into the war in 1917, Mary hosted numerous teas and dinners for Red Cross nurses, Allied officers, and American students from overseas. Her husband's church, St. Margaret's, was generally considered the "Abbey for Americans" abroad, as well as many members of Parliament, providing yet another setting in which Americans and Britons could interact.[103] Reflecting on a particular group of American students who attended one of her teas and had enjoyed a personal tour of the Abbey, Mary suspected that it made them conscious of a "common heritage" and hoped "their first experience of the 'allies' will be a happy omen. . . . [B]ehind it is the call of the blood which differentiates them from all the others."[104] Mary's nuptials to Reverend Carnegie reinforced both her ties to the United States and her position as a personal ambassador to Americans and Britons alike.

As the war continued, Mary reflected, "These last weeks have been filled with heartfelt rejoicing that at last the beloved land of my birth is ranged side by side [with Britain]." She expected greatness from this union: "I cannot but feel that to have America & England fighting in a common cause is fraught with great things for the future—better understanding, closer relations must be the outcome—a friendship sealed in blood between blood relations must mean a different attitude each toward the other in the days to come."[105] Even after the war ended, Mary pushed for proof of Anglo-American amity and saw to it that her husband held regular memorial services at St. Margaret's for American officers and soldiers who died and were subsequently buried in the British Isles. As had Lady Churchill before her, Mary continued to work for and identify with both of her countries after her first Anglo-American marriage had ended.

Mary's second marriage did not last as long as the first: Reverend Carnegie died in 1936, the same year as Mary's brother, William, and her beloved Austen died less than six months later. Shaken by the loss of so many in such a short time, Mary turned to her Anglo-American correspondence for comfort. Writing to her sister-in-law in the United States, she confided that she had "been so accustomed all my life to find in men [with] stimulus and purpose . . . [men] who have been so close to me in both countries." In a moment of candor, she lamented the "loss of the three who have shared most closely everything, in the three periods of which my life has been made up, so near together in five short months, [and that] I [feel] like a ship without a rudder."[106]

Even as Mary mourned her losses, she celebrated Neville's becoming prime minister in 1937. Just as Lady Churchill refocused her political efforts onto her son's career after her first husband died, Mary did the same with her stepsons. Like Mary, and partially due to her presence in his life, Neville shared a desire for closer Anglo-American relations, which would prove a critical alliance on the eve of World War II. In private correspondence, he pledged to "promote Anglo-American understanding and cooperation. Not because I want or expect America to pull our chestnuts out of the fire for us; in any cooperation we shall always do our part and perhaps more than our share." Based on a lifetime of interaction with Mary and all of her American family and friends, he believed "that America and Britain want the same fundamental things in the world—peace, liberty, order, respect for international obligations, freedom for every country." Above all, he deemed the "U.S.A. and U.K. in combination represent a force so overwhelming that the mere hint of the possibility of it was so sufficient to make the most powerful of dictators pause." Neville considered "cooperation between our two countries [as] the greatest instrument in the world for the preservation of peace and the attainment of those objects of which I spoke just now."[107] Mary's obvious influence concerning Anglo-American relations extended to all members of her family.

As Neville used his position as prime minister to pursue strong Anglo-American relations, Mary continued to serve as an informal ambassador for the United States. After dining with Ambassador Joseph P. Kennedy and his wife, Rose, in 1938, Mary reflected on meeting with almost every American ambassador to the United Kingdom since her marriage to Chamberlain. Having missed but one ambassador from her home country in fifty years demonstrates Mary's formal and informal Anglo-American connections—political, social, and diplomatic.

When war broke out again in Europe, Mary proudly pronounced, "England will give a good account of herself, with the Empire at her back and the co-operation of America in hastening the much-needed supplies." Specific to the war cause, England was most appreciative of the "ambulances, on their mission of mercy, [which was more] proof of the interest and sympathy which comes to our aide in Old England from New England."[108] She relayed that her fellow Britons were "tremendously touched by the great hospitality . . . offered [by] friends and relations and from strangers in America."[109] Gratefully, she noted the Americans' sympathies for England evident in the daily papers: "Now I think the people of my Native Land are thoroughly roused and realize more and more." Longing for her two countries to again fight side by side, she pressed for the United States to enter the war and reasoned that American involvement "cannot afford to be postponed."[110]

Following the attack on Pearl Harbor and America's entry into the war, Mary seemed almost giddy with excitement. "In one sense the Japanese could not have rendered a greater service had they tried to than their treacherous attack, for it is wonderful how absolutely it consolidated everybody to rally to the defence of the country."[111] As the war progressed, she was "more proud than words can say of the part my two countries have been playing."[112] Moved by Anglo-American military cooperation, she hosted a Christmas party for American officers and guests in 1942, which was "but one of thousands and thousands . . . given throughout England, and I hear the Americans are very much touched by the hospitality which they have received." She noted their generous gift of "money and goods and sweets and entertainments for British children . . . Christmas trees, and the warmth of their kindly feeling has been greatly appreciated."[113]

As the war continued, Mary enjoyed observing the "American soldiers, [the] R.A.F. in their grey-blue uniforms, sailors of all nationalities of the Allies, overseas troops, and of course a good sprinkling of British troops" at St. Margaret's on Sundays. Most pleased to hear of British and American "successes in Normandy of the combined forces and the commendation of the fighting qualities which have been so well displayed by the U.S. Army," Mary was "very proud of my countrymen." As a friend's son reported from the front lines at D-Day, "he could not say enough of the co-operation and untiring energy of the American troops on his flank . . . [and] spoke of their readiness to help." According to this unnamed British soldier, "when one asked [the Americans] to do something, they *did* it, and without delay."[114] Once the war ended, Mary was determined to mark the occasion. Despite continued rationing, food from the United States enabled Mary to host a truly Anglo-American dinner: turkey, cranberry sauce, plum pudding, and mince pies.[115]

In 1954, years after the war's end, Mary celebrated her ninetieth birthday in London with her families from both sides of the Atlantic. Encapsulating her life, an American cousin posed a somewhat rhetorical question: "How is it that she is able to bind to her with ever strengthening bonds the ever increasing members of her various families?" Considering her Endicott, Chamberlain, and Carnegie kin, maintaining timely correspondence proved a demanding task! He also noted not only her devotion to her three families but their reciprocal devotion to one another despite the ocean between them. "Not only that but by what ledger does she make these families feel such a strong bond with each other?" He postulated that Mary "may have some secret process or weapon but I think it is accomplished by the bounteous love she bestows on all of us and the great love we all feel for her."[116] Such love was a reflection of Mary's dedication to her Anglo-American identity and life, spanning some seven decades.

Mary Endicott Chamberlain Carnegie died in her sleep on May 17, 1957, at the age of ninety-three. Like those of her husbands before her, her memorial service was held at St. Margaret's. She was buried next to Reverend Carnegie, just feet from a bust of her first husband.[117] Newspapers on both sides of the Atlantic discussed the passing of Mary Endicott, the widow of Joseph Chamberlain, and the great hostess, Mrs. Carnegie.[118] According to the *New York Times*, "no American woman married to an Englishman [had] succeeded in winning the good-will of Great Britain as Mrs. Chamberlain."[119] As a testament to her life, her portrait was hung in the National Gallery in Washington, D.C., after her death.[120]

As the *London Times* noted, Mary "represented a link, spanning five generations, between London and American circles." Obituaries repeatedly described her as a "remarkable person" who would be "remembered in particular as being one of the great hostesses of her day." But Mary was much more than simply an American who married well and spent her life giving parties and attending dinners in London. Her dual identity as an Anglo-American and her commitment to both of her countries made Mary more than a successful drawing-room diplomat. As an informal ambassador, she was "able to play a special, though she preferred it to be a modest, role in British-American affairs."[121]

Given her elite families, affluent friends, and uniquely Anglo-American life, Mary was asked on more than one occasion when she planned to write her memoirs. Scoffing, she replied, "If I spent all my time looking backwards at the past, I'd have no time for living in the present and future."[122] Though she had no interest in reflecting on her life and the role she had created for herself as a true Anglo-American, historians must reconsider her relationships and activities throughout her decades abroad. Rather than living a life between the United States and Great Britain, Mary created a new dual identity as Anglo-American, just as hundreds of other American-born, British-wed women did at the turn of the twentieth century. In her countless conversations, dinners, teas, and daily interactions with Britons and her contributions to Anglo-American networks connected by personal contacts and overseas correspondence for decades, she indeed acted and engaged in traditional consular behaviors. By doing so, she played a role—official and unofficial, conscious and unconscious—as an informal ambassador and moved the United States and Great Britain toward their special relationship.

CHAPTER FOUR

Devoted Mediator

Mary Leiter Curzon

One's country is always one's country. Laws may change one's nationality, but they cannot change the heart, and mine is *and ever will be* American.

—VICEREINE MARY CURZON

Shortly before the marriage of Mary Leiter and George Curzon in 1895, the *St. James's Gazette* published "some notes on the bride and bridegroom." The brief article predicted that Mary would be "a beautiful and charming wife" and that "London society [would] be reinforced by [such] a clever and attractive woman." The piece relayed the assessment of another periodical and "critical authority," *Woman,* which described Mary as "almost, if not quite, a beauty" but quickly went on to determine her as "very intellectual" and "superbly educated." The critique concluded, "It may be said that she is one of the few American women who have triumphantly solved the difficult problem, 'How to be admired on one's own account, though an heiress.'"[1] Thus, the editorial gave her the ultimate compliment an American woman could have received in this period of increasing numbers of Anglo-American marriages, even as the trend experienced a corresponding decrease in popularity. If ever there was a diligent diplomat flying under the radar of traditional international politics, a dutiful wife and mother who used her dual identities as spouse and parent, American and Briton, to conduct masterfully soft power abroad, it was Mary Leiter Curzon.

Mary's unique ability to please the unappeasable and pacify the most irascible, an envoy's chief skill in any mediation, was undoubtedly impressed upon her from a very early age. Born on May 27, 1870, in Chicago, Illinois, she was the second child and first daughter of Levi Zeigler Leiter and Mary Theresa Carver. At the age of twenty, Mr. Leiter moved from his home in Maryland and began working

Mary Victoria Leiter, Marchioness Curzon in Her Peacock Gown, 1909 (oil on canvas). William Logsdail, (1859–1944). Kedleston Hall, Derbyshire, UK. National Trust Photographic Library/John Hammond. The Bridgeman Art Library.

for merchants in Chicago. Despite his lack of formal education, he was incredibly ambitious and opportunistic.[2] Over the next decade, he befriended a like-minded young man, Marshall Field, and the two opened a store bearing the second partner's name.[3] As the Leiter fortune grew, so did the family. Brother Joseph was followed two years later by Mary, and they were joined by two more girls, Nancy and Marguerite, better known as Nannie and Daisy.[4]

While Mr. Leiter concentrated on protecting their newly acquired prosperity, his wife, the granddaughter of a Connecticut judge and a former schoolteacher, focused on transforming the new family wealth into social gain. Though Mrs. Leiter had enjoyed a solidly middle-class upbringing, she wanted more for her children—specifically, greater social success.[5] She saw to it her daughters were taught art, dancing, music, and singing. They learned French from a French governess. She employed a tutor from Columbia University to teach them chemistry, history, and mathematics.[6] But Chicago provided limited social opportunities. Thus, when Mr. Leiter split with his business partners in 1881, the Leiters' affluence made it possible for him to retire at the age of forty-six and move the family, at his wife's urging, to Washington, D.C. Their relocation enabled Mrs. Leiter to "create for herself and her family a brilliant social position in a more cosmopolitan scene."[7]

Life in the nation's capital provided near limitless opportunities to advance socially based on the family financial successes, from which Mary benefited immensely. As her father's favorite child and the eldest daughter, Mary enjoyed the unconditional love of both her parents and, for better or for worse, her mother's vicarious need to succeed. Consequently, it came as no surprise that Mary eventually befriended Mrs. Frances Folsom Cleveland, who at the age of twenty-two became the youngest First Lady in American history.[8] Also, in addition to enjoying the busy social season in Washington, Mrs. Leiter traveled annually with her children to Europe for the social seasons there, in an effort to succeed on both sides of the Atlantic.[9] The Leiter family routine was set for the next decade.

But social acceptance was slow to come. Mrs. Leiter came across as "bold, proud, ignorant and selfish, [and clearly] ambitious to make herself a great social position."[10] Her determination to climb the social ladder appeared her greatest detriment; Mary's friendship with the First Lady, rather, eventually opened the door to social acceptance. In 1888, when the Leiters traveled to New York at the end of the Washington season, Mary was added to the Social Register, which provided for significant letters of introduction to overseas balls and dinners in London.[11] As doors suddenly opened on both sides of the Atlantic, the social powers that be agreed Mary was destined for a brilliant career.[12] Over the next two years, her beauty and kindness earned her many influential friendships, specifically that of Vita Sackville-West, the writer, and Margot Asquith, the wife of future prime minister Herbert Henry Asquith. But it was the Duchess of Westminster's ball in the summer of 1890 that changed Mary's future. She enjoyed the incredible honor of opening the ball by dancing a quadrille with the Prince of Wales, noted for his fondness of American girls. One of the men watching was George Curzon, who later recalled that he never loved Mary more than at that very moment.[13]

George Nathaniel Curzon was born on January 11, 1859, in Derbyshire at Kedleston, which had served as the family estate for over seven centuries. His father, Lord Scarsdale, was particularly passionate about the manor and passed his love for it onto George, the eldest brother among five boys and six girls. George suffered a devastating emotional blow when his mother died when he was only sixteen, after which he was raised by a distant father and a cruel governess.[14] This difficult upbringing may explain his apparent lack of emotion toward others and his overwhelming desire to protect Kedleston at all costs. From the very beginning of their unusual relationship, George expressed to Mary both in person and in letters his undying devotion to and desire to improve the estate. And he made it no secret that his family, despite its rank in English society, did not have the money for upgrades. Typical of Mary's devotion to George and any of his desires, Mary promised to do everything she could to have her inheritance go to the improvement of Kedleston, should he die before they could marry.[15]

Well before he married or even met Mary, George pursued his formal education at Eton College and Oxford University, where his professors and classmates either revered or despised him, reactions that would enable and plague his eventual political career. Proving himself obsessively competitive and a driven intellectual, he won many scholarly prizes and honors and was elected to the prestigious All Souls College. But his ability to charm or repulse others resulted in a notorious poem that followed him the rest of his life.

My name is George Nathaniel Curzon,
I am a most superior person.
My cheeks are pink, my hair is sleek,
I dine at Blenheim twice a week.

In 1885, despite his reputation as a pompous elitist, or perhaps because of it, George's political career began when Lord Salisbury selected him to serve as his assistant private secretary. The next year, Curzon became a Member of Parliament representing Southport. But from an early period, he invested his time in the House of Commons in an effort to become not a politician but rather a great administrator. Shortly after meeting Mary in 1890, Curzon was promoted to undersecretary of state for India. His intense desire to achieve more in less time than any other man in British political history led to his vast travels around the world—Europe, Asia, India, the Middle East—which preceded his vow that the next time he returned to India, it would be as Viceroy.[16]

Catch Me If You Can

George Curzon's first contact with Mary shaped his perception of her. She was beautiful, charming, and ebullient. While her status as an American was not particularly appealing, her family's money more than made up for it. But at thirty-one years old, George was actively carving out a political career for himself, and he refused to marry until his place in British politics was assured. Still, he realized the significance of choosing the right woman to be his wife. He was determined to marry someone who not only understood her supportive role as his wife but could also support his political and financial quests without hesitation. He seems to have considered a potential wife from this early period, as he described her as "the dearest girl I have met for long."[17]

A quick engagement and wedding did not follow, however. Instead, the two played a game of "catch me if you can" for the next three years. In the few days after their initial meeting at the Duchess of Westminster's Ball, they saw each other frequently, but she enjoyed countless invitations to country houses. She even assisted a fellow American, Lady Jennie Churchill, with a tableau for the Londonderry ball. Soon, she returned to the United States and he to his worldly travels and political aspirations. On more than one occasion, the two were within a day's journey in Europe or the United States but made no attempt to see each other. While they exchanged letters, George sometimes failed to respond to Mary's correspondence for months at a time.[18] When Mary received word that George was pursuing other women, she often found subtle ways to remind him that she, too, was the interest of many desirable suitors. In an 1892 letter, she relayed the interest of a "princeling who came with equerries and a suite to study American institutions, and I had the misfortune to be the only institution he wished to adopt." Following a trip to Italy in early 1893, she wrote to him that there "is an absolute assurance about an Italian that one rarely finds elsewhere."[19] But this may have been more of a front to lure George to her or force him to consider what feelings, if any, he had for her. She candidly wrote to a friend, however: "I will have him because I believe he needs me."[20] In any case, for two people who reportedly enjoyed a devoted marriage, their protracted courtship closely followed a pattern of catch and release.

Finally, after three years of intermittent correspondence, the two found themselves in Paris at the same time. When Mary initiated a meeting at the Hotel Vendôme in March 1893, eighteen months had passed since their last encounter. Following dinner with the pair, Mary's mother politely excused herself, leaving her daughter to make her pitch. She candidly expressed her feelings and told George how she had rejected countless suitors because she longed for him to return her affections. Perhaps her borderline begging inflated his ego all the more. Conceivably, George's early emotional devastations demanded confirmation of Mary's devotion before risking the possibility of a rejected marriage proposal. In any case, he received Mary's plea and asked her to be his wife but with a caveat—the engagement remain a secret for the next two years as he completed his "Asiatic travel, which [he] resolved to do, and which [he] could not ask any married woman to allow her husband to carry out."[21] Ever devoted, Mary complied.

The morning after the two became engaged, George wrote to Mary.

> You were very sweet last night, Mary, and I do not think I deserved such consideration. While I ask you, and while you consent, to wait, you must trust me, Mary wholly, even as I would trust you, and all will be right in the end. I will not breathe a word to a human soul, and since that is the line we take, it will be well that I should not write too frequently for fear of exciting suspicions. You need not fear that I shall not think of you, and relay upon your fidelity as upon a rock. You will let me hear how you are going on, Mary won't you, and sometimes if you are down in your luck, you will remember that my kiss of love has rested upon your lips. God bless you, my darling child.[22]

In one concise letter, George managed to validate his engagement to Mary, secure her silence, justify his lack of writing, and condescendingly address her as a child. And, as if to solidify his superior and her subordinate roles in their future marriage, he disgustedly wrote to her three months later of the House of Commons being "crowded with women" and complained of how the "encroachment of the sex fills me with an indignation which no blandishments call ally." Praising and enforcing Mary's submissive responsibility to him as his wife, he went on, "Give me a girl that knows a woman's place and does not yearn for trousers. Give me, in fact, Mary."[23] If earlier Anglo-American marriages welcomed the involvement of and influence by the American-born, British-wed woman, George fanatically rejected such meddling. If Mary had somehow missed the template of her future marriage, these letters all but presented a blueprint of her life as Mrs. Curzon. And, as always, she agreed.

The next two years followed the preceding three—intermittent letters coupled with confusing behaviors and coy comments dropped casually in the midst of letters. George apparently continued to move through London circles as a bachelor but prided himself on knowing that Mary would wait—forever, if necessary. Six months after their engagement, he wrote to her that he was "spared all the anxiety of courtship, and I have merely, when the hour strikes, to enter into possession of my own."[24] But the two appear to have thrived upon such games and keeping their little secret even as their closest friends and family members pressed them to leave singledom behind. Mary responded to her fiancé with constant dedication, though she admitted to never speaking his name: "You are so much in my thoughts that I fear my voice will give away too much tenderness." Rationalizing their extended engagement to him and likely herself, she concluded, "It is not a question of whom you could live with, but of whom you could not live without; and who in every condition of life, great or small, is the one to whom every fibre of your body and mind responds with devotion and love." Largely based on Mary's saintlike devotion, the two kept up their ruse until six weeks before they finally wed in 1895, having seen one another only for two days and some hours between their engagement and wedding.[25]

Shortly before the simultaneous wedding announcements in Washington and London on March 4, 1895, George made a special trip to Kedleston to tell his father of the engagement. More than anyone else's approval, George wanted and needed his father's, which he received largely based on a picture of Mary. Accordingly, the nuptial mediations began in earnest. The nuptial "treaty," as it was discussed, required two days of legal negotiations by trustees for both parties. The mere use of the word "treaty"—which conjures notions of international negotiations—proves interesting, as the same was used in reference to Joseph Chamberlain's "treaty" with Mary Endicott. In any case, the Leiters agreed to provide a marital "trust fund" of $700,000, wisely invested in railway stock, which generated an annual income of $33,000 for their daughter, like the "pin money" Lady Churchill's father designated for her. If Mary died before George, he would receive one-third of the income with another third going to any of the couple's future children. The recipient(s) of the remaining third was (were) left up to Mary and George. Finally, her father agreed to an additional $1 million upon his death. Lord Scarsdale agreed to provide his son two payments per year of £500 and landed wealth worth £7,000 annually.[26] The sum total of the Curzon and Leiter families' contributions allowed George and Mary to socialize comfortably as his political career demanded. Curzon's "paltry sum" amounted to a mere fraction of their joint income, but, George explained, "my family is poor."[27]

Following the wedding announcement, reactions from both sides of the Atlantic poured in. George cabled Mary that London had responded with "universal delight," based on Margot Asquith having described Mary as "a lovely sunny companion" and Mr. Gladstone's "blessing upon the coming union." The journalist G. W. Smalley, who had known both Mary and George for some years, described his recollections of the two over the years as seeming "to fall naturally into place together, as if the two lives were made to be lived together, and as if each had found the twin soul which halves their own."[28] The American press, however, expressed mixed emotions. As "elaborate preparations" were made, the New York Times predicted the wedding would be "a brilliant social affair."[29] Most editorials rejoiced, "The lady whom the country is proud to call her fairest daughter is marrying a man of splendid ability." Other newspapers disgustedly scoffed at yet another American girl marrying outside the country. Upon hearing the news of Mary's upcoming nuptials to a Briton, President Cleveland, having witnessed many of these marriages firsthand, simply grunted.[30]

Mary bitterly resented the transatlantic speculation and discussion of her relationship with George. She resisted being lumped in with the plethora of American girls who refused to marry American boys and "devote their talents and money to their own country."[31] Since many American girls had done just that, the general impression that Mary simply followed in the same path was somewhat justified. Like Mary Chamberlain before her, Mary Leiter did not receive a title upon her marriage, as her husband did not yet enjoy one. And despite his "poor" family, George was hardly impoverished. As with so many of these Anglo-American marriages, upon examination, this specific union and the individuals within it defy the conventional wisdom of transatlantic marriages.

Most Anglo-American marriages can be filed in one of two categories: love match or strategic alliance. While George and Mary's biographers would place their union in the former category, often describing them as a "devoted couple," a comment from George about marriage may complicate this classification.[32] He once surmised that the day a man married was "the commencement of extreme happiness, discreditable indifference or superlative misery."[33] Was George speaking of his own happiness or misery when he uttered these words? In which category George would have placed his own marriage? While most historians would consider it a love match, Mary's wealth and willingness to give herself to him and his ambitions without reservation certainly benefited George immensely.

Chosen Object of Affection

The wedding took place on April 22, 1895, at St. John's Church in Washington, D.C., a notable location just opposite the White House and the very church where Joseph Chamberlain and Mary Endicott had wed some years earlier.[34] As the two exchanged true transatlantic nuptials, the guests included the British ambassador, the First Lady of the United States, justices of the Supreme Court, and Cecil Spring Rice of the British embassy.[35] Following a short honeymoon in Virginia, George and Mary boarded a ship for England. Though Mary was more than ready to become George's wife, she was surprised at how much she already missed the United States. As Miss Leiter became Mrs. Curzon, she surrendered her American citizenship, as dictated by law. According to her biographer Nigel Nicolson, "never again would [Mary] quite belong." Instead, "for the rest of her life she would be acting a role, the role of pseudo-Englishwoman." And despite her devoted American sentiments, this pseudo-Englishwoman now known as Mrs. Curzon never saw her homeland again.[36]

When George and Mary disembarked in England, Lord Scarsdale gave them an extravagant reception. Meeting his son and new daughter-in-law at the station, he arranged for horse-drawn carriages to take them to the family estate as church bells announced their arrival and people lined the streets to welcome them. A feast and band awaited the new Mr. and Mrs. Curzon, and more than five hundred of Lord Scarsdale's tenants were invited to enjoy the festivities. The tenants presented the newlyweds with a silver tray and greeted the newlyweds warmly, as evidenced by a letter written to George and Mary. The also praised their current landlord, of thirty-nine years, George for his "conspicuous success" and "arduous public works," which had made his "name a household word throughout the British Empire." They went on to express their great concern for his "domestic happiness which we pray may be blessed to the fullest extent." Likewise, they extended Mary a "hearty greeting and cordial welcome." They promised her that as the "chosen object" of George's affection, "no efforts shall be wanting on our part, and in our humble way to add to your happiness and felicity." Apparently, word of Mary's analogous successes had reached the tenants of Kedleston from her "early and distant home," thus assuring them that their "future landlord has chosen as his life companion one whom we shall all regard and honour with the affection which has ever existed between the owner and tenantry of the Kedleston estates."[37] Apparently, most Americans and Britons found Anglo-Americans increasingly distasteful, but they somehow distinguished their personal interactions with these informal ambassadors and very much liked the individual women who lived their lives abroad by virtue of their marriages.

Shortly after the newlyweds settled into their own home in London, Lord Salisbury promoted George to undersecretary of state at the Foreign Office. Despite this advance in his career, George expressed great disappointment that he was not given a cabinet post. In an effort to pacify the obsessive overachiever, Salisbury appeased George's ever-needy ego by naming him a privy councilor. At thirty-six years old, George became the youngest man in living memory to hold the honor.[38] The next month brought more political activity, as George ran in the general election from Southport. He was reelected with an increased majority and owed "much more to the bright smiles and graces of his American wife than he did to his own speeches."[39] Almost immediately, Mary began exercising her soft power style as the wife of an influential political representative, whereby she influenced political decision-making as well.

In writing to her father, who was paying for the campaign, George assured him that Mary "has never been so happy in her life." But in true diplomat style, Mary kept her most intimate thoughts on life abroad to herself so not to damage the carefully crafted impression she wanted to impart to her husband and his country. Dependent on her transatlantic correspondence for comfort, as had been Mary Endicott before her, in her letters to her family Mary presented a very different perspective of life in England. That same summer, she wrote, "I think I must pour out my heart to you, and tell you how I *loathe* this place. The people are an ungrateful lot of vulgar cockneys, provincial to a degree and very stupid, and they do not half appreciate George." She described Southport as a "miserable 3rd-class seaside resort, a 4th-rate Brighton, . . . full of idle loafers. My only regret if he is elected here is that we shall have to spend part of every year among these people, frowsy women and horrid men."[40] Another letter followed a few days later in which Mary confessed that she "loathe[d] this place more than any other I have *ever* been to, but this I can only say to you. The people are an idle ignorant impossible lot of ruffians. I smile at them and look sweet because it would be the end of us if they knew all that I thought."[41] Undoubtedly, Mary understood the need to present a positive impression at all times and to all people, including her husband.

Although the election ended successfully, George felt no need to celebrate the moment. Regardless of his continued successes and promotions, he never socialized outside of work to further boost his political career or simply for the sake of enjoying himself. He repeatedly turned down invitations to various events such as dinners, balls, or races at Ascot because he had to work. As Mary could not attend an event without her husband, she remained at home; consequently, she went from being one of the most celebrated and admired debutantes in transatlantic history to living as a recluse, and not by her own choice. As she sadly wrote to her family, "G's work defeats all form of amusement." In the year after her marriage and move to London, she and George dined once with Lord and Lady Churchill and once with Sibell Grosvenor and hosted one party. That was Mary's whole 1896 London Season. Having agreed years before to George's superior role in their marriage, she was in no position to challenge her husband now. The die had been cast, and London society seemed to forget quickly about the Curzons. As was her custom, Mary used her letters to her family as therapy. Rationalizing her defenseless position and her husband's domination of their marriage, she explained to her mother, "George will do . . . what he chooses and nothing on earth can alter his iron will. I have long since realized George's iron will and never crossed it."[42]

A Difficult Transition

In addition to feeling unhappy in her marriage, Mary found it difficult to adjust to life in England in general. Despite all the money her father provided her and a fashionable home in London, she found *living* in London very different from *socializing* in London. She reflected, "London life is a continuous, striving, striving, striving to keep going, the little people praying to be noticed by the great, and the

great seldom lowering their eyelids to look at the small." Although by English standards Mary had married well, she apparently had to prove herself again following
her introduction to British society as a wife. One of her duties included running
a household, which, because of the staff, she found much more demanding than
she originally imagined. She wrote, "English servants are fiends. They seem to plot
among themselves. They are malignant and stupid and make life barely worth living." Although the women in George's circle seemed to welcome Mary initially,
such warmth did not last. As Mary saw it, she was "so much more sensitive and reserved than English women, and I never feel any sympathy with them, and I don't
feel that they do with me, so that my life centres on my own house."[43] Whether
they found fault with her lack of socializing or her total submission to George, she
could not count on such "unforgiving women" as friends.[44]

Mary's homesickness intensified as she began her second year of marriage.
Although she praised her husband, describing him as "devotion itself to me," she
conveyed her longing for the familiar when she confessed, "England can *never,
never* take the place of home to me. . . . There is nothing in the world I care for
but my own family and George." And while Lord Scarsdale invited Mary to look
to him and call him Papa, she rejected the mere notion: "For anyone less like my
own beloved Papa I cannot imagine."[45]

The transition to marriage, eventless days and nights, George's unceasing dedication to his work, and relocation to England began to take its toll. After a series
of insulting questions from her husband regarding the presence of sea fish in the
United States and whether or not she knew how to make a mince pie or serve
a good cup of tea, Mary reached her limit. In a rare outburst of frustration, she
retorted, "Why don't you ask me if there are any civilized or white people in America?"[46] George and Mary were no longer newlyweds, and the transition to married
life was more demanding than either had anticipated.

A great deal of the difficulty was due to Mary's American heritage. Now married,
George felt the need to tease or ridicule his wife for being an American. And while
she always identified as an American, she no longer enjoyed that right as a citizen.
She was truly a woman between two countries—not accepted in one and no longer
welcome in the other. According to Mary's biographer, "People were annoyed with
George for marrying an American, and with her for being one." Despite that Mary
was no longer an American citizen, she did not feel as though she was, or ever
would be, English. In a dramatic understatement, she confessed to her mother, "As
yet I am not attached to my new country." Her longtime friend, American journalist G. W. Smalley, summarized the situation with the greatest clarity; "You are an
American *au bout des ongles,* and you can never be anything else, with your American brilliancy, your American beauty and American intelligence. . . . You have had
perhaps too much homage; it might do you good to be neglected a little."[47]

Her life in England was about to take a turn. As Mary began a new year, her first daughter, Mary Irene, was born on January 20, 1896. To have someone in her life to tend to on a daily basis brought Mary a sense of duty she desperately needed. Shortly after Irene's birth, Mary wrote to her mother, "You are the only person in the wide world who knows how I have suffered this year. . . . George and [the] baby are the only people who exist for me in England."[48] Although problems remained with life in England, Irene, and a sense of family on her side of the Atlantic, brought Mary a renewed sense of identity and happiness.

Just as her personal life seemed to take a turn for the better, there came an international event that threatened to turn her precious families against one another. In the fall of 1895, the United States threatened war with Great Britain over a boundary dispute in Venezuela. War between the two countries would have sent shockwaves throughout the international community. but the reality of war meant something else entirely for hundreds of American-born, British-wed wives in England. Like Lady Churchill and Mary Chamberlain, Mary Curzon feared the possibility of war. But unlike her contemporaries, she did not take a visible position against war, nor did she not adopt a pro-British stand on it. Rather, she remained steadfastly American, albeit silently as far as her British family and friends knew. Writing to her mother that autumn, she pondered her difficult situation. "I am wondering what I should do if England and America followed [Republican senator Henry] Cabot Lodge's advice, and went to war about Venezuela. I should wear the American flag under my jacket if I could not wear it on the outside as the wife of an English cabinet official." One can only assume what George's response would have been to such behavior. But, in a bold move, Mary explained, "One's country is always one's country. Laws may change one's nationality, but they cannot change the heart, and mine is *and ever will be* American."[49]

Mary's situation held many more complications than that of her loyalty in the event of war. While Irene had given her great happiness on many levels, the creation of a family on the other side of the Atlantic changed her identity from American bride to British mother. As she reflected in a letter to her family, she was forever torn between the ties that bind. "Nothing could have kept me from bundling home, baby and all. Nothing but dear George could anchor me here."[50] Torn between her family by birth and her family by marriage, Mary forever found herself a woman between two countries.

And yet, given the emotional ties pulling on Mary and all Anglo-American wives in England, the case against war arguably came down to the single most straightforward explanation—money. In October 1895, the *New York Journal* asked whether the "American wives" in influential positions in Britain might not settle the matter. As previously noted, there were at least ten of them, including Jennie Churchill, Mary Chamberlain, and, of course, Mary Curzon, who was in a prime position to make her case known as the wife of the undersecretary of state for foreign affairs. But even the briefest examination reveals that Mary did not lean on her husband, or utilize his position, for her own interests or desires. Chief among George's interests and desires, however, was financial stability, with the long-term goal of updating Kedleston. A war with the United States would threaten, if not ruin, such intentions. As the *Journal* determined, "If war were thrown upon England, Mr. Curzon would lose immediately, through his wife's $15,000,000 in American securities alone. This was Miss Leiter's private fortune when she married Curzon last spring, and at the first nod of trouble her stock would drop to $2,000,000, and, at more trouble, to probably nothing at all." Clearly, Mary never had control over any sizable fortune of her own; thus, these numbers appear seriously inflated based on the original treaty negotiated shortly before her wedding. The *Journal* boldly concluded, "This is a solid and substantial reason why Mr. Curzon would not favour war, and why Lady Scarsdale, as Mrs. Curzon's title will be some day, would work against such a calamity."[51] The newspaper's statement would certainly be considered libel today, but in an age of increasing yellow journalism, such tales certainly made for a compelling story. Just as diplomatic history has shown repeatedly, though, economic ties and tenuous financial interests are often as influential as official diplomats in determining the course of foreign relations—if not more so. The hundreds of American-born, British-wed women torn between their two countries at this critical juncture, given their money and position as informal ambassadors, strongly influenced Anglo-American relations.

Nevertheless, the newspaper raises an excellent point as to the potential fortunes that would have been lost in England due to an Anglo-American war. In the event of such a dispute, how many fathers of former American heiresses would continue to send their hard-earned millions across the Atlantic? In 1893, five years before the Venezuelan boundary dispute, the *New York Times* estimated, "English noblemen alone have captured by marriage with American women, in round numbers, $50,000,000 of enviable American cash."[52] Granted, the original agreement for many of these marriages was a trade of fortunes for titles. But even the most socially ambitious mothers and fathers would not have continued along such lines in the event of a war with Great Britain. Would a rash of international divorce have followed? While such a scenario is difficult to imagine, it is safe to say that American patriotism would have trumped even the most title-driven nuptials.

Much to Mary's relief, in late 1895, the Venezuelan dispute ended peacefully, just as another heiress joined the ranks of American-born, British-wed wives. According to Mary, "Everybody raves about Consuelo [Vanderbilt], and she is very sweet in her great position, and shyly takes her rank directly after royalty." Consuelo's marriage to the 9th Duke of Marlborough on November 6, 1895, exemplified the epitome of American dollars for English rank. But few realized the depth of her misery at this point and merely focused on her appearance. Mary remarked, "She looks very stately in her marvelous jewels, and she looks pretty and had old lace which makes my mouth water. I never saw pearls the size of nuts." Without a doubt, the Vanderbilt-Marlborough fortune far exceeded the annual Leiter contribution. But, as far as Mary was concerned, "In a grand party like this, George and I have rather to tag along with the rank and file, but we are very happy and don't mind being small fry."

In the wake of Consuelo's arrival in England, Mary was no longer the newest or shiniest American bride in England. While she relished her role as mother, she needed something more in her life. But, as usual, George was either unaware of or unconcerned with Mary's discontent. Her health began to decline, and she candidly shared her unhappiness with her family.

> I hope to get fat some day, though I don't know quite how I am going to do it, for I get thinner and thinner. I do very little. There are things I cannot help doing, married as I am, but I do nothing that is not absolutely necessary. I never rush about London seeing people and exhibitions and concerts and theatres and charities and the hundred things the world expects you to do. I wish I had the strength, for no one would enjoy more than I the vast amount of interest and amusement that London affords. I do nothing outside my own house, and only see people on a visit like this or if they come to the house. I quite realise that I shall never be able to take my place and be a help to George unless I get strong, for an ailing wife is no help to a politician. She must always be ready to be a kind of smiling hand-shaking machine.[53]

Mary's traditional, unpaid work—as wife, mother, and unofficial diplomat—was critically necessary to her husband's career, a fact of which both parties were acutely aware.

The American Vicereine of British India

Just weeks after Mary wrote these lines to her family, George became viceroy of India.[54] As a result of his appointment, Mary became vicereine, a rank superior to that of any other American woman in history. As her husband now ruled some 300 million people, his wife now bowed "to but one other woman in the world—Queen Victoria." India, as the jewel in the imperial crown, operated via a rigid hierarchal system. While some might mock Mary's post as superficial, the British raj regarded it with great veneration and held high expectations for the recipient. As one former Indian servant described, "the princes and peoples of India" held "sacred reverence" for the Viceroy's consort. "This divine womanhood can only be fitly represented by a woman. . . . [We] desire to see the new Viceroy accompanied by a consort beautiful, gracious and accomplished, who will place all her fits, all her talents, unreservedly at the service of India." Suddenly, this American interloper into British society found herself at the pinnacle of a numerically inferior elite ruling one of the empire's most complex geopolitical regions. The same Indian servant surmised, "We should accord the very warmest welcome to the fair American." Consequently, the appointments of both George and Mary were met with great hope and the highest expectations. As one journalist described, their joint selection testified "in the highest possible way to England's regard for an Anglo-Saxon alliance, and will be the finest compliment the British nation could pay an American."[55]

And yet the appointment could not have occurred at a more inopportune time. In a failed quest to corner the wheat market, Mary's brother Joseph, formerly the "King of the Wheat Pit," lost more than $1.5 million of the Leiter family fortune practically overnight.[56] George and Mary could no longer count on family connections to underwrite their cost of living, a sum that could well prove financially debilitating, if not devastating. A successful reign on the subcontinent necessarily involved considerable expense on the part of the Curzons, who would be expected to entertain expatriates and the upper echelons of Indian society in a traditionally lavish manner, lest their financial situation compromise George's career and reflect poorly not only on Britain but also on the United States, as Mary now represented both countries to India. Much like Lady Churchill's position in Ireland as a representative of England and the United States, Mary's ambassadorial role embodied a triangular manifestation of the British Empire—from the old colonial holdings in the United States to the current powerhouse empire in India.

The Curzons' ascent to their exalted position in India was not without skeptics. At thirty-eight and twenty-eight years old, George and Mary became the youngest viceroy and vicereine in British history. Newspapers on both sides of the Atlantic stressed his educational achievements, vast experience, and ability as a diplomatist, a specific point that proved ironic in the end, as Mary demonstrated vastly superior mediation skills. Her "character . . . personal charm . . . [and] rare intelligence provided Mary with the label 'always a diplomat.'"[57] Clearly, George's aristocratic and politically successful background, in addition to his extensive travels to and knowledge of the area, identified him as an excellent choice.[58] Mary, however, was neither British nor an aristocrat. Many Englishmen and women wondered aloud how an American could possibly represent Britain at the zenith of the imperial raj. Queen Victoria herself asked her prime minister, Lord Salisbury, if "Mrs Curzon, who is an American, [will] do to represent a Vice-Queen?"[59] Much like how the U.S. president approves an ambassador, the queen questioned Mary's worthiness as an unofficial diplomat. The prime minister assured her that Mary's beauty and

charm would serve her well in India; thus, the Queen consented to the appointment. In fact, Mary's status as an American-born, British-wed woman proved a
mark in her favor. One British representative in India concluded, "An English Viceroy and an American consort occupying the throne of the great moguls would be a
living, splendid testimony that an Anglo-Saxon alliance is no mere passing phrase.
India would be glad thereof."[60] The *New York Times* focused on the strength of
an Anglo-American couple in India and stressed the timing of the appointment,
"for there can be no doubt that the pendulum of British-American friendship has
swung far over to the warm side. There is no denying the quickened pulse of Briton
and American when they meet."[61] Given this perspective, Mary's American heritage and Anglo-American marriage created a diplomatic opportunity unparalleled
in British-American history.

Excited at the selection of her husband as viceroy, Mary wrote to her family his
new post "takes my breath away, for it is the greatest position in the English world
next to the Queen and the Prime Minister, and it will be a satisfaction, I know to
you and Mamma that your daughter . . . will fill the greatest place ever held by an
America abroad." Even Mary wondered if she would be able to rise to the occasion: "Heaven only knows how I shall do it, but I shall do my best to be a help to
George and an honour to you and Mamma, and I shall put my trust in Providence
and hope to learn how to be a ready-made Queen." In short order, Mary received
a letter from John Hay, the American ambassador to London from 1897 to 1898
and future secretary of state. Buoying up her confidences as an informal attaché
abroad, he concluded, "No Vicereine has ever gone to India with so full an equipment of knowledge and capacity. No Vicereine with such recourses of radiance
and charm."[62] Solidifying Mary's position, one British newspaper pronounced
her "the most important woman socially, in a country of two hundred and ninety
millions of people. . . . She gives fresh point to the Anglo-American Alliance."[63]

Amid the talk of India, Mary bore a second child, Cynthia Blanche, on August
28, 1898, just two weeks after George was named viceroy. In addition to caring for
a newborn, she read about the geography and history of India even as she made
plans to move her family there. While George's position provided for a sizeable
staff and hundreds of servants, Mary's position required that she be dressed in the
style of a queen, complete with extravagant clothing and opulent jewelry. The viceregal's annual salary totaled a pitiful £25,000, ensuring that anyone who accepted
the position possessed additional wealth, which had long been the unwritten rule
for all diplomats. As always, Mary's father provided for his daughter and son-in-
law's necessities—diamonds and a tiara for Mary and £3,000 for the couple. Additionally, he guaranteed George's bank loan for a twenty-five-year lease on their
London home and much needed repairs. While in India, they leased the home for
£2,000 a year to Mr. Joseph Choate, the American ambassador to London from
1899 to 1905, a practical decision on both financial and diplomatic levels.[64]

When they left for India in December, Mary traveled with Irene, who was almost three years old, and "Cimmie," as she was always known, now four months old. As her primary identity at this point in her life was of mother, Mary focused on that to make the voyage to India a pleasant experience. She arranged for a Christmas tree, which she and some of George's staff decorated, and presents for the children to be brought aboard the ocean liner. Despite the "sweltering heat," Mary and the others "were paid for our trouble because the children were wild with joy." Clearly pleased with her first efforts to win over the staff and press, Mary wrote to her family, "You can't think how much pleasure that gave everyone and votes of thanks were passed & the Queen's and my health drunk amidst cheers."[65]

Upon their arrival in Bombay, George and Mary were received in extraordinary fashion. Bands played "God Save the Queen" while large crowds and soldiers lined the streets along with alternating American and British flags. Seeing the ensigns of both her nations overjoyed Mary, but she was careful to keep her American eagerness in check, lest the staff and populace at large regard her primarily as an American rather than their vicereine, though she readily admitted to her parents that she was adjusting to her new life. Elaborate receptions and dinners followed, with Mary reflecting, "We might as well be Monarchs."[66]

While Mary's appearance and enthusiasm made her popular with some, the same qualities incurred criticism from others. Mary's initial lack of confidence as vicereine stemmed from "her American heritage and her relative youth," in addition to an "overbearing if devoted husband." At the same time, her "considerable charm to smooth troubled waters" served her and George well, a counterbalance to his political personality as a "demanding and highly critical Viceroy."[67] Clearly, her nouveau riche background and American heritage had not prepared her for such a position. From a colonial perspective, she often appeared far too eager about her husband's reign as viceroy. While she claimed to despise "wearing my india-rubber smile," for hours on end, Indians and Britons alike criticized her for her eagerness to support her husband and his position.[68] Rumor had it that she enjoyed curtsying to her husband every morning and was far too happy "to jump up every time he" comes into a room. Etiquette called for the couple to enter a room side by side, but Mary insisted on entering several steps behind her husband. She adored him and wished only to boost his ego at every opportunity. As she wrote to her father shortly after their arrival in India, "George is like a reigning Sovereign. . . . The only difference is that he has a great deal more power than most kings."[69] Her visible pleasure with British protocol garnered the critical eye of more than one British politician. As St. John Brodrick, secretary of state for India from 1903 to 1905, later commented, "Lady Curzon, though possessing brilliant qualities, had not been brought up in England and had none of the traditional knowledge that many English women possessed of the 'give and take' of public life."[70] Undeniably, Mary did not possess the same level of poli-social ease as would woman with a noble background. Writing to St. John Brodrick, she teasingly spoke of the "absolutely aloofness [of the viceregalship] and [noted that] everyone is in mortal fear of the august being." She candidly admitted, "Being a Yankee I can't understand it, but I manage to assume the necessary amount of awful respect for His X when we appear in public."[71] Mary acknowledged her difficult situation; much of the criticism she endured as vicereine stemmed from the fact that she was an *American* woman acting as the *British* First Lady of India.

Acutely aware of her sometimes helpful but more often problematic heritage, Mary pledged "to keep up the dignity of this position [and to demonstrate] how nice and quiet Americans could be."[72] Unfortunately for Mary, her younger sisters, Nancy and Daisy, arrived in India for a seven-week visit. Admonishing them before they arrived, Mary wrote to her father that she would not "allow any flirtations as here I am a kind of Queen of Seringapatam and can't have any flirtations at my court!"[73] Unfortunately, her sisters did not share Mary's desire to represent the United States well and failed to heed her. Shortly after their arrival, Nancy asked one of George's aides-de-camp, wearing the rank and seasonally appropriate short breeches, if he had outgrown his pants. In short order, another aide-de-camp, Raymond Marker, proposed marriage to Daisy, and she accepted. The engagement, however, did not meet her elder sister's approval; Mary dissolved the match, believing that her sister could do better, due to her own position as vicereine.[74]

Despite the impression her sisters made in India, Mary quickly earned the love and respect of the British and Indian people. Less than a month after becoming vicereine, she began visiting hospitals as part of her duty related to the Dufferin Fund. Lady Dufferin, the wife of the first Marquess of Dufferin and Ava, had initiated a program for developing medical aid for Indian women while her husband was viceroy, from 1884 to 1888. The philanthropy aimed to provide Indian women medical care by giving them medical education, as cultural norms forbade Indian women from being examined directly by male physicians; thus, historically, "Indian women [suffered needlessly] and died from ignorance of sanitary principles" because their "caste, customs, and prejudices cut them off from the services of male physicians."[75] On special instructions from Queen Victoria, Lady Curzon "expressed her intention of making the fund prosper under her guidance" and was "determined to do her utmost to brighten and alleviate the lot of the women of India."[76] As vicereine, Mary made the Dufferin Fund a priority. Her engaging sympathy was noted in papers in India, Britain, and the United States, which won her quick approval in all three countries as she skillfully utilized soft power and consistently won people to her side, and George's as well, through attraction rather than coercion.[77] Her serene and gentle approach to people and policy illustrated the old adage that one can catch more flies with honey than vinegar. Similarly to Lady Churchill in Ireland, Lady Curzon worked tirelessly for the less fortunate in India. As the *New York Times* announced, "Lady Curzon's beauty, grace and geniality are the theme of general admiration. Her popularity is assured."[78] Winston Churchill confirmed the declaration when he stayed with the Curzons in February 1899. As he wrote to his American mother, he found the couple "very pleasant and . . . found [George] very delightful to talk to. His manner is wonderful. All the aggressiveness which irritated me at home is gone." Winston concluded, "They have both won everybody's heart." But in the same letter, he made a haunting observation: "You would be shocked to see how Lady C. has changed. She has had a sharp attack of fever and will not, I think, stand the climate which will spoil the whole thing."[79]

Another change for Mary also coincided with the move to India—her marriage became stronger. Due to the distance and isolating nature of life in India, George and Mary became closer than ever. While their staff and servants waited on them around the clock, they were neither friends nor family. Just as George and Mary had a duty to fulfill in India, so did their staff; thus, employees were not to be confided to or trusted. So the pair had a choice—disappear into utter isolation in India due to the extreme climate and overwhelming responsibilities or turn to and lean on one another solely. They chose the latter, and they benefited as individuals and as a couple. In their lengthy and frequent correspondence while he worked alone at the Government House in Calcutta and she stayed in Simla, they lovingly referred to one another as Pappy and Kinkie. Even brief separations took a toll on them: writing to George, Mary confessed, "The void in my breast never stops aching. . . . I miss you every second, and wish I had never come away. I never will again; life is too short to spend any of it apart." His opinion meant everything to Mary, and even the slightest compliment stirred her to action for weeks. "You made me so happy by telling me you thought I had made a good start the first two months in India. Anything I do seems minute besides all I want to do is help."[80] Noting his wife's work and high esteem as vicereine, he praised her as "the most humble, the most unspoiled creature in the world. I have never detected in you a ray of vanity, and it is your sublime unconsciousness of all that is most remarkable in you that is one of your incomparable charms."[81]

The transformation in their marriage directly affected George's work, as Mary increasingly became his eyes and ears while they endured separation. She took a greater interest in the political machinations and began reading British and Indian newspapers and dispatches when possible and subtly advising and providing increased support for her husband behind the scenes. Her Indian correspondence in this period served two purposes: to provide George continued support for his work and supply a new perspective on international issues. In some instances, she warned him that the Foreign Office would try to make him "the scapegoat" while pleading with him to not work so hard as his "life and strength are so precious."[82]

Her soft power persuasion within and from India proved invaluable to her husband's career and solidified her position as devoted mediator.

Without a doubt, Mary enjoyed more influence on George while in India than at any other time in their marriage. His previously domineering nature seemed to abate, which gained him widespread approval in India and Britain. As Mrs. Pearl Craigie wrote to him, "It seems to me that you have gained so much in sympathy—at one time it seemed the one thing lacking. But I observe now in your actions and speeches that winning note of human feeling which, with intellectual gifts must always command a country." In another letter, she acknowledged that she had "studied [his] speeches with great care. They show a remarkable development of your tact and . . . wonderful adaptability."[83] Ostensibly, Mary's "engaging sympathy" affected George positively as she served as nongovernmental official, working tirelessly through women's vocations, which quietly masked labors similar to men's diplomatic occupations.

While Mary enjoyed her new influence upon George, she discovered that being vicereine was truly demanding. The constant dressing and undressing for in addition to the preparing and performing at one event after another in the Indian heat proved arduous. She found the "strain [of life in India] very great," as "our days are filled with politics, philanthropy and charity, and our evenings with society." While she enjoyed the philanthropic aspect of being Vicereine, dealing with the "critical" and "chilly" British women in India proved daunting. As Mary explained to her mother, she could never afford a mistake: "English women are ready to pounce as my being here excites such jealously in many hearts." While she had missed participating in the Season in London, official duties in India resulted in "the fatigues of night after night of dinner-parties, frightful music, worse food, and company with whom you have nothing in common. It is all I can do to fill my part."[84] Lest her American family and friends assume her life in India amounted to one grand party after another, she assured them, "My life is real hard work I can tell you."[85]

Adding to the continual demands of viceregal life were constant threats to one's health. Mary acknowledged that her family was "surrounded by plague and cholera, but every precaution is taken for us."[86] Regardless of such protections, Mary received a stark reminder of the realities of life in India in the fall of 1900. Writing to her mother, she recounted the story of her godchild, aged three months, who "died suddenly on Sunday through neglect of the nurse & I went down . . . and actually buried the baby. There was no one but another woman & me to put the dead baby in its coffin. . . . it was the saddest baldest most miserable funeral."[87]

Fortunately, Mary was able to escape the realities of life in India for several months in 1901. Though custom forbade the viceroy from leaving the country during his five-year term, the same did not hold for the vicereine. Traveling with her two daughters, Mary left in March, spending some time in Continental Europe before arriving in London in May. A welcome break from India also provided Mary with an incredible opportunity in England—to serve as George's informal ambassador. Her presence in England allowed her to deliver messages to friends and officials, many of whom now occupied high positions, while observing the personal and political developments at home and countering any misinterpretations such as the "foolish formality" of India, which might harm George once he returned to London. In one conversation with Lord Alfred Milner, who served as governor of the Cape Colony and high commissioner for Southern Africa in 1901, he told Mary that it was "bad luck that the South African war had diverted attention from India." Mary quickly corrected him; the timing allowed George to carry out his duties without "foolish criticism." In another case, she candidly informed her husband that Secretary of State for India George Hamilton had criticized George and the weakness of the Indian Civil Service. Critical of her husband's frontier policy, Hamilton spoke only of his own policy for the frontier to Mary. She promptly declared him a "hopeless dotard" and "small-minded ferret-faced roving-eyed mediocrity."[88] This type of information, both good and bad, provided George the insight of political life in London that he had lost touch with based on the sheer distance between Britain and the British raj.

Powerful men who would never sit down and write a letter to George would converse with Mary for hours on end. For example, Arthur Balfour, less than a year from becoming prime minister, told Mary, "I never write, but I love George."[89] Though she playfully dismissed her letters as "tittle-tattle," Mary's correspondence to George in this period was invaluable in keeping him abreast of the perspective of India from London.[90] Her grateful husband wrote, "I love all the gossip you picked up from your various friends & passed on to me. In half an hour's talk one learns more than in half a year's correspondence."[91] For the next six months, Mary served as her husband's envoy and liaison, and he could not have asked for a better personal representative. In a rare acknowledgment of Mary as a wife and partner, Curzon admitted that his career demanded "considerable self-sacrifice and some subordination" of Mary, quite a transformation from the man who once hailed a woman who knew her place. He wrote candidly to her that summer, "that in our life there is a sense of comradeship almost as great as love."[92]

Widespread ignorance of India enabled Mary to play a tremendously influential role as vicereine. While most Britons expressed great pride for their empire, and particularly India, Mary now realized that it was "the great unknown: The moon seems nearer to the great majority." Misconceptions and false presumptions about the country plagued England, which she used to her full advantage. Their close friends and political allies had no idea where George and Mary lived, how they traveled, or even the religion of India. And yet Mary relayed to her husband, "There isn't a person I meet who doesn't speak of the great work you are doing.

They don't know what it is, but they know that it is something." Such ignorance in Britain, coupled with intense curiosity, provided Mary with near limitless diplomatic authority. By the time she returned to India in the fall of 1901, Prime Minister Salisbury had declared George's reign as viceroy a huge success, owing most of it to his "frontier policy [that] will keep us in India 50 years longer than we should have kept it otherwise." With what some might consider her feminine wiles, Mary used her time in London to renew and fortify political friendships and construct an "unofficial channel of communication" with individuals who were presently, or soon would be, her husband's superiors.[93] Always seen as a beautiful and graceful woman, Mary used her physical appearance and friendships to champion her husband's work in India and to challenge any potentially negative reports that might hinder his policies as viceroy and his eventual return to the House. Her utilization, and even manipulation, of both public and private diplomacy would offer skillful lessons to even the most seasoned consul. Even St. John Brodrick, who later criticized her deportment in India, praised her time in London. Writing to George, he explained that he could not "let another mail go without telling you how great a success your dear wife has had in England—confirming friendships, making many more, charming all." He complimented her "interest in big things and the great problems without losing that delightful simplicity which adds so much effect to her beauty and sweetness."[94] Again, her traditional duties as a woman, always unpaid, were necessary to George's career and her establishment as an informal ambassador. Mary's physical attractiveness and appealing character were mighty tools as she wielded soft power in Britain and India. Like her American-born, British-wed sisters before her, due to her British marriage and imperial rank Mary exhibited a degree of influence impractical in the United States; it would have been impossible for an American woman to hold a colonial post. She had such seemingly effortless influence because British politicians and even her own husband appeared largely oblivious of her power as a negotiator, mediator, and peacekeeper.

Mary's popularity and apparently invisible use of soft power resulted in a final and incredibly influential connection. In addition to wooing the political elite, she spent a considerable amount of time with the new monarchs, King Edward and Queen Alexandra. The latter was so taken with Mary that she commissioned her to order her coronation robe and several additional dresses to be made in India. For Mary, a woman of the antipodes, and an American at that, to be asked was the ultimate endorsement of her success abroad. She focused considerable time on the project, an enormous accolade to both Mary and India, and provided extraordinary dresses that met with the queen's great approval.[95]

Before Mary left London, however, George encouraged her to consider staying if she thought it would improve her health. Realizing the toll India had taken on her, he pressed her to "recover [her health], build it up, lay the scaffolding for itty boy—sacrifice everything to that."[96] An ever-present pressure in their lives, and especially Mary's, was the need to produce a Curzon heir. While a doting father to his two girls, George longed for and needed a male heir to carry on the Curzon name and Kedleston estate.[97] In an attempt to increase her fertility, Mary undertook some type of bath treatment in Ems, Germany, to "work the miracle of an *almost* immaculate conception!" So sure was she of the therapy that she hoped that the "patron saint of Ems will not retaliate & give me no twin sons because I hate the place so."[98]

Upon her return to India, Mary gave serious consideration to her imperial legacy. Building on her success with the Dufferin Fund, she created the Victoria Memorial Scholarship Fund, which aimed to train female physicians, midwives, and nurses and provide "practical knowledge," in an effort to improve the health of women throughout India.[99] In 1902, she successfully raised £50,000 within India and then turned to Europe for additional funds. In 1904, Curzon's Council approved the program, which was on the cusp of fruition when George resigned as viceroy. Following the Curzons' return to London, the Victoria Scholarships were made a reality by the following vicereine, Lady Mary Minto; hence, the scholarship earned the nickname "Lady Minto Scheme" much to Mary Curzon's disappointment. With four years in India behind them, George and Mary should have been making plans to return to England, as a viceroy's term lasted five years. But rather than concluding his policies in India, George threw himself into this work all the more, which coincided with the reports of Mary's failing health that appeared across American newspapers. Mary begged her parents to contradict these, but she admitted that she had taken on an increasing number of George's duties in the way of "races, parties, concerts, weddings, prize-gatherings, polo-matches, and the Lord knows what. It is all work and very little pleasure." Both she and her husband recognized her superior skills in this arena. But more specific to her deteriorating health, she confessed to her mother, "No one knows how I loathe Simla and its cruel climate. I never feel well here."[100] Mary's worsening health was no secret to her husband. In a letter from late 1902, she wrote to him, "Every bit of my vitality has gone, and I am iller than I have ever been and simply can't get back to life." But in typical Mary fashion, she pressured herself to rise to the occasion and to George's assistance, believing "absolutely in my power of 'coming up to time' or 'answering my ring' as an actor does in the wings of a theatre." In the same letter, she made an ominous prediction: "Some day, though, the bell will go and I shall not appear, as India, I knew, slowly but surely murders women."[101] She viewed her place in this world as one of the "many humble and inconsequent lives [that] always go into the foundations of all great works and great building and great achievements."[102]

Despite her failing health, Mary continued to pay great attention to her physical appearance, which carried great significance in India. Indian culture considered elaborate dresses and jewelry tremendously important. As Nicola Thomas has argued, "Mary Curzon's clothed body . . . demonstrates the ways in which she negotiated public space through her clothing practices." The tension of British imperialists in India demanded that materiality of clothing was taken seriously.[103] Consequently, Mary's consideration of her appearance meant much more than a dress and earrings. In a post-Victorian imperial world, prescriptions of especially feminine and masculine dress and behavior for women and men held particularly for the viceroy and vicereine. In an effort to negotiate the complexities "of empire in both domestic and political terms," Mary had to become a colonial spectacle, attempting to please both British and Indian audiences by wearing exquisite gowns from Paris with Indian ornamentation wherever possible.[104] For all of these reasons, the vicereine's dress for the coronation celebration in January 1903 to announce formally Edward VII as King held great importance. Mary did not disappoint, as she unveiled her famous "Peacock Dress," at one point the most well-known gown in the world.[105] In Anne De Courcy's words, her dress had "cloth of gold embroidered with tiny peacock feathers, each eye an emerald, the skirt trimmed with white roses and the bodice with lace. She glittered with diamonds, pearls and precious stones: a huge necklace of diamonds around her throat, others of diamonds and pearls and a crown-like tiara, a pearl tipping each of its high diamond points. As she walked through the hall, Curzon beside her in white satin knee breeches, the gasps were almost audible."[106]

Though her dress, demeanor, and deportment, Mary had managed to win over both her British and Indian counterparts as vicereine and was increasingly considered the "American Queen of India."[107] Unfortunately, the same could not be said of the viceroy. The more George achieved, the more he demanded of the Indian council. While his vigor, enthusiasm, devotion to duty, and apparently unlimited work ethic made him an ideal statesman, the same characteristics resulted in what seemed unattainable standards for others.[108] His previous career and knowledge of the Middle East actually complicated his perspective, as he believed no one knew or could possibly understand India as he did. Eventually, his domineering nature alienated his colleagues in India just as it had in London. Writing candidly to Mary in 1902, Lord George Hamilton, secretary of state for India from 1895 to 1903, explained, "George has had his way more than any Viceroy of modern times. . . . I have a deep and growing admiration for your husband's talents and force of character." To encourage Mary to speak kindly to her husband, and a clear acknowledgment of the influence she had over him, Lord Hamilton reminded her, "In public life you must give as well as take. The Council here are the final authority in all Indian matters." He warned Mary, and thus George, that the council included "the most distinguished, experienced men, and they cannot be expected to acquiesce in everything suggest to them without comment."[109]

Unfortunately, Hamilton's words fell on deaf ears. Though a diplomatic liaison between her husband and his colleagues, Mary could see George only as a great and wise leader and failed to acknowledge that he had any personality traits that could undermine his career. Unfortunately, they shared this blind spot, a fault that eventually cost George the viceroyship when he decided to place his entire Indian record on the line in a battle of wills with the famed military leader Horatio Herbert Kitchener. While she had functioned as a critical peacekeeper, like Lady Churchill and Mary Chamberlain, Lady Curzon was unable to maintain amity in what became the final scene of their joint term as viceroy and vicereine.

In 1902, Kitchener became commander in chief of India. During his term, he reorganized the Indian army. Initially, George supported many of Kitchener's reforms, and Kitchener became a close companion of both George and Mary, with the vicereine often serving as mediator. Enjoying her new role, Mary explained to her father in 1903 that she had "become a sort of necessary companion to statesmen. I talk to George literally by the hour about every one of his political plans; and the other Sunday, Kitchener sat in the garden and talked business with me for 3½ hours. It is only after vast study and reading that women can become good companions, but it is far greater satisfaction than frivolity."[110] Unfortunately, the newfound friendship did not last long, as "a Homeric conflict of personalities" seemed almost destined.[111] In a prophetic statement to her mother, Mary wrote that Kichener "and George both have indomitable wills, and it is frequently my diplomacy which keeps them great friends."[112] But even Mary could not prevent the deterioration of the relationship between her husband and the commander in chief as they struggled for ultimate power in India.

Mary took a brief hiatus from her role as negotiator between Kitchener and George in early 1904 when she returned to England in January for the birth of their third child. Writing from India shortly before the baby's birth, George presented contradictory sentiments about the potential birth of a son: "Darling, it doesn't matter if sweet Nalder is a girl. Don't fuss about that. Girls are very loveable"—and with his next breath, however, sharing a very different feeling: "I pray in these same words every day: "May she bear a child to thy honour and glory and to the good of the kingdom, and may it be a male child." Alexandra Naldera was born on March 20, 1904, named for the queen who was her godmother and the city in India where she was likely conceived. She was always known as "Baba," the Indian word for baby or little one, or sometimes "Baba Sahib," which meant "the Viceroy's baby."[113] Upon hearing of the birth of his third child, George wrote to Mary in to console her on not bearing a son. "Darling, I felt how miserable you would be, and though of course I was too somewhat disappointed, I really felt it much more for you than for myself. . . . So we will be content with our little Naldera and postpone

Irian-Dorian till some future date."[114] Even in her delicate postpartum state, Mary
felt pressure to produce an heir. As she had not yet birthed a son, she knew keenly
that she was not finished having children.[115]

Just a few short months after Baba's birth, Mary's father died of heart disease.
As he was most important man in Mary's life next to George, his passing proved
devastating. Despite that Mary had not seen her father since 1898, their frequent
correspondence allowed them to maintain a close relationship. His absence left a
tremendous void. Yet, the emotional loss was slightly counterbalanced by an economic benefit, as his death increased Mary's annual income by £20,000 a year.[116]

Exhausted by years of service in India, the birth of a third child, the continued
lack of a male Curzon heir, and her father's death, Mary dreaded a return to India.
In conversation, Lady Lansdowne, a friend and fellow political wife, said to her,
"I hear you are the most helpful wife a public man ever had and a most wonderful ambassador!"[117] Having served as an informal diplomat to Britain and India,
Mary decided to utilize her status in London and correspondence to George in
this period to convince him to return home to a promising political career. She
frequently discussed the endless possibilities that existed for him: "You do loom
so great and big and strong out there in India, away from the miserable muddles
here, where each day seems to add to the failures of your friends. . . . Here you are
looked on as a giant—and a frightening one." He responded that he felt "so happy
and proud when I see you run after, admired and adored. You hold a really unique
position in this respect. For what other woman in London combines great beauty
with exceptional intelligence as well as a tact which is an inspiration?" Recognizing what she had done for him not only in London but also in India, he continued,
"There is no limit to the influence you can exercise at home, as you have done in
India, smoothing down those whom I ignore and offend, and creating our own
atmosphere of refinement and devotion."[118]

Despite her best efforts to lure him back to a conventional life in London,
George took an extension as viceroy. Most English administrators concur that five
or six years of service are the most one can provide and function at a high level;
this proved especially true for the viceroy of India, as the country's intense climate,
brutal workday, and demanding social calendar quickly wear down even the most
dedicated public servant.[119] Yet, after a summer visit to London, George returned
to India more determined than ever to put his stamp on the colony. Defeated, Mary
admitted to her close friend Pearl Craigie, "India suits him [as] the air of the House
of Commons never did." Ever devoted to George, she pledged that she would "never
let him know how much I regret the decision."[120]

Shortly before George returned to India, Mary became seriously ill. That autumn, she suffered a probable miscarriage, complicated by peritonitis and phlebi-
tis. Following a botched operation, she remained comatose for several days. She

recovered to some degree the next month, after which George decided to return to India. He wrote, "I felt it a duty to the Government of which I had been the head of for so long not to desert it in the hour of trial but to sacrifice all personal considerations to the necessity of fighting its battles."[121] Acknowledging the incredible challenges they had faced together, he wrote to her, "Amid all the great misery that we have been through, there shines out the consolation of many happy hours and tender moments and the memory of your beautiful and ineffaceable love. We have been drawn very close by this companionship in the furnace of affliction and I hope that it may leave me less selfish and more considerate in the future." In what appears a confession of guilt following his return to India, George pledged to "go on existing in order to come back and try to make you happy." And yet, focusing on himself, he continued, "It is with a sad and miserable heart that I go leaving all that makes life worth living behind me and going out to toil and isolation and often worse. But it seems to be [my] destiny."[122]

In her devoted manner, Mary decided to return to India after a year away. In early 1905, she arrived in Bombay to receive an overwhelming greeting and out-pouring of support. As she described to her mother, "People treat me as though I were a miracle returned from the dead, & the affection is affecting. No one ever had such a welcome to India. . . . My heart is very tender towards India—and I shall do my best to get well here."[123] Validating her transnational influence and perspective, the streets were once again lined with American and British flags. One Indian newspaper described her return as one "neither Lady Curzon nor the people who witnessed her arrival would easily forget."[124] Weeks later, she barely survived a massive earthquake at Viceregal Lodge with the children.

Upon her return to India, Mary resumed her utilitarian friendship with Kitchener, and she described her conversations with him as among the happiest memories of her life in India. In writing of this relationship to her mother, she explained, his "utter dependence upon me appealed so strongly to me—more so because liking me as a woman, he talked to me as a man."[125] This apparent give-and-take dialogue and true equality in conversation was what Mary had long wished for from her husband and the very thing he could never give her. This proved ironic, as Kitchener dealt the final blow to George's career in India and gave Mary the ultimate exit from India.

In the end, Mary's friendship with Kitchener was not enough to keep the jealous competition between the viceroy and commander in chief at bay. The mounting conflict between them resulted from the question of dual control that began when Kitchener demanded that the role of the military member of the Viceroy's Council should be redefined as subordinate to the commander in chief of the army; thus, making the commander in chief as important as the viceroy.[126] George regarded Kitchener's "proposals as a positive menace to the State." Kitchener believed the change was necessary to strengthen the army, lest his soldiers be "sent to fight the battles of the empire all unprepared and without leaders to guide them." Both men poured their hearts out to Mary, in validation of her influential position as the only remaining diplomat who could find a way to avoid war between them. George saw the move as Kitchener's attempt to become "an autocrat in our administration." Kitchener described the situation to Mary as "next door to whole sale murder. Well, it cannot be helped, and I shall at least have the comforting thought that I have done all I could for them, so I am starting my packing-up."[127]

Both George and Kitchener threatened resignation, which put the home government in a difficult situation. One policy would be chosen over the other; one man would be chosen over another; accordingly, one career would end in defeat. While George had the upper hand politically, Kitchener enjoyed popular support as a military hero; in the end, the latter won the support of the press and the people. When the home government sided with Kitchener, George resigned in August 1905.[128]

While George's viceroyship came to a disastrous end, Mary earned great praise for her time as vicereine. Quickly evaluating the situation in India upon their arrival in 1899, Mary "understood how to make herself no less popular in India than her husband."[129] One newspaper commented that George, in his "marriage, as in all things else, [had] drawn a prize in life's greatest lottery. . . . From the earliest days of your wedded life your lovely bride proved herself a true helpmeet. As Vicereine she has won nothing but golden opinion, and undoubtedly fresh triumphs are in store for her when she takes her rightful place as a leader of English society. It is quite possible that she may, if she so chooses, restore the political *salon,* which has so nearly disappeared, to its earlier importance."[130] Consequently, George left India vanquished while Mary left victorious.

In his final speech in India, George bade the people farewell and urged them to remember the "seven long and happy years." Noting his wife's invaluable role, he admitted, "No one knows better than the Viceroy the part, not merely in private life but in public responsibilities, that is capable of being borne by the Viceroy's wife. No Viceroy has ever had more cause to feel that woman is the better part of the man than myself." He continued to shower his wife with praise and described her work as her full focus, proclaiming that nothing "absorbed her more completely than the organization which she started for providing nurses . . . to Indian mothers, or the effort to which she has devoted so much labour for creating an Indian Nursing Service for Europeans and which we still hope will be crowned with success." In typical postmortem fashion, George seemed to apologize for neglecting his wife by demanding public adulation for her effort when he surmised, "From both these classes of the community, and indeed from every class, anything she has done came back to her tenfold in sympathy and tenderness."[131] Unable to give his wife the love and devotion she needed from him, he commanded that the populace do it for him.

Upon their departure from Simla, the people physically conveyed George and Mary's carriage through the streets in a final tribute to their departing Viceroy. Unfortunately, their arrival in December in England was not nearly as celebratory. No one—not King Edward VII, not a single member of the government, or a solitary friend—met them at the station.[132] George did not receive an earldom, which had been presented to every previous viceroy. Not even Arthur Balfour, who just a year earlier all but begged Mary to bring George home to a position in the prime minister's government, supported George in any parliamentary election.[133] Hurt by their involuntary departure from India and humiliated by their arrival in London, the couple retrieved their children from southern France three weeks later and did not return to England until March 1906.

Return to London

Upon their homecoming, it was clear that Mary's health had significantly deteriorated. Writing to her brother in June, she confessed, "I sometimes fear and feel I shall never be well again" and discussed suffering from "devilish ills." In what would be her final letter to George, she wrote, "what causes me such acute agony is that I should be a burden to you whom I worship, just when I would give my soul to be a help. I will be brave, beloved and when I am naughty, you will know it isn't your Kinkie but all these devilish ills! There is plenty of hope and light ahead, and I won't always add to the shadows in Pappy's life, but pray that I may yet bring him the sun in all its glory. Love. M."[134]

On July 17, 1906, Mary took a sudden and drastic turn for the worse. As her heart began to fail, doctors responded with rounds of oxygen, champagne, and strychnine, which worked only for a short period. By the end of the day, Mary was clearly fading. Late that evening, she collapsed in George's arms and died.[135] The official cause of death was listed as heart failure, but Mary's demise had been ongoing for at least two years.[136] Following a funeral in Derbyshire, George buried his beloved wife at Kedleston. Flowers and wreaths were sent by, to name but a few, the president of the United States, the viceroy of India, the United States ambassador, the American Society in London, and the staff of the Kedleston estate; other tributes included a handwritten card from Queen Alexandra.[137] George spent the next six years building a memorial to Mary, complete with Serravezza marble and Spanish spires. Upon its completion, he had a tablet laid at the north wall that read:

MARY VICTORIA
LADY CURZON OF KEDLESTON
BORN MAY 27, 1870   DIED JULY 18, 1906
PERFECT IN LOVE AND LOVELINESS
BEAUTY WAS THE LEAST OF HER RARE GIFTS
GOD HAD ENDURED WITH LIKE GRACES
HER MIND AND SOUL
FROM ILLNESS ALL BUT UNTO DEATH
RESTORED ONLY TO DIE
SHE WAS MOURNED IN THREE CONTINENTS
AND BY HER DEAREST
WILL BE
FOR EVER UNFORGOTTEN[138]

The outpouring of grief that followed Mary's death was shared around the world. Curzon received more than eleven hundred letters and telegrams expressing sympathy, and in an effort to assuage his grief he personally answered some eight hundred. To Mary's mother he expressed his most profound sorrow: "There has gone from me the truest, most devoted, most unselfish, most beautiful & brilliant wife that a man ever had. . . . Somewhere my previous darling is happy and blessed. I owe to her all the happiness of my life."[139]

In her hometown, the *Chicago Tribune* reported, "It was remarked that she had none of the aggressive self-confidence which, rightly or wrongly, is usually attributed to ambitious American girls, but she attracted by reserve and a thoughtful, studious manner and an engaging sympathy."[140] Even the *London Times* reflected on her unique role as an informal ambassador, describing her as "the girl whose subsequent career has been so brilliant."[141] Upon the request of an anonymous letter to the editor of the *New York Times,* Rudyard Kipling's poem "The Song of the Women" was reprinted. Originally written for Lady Dufferin, for her efforts in India, the poem could have easily been written for Mary.

How shall she know the worship we would do her?
The walls are high, and she is very far.
How shall the woman's message reach unto her
Above the tumult of the packed bazaar?
Free wind of March, against the lattice blowing,
Bear thou our thanks, lest she depart unknowing.

. . . .

By hands uplifted to the Gods that heard not,
By fits that found no favor in their sight,
By faces bent above the babe that stirred not,
By nameless horrors of the stifling night;
By ills foredone, by peace her toils discover,
Bid Earth be good beneath and Heaven above her!
If she have sent her servants in our pain
If she have fought with Death and dulled his sword;
If she have given back our sick again.
And to the breast the waking lips restored,
Is it a little thing that she has wrought?
Then Life and Death and Motherhood be nought.

. . . .

Haste, for our hearts are with thee, take no rest!
Loud-voiced *ambassador,* from sea to sea
Proclaim the blessing, manifold, confessed.
Of those in darkness by her hand set free.
Then very softly to her presence move,
And whisper: "Lady, lo, they know and love![142]

Following Mary's burial on July 23, 1906, George suffered mightily. In accordance to their 1895 marriage settlement, he received one-third of the income from a $1.75 million real estate and bonds investment, and the remainder was divided among their three daughters.[143] A Washington, D.C., judge later named Lord Curzon ancillary guardian for his daughters and ordered him to collect the interest on the marriage settlement and on the Leiter estate, which amounted to $36,000 per year for each daughter.[144] The Leiter fortune and comparative Curzon paucity, which lay the foundation for the initial match, fueled the bitter hostility between Curzon and his daughters that would continue for years.[145]

After Mary's death, George withdrew from politics and society for essentially the next decade and became something of a hermit. Though he served as chancellor of Oxford for many years, without his devoted Mary at his side he was no longer a force of nature. He did marry again, and to another American heiress, no less. In 1917, George wed Grace Elvina Hinds, who knew firsthand the intricacies of American diplomacy and transnational relationships. She was the daughter of J. Monroe Hinds, the former U.S. Consul General in Rio de Janeiro, and the widow of Alfred Hubert Duggan of Argentina. Based on her wealth, more than one politician unmercifully remarked that George survived financially by the means of Grace.[146]

Focused on raising his three daughters, George was both a dedicated and aloof father. Their relationship did not improve over the years, and until his death in 1925 the four fought nearly nonstop over the remaining Leiter fortune. Desperate to update his beloved Kedleston, he tried valiantly to have his daughters turn over their respective riches to him for this end. On differing levels and for a variety of reasons, they all refused. Never having received rejection well, George considered this the ultimate betrayal and even refused his eldest daughter when she came to him at his deathbed.[147]

Following his passing, the *London Times* lauded George for his great career and fierce devotion to country at home and abroad. The same adulatory article also noted that Lord Curzon was "one with whom it was very hard to deal," concluding that he was "not a diplomatist."[148] Clearly, that duty had always resided with Mary. Nearly twenty years after his beloved's death, George's widow and daughters found that he had already handled most all of the arrangements for his funeral. To no one's surprise, his wishes were to be buried next to Mary. While visiting her deceased husband, Grace found a slip of paper that indicated where she would one day be buried, marked with the words "Reserved for the Second Lady Curzon." As Nigel Nicolson has succinctly observed, Grace was the second Lady Curzon in more ways than one.[149]

In every way possible, Mary Leiter Curzon used her life as an ambassadorship. First, representing the United States to England, she aimed to present a docile and reserved image as an individual American woman to counteract the collective impression of American-born, British-wed women as loud, impulsive, boisterous title-hunting women. Next, as the vicereine of India, she represented imperial England at the height of the British raj. Finally, throughout her marriage to George Curzon, she acted as his personal mediator, liaison, representative, emissary, and negotiator to a wealth of men and women, British, Indian, and American. Though her absolute devotion to her beloved husband blinded her at times from seeing him through another's perspective, she never failed to serve his interests and push for his policies and career at home and abroad. In every sense of the word, Mary Curzon—American, Briton, and Indian—was an informal ambassador.

CHAPTER FIVE

Elegant Envoy

Consuelo Vanderbilt Marlborough Balsan

So is it surprising that an American girl who held democratic views found it difficult
to accept the assumption that birth alone confers superiority?

—CONSUELO BALSAN

*A*s the nineteenth century came to a close, Great Britain and the United
States teetered on the brink of war. While Anglo-Americans looked to Lady
Churchill, the British colonial secretary's wife, and the vicereine of India to calm
fears on both sides of the Atlantic in the midst of the Venezuelan boundary crisis,
a new American heiress reluctantly prepared to join the ever-growing number of
American-born, British-wed wives living abroad. Unlike the transatlantic marriages presented thus far, neither party here wanted the union. The nuptials took
place under duress even as newspapers followed the public and, to the degree
that was possible, private activities of Lady Churchill, Mary Chamberlain, and
other American Amazons as the best behind-the-scenes ambassadors worked to
mitigate a significant Anglo-American crisis. Nevertheless, the ceremony proved
the social event of year in New York and had a much-needed calming effect on
British-American relations. As Charles S. Campbell argues, the ostentatious wedding "created an unintended tranquilizing effect on the contemporary Venezuelan affair by providing the American public with a far more fascinating spectacle
even than the most provocative of Secretary [of State Richard] Olney's notes."[1]

Almost from the beginning, the union disintegrated. Neither Consuelo Vanderbilt, great-granddaughter of Cornelius "Commodore" Vanderbilt, nor her fiancé,
Charles Spencer-Churchill, the 9th Duke of Marlborough and Winston Churchill's
cousin, voluntarily chose the other; both professed to be in love with other people.
In the end, both parties succumbed to pressure from their respective families and

Consuelo Vanderbilt Sitting in Chair. BE034819. © Bettman/CORBIS.

proceeded with a union that epitomized the worst stereotypes of Anglo-American marriages. Consuelo's mother forced upon her daughter what she had always wanted for herself. The Duke of Marlborough's family urged their son to make a strategic match with a wealthy American heiress, as their own financial condition demanded such security. After such an inauspicious beginning, much to the surprise of Consuelo and both of her families, American and English, her life abroad significantly influenced British and American opinions, especially after her marriage ended.

Regardless of the Duchess of Marlborough's eventual high-profile divorce, her life and pursuits as an American-born, British-wed woman broadened the prospects for all Anglo-American women living abroad by virtue of their transatlantic marriages and demonstrates the spectrum of pursuits and possibilities available to them. As a British wife, Lady Randolph did all she could under the guise of traditional women's work—hosting dinners and instigating dialogue between critical individuals—both in her home and through her attendance at Parliament meetings, to promote positive perceptions among Britons. She increasingly united other American-born, British-wed wives as a self-identified legion of women working to promote a united Anglo-Saxon identity and improved Anglo-American relations. Mary Endicott Chamberlain continued these efforts as a member of the American Amazons and in her own right by pursuing professional meetings and important dinners with American emissaries to Britain and advancing contemporary definitions of public diplomacy for Americans in Britain through services at St. Margaret's. The correspondence of both Mary Endicott Chamberlain and Mary Leiter Curzon served to create an Anglo-American network to enhance and rival Lady Churchill's *Anglo-Saxon Review* while securing both the private and public identification of an Anglo-American leadership on both sides of the Atlantic. But all of these women's activities remained largely behind the scenes and were therefore essentially protected from most censure, as their work was conventional, unpaid, and acceptable under the guise of elite women's work. While Consuelo's initial impact began in this protected category, like Lady Churchill and Mary Chamberlain she had her greatest influence after her marriage had ended and, as she pursued more overtly political opportunities, much like Lady Nancy Astor, who also increasingly focused her endeavors on improving the lives of women. Building on the successes of her Anglo-American sisters, Consuelo's initial ventures into the national and international political arenas laid the groundwork for Lady Astor to secure a political seat in her own right and exert a public, forceful, and unapologetic influence like no other American-born, British-wed woman before her. Their individual and collective activities and efforts served to change the perspectives of Anglo-Americans on both sides of the Atlantic while cracking a glass ceiling of sorts by redefining who could serve as an informal ambassador and how.

Like Lady Churchill, Mary Curzon, and Lady Astor, Consuelo Vanderbilt Marlborough married a leading member of the British peerage. But these American women approached their lives in Britain very differently. While Lady Churchill's life serves as an excellent example of one woman's efforts to improve Anglo-American relations, Consuelo did not initially use her position in Britain to pursue openly the same cause. Instead, her life provides an opportunity to analyze the question of personal and national identity, akin to Mary Curzon's negotiation of identity in Britain and India, as Consuelo skillfully manipulated the limits of her countries by birth and marriage. Similar to Mary Chamberlain, who appeared reticent to engage publicly a political audience but was increasingly willing to participate in behind-the-scenes dinners as a drawing-room diplomat, particularly after her first husband's death, Consuelo increasingly pursued opportunities as an elegant envoy to Britain as a result of her Anglo-American marriage, and even more so after its conclusion; without a doubt, she was a leading informal ambassador at the turn of the century.

Born in the early hours of Friday, March 2, 1877, Consuelo Vanderbilt was the first child and only daughter of Alva Erskine Smith and William Kissam Vanderbilt. Her mother, originally from Mobile, Alabama, met William K. Vanderbilt through a close childhood friend, Consuelo Yznaga of Natchez, Mississippi. Determined to marry well and escape the South's post–Civil War devastation, Alva approached William as she did everything in her life—with strategic poise and deliberate calculations. The two married on April 20, 1875, and the bride later bragged, "I was the first of my set to marry a Vanderbilt."[2] She had accomplished her dream of permanently leaving the South and entering New York society by her marriage to a wealthy man. Or so she thought.[3]

Shortly after her wedding, Alva quickly came to two startling realizations. First, New York society did not welcome new money into their elite circles; thus, her marriage to a Vanderbilt guaranteed her nothing in terms of mingling with the upper crust. Second, marriage to a rich American man no longer marked the pinnacle by which a young and beautiful American woman could direct her marital ambitions. While Alva's marriage to William K. Vanderbilt seemed quite impressive in 1875, the wedding paled in comparison to the splendor of her best friend's wedding a year later. On May 22, 1876, Consuelo Yznaga married Viscount Kim Mandeville, the future 8th Duke of Manchester, which made his wife Viscountess Mandeville and eventually the Duchess of Manchester. While Alva could only hope to receive the approval of *the* Mrs. Astor in New York City, her best friend mingled on a daily basis with members of the British aristocracy.[4]

At that point, Alva decided that should she have a daughter, this girl would conquer British society, and Alva would secure the best possible match for her, one that would not only make her daughter the envy of families like the Astors but also demand respect and inclusion from the very leaders of New York society who had once rejected Alva. Approximately one year later, the young Consuelo entered the world, completely oblivious to the fact that her mother had all but planned her entire life. Alva named her child after her best friend, who also became her godmother. Years later, Consuelo reflected, "It was her [Alva's] wish to produce me as a finished specimen framed in a perfect setting. . . . My person was dedicated to whatever final disposal she had in mind."[5]

Consuelo's childhood consisted of a seemingly endless experiment in superior education and cultural training that would rival the edification of any ambassador. Alva took pride in the fact that her daughter never attended school; she saw to her education by hiring a team of English, French, and German governesses. On Saturdays, Consuelo recited poetry to her mother in each of these languages; thus, by the age of eight she could read and write in three languages, a skill necessary for any attaché. When Consuelo was seventeen, her mother requested the entrance exams for Oxford University, and her daughter passed with ease.[6] Additionally, her mother arranged for daily music lessons, during which Consuelo learned French and English songs, and she exercised in Central Park every day. Once a week, she took lessons in dancing and deportment. At an early age, Consuelo was a beautiful girl who never wanted for dancing partners. This experience boosted her ego; she remembered, "The competition gave me a sense of superiority I did not often enjoy at home."[7]

Consuelo's life at home was another matter entirely. Alva rarely praised her but instead treated her like a work in progress. Consuelo received love and affection only from her father, a wealthy and powerful man who relinquished the management of the home and development of their children to Alva, who constantly looked at her daughter with a judgmental eye. In front of her, Alva frequently discussed Consuelo's nose with her friends, saying it was too upturned. Consuelo was never allowed to choose her own clothes. When her mother thought she needed to improve her posture, she forced her to wear a back brace consisting of a steel rod that extended the length of her spine, held in place by belts around her waist, shoulders, and forehead. This apparatus made reading and writing exceeding difficult, though reading was Consuelo's one escape from her overbearing mother. Alva, however, credited her daughter's magnificent carriage as a young woman, commented on frequent by strangers and friends, to this brutal device. While Consuelo became quite a stunning young woman, she was also incredibly introverted and hypersensitive to any sort of criticism.[8]

In 1893, at the age of sixteen, Consuelo took a sailing trip to India with her parents and several family friends. She was drawn to Winthrop Rutherford, one of the other guests; in fact, she fell in love with him—thirteen years her senior.[9] Descended from distinguished families such as the Stuyvesants and Winthrops, Rutherford mingled in New York's best circles. His ancestors included Peter Stuyvesant, the governor of colonial New York, and the first Massachusetts governor, John Winthrop.[10] The two kept their growing attraction hidden, so as not to draw Alva's attention. They continued to see each other secretly after they returned to New York. Several months later, Rutherford proposed to Consuelo and she accepted. When her mother realized what had transpired, she threatened to kill Rutherford.[11] The next day, Alva and Consuelo left for Europe. In an effort to prevent any marriage from taking place, in less than twenty-four hours, Alva had arranged for herself and her daughter to spend the next several months abroad. She had not spent sixteen years preparing Consuelo to marry a simple American man; rather she had spent the time and countless dollars on molding the perfect American heiress to enter the highest echelons of the British aristocracy. As one paper later reported, "Winty was outclassed. Six-foot-two in his golf stockings, he was no match for five-foot-six and a coronet."[12]

Consuelo and her mother spent the next several months abroad, beginning their journey in France and eventually spending several weeks in England. Alva arranged for her daughter to make her formal debut in Paris through a series of several small and informal receptions rather than an elaborate social function. Being young, beautiful, and, thanks to her mother, submissive, Consuelo garnered many proposals of marriage; the suitors made the proposals to Alva and not to Consuelo, as French custom dictated. This position of power over socially and politically prominent men reinforced her control over her daughter. Alva turned down all of these proposals; she felt it "better for an Anglo Saxon woman to marry in the Anglo Saxon race."[13] Thus, France served as a gauge for her daughter's success in England and a precursor to her daughter's real debut during the London Season.

Over the course of the next year, Alva took her daughter to England several times, with the goal of terminating any relationship with Rutherford while making contact with Charles Richard John Spencer-Churchill, the Duke of Marlborough. Born in 1871, the Earl of Sunderland, his second title, was always known as "Sunny," though he had anything but a sunny disposition. Educated at Winchester and Cambridge, he fit the Oxbridge stereotype. As the eldest son, thus first in line to inherit his father's title, Sunny had few goals in life and little reason to develop any ambition. His duty was to marry and continue the family line. But in the aftermath of decreasing agricultural prices and a declining economy, the family looked to him to marry well and bring some level of prestige (i.e., money) back to the Marlborough name and Blenheim Palace, the family estate. Sunny's family pressured him to marry soon and marry well. Like Consuelo, he never wanted to go through with this marriage; he received intense pressure to marry a girl not of his choosing in order to pacify and elevate his family.[14]

Alva approached her daughter's engagement in the same manner as she had arranged for her enviable education and cultural training. Months of scheming paid off when the duke proposed to Consuelo during a trip to Marble House, the Vanderbilts' magnificent summerhouse at Newport.[15] Consuelo accepted, burst into tears, and ran out of the room. Within hours, Alva had notified the New York newspapers that "a marriage had been arranged" between her daughter and the duke.[16] When Consuelo told her younger brother that she had agreed to marry the duke, he bluntly responded, "He's only marrying you for your money."[17] Even a twelve-year-old could see through this arrangement. Alva had finally achieved her dream, by forcing it upon a naïve, subservient, and miserable eighteen-year-old girl. Some years later, she justified her actions: "My idea was that Consuelo should take a place in a life of whose firm establishment there could be no question. It was such a position that the House of Marlborough offered her through the present Duke at that time a young man of promise."[18]

Marriage to Marlborough

The first wedding date for the Anglo-American marriage of the century had to be changed; the Duke of Marlborough explained to his fiancée that November 5, their original wedding date, was unacceptable, as it was Guy Fawkes Day. Consuelo, in reality Alva, quickly rescheduled the ceremony for the following day, November 6, 1895.[19] But, as Consuelo wrote in her memoirs, she did not "understand why Guy Fawkes's attempt to blow up Parliament almost three centuries before should affect the date of our marriage, but this was only the first of a series of, to me, archaic prejudices inspired by a point of view opposed to my own." Perhaps this cultural difference should have indicated that the marriage would be difficult, at best, but Consuelo did not dare challenge her mother. Clearly, Alva was in charge of the wedding: she did not even allow her daughter to choose her own bridesmaids.[20]

The Vanderbilt-Marlborough wedding created a great deal of interest, as it was the epitome of conspicuous consumption in the midst of elaborate Anglo-American weddings. In many ways, the printed press did much to sensationalize these marriages and almost glorified, only to later disparage, the American women who left the United States for the British aristocracy. To keep their readers informed of every minute detail concerning the bride and the wedding, the New York newspapers published frequent updates on the impending nuptials. The *Times* published an article discussing the bride's trousseau in detail—from the corsets, chemises, robe, low V-back gown, underskirts, to petticoats.[21] The British magazine *Punch* concluded, "not even the bride's underclothing is spared from publicity."[22] A week later, the *Times* presented the details of the wedding, including music, procession, and minister. The same article informed the public that the bride's family sent out nearly four thousand invitations for the church ceremony but had limited the breakfast following to two hundred people.[23] In late September, the *New York World* published a list describing Consuelo's physical characteristics: "Chin: pointed, indicating vivacity. . . . Eyebrows: Delicately arched. . . . Length of hand: six inches." And, as with other transatlantic marriages, the two most important numbers followed. "Waist measure: Twenty inches. . . . Marriage settlement: $10,000,000."[24]

The bride's tiny waist measurement and her father's vast fortune seemed to impress the public on both sides of the Atlantic more than any other pieces of information. But the Vanderbilt-Marlborough settlement exceeded that of any previous transatlantic marriage, illustrated by the fact that the final papers required the attendance of the reluctant couple, her father, the duke's counselor, Mr. Vanderbilt's lawyer, and a former judge.[25] William K. Vanderbilt conferred upon his new son-in-law some $2.5 million in fifty thousand shares of railroad stock, with a guaranteed annual payment of 4 percent. They agreed that should Sunny precede his wife in death, Consuelo would receive the interest. Her father also gave the couple £500,000 to buy a house on fashionable Curzon Street in London. In total, Sunny received approximately $15 million—in the currency of that period. But he apparently needed such funds, as the payroll of Blenheim Palace alone exceeded $100,000 per year.[26] Referring indirectly to the immense amounts of money and stature involved in this marriage, the *New York World* declared, "Miss Consuelo Vanderbilt is one of the greatest heiresses in America. The Duke of Marlborough is probably the most eligible peer in Great Britain.... From the standpoint of Fifth Avenue it will be the most desirable alliance ever made by an American heiress up to date."[27] Without a doubt, this marriage garnered a great deal of public attention as the means of the bride's "burnishing her husband's coronet."[28]

The *New York Times* incorrectly predicted, "The Vanderbilts, with their characteristic reserve, will avoid as much as possible the publicity that attached to an international match of such importance."[29] This author of this statement obviously did not know Alva Vanderbilt. Consuelo's marriage to Sunny was a spectacle even by New York standards. As fifty policemen patrolled the Vanderbilt mansion and twelve detectives attempted to hold back the growing crowd, a detailed article laid out the particulars for the wedding rehearsal.[30] Some two thousand spectators gathered to watch the event of the decade—which had brought a hasty end to the Newport social season—fully equipped with lunch bags and stools.[31] Curious eyes stared out from every window in the neighborhood toward the Vanderbilt home, with some eagerly staring through their opera glasses for a glimpse of the bride. The scene at the church was no different. The guest list read like a who's who of New York society and national government officials. Even President Grover Cleveland attended the ceremony, which caused the *London Times* to comment that he was "something more than a private individual, and his presence at an Anglo-American wedding is certainly something more than an expression of personal good-will."[32]

Amid such commotion and intense pressure, Consuelo despondently spent the morning of her wedding "in tears and alone; no one came near me. A footman had been posted at the door," so that she could not escape from the fate her mother had chosen for her.[33] Arriving twenty minutes late, Consuelo reluctantly married the Duke of Marlborough at St. Thomas Episcopal Church in New York City. She remembered that Sunny's "eyes were fixed in space," and she reportedly wept at the altar while taking her vows.[34] Despite their obvious and shared reluctance, the young couple married and attended a reception in their honor afterwards. But none of these ominous details were reported in papers on either side of the Atlantic. A London correspondent wrote that "no American or Anglo-American wedding ever excited so much interest among people of all sorts and conditions, nor was any such ceremony in this city ever so splendid and elaborate." He went on to report that if there were "any prejudices in this country against rank and wealth, or against the union of the two, they have on this occasion been suppressed. The marriage is extremely popular." Americans read about the event of the century while

Britons were told that the marriage "was celebrated with much splendor."[35] Despite the omissions, the truth was clear to the immediate families. When Conseulo and her new husband left for their honeymoon, she looked back longingly to her home and saw her mother, hiding behind a curtain but obviously in tears. Perhaps Alva finally realized what she had done, but it was too late. "And yet," Consuelo thought, "she had attained the goal she set herself, she has experienced the satisfactions wealth can confer, she has me in the niche she so early assigned me."[36]

The next day, the *New York Times* praised the bride, asserting, "No fairer or bonnier a young woman ever became the wife of a member of the house founded by England's great military commander." It described the wedding as "without exception the most magnificent ever celebrated in this country."[37] It certainly included all of the most negative stereotypes of Anglo-American marriages: a title-hunting American mother, a bankrupt duke, a loveless union. Similar to Lady Churchill before her, Consuelo Vanderbilt left her country and previous identity behind her upon her marriage. Although, like Lady Curzon, Consuelo expressed her undying love for "America and always shall," and she was "not quite sure that she will altogether like turning Englishwoman," the article warned, "although of course she must as an English peeress."[38] Formerly Miss Vanderbilt, as the newspapers now described her, Consuelo now became the Duchess of Marlborough.[39] The act of marrying Sunny transformed her into the wife of the 9th Duke of Marlborough.[40] Throughout her life, she would forever be identified in this capacity. Confirming her transformation and new identity, the *New York Times* reported, "She is now a Duchess."[41]

New Home, New Country, New Identity

If Consuelo's honeymoon served as an indicator of what her life in Britain would bring, she likely dreaded her eventual arrival. While on the train to Oakdale, the first stop in their four-month-long honeymoon, the Duke and Duchess of Marlborough read numerous congratulatory telegrams. The duchess received her first lesson in British class-consciousness through gauging the importance of each person by reading the manner in which the duke presented the telegram to her. "Unfortunately," the duchess remembered, "there was no silver platter on which to present Her Majesty Queen Victoria's missive, but it was read with due respect, and a sense of her intimidating presence crept into that distant railway car."[42]

While the duke finished reading the many telegraphs, the duchess felt the need to address one matter. Summoning the courage to speak candidly about the circumstances leading up to their marriage, she said, "I am sure that we shall both do our best to make the other happy, but there is something you must believe. Our marriage was my mother's idea, not mine." The duchess waited a moment before continuing. "She insisted on it, even though there was another man who wanted me. She made me turn him away." The duke stopped opening telegrams for a moment and looked at his wife. "Really?" he replied. "I take it he was an American. I don't see much point in discussing it any farther."[43] The couple never again discussed the prelude to their unfortunate union.

Over the next four months, they traveled widely, as renovations on Blenheim Palace would not be finished until March. Clearly, the Vanderbilt fortune was already being put to good use! The newlyweds left New York and began a European tour that would make any American heiress envious. They visited Spain, the French Riviera, Egypt, Italy, Cairo, Marseilles, and Paris. In early spring, they crossed the English Channel and headed for the duchess's new home in England. Before they reached the duke's home country, he gave his wife a copy of *Burke's Peerage,* a published guide to the British aristocracy, and instructed her to learn all the families, their titles, and their histories before they reached home. She remembered that her "husband spoke of some two hundred families whose lineage and whose ramifications, whose patronymics and whose titles I should have to learn." The duke had grown up within aristocratic circles and had known the various distinctions and titles from a very early age. Fulfilling this request, or, rather, order, was at the least challenging and at the most impossible. Her marriage had, unfortunately, not provided the duchess an escape from the demands of a harsh mother; rather, her husband had simply replaced her. Upon their arrival at London's Victoria Station, the duchess readied herself for her official presentation to a throng of the duke's relatives: Lady Blandford, her mother-in-law; Lillian and Norah, her sisters-in-law; Ivor Guest, a cousin; Lady Sarah Wilson, an aunt; Lady Randolph Churchill and Winston, now her cousins. Analogous to Mary Curzon, who yearned for the United States, the duchess suddenly felt homesick. "Like a deserted child," she later remembered, "I longed for my family."[44]

As the duke and duchess stepped off the train, the group awaiting their arrival began to talk in hushed voices and strange accents, which the duchess noted "I knew I should have to imitate. . . . I felt thankful that I had no nasal twang."[45] From the station, the group went to the family borough of Woodstock, where some twenty thousand sightseers gathered in hopes of catching a glance of the new duchess. A red carpet emerged, on which the mayor stood with other dignitaries of the town to greet them. A crowd sat down to lunch together, and as the *Illustrated London News* described, "the day closed amidst brilliant illuminations and general rejoicings." The duchess, however, "felt distraught . . . with a wild desire to be alone."[46]

Another formal gathering followed that evening at dinner, but only the Marlborough family were in attendance. Not surprisingly, dinner discussion turned to the United States, and the duchess's new family began commenting at length on America and Americans. Lady Blandford did not share her son's disdain for Americans, but she was quite ignorant of the United States and its citizens.[47] She made a number of comments that revealed to the duchess that she believed that all Americans "lived on plantations with Negro slaves and there were Red Indians ready to scalp us just round the corner." Another dinner guest expressed his inability to understand the war between North and South America. When told that such a war had never occurred, he answered indignantly, "Oh yes, [it] did. It was in 1861."[48] The duchess retired to bed that evening at a complete loss for what she had experienced in the previous several hours.

The next morning, the Duchess of Marlborough met her husband's grandmother, the dowager duchess, who closely inspected her new granddaughter by marriage before explaining what she expected in the coming years. At the top of the list, the dowager duchess candidly expressed her wish "to see Blenheim restored to its former glories and the prestige of the family upheld." The young duchess took this to mean that she expected a certain level of behavior from the American who had joined their ranks. The duchess could never forget what followed: the dowager duchess locked eyes on the duchess and explained in no uncertain terms, "Your first duty is to have a child and it must be a son, because it would be intolerable to have that little upstart Winston become Duke." She then inquired of the young woman she had just met, "Are you in the family way?"[49] Clearly, the Marlborough family had three expectations of this dubious American girl: a behavior becoming a duchess, the restoration of Blenheim Palace, and the production of "an heir and a spare," in quick order. The duke had married, and renovations had begun; thus, the time had come to beget a son.[50]

Like Lady Curzon, Consuelo quickly felt pressured to become pregnant with a boy, as both sides of the duke's family needed sons to maintain the family line. When she met him, the duke's uncle looked the duchess up and down and then asserted, "I see the future Churchills will be both tall and good-looking." The duchess had arrived at her new home one day before, and, as she recalled, several family members had already expressed their concern "with the immediate necessity of an heir to the dukedom, and were infecting me with their anxiety."[51] For years, the dowager duchess complained that Consuelo did not understand the importance of her position.[52] But like the American-born, British-wed brides before her, she eventually found a way to meet and exceed the British expectations of her Anglo-American shoulders.

Closely related to these demanding obligations was an intense level of British class-consciousness that she had not experienced as an American. First, the duchess paid official visits to all of Marlborough's family, then country neighbors, and finally the tenant farmers on the estate. Echoing the presentation of congratulatory telegrams on their honeymoon, a clear sense of the importance of the persons based on their position within the hierarchy of the borough dictated the length and formality of each visit. Some families genuinely wanted to meet the new American duchess, but others simply wanted to earn favor with the Marlborough family and had no real interest in Consuelo herself. But of all the people she met in paying these calls, the duchess greatly enjoyed her time with the farmers and came to admire them as hard workers and trusted friends. But each time she returned to Blenheim, indirect but frequent references to her wealth and reproductive capabilities reminded her of her duty as a duchess and to the family. Even as her new family members unofficially demanded her fortune for the refurbishment of the place, they never allowed her to participate in planning such renovations; they simply expected the rich American heiress to finance it without question. Additionally, the Marlboroughs regularly reminded her just how fortunate she was to have become one of them, while hinting just as frequently that her American-ness was not a point in her favor. The duchess found their collective British belief in their own class-based superiority confounding.[53] "But in time I learned," she recalled, "that snobbishness was an enthroned fetish which spreads its tentacles into every stratum of British national life."[54]

The one advantage to the duchess's so-called Americanness was Lady Churchill. Consuelo's arrival at Blenheim, and the eventual birth of her sons, ended any chance of Winston becoming the Duke of Marlborough. Yet, Lady Churchill never treated the duchess with contempt but rather served as her protector and counselor. In later years, the duchess confided to Lady Churchill about her failing marriage; when Consuelo became the Duchess of Marlborough Lady Churchill had twenty years of marital and British experience. Understandably, the two American women became quite close. While Lady Churchill appeared to adapt quite well to British life, the duchess never fully adjusted to her surroundings at Blenheim and what she found a staid, stuffy, and snobbish atmosphere. While she had mastered the social complexities and hierarchical games in the United States and in France, she always regarded the class-obsessed British version as full of hypocrisies, later describing it as "a society whose conventions were closer to the eighteenth century than to the twentieth century."[55]

The one area through which Consuelo enjoyed a degree of autonomy was the Woodstock community. Had she married a rich American man and stayed in the United States, her desire to participate in charitable organizations or assist her husband if he entered politics would have received disapproval. But in Britain, as the wife of the Duke of Marlborough, she had a nearly endless stream of opportunities to enter the public sphere by either assisting her husband if he were in politics or by performing good deeds on a local level. Again, this type of traditional women's work was acceptable for elite British women, but it also provided American brides with a degree of freedom and opportunity to create an identity

ostensibly independent from their British husbands. Having enjoyed a lifetime of
affluence, Consuelo pursued charitable work with the needy. She enjoyed visiting the poor and reading to the blind at the almshouses. The Marlboroughs had
long supported the local poor from a distance, but the duchess's physical presence and sincere desire to interact with and aid the destitute within Woodstock
was a first. Blenheim Palace had long distributed containers of its leftover food,
just crammed into tins. It occurred to the Duchess that simply separating meat,
vegetables, and desserts into separate containers would be a thoughtful gesture.[56]
As hard as she tried, Consuelo rarely pleased her British family, but the poor absolutely adored her compassionate methods of soft power.

Like her new friend and American compatriot Lady Churchill, Consuelo found
ways to negotiate her American identity within the repressive world of aristocratic Britain. When Lady Churchill organized the American Amazons, Consuelo
quickly joined the cause. While American-born, British-wed women had been active for some years, this marked the first time that individual American women
living in Britain had identified themselves collectively. The group, which let affluent women enjoy some level of freedom and meaningful interaction with other
women from their homeland, was Consuelo's first venture into philanthropy. At
this point in her life, Consuelo had little knowledge of charitable committees or
fund-raising. In fact, Lady Churchill's sister Clara described her as "about the most
useless member of all."[57] In any case, the group gave her "a glimpse of what could
be done by deploying American energy and English aristocratic connections."[58]

Just as Lady Churchill had discovered she could use her American identity to
her advantage, Consuelo began to hone her ability to negotiate her British and
American identities. Over the next several years, she discovered that she could
manipulate her national identity depending on the circumstance. When she did
something that found favor with the Marlboroughs, she praised her British family.
To an increasing degree, she sought to diminish her American identity on a public level, but like Lady Curzon, she never denied or disparaged her home country.
Over time, the Duchess of Marlborough learned to maintain both identities but
recognized when to downplay or amplify one over the other.[59] After several years
of marriage, she had endeared herself to Lady Blandford, who once praised her,
"I must tell you that no one would take you for an American." Consuelo quickly
answered, "I suppose you mean that as a compliment, Lady Blandford, but what
would you think if I said you were not at all like an Englishwoman?" Lady Blandford explained that *that* was quite a different situation, to which Consuelo replied, "Different to you, but not to me."[60] An Englishwoman by marriage, like
Mary Leiter, Consuelo remained proud of her democratic American heritage.[61]
But while Lady Curzon kept virtually silent about it on all but a few occasions,
the Duchess of Marlborough, slowly and cautiously, found a way to balance her

two identities simultaneously without alienating either country. Increasingly, she spoke up for herself and her homeland.

Consuelo found even more favor with her British family when she gave birth to a son on September 18, 1897. The duke and duchess named him John Albert William Spencer-Churchill, but he always went by "Blandford," his family title. The *New York Times* reported the birth under the headline "Consuelo, the American Duchess, Gives Birth to a Son."[62] Approximately a year later, the American duchess produced "the spare," when she gave birth to her second son, Ivor, on October 14, 1898. Again, the *Times* carried word of the birth to its American readers: "Second Child Born to the Duke and His American Wife, Formerly Consuelo Vanderbilt."[63] The press and the public never missed an opportunity to celebrate "our duchess" and noted her gifts to her sons of her "wonderful heritage of American spirit, American courage and American wealth."[64] And papers on both sides of the Atlantic continued to confirm the duchess's former identity. As a duchess, she was the wife of a duke and mother of the future duke, though consistently identified as the former Miss Vanderbilt.[65]

Consuelo visited the United States for the first time after her marriage during the fall of 1902. She spent only a month there, but the *New York Times* happily reported that "her seven years as one of the leaders of the British aristocracy has in no way changed her American spirit."[66] At the same time, she had developed into a leading woman in British society, largely due to her increasing interests and participation in philanthropic activities. As her public life thrived, however, her private life crumbled. Consuelo saw herself and the duke as "people of different temperament condemned to live together."[67] They picked on each other in public and criticized each other to friends and family, thus breaking a rule of aristocratic marriages. Tradition required marriage, and custom permitted adultery, but problems remained private. Above all, divorce was never acceptable. In 1906, the duke and duchess finally separated, driving a wedge between Consuelo and Lady Churchill and for a short time between her and King Edward, long fond of American heiresses and particularly Consuelo. Lady Churchill believed that even if the duke and duchess did have problems, they should simply spend more time traveling and away from one another, as she had done in her marriage to Lord Randolph Churchill. Likewise, King Edward announced that neither of them would be welcome in his presence and that he would not attend any function if either was present. Thus, a great deal of pressure fell on the Duke and Duchess of Marlborough to stay married, if only in name.[68] But neither party had ever wanted to marry the other, and neither felt the need to acquiesce to others' suggestions now.

"A Credit to Her Country"

Shortly after her separation from her husband, Consuelo went to live in Sunderland House on Curzon Street in London, a house her father had built for her a year earlier, which served as her base for the next decade.[69] Early the next year, Consuelo made another trip to the United States, which was announced in the *New York Times*. Although she likely wanted to spend some time with her family, she had another reason for coming home now. For at least part of her stay, the duchess lived at the Martha Washington hostel for women, to gain first-hand knowledge of women in poverty and how best to help them.[70] As she took an increasing interest in philanthropy, the Progressive Era in the United States influenced her activities in Britain as she participated in and learned from both American and British forms of charity. In Britain, society expected aristocratic women to support philanthropic work, but this generally meant that they donated a great deal of money in lieu of their own time or work. Such "traditional political tasks of patronage, [and] networking, . . . often fell to the female members of the family."[71] But with the participation of her mother, who had become a leading force in the burgeoning Progressive movement in her home country, specifically in regard to woman's suffrage, Consuelo had an opportunity to learn from women leading philanthropic movements in both of her countries. Her experiences in each country allowed her to convey organizational styles and fund-raising techniques as something of a transatlantic Lady Bountiful. Given her notable standing in both countries, the press in each followed her international efforts and philanthropic activities.

Consuelo's philanthropic leadership began in earnest after she separated from her husband. The pair agreed to share custody of their two sons, but several private nurses and nannies tended to the boys' daily upbringing. This Victorian approach to childrearing allowed the duchess to pursue her own activities, and after their separation this freedom meant an increasing participation in and direct leadership of charitable causes. King Edward had closed the door of London's social circles to the American duchess, but she did not respond by mourning her lack of invitations to dinner parties and balls. She had had her fill of such social activities since the age of sixteen. "A purely social life had no appeal" to Consuelo at nearly thirty years old, and she looked for something more substantial to fill her time.[72] Having enjoyed a life of fine clothes, beautiful houses, and ample wealth, she wanted to spend her fortune not on tea parties and trips to Paris but rather on a number of personal projects aimed at helping the poor and disadvantaged. Over time, she shifted the focus of her philanthropic missions to help women specifically.

While some may dismiss the duchess's efforts as little more than "emotional therapy for an unhappy aristocrat" or an attempt to reinstate "her social position after a much-discussed marital breakdown," her involvement in charitable works went far beyond simply writing a check or lending her name to an institution. She donated her money and time and the leadership skills she had learned as an American Amazon to address major problems that affected Britons overall and women especially. This practice of serious philanthropy has earned the attention of scholars: Amanda Mackenzie Stuart asserts, "Historians have re-examined nineteenth- and early-twentieth-century female philanthropy and come to see it as an important factor both in an extension of female power in general and the campaign for the vote in particular."[73] Women used "philanthropy as an entry point into *public* life without agitating conservative elements because it was seen as an extension of their role as wives and mothers and, in the case of rich or aristocratic women, as part of their traditional role."[74] Consuelo's philanthropic works were not an attempt to reestablish her membership in London society; she genuinely cared about changing the lives of the women, children, and the poor. She did not merely show up in an inner-London slum, announce that she planned to bestow ample money on the poor, and walk away. Rather, exhibiting great courage and unprecedented personal dedication, she earned trust over time by working directly with disadvantaged people on a daily basis and, through kind deeds rather than disdainful donations, the equivalent of soft power, proved her sincerity.

Consuelo's first charitable exercise came at the invitation of Prebendary Wilson Carlile, the head of the Church Army. Originally established in 1882, the Church Army hoped to reconnect the Church of England with the working-class men and women of inner-city London. Together, Carlile and the duchess leased two adjoining houses in London and established a Home for Prisoners' Wives. The home, which opened in May 1907, provided the wives of first offenders laundry and sewing rooms and a chance to earn a standard wage, thereby giving them a degree of financial independence, the importance of which Consuelo realized after her own divorce. The women worked while their children played in the day nursery next door. Consuelo, who argued that "to be punished for the guilt of others is essentially unfair," closed every day with a prayer. This endeavor gave her a great deal of hands-on management experience and earned her recognition as the new Lady Churchill in London. Like Lady Curzon in India, she put a great deal of effort into health and medical improvements for women—an act of soft power, as the British public found themselves under the American-born, British-wed spell of attraction. Consuelo now became *the* Anglo-American woman in Britain.

By establishing herself as a ready leader and financially able philanthropist, the Duchess of Marlborough now received a barrage of invitations and requests from other benevolent groups. Invited to serve on the National Birth Rate Commission, she worked as a lay member with "a conclave of clergy, doctors, eugenists, economists, and social workers," who investigated the declining birthrate in Britain. "The men, who predominated, maintained that the declining birthrate in the middle classes was entirely due to the higher education of women," Consuelo re-membered, "an argument so conspicuously prejudiced that I immediately deter-mined to champion the cause."[75] In response, she made a mental note of another cause that needed her support: birth control for wives and mothers.[76] Rather than simply focusing on the declining birthrate and supporting the masculine need to blame the education of women, Consuelo sought to provide free prenatal and in-fant care to the poor. In 1916, she delivered the Lady Priestley Memorial Lecture to the National Health Society; the first woman to give the lecture, she spoke on the annual mortality rate in Britain. According to the *New York Times,* the "former Miss Vanderbilt" stressed that the 320,000 babies lost every year surpassed the number of Britons killed in World War I.[77] Notably, her Anglo-American identity influenced her views; her concern was not only for women and children, rather, as "a supporter of racial theories, she spoke out publicly for the need to preserve and increase the Anglo-Saxon stock of the world." Many of the American-born, British-wed women shared this personal identification as Anglo-Saxon and belief in its supremacy and common destiny. To Consuelo, Christian ethics dictated "the preservation of infant life," provided that that child was an Anglo-Saxon life.[78] Like her predecessor Lady Churchill, Consuelo enjoyed philanthropic activities center-ing on Anglo-Saxon ideals, which contributed indirectly to a closing of the gap between the United States and Great Britain.

Taking what she had learned in Britain, Consuelo traveled to the United States in 1908 and spoke at a dinner at the Waldorf-Astoria Hotel. Returning to her "native land deeply impressed with the civic service English men and women so wholeheartedly gave their country," Consuelo felt "an obligation to tell [her] coun-trywomen what [she] had learned."[79] Unofficially designated a nongovernmen-tal envoy between her two countries, Consuelo asserted in her speech that "rich American [women] were idle . . . [and that] they should follow the example of their English counterparts to make a useful contribution to society." Serving as an Anglo-American liaison, she challenged her audience, "Is it not possible for the women citizens of this great Republic to recognize that personal obligation on its ethical ba-sis and to turn it to account in practical works?"[80] Not all Americans took kindly to the duchess's advice. The next day, the New York newspapers ran headlines reading "Consuelo in Dinner Talk Criticizes U.S. Women," and "Duchess of Marlborough Delivers an Eloquent Speech." Articles below each headline presented verbatim re-ports of her lecture.[81]

After returning to Britain, Consuelo edited her American speech into three articles that appeared under the title "The Position of Women," published in the *North American Review* in the spring of 1909.[82] The articles gave her an opportu-nity to reflect on her philanthropic achievements and personal views on the role and duty of affluent Anglo-American women. Through her frequent trips to the

United States, Consuelo observed that, when compared with her experiences as a woman abroad, rich American women's lives were incredibly empty. Appalled by their "vapid and meaningless, starved and bored" lives, she reflected that her life in Britain had given her the opportunity to accomplish great things. She confided to her mother, "In spite of all that has happened I am glad I married an English-man."[83] One should note, however, that only after her separation from the duke did Consuelo begin her philanthropic life wholeheartedly and redirect the Vanderbilt fortune toward her new independence and ambassadorial identity. Nevertheless, none of these endeavors would have occurred without her marriage.

Becoming ever more concerned about the lives of women, Consuelo continued her philanthropic quest in Britain. Her next project forever tied her to the former American vicereine of India. The Mary Curzon Lodging House for Poor Women, which Consuelo established in 1914, gave working girls a home and a hospital for women only, staffed by female physicians.[84] Providing women with medical care practiced by women echoed Lady Curzon's efforts in India. Along the same lines, in an effort to curtail the traffic of women as "white slaves" to overseas brothels, Consuelo identified potential donors for the Young Women's Christian Associa-tion and Sunderland House.[85] This type and level of personal philanthropy did much to shape the perception of Consuelo specifically and American women overall as dedicated, caring, and focused individuals who had much to offer Brit-ons, and women especially, beyond their fortunes as heiresses.

In addition to engaging in philanthropic activities on behalf of women, the duchess accepted the post of honorary treasurer of Bedford College, a women's college in London. As a supporter of higher education for women, she became the college's primary fundraiser and quickly secured a "magnificent donation of 100,000 guineas . . . [,] which enabled the college to be moved from its cramped quarters in Baker Street to a beautiful site in Regent's Park."[86] Consuelo believed educating girls would result in women being better mothers, and thus produce and care for healthier children, all of which fell neatly under the category of tra-ditional women's work. When asked why she believed Englishmen objected so strongly to the education of their daughters and sisters, she replied, "There must be some secret fear that, hard as they found it to understand a woman now, it would be absolutely beyond their ken were she highly educated."[87]

Continuing her fight to improve women's lives, in 1913 Consuelo attempted "to do something about the shameful conditions under which women worked in the sweated industries."[88] Working with Winston Churchill, she sought a minimum wage for such women, a personal and political cause illustrative of "how she used her status at the top of the ladder to combat social evil at its foot."[89] Further, in November she organized a conference and invited a number of influential Brit-ons who likely thought they would spend an afternoon lamenting the terrible lives of such women, make a modest donation to the cause, and be on their way. Little did they know that Consuelo had invited twelve women to give testimony regarding their lives "bearing the yoke of industrial slavery in its cruelest form."[90] Rather than allow her fellow aristocrats to converse ignorantly about such situations, Consuelo brought the victims to the forefront and demanded that their lives receive the attention from the very people who could force change in Britain. As a result of the so-called Sunderland House Conference, eight more sweated industries became eligible for the trade boards in London.

In the midst of the duchess's many charitable activities, she wrote an article titled "Hostels for Women," published in a leading journal of the period. In the editorial, the Duchess called Britons' attention to "the necessity of providing clean and respectable lodgings for working women . . . and suggested an extension of the system of municipal lodging-houses at present provided for men of a similar class." She exclaimed that in the entire country of England, only Manchester provided "respectable accommodation for women." Knowing firsthand the value of independence, she argued that providing them the opportunity to live on their own, work, and pay for their own lodging gave women "the pride of decent self-support—the love of liberty—the satisfaction of standing alone—unaided." She ended her article by asserting that the most critical years in a young woman's life, between thirteen and twenty, determined the course of the rest of her life, something she knew all too well. She pressed national and local agencies to come together in an effort to provide "respectable lodgings . . . so that the self-respecting woman worker shall be at least as fairly treated as the self-supporting man."[91] Thus, Consuelo had turned her philanthropic activities toward the pursuit of women's rights, later to include women's suffrage. Like many women before her, she used the traditional avenue of philanthropy to make a political statement.[92] In the years to come, this Anglo-American woman would take on an increasingly prominent role in British politics.

Continuing with her political passions, Consuelo served in 1913 as a delegate to the International Women's Suffrage Alliance Convention in Budapest, Hungary. The conference had a significant effect on her views of suffrage. Afterward, she traveled to the United States and participated in a meeting hosted by the Political Equality Association. As she traveled across the Atlantic with growing frequency, her journeys increasingly mimicked a traditional ambassador's. Although Alva Vanderbilt, Consuelo's mother, viewed suffrage in terms of human rights, Consuelo considered the right to vote an appendage of citizenship and "a privilege for which women should prepare and educate themselves."[93] The *New York Times* quoted the "Former Consuelo Vanderbilt," in New York on yet another trip to support the suffrage movement as supporting suffrage, though not militant suffragists.[94] While many people saw her activities strictly as those of a woman helping other women, she quickly corrected them. In a statement that eerily foreshadowed

Secretary of State Hillary Clinton's demand a century later to see "women's rights as human rights once and for all," Consuelo announced, "This is the age of feminism . . . [but] not so much feminism as humanism."[95]

Because of all of her efforts as an informal ambassador, the American duchess simultaneously endeared herself to her new countrymen, maintained an admiring public in the United States, and relied on a "wide circle of aristocratic and American friends in her philanthropic ventures," which allowed her to "reinforce friendships and open up new vistas."[96] In the decade or so since her marriage, she had spent approximately $2 million of her own American inheritance supporting her charitable British interests, thus investing her Anglo-American self permanently on both sides of the Atlantic.[97] Through her traditionally female and increasingly ambassadorial efforts, she managed to win over the hearts and minds of both Americans and Britons. She had earned the love and respect of the Blenheim tenants while making the palace itself livable. She had hosted a number of weekend parties, "which are never wholly American and never wholly English, but a blending of the two," which met with great success.[98] According to Mary Curzon, Consuelo was "a triumph & she must be a nice woman . . . [and] the best brought up young woman we've seen for many a day. . . . [H]er simplicity and brightness have won her a great position." Even Mary's husband, George, praised Consuelo: "She never pushes herself and everyone tries to know her & entertain her. . . . She is everything that is nice."[99] Consuelo had succeeded Lady Churchill as the leader of the American-born, British-wed colony of women in London, but her growing notoriety grated on her husband's nerves. Bewildered by her popularity, he asked, "Philanthropist, Patriot Yank, Beauty, the used wife, what else!!!"[100] Even her in-laws took her side over the duke's in their very public separation.[101] Based on all of her efforts in English communities, a contemporary magazine remarked of Consuelo, "The Duchess? Oh, she's a *credit* to her country."[102]

American Women's War Relief Effort

Consuelo learned a great deal from being an American Amazon and engaging in her own philanthropic projects; she needed this sort of knowledge and experience especially after World War I began in the fall of 1914. During the war, she led three different groups, all composed of women and all aimed at relieving Great Britain from the strains of war. The American Women's War Relief Effort was originally conceived in November 1898, when twenty-five American women gathered for tea and discussed the idea of bringing "together [an] organized group [called] the Women of America resident in London."[103] Over the next six months, the women created such a group and in May 1899 officially founded the "Society of

American Women in London." They held their first luncheon in the spring, which some seventy-nine women attended, a gathering that promoted an individual and collective identity of these women as a validated and viable unit that could promote improved understanding and relations within the Anglo-American world. The society kept its name until 1916, when the members voted to change it to the "American Women's Club." This evolving group contributed significantly to aid the British war effort by working across national lines fully three years before the United States entered the war.[104] Formally and informally, their liaison status between their two countries certainly earned them recognition as ambassadors.

The group drew upon the increasing numbers of American-born, British-wed women living in England. The loose but established organization of an Anglo-American elite network on both sides of the Atlantic was already identified by Lady Churchill's transatlantic publication, both Mary Chamberlain's and Mary Curzon's correspondence and activities, and the Duchess of Marlborough's philanthropic efforts. According to its constitution, "the object of the Society is to promote Social intercourse between American women, and to bring together women who are engaged in literary, artistic, scientific, and philanthropic pursuits," all of which had occurred formally and informally under the hundreds of American-born, British-wed women and the hundreds of American-born, British-wed women they represented. The constitution provided numerous articles and bylaws, including a lengthy list of standing and house rules.[105]

Membership in the society required a formal application and that one or both parents of the applicant be "of American birth and an American citizen, . . . unless the candidate for membership, if of foreign parentage, was born in America and lived there until the age of 21," with the exception of Honorary Members. Membership did not require permanent residency in England, a departure from previous efforts and groups, such as the American Amazons. But as the president of the society, Jeannie T. Comings reported in 1914, "the great majority of Americans in London are the wives of businessmen who come to represent American firms, and come without Social introductions, and who—strangers in a foreign land, are very grateful for the American hospitality, and the American atmosphere which we have tried to create in a little bit of London." The society gathered its original membership from the American Amazons and quickly increased its numbers and organizational hierarchy in its first years of existence. By 1908, it had numerous officers—including president; first, second, and third vice presidents; executive committee chair; ex officio members of executive committee; recording and corresponding secretaries (both with assistants); treasurer (with an assistant); and auditor—and various committees such as house, reception, membership, music, art, education, philanthropy, and visiting. Society members were categorized as "honorary," "foreign," "town," and "country." Clearly, the society had grown a great deal since Lady Churchill's days as leader of the American Amazons. Its complex and intricate hierarchy speaks to its overall growth in scope, participants' contributions, and expectations.[106]

While Lady Churchill was an active member, the transatlantic torch had passed to Consuelo, the new leader of the Anglo-American community in the years that preceded World War I. At the society's eleventh anniversary luncheon, where the attendees sang both "God Save the King" and "My Country 'Tis of Thee," she served as the guest speaker.[107] She titled her speech "The Need for Cooperation Amongst Women," appropriate, given the increasingly visible face of the American woman in England.[108] With the outbreak of World War I, the Duchess of Marlborough became a major leader of London's transatlantic community.[109]

Another new leader of Anglo-American women emerged in London shortly before war began in the summer of 1914. As vice president of the Society, Lou Henry Hoover, the wife of future president Herbert Hoover, became president in May 1914, following the sudden death of the current president's husband, Consul General John L. Griffiths. Notified of her new position by telegram at her home in Palo Alto, California, Lou relocated to London in December and remained there for several years. Because of her extensive travels with her husband, and to London specifically, she had joined the society in 1908, eager to meet other American women and participate in its charitable and social activities. But the society's social attraction was replaced by more serious concerns following the outbreak of war in 1914. In the first two months of the war alone, it aided over twelve hundred unaccompanied women traveling in Great Britain. By 1916, it had arranged for the safe return of some twenty-six thousand women to the United States.[110] Already familiar with the realities of war and necessities of relief work, Lou decided to refashion the society as a largely philanthropic, rather than social, organization. In 1915, she wrote, the "only way I could consent to take on the work as President [was to] turn all fees and dues . . . into philanthropic work . . . [as] one cannot ask anyone to join a social club in these times."[111] Consuelo now had an American counterpart in London, and their shared liaison status established their transatlantic leadership and informal diplomatic presence.

When World War I began, the Society of American Women in London established a purely charitable organization under its supervision, the American Women's War Relief Fund (AWWRF). The AWWRF served as a subagency exclusively dedicated to relieving military and civilian ailments due to the war. A longtime member of the society and chair of its philanthropic committee, the Duchess of Marlborough was a natural choice to lead this new initiative.[112] As an American who married into the British peerage, she provided the organization a greater degree of authority and notoriety than it likely would have received under other leadership. Together, Lou Henry Hoover, the American, and the duchess, now a Briton, led their two interdependent and truly transnational organizations.

In response to this development, Lady Churchill remarked, "it is a source of pride to me personally that the women of America have proved . . . that their hearts are always ready to respond to the call of suffering humanity."[113]

Under the society's philanthropic umbrella, the AWWRF established numerous committees focused on wartime issues. Its Executive Committee counted among its members the Duchess of Marlborough, Lady Randolph Churchill, Lou Henry Hoover, Mrs. Reginald Owen (William Jennings Bryan's daughter, who had married a Briton), and Mrs. Walter Hines Page (the wife of the current American ambassador to the United Kingdom, 1913–18) who spearheaded the AWWRF, which supervised a range of committees.[114] Owing to her experience with the American Amazons, Lady Churchill served as chair of the Hospital Committee, which originally opened an American Women's Hospital at Oldway House at Paignton, the private home of an American businessman, and a second American Women's Hospital for Officers at Lancaster Gate as "a further expression of the sympathy felt for Great Britain by American women."[115] It also managed and equipped ambulances for the army.[116] This particular committee worked closely with the American Red Cross and its commissioner for Great Britain, William Endicott, the brother of Mary Endicott, widow of Joseph Chamberlain; thus, the Anglo-American network publically identified by Lady Churchill and enhanced by the transnational correspondence of Mary Chamberlain and Lady Curzon proved most valuable at this diplomatic crossroads. Additionally, these women took classes sponsored by the AWWRF in basic first aid: bone-setting, compound fractures versus dislocations, and the dangers of sepsis.[117] The Duchess of Marlborough chaired the Economic Relief Committee, which included the clothing committee and knitting factory committee. Overall, the committee helped the British people adapt as the economy shifted from peacetime to wartime, especially in the production of military provisions. The war caused the unemployment of many women, as nonmilitary factories closed around the country, and, in an effort to provide jobs and income to these women, who were "quite without resources of any kind," the Economic Relief Committee opened a knitting factory in Islington, an exceedingly poor area of London.[118] By January 1915, the society and AWWRF were hailed as "this new Angel of Islington."[119] The Clothing Committee, also under the Economic Relief Committee, made direct requests to the United States for "suiteable [sic] clothing" for "England's poor" and "better class people, both English and American, [who] have suffered greatly in the present crisis and in desperate straits . . . in which to pursue their professions." The committee specifically requested "odd quantities of wool [as] any quality or colour are most useful."[120] Finally, the Collection Committee boasted the most members, not surprisingly, as it was responsible for fundraising efforts.[121] In the *American Bulletin*, the committee solicited and advertised donations made by Americans, with a list of subscribers similar to the ones listed in the *Anglo-Saxon Review*. Published free of

charge by the Committee of Americans Resident in London, the *Bulletin* provided a
list of sailing dates to the United States, changing passport regulations during wartime, and other notices pertinent to Americans in London. Overall, it acted as a
reliable source of information for travelers during World War I.[122] The influence of
and work by the hundreds of American-born, British-wed women who now lived
abroad now reached a new apex.

In 1916, midway through the war, the society voted to change its name to the
American Women's Club, dropping the word "society" and any indication that the
group was primarily socially inclined during a time of war. At this point, the American Women's Club and the AWWRF managed some ten committees and claimed
more than two hundred active members.[123] In 1917, when the United States finally
entered the war, in an effort to address the expansion of wartime ills, the American Women's Club and the AWWRF created additional committees—including
the Convalescent Home Committee, the American Citizens Relief Committee, the
American Benevolence Committee, and the American Care Committee for Soldiers and Sailors.[124] The reach of the Anglo-American cohort seemed to grow almost daily.

By 1917, Hoover trusted in the capable leadership of the American Women's
Club and the AWWRF; she submitted her resignation as president shortly before
the war's end. After three long years of relief work, she looked forward to her
return to the United States; she had not seen her two young sons in many years—
something Consuelo could empathize with fully. In January 1917, she sailed back
to California. Her longtime compatriot, the American Duchess of Marlborough,
now led the AWWRF.

The duchess supervised an American-sponsored military hospital of four hundred beds in Devonshire and arranged for a contingent of nurses from New York
to staff it.[125] Related to her supervision of the Devonshire hospital, the duchess also
became the honorary treasurer, another term for chief fundraiser, for the Medical
School for Women at the Royal Free Hospital in London.[126] By 1915, many Britons
offered the British War Office their homes to serve as additional hospitals for the
sick and wounded. Noting the need for labor and birthing wards in hospitals, as
obstetric wings were largely neglected during the war, the duchess transformed the
British Home for Prisoners' Wives into a labor and delivery annex for the Royal
Free Hospital. Her continued interests in helping women and children earned her
the nickname "Baby Duchess."[127]

The duchess also oversaw the Woman's Emergency Corps, which coordinated
the employment of women to fill men's jobs in factories and in offices as they left to
fight the war. These included everything from caring for horses and feeding Belgian
refugees to making toys to replace those once imported from Germany.[128] A few
days after the war broke out, the duchess made a request for volunteers to fill men's

tasks. Following her solicitation, "ten thousand offers of personal service were received from doctors, dispensers, trained nurses, interpreters and others . . . while bus drivers and sportswomen who understood the care of horses volunteered to assist in transport work."[129] Her reach across British class lines and wartime categories appeared limitless.

Finally, a Committee of Mercy emerged as another means by which Americans aided Britons during the war. In October 1914, the *New York Times* ran an article explaining that the "former Consuelo Vanderbilt" had requested funds to relieve women and children in Great Britain. In a few short weeks, her homeland had donated more than $180,000, whose thanks the duchess diplomatically telegraphed, "War refugees' committee delighted to hear of movement in America to aid destitute. Your assistance gladly received."[130] Even though the newspapers constantly identified her as the *former* Miss Vanderbilt, Americans responded to *their* American duchess's call for help in the midst of war.

The duchess continued her work with the American Women's Club and the AWWRF until the end of World War I, at which time the relief agency was dissolved.[131] The sheer scope and size of the AWWRF demonstrates the increasing complexity of the transnational work of American women in Great Britain. Their numbers and efforts grew steadily as international conflicts in Latin America, Africa, and Europe presented opportunities to work across national boundaries and patriotic lines. The AWWRF rested on the foundational work of individuals such as Lady Churchill, the Duchess of Marlborough, and Lou Henry Hoover; the network established by the *Anglo-Saxon Review;* the vast correspondence of Mary Chamberlain and Lady Curzon; and the collective labors of the American Amazons. After the war, the American Women's Club continued its philanthropic efforts but also reinstated its social purpose.[132] The war's end terminated the need for the relief fund, but the transatlantic organization continues today.

The Political Duchess

In addition to her philanthropic and war efforts, the "former Consuelo Vanderbilt of New York" founded the Women's Municipal Party in 1913. This party attempted to interest women in municipal affairs within London and promoted the election of women in local government so they could address issues concerning women and children in London. Her political career, though it was short, reflected her years of philanthropic interest in England. As the party's mission statement put it, "We want for our women and children reform in housing, to include cheap, decent municipal hostels for women, such as are provided for men, and education reforms, to include grants for play centres and gardens and the utilization of waste spaces. We want a great number of women inspectors in all municipal services, supervision of women of the female wards of lunatic asylums, inebriate homes for women, day nurseries and baby farms, and better administration of children's acts."[133]

The Women's Municipal Party rewarded Consuelo's efforts on behalf of women and children after the war, asking the "Baby Duchess" to run for the London County Council.[134] Already popular among the poor, she easily attracted large crowds to her campaign appearances, with young children singing "Vote Vote Vote for Mrs. Marlborough," to the tune of "Tramp Tramp Tramp the Boys Are Marching."[135] Even the *Manchester Guardian* supported her candidacy, reporting that she was "the most energetic of all our duchesses," knowledgeable in issues of child welfare, working women, and local politics.[136] She also had earned the respect of the working-class voters. Additionally, many English women had earned the right to vote in January 1918, two years before their American sisters, which came as something of a surprise to both countries. Given these two voting blocs, she successfully won the election in March 1919, which made her the first woman to ever serve on the council.[137] Unfortunately, her term was brief. The marriage that had first brought her to England and made all of her efforts and activities possible also ended her time as the public face of Anglo-American women.

Life under Three Flags

In 1920, the duke and duchess began a series of legal battles that revealed Britain's depth of social ostracism for divorcees. Their official divorce forever placed Consuelo and Sunny outside social circles in England and ended Consuelo's political career.[138] The two received a divorce in May 1921 and then in 1926 annulled their marriage after her mother, more than twenty years after the fact, testified that she had forced her daughter to marry the duke.[139] Following their divorce, both remarried. He wed Gladys Deacon, another American woman, in the summer following the divorce, but it too was an unhappy marriage. Consuelo married Jacques Balsan, a French aviator, that same summer, on July 4, an auspicious choice for a wedding date, marking a union that would tie the American duchess with none of the oppression that colored her first marriage.[140] On her second marriage certificate, Consuelo listed her profession as "Duchess of Marlborough." Few would have argued that her position in Britain was not an occupation.[141]

For the rest of their life together, Consuelo and Jacques split their time among Paris, Southampton, New York, and south Florida and enjoyed a very happy marriage.[142] Even after she became Madame Jacques Balsan, American newspapers continued to identify her as the former Consuelo Vanderbilt.[143] Her second husband died at the age of eighty-eight in 1956.[144] Nearly a decade later, at the age of eighty-seven, Consuelo suffered a stroke and died on December 6, 1964, in New

York, where her life had started in the previous century. The funeral of Mrs. Jacques Balsan, the first wife of the 9th Duke of Marlborough, the former Consuelo Vanderbilt, was held at St. Thomas Episcopal Church, the same place where her transatlantic marriage had taken place almost seventy years before.[145] Making one last transatlantic journey, she was buried next to her sons at the Marlborough estate at Blenheim Palace. That the Marlborough family agreed to have her buried there, following such a public divorce and the publication of an autobiography critical of Britain and the Marlborough family, speaks volumes about her personal character and what the British thought of the American duchess. At her burial, one servant remarked, "She's the best woman ever to be buried here."[146]

Consuelo Vanderbilt reluctantly entered a transatlantic marriage, as did her husband, under family pressure. Their marriage deteriorated almost immediately, although they maintained the facade of matrimony for almost a decade. After dutifully producing two sons to continue the Marlborough line, the duke and duchess separated and pursued separate lives. Only at this point did Consuelo begin to identify herself through philanthropic works in Britain "in a decisive, demonstrated way, able at long last to take possession of her homeland and herself."[147] Spending her own money and investing herself in a variety of charitable projects, Consuelo created a new identity in Britain, one that did not rely on her identification as the wife of a duke. Working to improve the lives of the poor, especially women and children, she interacted with the lower and working classes on a daily basis. Over time, her philanthropy took on an increasingly political tone as she participated in the suffrage movement in the United States and Great Britain. As her philanthropy merged with World War I, the former Miss Vanderbilt led a number of projects that relied on her transatlantic contacts and clearly placed her at the head of London's Anglo-American ambassadorial contingent.

George Curzon, the husband of two American wives, once asked Consuelo if it had been worth the sacrifice. She did not understand his question, so he explained himself, "Yes—to give up being the beautiful Duchess of Marlborough and all it meant." She answered him, "But of course, George, I willingly gave up and have never regretted no longer being Duchess."[148] Having enjoyed a lifetime of wealth and affluence, she found her own identity and happiness outside of the walls of Marble House in Newport, Rhode Island, and Blenheim Palace, Woodstock. Her marriage to the Duke of Marlborough placed her in England with the name of a leading family. But during her time in England, she made a name for herself—Consuelo, duchess, American—and influenced millions of people throughout her new country through her own means of soft power.

Nevertheless, she would be identified throughout her life by a marriage she never wanted. And the demise of the same marriage ended her career as a public servant, women's advocate, and Anglo-American envoy. As she recalled, when "divorce brought complete freedom," her life in England came to an end.[149] And only through her efforts on behalf of British women, individually and with hundreds of other leading Anglo-American women did Consuelo, formerly Miss Vanderbilt, the Duchess of Marlborough, carve an identity for herself and serve as an informal ambassador for and between her two countries.

CHAPTER SIX

Candid Consul

Nancy Langhorne Shaw Astor

"America's Daughter"
America's Daughter—Entwined with our race
Has Struck the right path for women to pace
The cry of the children—the sad long call
Will be answered with feeling at Westminster Hall.

*J*ust as Consuelo Vanderbilt's high-profile life in England came to an end in 1920, one of the final American-born, British-wed women had just begun to make her impression on Great Britain. Lady Nancy Astor, wife of William Waldorf Astor, 2nd Viscount Astor, and the first woman to take a seat in the House of Commons, made significant contributions to the way Britons felt and thought about Americans during the first half of the twentieth century. Her Anglo-American marriage put her in contact with some of the principal political leaders and socialites of the period. Her candid personality and quirky sense of humor met with either howls of laughter or great disparagement from her fellow Britons. Her life functioned as nothing less than a bundle of contradictions. "She was an American divorcee who married a British peer, stood for Parliament as a Conservative, was elected seven times," explains John Halperin, "lived in a house next door to the Libyan embassy that now sports a blue plaque with her name on it, and was buried under a Confederate flag."[1] This flood of paradoxes only begins to explain the Anglo-American life and legacy of Lady Nancy Astor.

Nancy Witcher Langhorne was born in Danville, Virginia, on May 19, 1879, the same day that her future British husband came into the world, in New York City. Her parents, Chiswell Dabney Langhorne and Nancy Witcher Keene, both hailed from Virginia and held strong Confederate convictions throughout their lives.

151

Lady Astor. PL2023. © Bettmann/CORBIS.

Her father, known as "Chillie" (pronounced "Shilly"), served in the Confederate army and married Nancy Keene in 1864, in the midst of the Civil War.[2] The couple had eleven children, three of whom died in infancy. As the fifth surviving child and third of five daughters, as a child Nancy enjoyed the company of several siblings, a happy family, and the open spaces of rural Virginia. She reminisced fondly about her youth: "Nothing could be quite as lovely as that."[3]

Following the war, in an effort to support his ever-growing family amid the financially and physically destroyed South, Chillie Langhorne held a number of jobs. The one-time tobacco planter and slave owner worked as a hotel porter, security guard, auctioneer, and poker player. When the railroad industry materialized as a viable means of financial independence during Reconstruction, Langhorne threw himself into the enterprise, making valuable contacts to win bids for various railroad projects and taught himself about the engineering side of the business along the way.[4] The family experienced numerous financial ups and downs over the next several years. By 1892, Chillie had managed to attain a level of fiscal stability that allowed the Langhornes to move from the state capital of Richmond to Mirador, a sprawling, traditionally southern estate outside Charlottesville near the Blue Ridge Mountains.[5]

Nancy relished her years at Mirador, spending many hours a day on horseback with her four sisters: Lizzie, born in 1867; Irene, 1873; Phyllis, 1880; and Nora, 1889. Nancy also had three brothers—Keene, born in 1869; Harry, 1874; and William, always known as Buck, born in 1886—all of whom developed drinking problems. As the oldest sister, Lizzie acted as a second mother to all of the children. Irene, often considered the last great southern belle, married the artist Charles Dana Gibson, creator of the Gibson Girl. Closest to Phyllis, her immediately younger sister, and fiercely protective of her throughout her life, Nancy became very jealous of anyone or any relationship she perceived to challenge her position in Phyllis's life. Phyllis remained the only person Nancy loved throughout her life.[6] All of the children spent their days and nights doing little but riding horses at Mirador. Unlike Nancy's Anglo-American sisters who typically received remarkable educations, the Langhorne girls received little in the way of formal tutelage, as the position of and expectations for most American women, particularly in the South, presented little reason for schooling. Throughout her life, Nancy lamented her lack of education and spoke openly about her own ignorance.[7]

The only training Nancy ever received fell under the category of "finishing school." At the age of seven, she attended a school in Richmond run by Julia Lee. Proud southerners, her parents may well have chosen this school because Lee was a relative to the Confederate general Robert E. Lee. Two years later, Nancy attended another school in Richmond. Finally, at seventeen, she left the South to attend Miss Brown's Academy for Young Ladies in New York City. Learning for the first time that "Damn Yankee" was two words, Nancy did not adjust well to life in the North.[8] Surrounded by rich northern girls who seemed obsessed with their wardrobes and their fathers' fortunes, Nancy responded by playing up her Virginia roots and acting like a country bumpkin. She overemphasized her southern accent, wore unflattering clothes, and told exaggerated stories about her family and home, including bogus tales of her mother washing other people's clothes for money and her father's drunken rages. She quickly developed a reputation as an entertaining personality but a notorious one, a persona she resurrected during her later life in England. She later recalled, "I nearly finished the school instead of it finishing me . . . and I have never forgotten how it horrified me."[9] Her parents soon removed her, and Nancy gladly returned home to her beloved Mirador.[10]

Upon her return, Nancy began visiting elderly and disabled persons in her community. She enjoyed spending time with them and helping them with small tasks around the house or reading to them. She took pleasure from these good deeds and even considered becoming a missionary. Her mother, a very religious person, encouraged her daughter to pursue this, since it gave her such joy; she may also have wished Nancy to strive for something different from her own life. Nancy closely observed her parents' relationship: although her mother had the stronger temperament of the couple, her father controlled the finances and thereby held the power in the marriage. At the age of seventeen, Nancy had received sixteen proposals of marriage, none of which she accepted. She began questioning her role in the world as a woman and wondered what kind of husband and marriage she would have. Remembering her mother's dependence on her father, Nancy thought, if "Mother had had independent means she would not have had to stand for that. . . . I felt that men put women in this position for this very reason, that it rendered them helpless." She lamented that American women of her generation "had no kind of independence. It seemed to me wrong."[11] This sentiment remained central to Nancy's life in the United States and abroad.

While Nancy did not want to replicate her parents' marriage, she had watched her older sisters marry well and hoped to do the same. Upon visiting her sister Irene, now married to Gibson, in New York in 1897, Nancy met Robert Gould Shaw at a polo match. Shaw boasted a prominent Boston family, and appeared an ideal match for a beautiful and outgoing young woman from the South. Nancy described him as a "rather spectacular young man," and her parents encouraged the match.[12] He and Nancy became engaged, but she soon realized that she did not love him and that they shared little but their passion for horses. Under pressure from her family, however, Nancy agreed to go forward with the engagement and set a wedding date for that fall. Nancy later wrote of this impending wedding: "The engagement of any Langhorne was a sensation, and mine was announced with the usual enthusiasm and excitement." Yet she was frustrated that she "was supposed to be making a brilliant match, but noticed that I was alluded to, still, as 'the beautiful Irene Langhorne's sister.'"[13]

Shortly before the wedding, Chillie heard troubling rumors concerning his future son-in-law's personal habits. He traveled to Boston and met with Shaw's parents. Out of concern for his daughter, he bluntly asked if there was any reason his daughter should not marry their son. Shaw's parents assuaged his fears and assured him their son had done nothing that other young men did not do and explained that marriage to Nancy would settle him down. Chillie promptly returned to Mirador and advised his daughter *not* to marry Shaw. But Nancy never responded well to situations where she perceived someone pushing her into a corner. Her father's controlling relationship with her mother, what she saw as his attempt to guide her similarly, and her inability to shake her identity as Irene's sister combined to make Nancy determined to marry Shaw. The ceremony took place on October 27, 1897, in the drawing room of Mirador. Her younger sister Phyllis, who served as the maid of honor, later remembered the wedding "only for its gloom."[14] At the age of eighteen, Nancy Langhorne became Mrs. Robert Shaw of Boston transforming, much like Consuelo Vanderbilt had into the Duchess of Marlborough, by virtue of her nuptials.

The marriage lasted only a few years. As it turned out, Chillie's concerns were valid. Shaw had a terrible alcohol addiction and physically abused Nancy in his drunken rages, in addition to keeping a mistress on the side. Nancy left her husband several times in the first years of their marriage. Nonetheless, the two did conceive a child, a boy they named Robert (always known as Bobbie), born in 1898. Nancy left Shaw for good in 1902, at the age of twenty-three, and returned to Mirador with her son. Upon her arrival, she announced to her father, "Your beautiful daughter is back again, unwanted, unsought, and partly widowed for life."[15] A Charlottesville court finalized the divorce in early 1903 on the grounds of adultery. No proud southern man would marry Nancy, because she had married a Yankee. No northern man would take the same risk of marriage with a woman who had divorced and humiliated the son of a prominent family. Believing that her failed marriage and subsequent divorce had completely alienated her from public life, she settled into her solitary existence as a divorcée with a child. But her mother predicted, "Somehow I don't think the world has heard the last of Nancy yet."[16]

From Mirador to Cliveden

Following Nancy's divorce, Chillie thought a trip abroad would help her work through her sadness, so in February 1903 he sent Nancy and her mother to England, along with a family friend named Alice Babcock, who had also recently ended an unhappy love affair. On their transatlantic voyage, united in their disdain for the opposite sex, Nancy and Alice condemned all men and had a grand time ignoring them at every opportunity. The trio traveled first to Paris and then to England. Nancy loved England and later wrote that the country "always gave me a peculiar feeling of having come home, rather than of visiting a strange land."[17] During this visit, the women met up with Nancy's sister Irene and her husband, Charles, who had lived in London for several years. Nancy made the most of their British friends and contacts. During her time abroad, Nancy met Ava Astor, the wife of John Jacob Astor IV, a cousin of Nancy's future father-in-law. Astor took an immediate shine to the American and asked her and Alice to remain for an additional month. Mrs. Langhorne returned to care for her grandson, Bobbie, while Nancy and Alice stayed with Mrs. Astor. Nancy did not, however, meet her future husband on this particular transatlantic journey.[18]

Nancy returned to Mirador with a renewed spirit, but her happiness ended quickly with the sudden and unexpected death of her mother that summer. At the age of fifty-five, Mrs. Langhorne suffered a heart attack, and Nancy never fully recovered from the loss, writing, "The light went out of my life. I was ill for months, in a wretched, nameless fashion."[19] Some twenty years later, she still grieved over the loss of her mother. She wrote to her sister Irene, "Mother Oh how I long to see that woman, mother, mother the one love of my life, no one will know how I miss her, she dwarfed all other love for me."[20] At the age of seventy-two, Nancy wrote of her mother's passing, "The memory of those days is like a shadow on the heart still."[21]

Nancy continued to openly grieve throughout the next year. She tried to take her mother's place as the matriarch of Mirador, but her attempt met with little success. Since England had cheered her up in the past, Chillie suggested she take another transatlantic trip. Nancy and Phyllis returned to England in the winter of 1904–05, and Irene carefully choreographed their interaction with English society. Nancy enjoyed three months of the hunting season in Leicestershire. Having spent the better part of their childhoods on the backs of horses, the Langhorne women relished this experience and proved themselves excellent equestrians. As James Fox asserts, "To be praised on the hunting field was the highest accolade, which also absolved you of any other sin." Nancy did take a serious fall once during the season, after riding the biggest horse she could find, well over sixteen hands. As the horse jumped to miss a branch, Nancy fell and landed in a ditch. A British gentleman rode up and asked her, "Can you mount from the ground? Shall I get down to help you?" Nancy snapped at him, "Do you think I'd be such an ass as to come out hunting if I couldn't mount from the ground?"[22] Clearly, this woman was not nearly as docile as some of the other American women Britons had encountered. Nonetheless, the Langhornes meshed well with the leisure class in England. The Virginia gentry and British rural aristocracy held much in common: a high opinion of one's self-worth, a love for the outdoors, and a disdain for the working classes.[23] As Nancy reflected on this period, she recalled, "I began to live again."[24]

During this trip, Nancy began making a name for herself among the English elite. Her boldness and attractiveness impressed the men. British women, however, were less taken with this her. The initial excitement surrounding the arrival of American women in Britain in the late nineteenth century had passed. After several decades' experience watching similar American women, British women regarded Nancy as yet another American girl with daddy's money who had come to steal one of their men and, more importantly, his title. During a hunt one day, Edith Cunard, the wife of the industrialist Sir Gordon Cunard, haughtily accused Nancy, "I suppose you have come over here to get my husband." Nancy candidly responded, "If you knew the trouble I had in getting rid of mine, you would know I don't want yours."[25] The two became instant friends, and Edith provided Nancy a degree of protection from the other still suspicious wives.

As Nancy mixed with the same elite social and political circles patronized by her American compatriots Lady Churchill and the Duchess of Marlborough, she fiercely protected her personal privacy and reputation. She stayed away from gossipy circles and avoided being on a first-name basis with anyone. Although she attended numerous dinners and dances, she never drank or played cards, and she attended church regularly. She later reminisced, "I had suitors to spare, but with wisdom beyond my years I kept them all at bay and I had my own way of doing it." She always had her maid chaperone her to and from parties. One interested gentleman remarked on this: "Poor Mrs. Shaw. Not much fun, a maid to see you home." Nancy curtly countered, "If I had known who I was going to meet, I would have called a policeman."[26] Another man confessed that he wanted to kiss her but that he feared she would tell his wife. She bluntly explained to him, "I would not tell your wife. . . . I would tell the whole hunting field."[27] But overall, the expectations for and conduct of men and women in England matched Nancy's upbringing in Virginia, and Nancy increasingly felt at home.

Despite her best efforts to keep men at bay, Nancy had become increasingly interested in one English gentleman in particular. At the age of forty-one, John Baring was the chairman of his family's merchant bank, Baring Brothers. His family position bestowed upon him the title of Lord Revelstoke, but Nancy glowingly referred to him as "Apollo."[28] Lord Revelstoke was both spectacularly handsome and incredibly rich. Unfortunately, he was well aware of his attractiveness to women and acted like an arrogant snob. Although the two never became engaged, they did discuss a future together. But Lord Revelstoke ruined any chance of marrying the proud Virginian when he openly asked her, "Do you really think you could fill the position that would be required of my wife? You would have to meet Kings and Queens and entertain Ambassadors. Do you think you could do it?" As Nancy later recollected, "That was the death blow to my love for him. I said promptly I was quite certain I never could. That was the end of it, although he wrote to me for some time after I went back to Virginia."[29]

Clearly, Nancy was capable of anything to which she set her mind, a fact she later proved in her marriage to another British lord. Without a doubt, her later life and position demonstrated her ability to meet royalty comfortably, entertain diplomats, and impress others with her capabilities as a hostess, not only as the wife of a leading British man but also in her own right as an American woman. Lord Revelstoke clearly did not know Nancy very well and did not understand how to approach her or her proud and defensive personality. Otherwise, he would never have phrased his questions in such a way. A host of other American women—from Lady Churchill to the Duchess of Marlborough—had more than confirmed their extraordinary poli-social skills as the wives of leading British peers. And Nancy was more than competent to meet the bar her American-born, British-wed sisters had set as informal ambassadors in England.

She returned to Virginia with another serious relationship having ended. Lord Revelstoke wrote to her and tried to continue their courtship, but Nancy would not hear of it. He had offended her proud Virginian and American sensibilities, and no amount of apologies or gifts would mend her wounded heart. She did not return to Britain for nearly a year, but she maintained her personal transatlantic contacts by actively writing to her English friends, both men and women, in a style similar to Mary Chamberlain and Lady Curzon. One such gentleman was Herbert Asquith, the future prime minister, who was aware of her situation with Lord Revelstoke. Nancy asked Asquith if she should ever marry again and, if so, who he had in mind. He did not send a quick reply, which further injured her already sensitive spirit. She wrote to him again and scolded him for not having written to her promptly. He playfully responded:

> You must not reproach me, my dear Mrs. Shaw;
> It's not a like a Redskin selecting a squaw;
> For there's no tougher problem, in logic or law
> Than to find a fit mate for the lady called Shaw.[30]

Asquith had summed up what many Britons thought about the latest addition to their fashionable circles. Nancy Langhorne Shaw was beautiful, funny, witty, and a simply splendid person with whom to spend time. She knew how to ride, enjoyed hunting, and fit easily with the London Season crowd. But her sensitivity to her Virginian and American identities made her a prickly person at times. She could be moody, spiteful, and outspoken to a fault. While she regarded England as much home as she did Virginia, in many ways she was a woman out of place in not one but two countries. The heyday of Anglo-Americans marriages had passed, and few British men wanted to marry an American divorcée with an impulsive personality, not to mention a child. Little did Nancy know that her next transatlantic voyage would be her most important.

In December 1905, she sailed back to England with her father. Lord Revelstoke still thought he would marry Nancy, believing himself the frontrunner of the five proposals Nancy received that winter; thus, he planned to meet her at the dock in Liverpool. But a competitor had chosen not to wait for Nancy's next trip. Instead, William Waldorf Astor traveled to the United States and sailed back to England under the guise that his presence on the ship was merely coincidental. As James Fox explains, however, "in those days of competing steamships, the first-class passenger lists were available to any good travel agent." Waldorf, as he was known, asked to meet Nancy aboard the ship, but she put him off for several days. Undeterred, he took the opportunity to woo her father. According to his future wife, the man "knew what he wanted. A clever man can always find more ways than one of getting what he wants. Waldorf knew all the ways," Nancy remembered. "He was very good looking, and he had immense courtesy and very great charm. He soon had Father eating out of his hand." By the time they reached England, she was at least considering Waldorf a potential suitor. Writing home to her sister Phyllis, she approvingly noted that he was "the fourth richest man in the world."[31] Clearly, Nancy wanted to marry again, but any husband would have to bring a considerable fortune as well as be a second father to Bobbie. Nancy judged Waldorf able to meet both of these requirements.

Members of the Astor family had led prominent lives on both sides of the Atlantic. By great success in the fur business and trade with China in the early nineteenth century, John Jacob Astor had been the first to make the Astor name well known in the United States.[32] When he died in 1848, his fortune was estimated at $25 million, one-fifteenth of all the personal wealth in the United States.[33] Additional profits from real estate in New York and shrewd investments only increased the Astors' wealth. The family fortune remained intact for three generations but in 1875 was split between John Jacob Astor III and his brother, William Backhouse Astor Jr. The larger share went to John Jacob, making him the richest man in the United States. His son, William Waldorf Astor, moved to Britain in 1893, along with his wife and fourteen-year-old son, William Waldorf II. This transplanted American attended Eton and Oxford, like the other Anglo-American grooms. In 1899, at the age of twenty, he became a naturalized British citizen.[34]

Waldorf and Nancy shared not only the same birthday but also many common interests. They both enjoyed high-class leisure activities, such as hunting; raising, riding, and racing horses; and serving the public. But they did have very different personalities. "Restless, intuitive, relying on instinct, impatient with argument," Nancy was a force of nature. Few people dared to meet her head-on in any sort of disagreement. Waldorf, a kind and gentle soul, avoided confrontation with her except in rare cases. One friend later described their marriage as, "like watching an animal trainer with a rather dangerous animal."[35]

In any case, Waldorf courted her throughout the winter and showered her with letters and gifts. He proposed, she accepted, and the two announced their engagement in March 1906.[36] Nancy feared Waldorf's father might object to their union; since he had left the United States and become a British citizen, she thought he might prefer his son to marry an Englishwoman. But Waldorf's father raised no objections, and he became quite fond of Nancy and she of him. Waldorf and Nancy wed on May 3, 1906, at All Souls Church, at Langham Palace, in England. Notably, neither father attended the ceremony, as both were suffering from gout.[37] After she married Waldorf, Nancy called her father-in-law "Old Moneybags." But he apparently found this amusing, as he gave her the Astor family diamonds, which included the Sancy diamond, a fifty-five-carat stone whose prior owners included Elizabeth I, James II, and Louis XIV. The couple also received from William the family estate, Cliveden, as a wedding present, in addition to an annual income of $100,000 from Waldorf's father.[38] Before returning home to England, they honeymooned in Italy and Switzerland.[39]

Nancy threw herself into her new role as a wife to one of the best-known men in England. Fine-tuning her skills as a hostess at the level of Mary Chamberlain, Nancy made Cliveden an "international social center."[40] As Lady Churchill facilitated the Fourth Party and the *Anglo-Saxon Review* identified leading Anglo-Americans of the period, Nancy also supported her husband's political ambitions and fostered connections among Anglo-Americans as an American-born, British-wed wife. The guest book at Cliveden included the names of some of the period's most prominent Anglo-Americans: James Arthur Balfour, Charlie Chaplin, Winston Churchill, Lord Curzon, Henry Ford, Henry James, Rudyard Kipling, Lady Mountbatten, Sean O'Casey, Bernard Shaw, Edith Wharton, Edward VIII, George V and Queen Mary, the Queen of Rumania, the King of Sweden, and the Archduke Franz Ferdinand.[41] "In inviting guests to Cliveden the only policy Nancy Astor seems to have followed in these days," according to John Halperin, "was that of exposing as many Englishmen to as many Americans as she possibly could, believing as she did that the peace and happiness of the world depended in part on Anglo-American friendship." As an example of her strategic but soft power efforts on behalf of the Anglo-Saxon world, she always placed an American on either side of Winston Churchill when he dined in her home.[42] This unofficial emissary carefully calculated everything—from the guest list to the seating chart to the food served—in a manner akin to that of a seasoned diplomat in her formal entertaining, which was protected by the veneer of traditional women's work and expected from a wife of her ranking.

Although Nancy had failed at running Mirador after her mother's death, she excelled at Cliveden by blending her southern hospitality and her husband's riches. In traditional British fashion, she hosted elaborate dinners, as did Lady Churchill, and intimate teas, much like Mary Chamberlain. Guests knew that when they attended a dinner at Cliveden they would enjoy delicious food, "a blend of French cuisine and traditional Virginia fare such as corn bread and beaten biscuits."[43] Rather than push specific people into conversations, Nancy took a seemingly hands-off approach to discussions between her guests, as her soft power coercion proved more successful than formally contrived encounters. Instead, she simply allowed everyone to mingle and chat at his or her leisure. In addition to these time-tested polisocial strategies, she also kept Cliveden open to friends and family at all times. The candid consul with the buoyant personality attracted people to her and to Cliveden. She did not schedule her guests during their visits but rather encouraged them to move freely within the house and around the Cliveden grounds. Through her Anglo-American marriage and a blending of American and British entertaining, Nancy became "one of the leading hostesses in England."[44] As her neighbor Julian Grenfell once wrote to her, "You will go to heaven for keeping people cheery."[45]

In many ways, Nancy did not fit the stereotype of the American heiress buying her way into the British aristocracy. Her family, though comfortable, did not enjoy wealth to the same degree as the Jeromes, Endicotts, Leiters, or Vanderbilts. Rather, Nancy's husband held the riches. She hailed from the South, not the North like the large majority of American heiresses. Finally, when Nancy married him, Waldorf held no title. They genuinely married for love and enjoyed a life "full and fascinating, if not always happy."[46] Nancy never placed herself in the same category as previous Anglo-American brides, and she despised the so-called dollar princesses. Though she had little in the way of a formal education, she was exceedingly shrewd and likely deduced that she would do well to distance herself from her Anglo-American predecessors, at least on a formal level. She once wrote to Phyllis about these women in general and Consuelo Marlborough in particular: "They have the form, the taste, the desires of every single one of those rich N.Y. soulless sort of women, May Rox[burghe] the same, also Consuelo M."[47] Nancy had especially harsh and surprising words about Consuelo: "Her life has been spent with the smartest & fastest set England & I don't believe she has a single friend who's worth 'twopence' as a Thinker or a Reformer."[48]

Nancy's vehement disdain for this cohort of American-born, British-wed women arguably served as a method of protection. After the turn of the twentieth century, public opinion slowly turned against transatlantic unions. Always strategic in her personal and professional lives, Nancy may well have deliberately distanced herself from her compatriots so as not to generate suspicion among her fellow Britons and eventual constituents.

While she shared some similarities with her Anglo-American sisters, Nancy offered something very different. During meals at Cliveden, she frequently performed for her guests, her quirky sense of humor shining through. She often popped in an oversized set of false teeth, chewed gum, and impersonated various people. Her favorite characters included a "horsey, profane, toothless, shrewish, upper-class Englishwoman who hated Americans and a Southern belle telling stories about 'her' Negroes."[49] Sometimes Nancy pushed back her tiara as if it were an old hat or fanned herself with a dinner plate. Many friends knew her well enough to find these escapades entertaining. When a British ambassador and his wife visited Cliveden, the wife explained that Nancy simply "didn't care what anybody thought. She was a southern prima donna. She would do *cartwheels* in the hall at Cliveden."[50] But over time, her sense of humor and performances more often offended her fellow Britons. For better or for worse, Nancy Astor had made a name for herself in England.

In addition to becoming a well-known hostess in England, shortly after the wedding Nancy again became a mother. In 1907, Nancy and Waldorf welcomed a son, William Waldorf Astor III. Though she enjoyed a large family with Waldorf, much like her kin in Virginia, Nancy's son Bobbie always held a special place in her heart. Writing to Phyllis five days after the birth of her first English son, she confided to her sister, "He's not so nice as Bobbie. . . . We can never love any children like one's first borns, can we?"[51] Nancy's only daughter, Nancy Phyllis Louise, followed in 1909. The family added three more sons: Francis David Langhorne, born in 1912; Michael Langhorne, born in 1916; and John Jacob Astor, always known as Jakie, born in 1918.[52] Throughout this period in her life, Nancy continued to hunt "regularly, between babies."[53] Regarding her numerous offspring, she explained simply, "Babies are my hobby."[54]

As Nancy practiced her hand at motherhood, Waldorf tested the political waters. When he expressed an interest in standing for Parliament, the Conservative Association of Plymouth adopted Waldorf in 1908. To run for the House of Commons, he needed to meet the residency requirements by living in Plymouth. The Astors bought a house there in 1909, and Waldorf began his political campaign. Plymouth was also significant for its Anglo-American connection to the United States, as "the Pilgrim Fathers had set sail on the *Mayflower* from the harbour at Sutton Pool."[55] Nancy even held "a romantic notion of herself as the pilgrim returning to the place from which [Sir Francis] Drake had set off to reach Virginia," going so far as to state that "there might be divine inspiration at work in the choice of constituency."[56]

Plymouth had a large working-class population, thereby making the city a Liberal stronghold. When Waldorf campaigned in the fall of 1909, he and his wife canvassed the city. Like Lady Churchill, Nancy visited hundreds of working-class homes and spoke with hundreds of people in an effort to secure her husband's election. She enjoyed the opportunity to "go out to people in a friendly spirit," believing, "that is how they will receive and listen to you." But like Consuelo, Nancy found English people at times difficult to reach and to form a rapport with, a detail that Mary Curzon had observed when she expressed her inability to connect with or trust English women. Nancy explained this difficulty by saying, "The trouble with so many English people is that they cannot, however hard they try, be quite natural with other people. It is difficult for them not to be just a little patronizing." She concluded, "I don't know why that is. Maybe it has something to do with the climate over here."[57] Sadly, Waldorf lost his first political contest to the Liberal candidate, but another election followed in December 1910; he won this one. Plymouth reelected him several times to the House, where he even served as Prime Minister David Lloyd George's parliamentary secretary. Consequently, Nancy added Lloyd George to her list of prominent Cliveden guests. More importantly, Waldorf's entry to the House of Commons began thirty-five years of Plymouth's representation by the Astors.

Between their family and political duties, Nancy and Waldorf remained busy. During a conversation with the German ambassador at a July 1914 dinner party, she boldly asked, "Have you come to admire the very country I hear you intend to invade shortly?" According to Nancy, "it just popped out before I knew anything about it."[58] Of course, the ambassador feigned horror, but World War I began a month later. As custom dictated, many wealthy aristocrats opened their homes to the government for use as hospitals as their contribution to the war effort. The Astors offered Cliveden in November 1914. The house "was considered unsuitable," but Nancy oversaw the transformation of its covered tennis courts and bowling alley into a hospital for soldiers, much like Conseulo's supervised improvised hospitals. Three months later, the renovation was complete and the Cliveden hospital held more than one hundred patients. By the end of the war, the Astors' estate housed more than six hundred patients and functioned as a convalescent home; over the course of the First World War, more than twenty-four thousand men had been treated there.

Throughout the war, Nancy worked nonstop in both wings of the hospital and brought the soldiers a unique nursing style. But, consistent with her need to stand out, often attributed to her American identity, Nancy's bedside manner proved unconventional, to say the least. She often told men who had given up that they were "going to die because they had no guts. If you were a Cockney, or a Scot, or a Yank, you'd live. But you're just a Canadian, so you'll lie down and die."[59] When she heard that one Canadian soldier had lost the will to live after being badly burned, she leaned over his bed and whispered, "You're going to die, and I would too, rather than go back to Canada." The soldier responded by making a full recovery.[60] She used this technique on a number of badly wounded soldiers. Once she asked a soldier where he came from. When he answered, "Yorkshire," she replied, "No wonder you don't want to live, if you come from Yorkshire!"[61] The enraged soldier made a complete recovery and did indeed return to Yorkshire.

While Nancy tended to soldiers, her father-in-law donated what he could to the war effort: his money. In 1914, he gave $100,000 to the Red Cross, $175,000 to various funds, and $125,000 to aid the dependents of officers. In 1915, he gave another $100,000 to the Red Cross. Every $100,000 he donated would amount to approximately $1.7 million today.[62] As a result of his financial support of the war, King George V bestowed upon him a barony, and in 1916 he became Baron and then Viscount Astor. Thus, he now sat in the House of Lords, and Waldorf automatically became the 2nd Viscount Astor. Nancy and Waldorf disapproved of the title, believing that the aristocracy was unseemly. Nancy especially thought a former American should never have become a titled British aristocrat. It must here be noted that Anglo-American marriages had largely come to an end by now, and people on both sides of the Atlantic gradually turned against such unions. Clearly, Nancy did not identify with the American-born, British-wed women whose lives in England had, in many ways, made her political career possible; and she, an American, took a seat in the British Parliament before her compatriots in the United States achieved voting rights. Obtaining political office, by virtue of marriage or otherwise, would have been impossible in the United States. In any case, the British and American populaces watched her actions, activities, and associations just as closely as those of previous American heiresses who had married into the aristocracy. Nancy was now Lady Astor. Her husband's seat in the House of Commons and her father-in-law's presence in the House of Lords portended great changes and opportunities for her.

Lady of the House

On October 19, 1919, Waldorf's father died of a heart attack. His death transformed Waldorf into Viscount Astor and subsequently ended his career in the House of Commons. Waldorf, inheriting the title of Lord Astor, took his father's seat in the House of Lords, thereby vacating his seat in the House of Commons. For almost a decade, he had represented the people of Plymouth. Both he and his wife felt much attached to the people, and neither wanted to give up his or her position and relationship with these constituents. As a result of their leadership in the community, the local Conservative Party proposed substituting Lady Astor in her husband's place.[63] At first, Lord and Lady Astor agreed that she would retain his seat in the House of Commons while he found a way to drop his peerage title and seat in the House of Lords through legislation. Thus, Lady Astor's entry into the House of Commons was not initially an attempt to push a woman into British Parliament or advance a feminist agenda but merely to serve as a stopgap to hold Waldorf's seat until he could terminate his position in the House of Lords. Little did Lord and Lady Astor realize they had begun a new chapter in their lives.

Lady Astor's entry into the House of Commons was fraught with obstacles. Legally, she could run for a parliamentary seat. The Representation of the People Act of 1918, which gave British women of property thirty years old and over the right to vote and permitted them to stand for the House of Commons but not the House of Lords. A number of issues worked against Lady Astor, however: she was a wealthy, divorced American with little or no education, no experience running for a House seat in a working-class district as a Conservative and a woman. The *Sunday Evening Telegram* argued, "The first woman member really should be a native of the kingdom."[64] The *Saturday Review* suggested that Lady Astor could not take a seat in Parliament because she was an "American by birth."[65] Without a doubt, "Lady Astor had enough personal liabilities to make any thoughtful voter pause."[66] Few people believed her campaign would result in a victory.

At the same time, Lady Astor answered her opponents' every criticism. When a woman attempted to disparage her for her divorce and asked her if she would make a divorce as easy to achieve in England as it was in the United States, she leaned forward and asked, "Sister, are you in trouble too?"[67] When crowds told Nancy, "Go back to America," she answered, "I am pleased to do my duty in the State which it has pleased God to call me." In an attempt to emphasize her American and British identities in a positive light, Lady Astor explained, "I am of Virginia blood and come of good old Anglo-Saxon fighting stock." When attacked on the grounds of her wealth, Lady Astor put her critics on the spot. "Would you be doing what I am doing if you had what I have?" Other times she retorted, "I represent the working man. My husband was not elected by 17,000 millionaires living on the Hoe."[68] Throughout her campaign, Lady Astor showed that she had an answer for every liability. The experience "greatly strengthened her sense of the tie between her native and her adopted lands" and reinforced Anglo-American connections while representing a serious achievement along the spectrum of possibilities for American-born, British-wed women abroad.[69]

In the aftermath of World War I, Anglo-American relations seemed to have begun a new phase, a sentiment that functioned as the hub of Lady Astor's political campaign. Though she left the United States a southern belle and became an English peeress, Lady Astor did not forget "her American traditions, and [was] not ashamed of them." Heckled by crowds for not restricting herself to organizations such as the Society of American Women in London or the American Women's War Relief Fund, she retorted she was anything but "ashamed of my Virginia blood. I married in England; my interests for ten years have been in Plymouth; every drop of blood in my veins is Anglo-Saxon, and I am proud of my American birth." The *New York Times* argued that Nancy was against sexism and nationalism in running for a seat in the House of Commons but predicted that if "the election depends on Nancy's tongue, she will win." In a tone similar to that which identified Consuelo as the former Miss Vanderbilt, the same paper wished "Good luck to Nancy Langhorne that was—Lady Astor that is!"[70]

Now known by her British title, Lady Astor had lived in Plymouth for ten years and had met thousands of its constituents through her husband's campaigns and political career. Over the previous decade, she had acted as a Lady Bountiful, like the Duchess of Marlborough, to Plymouth and had "won the heart of the West county."[71] She had demonstrated her ability to meet people individually and in groups and speak candidly with members of the working class without the typical attention to class-consciousness. She gave rousing speeches, excited people to her side, and was determined to earn every Plymouth woman's vote—a total of 17,175—more than enough to win the election. Many of Lord Astor's efforts during her tenure in the House dealt with helping women and children, a cause that, like Consuelo Marlborough, she continued to work for throughout her own political career. While Lord Astor had represented Plymouth, Lady Astor had pushed her husband and his fellow members of Parliament to fight for pure milk, improved working conditions, and shorter hours for women and children. She told fellow mothers, "I want for your children what I want for my children. I do not believe in sexes and classes." In an echo of Consuelo as the "Baby Duchess," flyers with Lady Astor's picture appeared throughout Plymouth with the message, "Vote for Lady Astor and Your Babies Will Weigh More."[72]

In typical Nancy fashion, throughout her campaign she took political advice from no one and merely acted on pure instinct. She made no lofty promises but rather candidly told her constituents, "I am not one of those *asses* who tell you're going to have a new heaven on earth."[73] In another speech, she announced to the crowd gathered in front of her,

> I am not standing before you as a sex candidate. If you want an MP who will be a repetition of the 600 other MPs, don't vote for me. If you want a lawyer or if you want a pacifist don't elect me. If you can't get a fighting man take a fighting woman. If you want a Bolshevik or a follower of Mr. Asquith don't elect me. If you want a party hack don't elect me. Surely we have outgrown party ties. I have. The war has taught us that there is a greater thing than parties, and that is the State.[74]

Newspapers everywhere followed Lady Astor's campaign. Reporters from the United States followed their American peeress throughout her run for the House. Newspapers such as the *Chicago News, Boston Globe,* and the *New York Times* all carried reports of how their American daughter's campaign was progressing. Additionally, newspapers from all over Britain covered it: *Western Morning News, Birmingham Gazette, Liverpool Courier, Manchester Daily Despatch, Yorkshire Observer, Glasgow Herald,* and the *South Wales Daily News.* That she was an American made the story even more interesting and appealing to many readers. The possibility of the first woman, an Anglo-American at that, taking a seat in the House of Commons brought transatlantic following. Newspapers in the United States maintained a degree of objectivity the British papers did not. Americans were happy simply to read about Lady Astor's pursuit of the House, while British newspapers were highly partisan. But both, according to Karen Musolf, regarded Lady Astor as one of their own.[75] Together, the American and British publics were again following the life of an American woman who had taken a prominent role in Great Britain. Like Lady Churchill and Mary Chamberlain, she hosted dinners and worked for her husband's political career. Like Lady Curzon and Lady Marl-borough, she invested a great deal of time, energy, and resources in philanthropic, and specifically wartime, charities. In no small part, Lady Astor owed her po-tential political career to previous Anglo-American brides' successes as informal ambassadors. But she seized such opportunities on her own terms.

The night before the election, Lord Astor excited the Plymouth constituents when he told them, "In the past Plymouth sent out the Pilgrim Fathers. Tomorrow I believe Plymouth is going to send in the first Pilgrim mother."[76] After the final tally, Lady Astor had earned 14,495 votes, a margin of more than five thousand votes over the second place candidate and ten thousand over the next. In her acceptance speech, she admitted to the Plymouth constituents that the thought of running for Parliament had "knocked me out for a week." But her husband believed in her abil-ity to serve the people, and she came to agree with him: "I am a Virginian, so natu-rally I am a politician."[77] When Lady Astor, now known by the British public as "our Nancy," took her seat in the House of Commons on December 1, 1919, she became the first woman in British history to do so.[78] Her son Bobbie and sisters Nora and Phyllis watched from the spectators' gallery. Former prime ministers David Lloyd George and Arthur Balfour served as her sponsors, as ceremony required the for-mal introduction of new MPs to the House by a standing MP. Despite repeated attempts, the three never quite bowed in unison, as custom dictated. Instead of tak-ing a seat silently, Lady Astor turned and began talking with the various people she knew. In typical Nancy fashion, her entry into the House lacked the usual degree of solemnity and dignity.[79]

Many members of the House perceived Lady Astor's lightheartedness and at-tempt to make small talk as apparent disregard for the prestige of Parliament. From the all-male British parliamentary perspective, the American woman had no de-sire to uphold the decorum fitting an MP. Like Anglo-American grooms, the large majority of British MPs were Oxbridge men; having attended the finest schools in England and matured in the absence of women, they did not welcome a woman, much less one without a day of higher education. "They call it the best club in Europe," Nancy later recalled, "but it didn't seem like the best club to me. I can't think of anything worse than being among six hundred men none of whom really wanted you there."[80]

One member in particular resented Lady Astor's presence. Despite having dined frequently at Cliveden, Sir Winston Churchill, who had known Nancy for years, had never gotten along with her. The son of the American Lady Churchill deeply resented Lady Astor's entry into the House of Commons and chose to ig-nore her and any speeches she gave, believing the men "could freeze her out and be rid of the female sex for good."[81] When she pressed him on the matter, Churchill described his feelings: "I find a woman's intrusion into the House of Commons as embarrassing as if she burst into my bathroom when I had nothing with which to defend myself, not even a sponge." Nancy quickly replied, "Winston, you're not handsome enough to have worries of that kind."[82] In another case, the two exchanged harsh words over a petty issue. She spat at him, "If I were your wife, I'd poison your coffee," to which he snapped, "If you were my wife, I'd drink it."[83] During a particularly heated exchange, Lady Astor bellowed, "The trouble with you is that you have the worst blood of two continents in your veins."[84] Though the two remained bitter rivals for years, on one point they could agree. As Churchill once admitted, they both "like[d] to have everything both ways."[85]

Regardless of her hostile relationship with a fellow MP, Lady Astor, now age forty, entered the House of Commons and donned the sober costume she would sport for the next twenty-five years. Wearing "an elegantly cut black suit, long in jacket and skirt, her white shirt collar spread across her shoulders, and a three-cornered hat," Nancy appeared solemn and yet stylish.[86] If she ever varied her outfit, the gentlemen in the House rose to their feet upon her entrance to Parliament and shouted, "Bravo, Nancy!"[87] The other MPs treated her differently because she was a woman, but this humorous gesture demonstrated her ability to win over her colleagues.

Lady Astor gave her maiden speech in February 1920, opposing a bill to ease the wartime drinking restrictions. Her early life had given her a sincere hatred of liquor, but she also understood that she could not impose a personal belief on the British public.[88] "I am not pressing for prohibition. I am far too intelligent for that." In her address, she remarked on her presence in the House: "I know it was very difficult for some honourable members to receive the first lady MP," to which the House answered, "not at all." She continued, "I assure you that it was difficult for a woman to come in. To address you now on this vexed question of drink is harder still. It takes a bit of courage to dare to do it. But I do dare."[89]

Lady Astor's maiden speech set the tone of her career in the House, during which her efforts would fall into one of several categories that focused on women, children, and Anglo-American relations. While she may have voiced disapproval of Consuelo, her efforts as the leading Anglo-American woman in Britain shadowed her predecessor's dedication to women and children. Lady Astor constantly sought improvements in maternity care and infant welfare, fought for women's labor conditions, argued for health and sanitation progress, improved educational opportunities and the modernization of marriage and divorce laws, and focused her attention on transatlantic issues.[90] She even went so far as to push women to run for public office, an controversial proposition in the early twentieth century. When criticized for encouraging women to abdicate their responsibilities in raising a family, as the public saw it, she responded that they would do more for their offspring as politicians than as parents and simply needed to make a distinction between "mother love" and "smother love"; she believed women need not be mothers exclusively.[91] In explaining her approach to her leadership role, and women and children specifically, Lady Astor declared, "I don't like people I can't do anything for."[92]

As she had demonstrated in her private life, Nancy held little regard for formalities and did not feel the need to show kindness and concern toward her fellow MPs. She rarely followed the rules of exchange in the House of Commons; she typically addressed her fellow members directly, instead of communicating through the Speaker of the House, and frequently interrupted members when they gave speeches. When a fellow MP once said, "My opinion, for what it's worth," Nancy interrupted, "Well, what do *you* think it's worth?" When another addressed the House, "When I was walking in my garden, this is the question I asked myself," Nancy interrupted, "And I bet you got a silly answer." When a fellow Conservative MP opposed her drink bill, she verbally attacked him. "You're the village donkey and the House of Commons is the village where you bray." The Speaker of the House of Commons ultimately forced her to retract her remark.[93] Lady Astor's behavior taught her fellow MPs and Britain as a whole that a woman could hold her own in the House. Her presence also demonstrated a notion Britons had long held—that Americans were bold, brash, and outspoken to a fault; thus, as Anglo-American marriages came to an end, the perception of Anglo-American brides had come full circle.

An Embodiment of Anglo-American Unity

Although she had been elected in Britain, Lady Astor maintained strong ties to the United States. In 1920, she wrote an article titled "What Women Can Do in Politics That Men Cannot Do," published by the *Woman's Home Companion*. Its appearance in September was quite timely, considering that Congress had just passed the Nineteenth Amendment, guaranteeing American women the right to vote, on August 18. In her first contribution to any American magazine, she attempted to draw out the commonalities faced by American and British women. "American women also may be interested in the problems which we have faced in the British House of Commons," she wrote, "and which, after all, are universal to the whole Anglo-Saxon race—for England and America." She maintained that Anglo-Saxon women "cherish[ed] the same ideals of liberty, conscience, and clean upright living that are synonymous with the language we both speak." Lady Astor called on women to exercise their right to vote, arguing, "Women hold the balance of power." She expressed her disdain for alcohol, discussed her desire for peace, and encouraged American women to support the League of Nations and the United States' membership in it. Finally, she encouraged the United States and Great Britain to pursue close bilateral relations regardless of problems resulting from the

League of Nations. Calling on both countries to extend their "hands across the sea," she pleaded with Americans to "realize that England's desire for American cooperation [with the League of Nations] is a genuine one, without ulterior or imperialistic motives." At the heart of her essay, she appealed to her fellow American women from a British perspective.[94] In the upheaval following World War I and the Versailles Treaty, Lady Astor stood as an ideal informal envoy to reach out to the United States and Great Britain, and to women in particular, in an effort to bring the two countries together in the aftermath.

In the spring of 1922. Lady Astor received an invitation to speak at the Pan-American Conference for Women in Baltimore, Maryland, and another meeting sponsored by the English Speaking Union, a clear indication of her influential position regarding Anglo-American relations. On her journey back to the United States, Lady Astor received numerous requests "to speak, appear, lunch or banquet in every part of the country" and in Canada. Lord and Lady Astor arrived in New York on April 18, 1922. She rearranged their transatlantic visit and accepted invitations to various engagements in Chicago, Montreal, New York, Philadelphia, Ottawa, Toronto, and Washington, D.C., and planned an extended stay in Virginia. In the six-week span before they returned to England, on May 26, 1922, Lady Astor gave approximately forty formal speeches.[95]

During her time in Virginia, Lady Astor visited large crowds in Richmond, Danville, Scottsville, and Charlottesville. Bands entertained the throngs with songs such as "Carry Me Back to Old Virginia," "Dixie," and "Home Sweet Home."[96] In Danville, her hometown, she received a loving cup and a Confederate flag, and the city renamed her home street "Lady Astor Street." When she addressed a crowd of five thousand people, Harry C. Ficklen, a childhood friend, introduced her as "the sweetheart of two nations." He described her as "an angel with a flaming sword cutting the right of way for the mothers of men, dove of war and eagle of peace . . . [,] the first woman ever to sit in the British Parliament and last woman in the world ever to forget the sacred soil of Virginia that bore her." During her visit to Scottsville, Lady Astor charmed the mayor, who later expressed his hope that she would return to Virginia and run as a Democratic candidate for president.[97] Regardless of how long she had been abroad, her return home proved she would always be welcomed with open arms in her homeland.

Throughout her tour of the United States, Lady Astor continually stressed several themes in her speeches. First, she always opened by saying that she was not there to speak to the people as a Briton/American/Virginian, but then went on to do just that. Yet, she always found a way to juggle her dual identities and promote Anglo-American relations. In New York, she explained that she was there as "proof to all countries that England and America will give you a chance if you can prove to either of them that what you are striving for is something which will hurt no man, woman, or child of any country, but which you earnestly feel is going to help all countries." Like the Anglo-American brides before her, Lady Astor negotiated her national identity depending on her situation and audience. Second, she always made some sort of self-deprecating statement about not being up to the task but doing her part. In a speech to the League of Women Voters in New York, she said that her time in the House of Commons had given her "courage and strength. I won't say too much about wisdom." Third, she constantly pressed the United States to join the League of Nations. She appealed to a New York audience by saying, "I feel sure the fathers and mothers of America [think] that the safest and sanest way to get out of wars is to join some sort of association of nations for peace." She also urged women to take their part in politics and influence their homes, cities, or states, just as she did in Britain. She encouraged Convention of the League of Women Voters in Baltimore: "We must put into public life those qualities which women have had to put into their home life." Finally, she consistently stressed the power of the Anglo-American alliance and the necessity of Anglo-Saxons to remake the world through Christian civilization. During a speech in New York, she emphasized the need to build a "civilisation based on Christianity." Before the English Speaking Union, the leading attaché of the Anglo-American world accurately described herself as "a symbol—a sort of connecting link between the English-speaking people!"[98]

Lady Astor's trip to the United States came at an opportune time, immediately following the disastrous lecture tour of Margot Asquith, wife of former prime minister Herbert Asquith. Asquith told Americans how ridiculous they had been not to join the League of Nations. Advertising her ignorance of North American history, she told a Canadian crowd about *its* president, Abraham Lincoln. Her "demolition of Anglo-American relations," maintains Anthony Masters, gave Nancy a chance to offset the "appalling impression Margot had made."[99] Lady Astor's American tour met with great success and served as the high point in her first parliamentary term even as she functioned as a nongovernmental official against a transatlantic background. A Virginia newspaper praised her: "An accomplished and highly trained orator could hardly frame an address to a general audience with finer effect." The *New York Telegraph* wrote, "Her gifts are remarkable; her faculty for saying the right thing at the right time amounts to genius."[100] Supporting these comments, the *New York Times* wrote, "Lady Astor already symbolizes a condition of things that time has modified. . . . She was born in Virginia. And she sees England, not as a Parliament, but as a home." The newspaper encouraged its readership to "concede to her then, as to any other Queen, the divine right to do no wrong."[101] The American daughter had long considered herself "a symbol and embodiment of Anglo-American unity," but even she could not have asked for a more successful reception on her transatlantic journey or a better opportunity to act as an informal ambassador.[102] In 1923, after her return to Plymouth, she published her speeches from her tour, aptly titled *My Two Countries*, a formal acknowledgement of her position on the Anglo-American stage.

After her trip, Lady Astor returned to the House of Commons with a newfound sense of confidence. Continuing her fight on behalf of the women and children of Britain, she worked for the expansion of women's suffrage. The 1918 Enabling Act made approximately 8 million British women eligible to vote. Nancy wanted to drop the voting age for women from thirty to twenty-one. She had hoped to achieve such a goal during her first term in office, but this increase in women voters did not occur until 1928. She found a political soul mate in Margaret Macmillan, a Labour party member elected to the House in 1926. Together, they advocated the establishment of nursery schools across England.[103] Nancy's new project interested her husband so much that he purchased some land that eventually became the home for the Rachel McMillan College, which opened in 1930.[104] As the American woman in Parliament, Lady Astor used her position to improve the lives of British women and children, much like Consuelo Vanderbilt had before her.

When Lady Astor stood for reelection in 1929, she reminded her constituents of the various measures she had achieved in the House: equal votes for women; pensions for the aged, widowed, and orphans; a national electrical system; and European reconciliation on Locarno lines (a railway extending from Domodossola, Italy, to Lorarno, Switzerland).[105] She also told Plymouth that her representation in the House of Commons actually offered voters "double representation in Parliament," because they had both Lord *and* Lady Astor working for them. As a self-described "unrepentant believer in women," in combination with her new dedication to Anglo-American amity, Lady Astor announced that if wars were to be stopped, "women must stop them."[106] She also pledged to her supporters her continued efforts toward "Peace, Production, and Prosperity." She ended her open letter by reminding the people that while she was a Conservative, she worked with MPs of all parties on behalf of all Britons regardless of class: "I appeal for support to men and women of all parties, and of no party; and in particular to the new Women Voters. I have proved that I am ready and able to work for the general welfare, and not for any sectional interest. You took a risk when first you elected me. Since then I have taken many risks on your behalf. Let us once more stand by each other."[107]

Following her reelection, Lady Astor hosted a luncheon for all of the women now sitting in the House of Commons. She acknowledged to her fellow female MPs how exasperating it must be for them to have an American blaze the trail in Parliament. She then proceeded to tell the women gathered for what seemed an innocent lunch that they were to drop their political loyalties at once and join her proposed Women's Party. The newly elected female MPs were surprised and angry that she would place such demands on them immediately following their swearing-in ceremony.[108] Lady Astor's attempt to embrace a feminist cause failed miserably and foreshadowed her decline in her remaining years in the House of Commons. Her bold antics and rash but humorous behavior had been endearing in a private setting but did not fare nearly as well in a professional one.

Lady Astor enjoyed the pinnacle of her political career during the 1920s, during which she achieved many of her highest goals by improving the lives of women and children and increasing her overall popularity in the United States and Great Britain. But she did not enjoy the same level of success or esteem during the 1930s and 1940s. The Astors celebrated their twenty-fifth anniversary in 1931, an event noted in the "English-speaking world . . . [with] . . . ardent good wishes," but their heyday of Anglo-American influence had come to an end, evinced by an unfortunate international expedition.[109] In the summer of 1931, Lord and Lady Astor took a trip to Russia, along with friend George Bernard Shaw, to see Communist Russia.[110] Shaw, a professed communist, described the trip as "a bit of an accident. . . . The Astors suddenly took it to their heads to see for themselves whether Russia was really the earthly paradise I had declared it to be; and they challenged me to go with them."[111] Shaw recalled Nancy saying, "I am a Conservative. I am a Capitalist. I am opposed to Communism. I think you are all terrible." During one dinner with Stalin, the interpreter refused at first to translate her comments and questions. She reportedly asked, "When are you going to stop killing people?" Stalin answered, "When I think it is necessary to do so."[112] Needless to say, Lady Astor returned to Britain with a terrible impression of Russia. Stalin shared the same view of the brash American-born, British-wed wife. She had confirmed his worst impressions of Anglo-Americans.

In the years immediately preceding World War II, the Astors became known as pro-Nazi, pro-Hitler, and "friends of the Third Reich."[113] Lady Astor's fellow MPs referred to her as "the honourable member for Berlin."[114] Lord Astor's 1937 visit to Hitler was immediately suspect. Suddenly, Cliveden became known as a hotbed of communism, fascism, and appeasement. It was not until well after World War II that the manor finally shed this reputation. Before then, in 1942, the Astors gave it, along with a sizeable endowment, to the National Trust, with the stipulation that it be used for Anglo-American interests. In 1969, Stanford University began a twenty-one-year lease and transformed the estate into "an American campus," which would have pleased Lady Astor immensely.[115]

While the Astors were painted as unpatriotic pacifists, their efforts were largely due to their horrific experiences during World War I. Together, as individuals committed to both of their countries of birth and residence, they would have done almost anything to avoid another war. Given her inclination toward pacifism, both Americans and Britons now judged Lady Astor, once the darling of the Anglo-American world, harshly. American newspapers accused the couple of being "responsible for a new policy of determined efforts to make friends with Hitler and Mussolini."[116] In 1937 British journalist Claud Cockburn, a Marxist, equated the "Cliveden Set" with appeasement, which hurt Lady Astor's political career and her reputation as a liaison between the United States and Great Britain. Over the next several years, "the term Cliveden Set [became] a symbol . . . of not just appeasement but a failure to evaluate the world situation as it really was."[117] For the rest of their lives, Lord and Lady Astor denied that such a set existed but never completely rid themselves of the albatross.[118]

Although she had lost her popularity in both the United States and Great Britain, Lady Astor remained a heroine in Plymouth after the outbreak of World War II. She split her time between the military hospital at Cliveden and service as mayoress of Plymouth. At the age of sixty-two, Nancy appeared "immensely brave, outwardly fearless . . . she walked the street tirelessly and climbed the rubble often in highly dangerous circumstances," writes James Fox, "arranging shelter, food, clothing, evacuations, bullying the local authorities, talking to the remaining residents, the soldiers and sailors." She seemed to work day and night and remained visible to her loyal constituents. But she had indeed lost the love and support of the rest of Britain. A popular anti-Nancy song during World War II, "The D-Day Dodgers," sung to the theme of "Lili Marlene," follows:

Dear Lady Astor
    You're pretty hot
Standing on the platform
    Talking bloody rot
You're England's sweetheart and her pride
    We think your mouth's too bleeding wide
We are the D-Day dodgers
    In Sunny Italy.[119]

By 1944, the Astor family agreed that Lady Astor should not stand for reelection in Plymouth—or at least everyone except Nancy, who saw her family's request that she step aside as a male conspiracy and equivalent to her father's heavy-handed treatment. She announced to her Plymouth constituents, "I have said I will not fight the next election because my husband does not want me to. Isn't that a triumph for men?"[120] The truth was that not only had Nancy lost her base, she had become increasingly senile. Her notoriously candid personality had taken on a degree of maliciousness and acquired a bitter tone to even those closest to her. In 1942, during a debate at the House of Commons that was broadcast to the British public, Nancy calmly warned everyone about the dangers of Catholic influence: "The Foreign Office . . . was riddled with Catholics and there were far too many of these sinister zealots in active communication with Nazi-dominated Europe." In a speech in February 1942, she appeared incoherent and rambling, and her fellow MPs dismissed her as a "conspiracy scaremonger."[121]

Visibly upset, Lady Astor announced her retirement on December 1, 1944. One newspaper responded by stating the obvious: "The House will lose its most historic figure." The *Daily Mail* wrote, "Maybe there will never be another quite like her."[122]

On her last day in the House of Commons, June 14, 1945, a fellow MP told her how much she would be missed. Lady Astor replied, "I will miss the House: the House won't miss me. It never misses anybody. I have seen 'em all go—[David] Lloyd George, [Herbert Henry] Asquith, [Stanley] Baldwin, [Philip] Snowden, [James Ramsay] MacDonald—and not one of them missed." She lamented, "The House is like a sea. MPs are like little ships that sail across it, and disappear over the horizon. Some of 'em carry a light. Others don't. That's the only difference."[123]

An Extinct Volcano

After Nancy grudgingly left the House of Commons in 1945, she became a very bitter and unhappy person. Blaming Waldorf and her sons for forcing her to retire, she turned on her family members and accused them of making her quit something she loved so much because she was a woman, and, as men, they wanted to limit her life. Clearly, nothing could have been further from the truth. But at this point in their marriage, according to their son Michael, Lord and Lady Astor "fell out with each other."[124] As transatlantic voyages had helped assuage her anger in the past, she and her husband took a trip to the United States in 1946. When they arrived in New York, a throng of reporters met Nancy at the gangplank. When asked for a statement, she announced, "I am an extinct volcano." Her statements throughout her trip did not improve. After her visit to Savannah, Georgia, the press asked what she thought of the city. She complimented the city and described it as one of the most beautiful cities in America. But she went on to say, with an embellished south-ern accent, "But the way y'keep it. It's revoltin.' Never seen anythin' so revoltin' in m'life. Wherever y'go, there's litter. I'll tell you what I think of Savannah. I think it's a beautiful woman with a dirty face. One of the loveliest women in th' world who's forgotten to wash." While in Washington, D.C., she visited an all-black high school. She told the students that as a southerner, she learned to appreciate "colored people through her black mammy." As the United States stood on the cusp of the civil rights movement, she denounced Harlem culture, telling the students "No race can develop beyond its moral character" and urging them to return "to the simple faith of their 'Aunts and Uncles.'"[125] Neither the students nor the press, among whom were African American reporters, responded well to this. Lady Astor's objective in this tour, as with previous excursions to the United States, was to act as an Anglo-American ambassador. Clearly, this trip did not succeed as prior transatlantic jour-neys had. Nancy's time as an informal ambassador had passed.

In the end, Lady Astor blamed her husband of nearly forty years for her demise. Waldorf died in 1952, at the age of seventy-three. Nancy did not grieve in front of anyone and remained convinced he had been wrong to force her to resign her position as MP. In 1959, the Plymouth made Lady Astor a Freeman of the City, and she seemed happier for a time. But she never really accepted her absence from the House of Commons and began to mourn her husband's death only years after his passing. At the age of eighty-five, she suffered a stroke at Grimsthorpe, at her daughter Wissie's house. When the doctor asked her how she felt, she candidly answered, "Considering that I am dying, I am very well." Slipping in and out of consciousness, she lifted her arms and cried out, "Waldorf." She died in the early morning of May 2, 1964.[126] A memorial service followed on May 13, and the current prime minister, Sir Alex Douglas Home, attended. But Lady Astor's friends— Lloyd George, Asquith, and Balfour—had all died long before. Nancy truly had become an extinct volcano.[127]

Upon Lady Astor's death, former prime minister Lord Clement Attlee recorded his thoughts about her, published in the *Observer*. He recollected,

> Nancy Astor could be bold as brass; but she was in fact a kind and compassionate woman with, especially where women were concerned, a great sense of justice. She was no respecter of persons, and would take you down a peg as soon as look at you, but not if you were getting a raw deal or down on your luck. . . . Her most valuable work was to make it possible, often behind the scenes, for able and worthy people, welfare workers and social reformers, to get a hearing and a chance to act. She was amongst the impresarios of the Welfare State. . . . People like Nancy Astor, quite apart from their good works, are atmospheric. They make things hum.[128]

Lady Nancy Langhorne Astor left behind a mixed legacy. Like the other American-born, British-wed brides of the late nineteenth and early twentieth centuries, she took on a very public role due to her marriage to a leading British man. Like Lady Churchill and Mary Chamberlain, Nancy supported her husband's political career by hosting numerous dinner parties and making valuable contacts. Like Mary Curzon and Consuelo Vanderbilt, Lady Astor showed a keen interest in improving the lives of British women and children through a variety of projects, both philanthropic and political. But unlike her Anglo-American predecessors, she entered the world of British politics and forged a career in Parliament. Her entry into the House of Commons was significant not only because she was the first woman ever to take a seat as a Member of Parliament but also because as an American woman she earned this honor before a British woman. She worked tirelessly for women and children and improved Anglo-American relations. At the same time, her candid personality cost her friends, family, and constituents. Her once-entertaining commentary wore thin and eventually brought her political career to an end. She promised to "not be silent" in her political career, and that was a promise she most certainly kept. Though she was a "creature of impulses," the *New York Times* concluded, all of her "impulses [were] noble."[129] Throughout her life, the American and British public followed her evolution from wife to mother to campaign manager to political candidate to civic leader. Her consular position in Great Britain gave her the opportunity to work for an amelioration of Anglo-American relations, but her decision to pursue this goal with her own style and personality made her an invaluable informal ambassador between her two countries.

CHAPTER SEVEN

The American Invasion

It may with justice be said that it is by the American girl that we have been conquered.

—LADY DOROTHY NEVILL

*T*ransatlantic marriages, and the informal ambassadorships that resulted from them, began in earnest in the 1870s, after the union of Lord Randolph Churchill and Jennie Jerome. Often regarded as the pioneer in the Anglo-American marital market, Lady Churchill married into the British aristocracy when the American and British publics regarded such nuptials as something new, exciting, and symbolic of the growing friendship between the two countries. When such marriages began, one observer maintained, "The average American citizen is . . . pleased when he hears that another American girl had entered the exclusive circle of the British aristocracy."[1] Over time, Anglo-American marriages became something of a local-girl-makes-good story, which certainly seemed the case for both Mary Endicott Chamberlain and Mary Leiter Curzon, as their successes were celebrated in the United States and Great Britain. But the very nature of such unions implied that "materialistic motives were necessarily present in most marriage choices." As Sondra Herman contends, the mere use of the word "market . . . suggested a terrible impersonality in the exchange of love for support. The harshness of the business world was invading the home itself. Home was no longer a refuge from the cold world, but rather its extension."[2] According to her assessment, ambitious marriages, motivated solely by financial and social advancement, actually encouraged husbands and wives to engage in adultery.

A Titled American Is Not an American

As the Anglo-American marital market continued to grow throughout the late nineteenth and early twentieth centuries, the novelty of such nuptials gradually wore off. Both Americans and Britons began to view such matches as suspect and loveless unions, epitomized by the ostentatious wedding and strategic marriage of Conseulo Vanderbilt and the 9th Duke of Marlborough, which exchanged little more than capital for class.[3] Americans became increasingly convinced that transatlantic marriages unwittingly threw innocent democratic daughters from the land of opportunity into the hands of financially and morally bankrupt dukes from the land of heartless nobility. Conversely, Britons viewed such unions as the socially hungry Americans buying their way into the centuries-old British aristocracy and ruining the prestige of such an establishment. In considering Anglo-American marriages, Americans focused on the transference of money and the question of citizenship, while Britons expressed their disdain for *American* women holding *British* titles, as in the cases of Lady Jennie Churchill, Viscountess Mary Chamberlain, Lady and Vicereine Mary Curzon, the Duchess of Marlborough (Consuelo Vanderbilt), and Lady Nancy Astor. By the beginning of the twentieth century, the American colony had become an American invasion.[4]

Although the sentiment against such marriages began in full after 1895, particularly after the Vanderbilt-Marlborough wedding, some latent resentment toward Anglo-American marriages had existed earlier. When Lady Churchill's sister Clara married Moreton Frewen in 1881, Lord Stafford, heir to the Duke of Sutherland and a good friend of Frewen, attended the wedding in New York. Following the service, the mayor of New York City boldly asked Lord Stafford, "Did the pretty service not incline you to carry off some daughter of our Republic?" He answered brashly, "But no, my brother Francis is married and has children."[5] Why would he sacrifice his own marital independence if his brother's children could inherit the family title? This showed that he saw himself as the prey of beautiful, rich, predatory American heiresses.

Just as money played a central role in instigating Anglo-American marriages, it also helped evolve such nuptials into distasteful unions as perceived on both sides of the Atlantic. When George Charles Spencer-Churchill, the 8th Duke of Marlborough and Lord Randolph Churchill's brother, married Lillian Price Hammersley in 1888, attention returned to New York heiresses and the Churchill family. Lillian's own family was quite wealthy, and following the death of her first husband, Louis C. Hammersely, she received a fortune estimated at $6 million.[6] When she married the duke, she reportedly changed her name to Lily, since her birth name, Lillian, rhymed too easily with million—an attempt to distance herself from the negative connotation that had become associated with Anglo-American marriages and money.[7]

Conspicuous amounts of cash and capital continued to taint Anglo-American marriages through the end of the nineteenth century. When Miss Cornelia Bradley-Martin married the Earl of Craven in 1894 at the age of sixteen, many an American raised a disapproving eyebrow. Elizabeth Cameron, the wife of the senator from Pennsylvania, wrote to Cecil Spring Rice, "The wedding of Miss Bradley-Martin, aged sixteen, to the Earl of Craven has been one of the most disgusting exhibitions of American snobbery I have ever seen. Even New York was disgusted at such a palpable sale."[8] Miss Bradley-Martin's marriage to a titled Briton transferred a settlement in the amount of $1 million from one side of the Atlantic to the other. Shortly after her wedding, the *New York Times* published an article titled, "American Women Who Have Given Their Hearts and Money to Foreigners." It estimated "that English noblemen alone have captured by marriage with American women in round numbers $50,000,000 of enviable American cash."[9] In 1909 an article appeared in the *New York Journal* with the title "How Titled Foreigners Catch American Heiresses."[10] Americans appeared most distressed about the waves of financial resources of wealthy heiresses traveling across the Atlantic, which was ultimately the most important factor in the turn against such marriages.

A key signal of Americans' increasing resentment toward Anglo-American marriages came in 1896 when Gertrude Vanderbilt married Harry Whitney. The *New York Journal* declared, "From an American standpoint [this is] the greatest wedding this country has ever known. Money will marry money next Tuesday. Broad acres will be wed to broad acres. Railroads will be linked to railroads." The journalist celebrated: "It will be an American wedding. There will be no foreign noblemen in this—no purchase of titles. The millions all belong in America and they will all remain here. . . . An American boy, an American girl, [and] an American courtship." As Gertrude's marriage took place a mere nine months after her cousin's forced marriage to the 9th Duke of Marlborough, such negative comments clearly indicate that the tide had largely turned against Anglo-American unions. At the Vanderbilt-Whitney wedding reception, the bandleader could not restrain himself from playing "The Star-Spangled Banner."[11]

Clearly, many Americans had become increasingly frustrated by the flow of money to Great Britain via Anglo-American marriages. In 1895, a founder of the National Association of Manufacturers (NAM) expressed a perspective many Americans shared. He asserted the British "come over here every day and trade us a second-class duke or third-class earl for a first-class American girl, and get several million dollars to boot." Disgusted, he continued, "The very next day the entire outfit goes back to Liverpool on a British vessel. We didn't even get the freight back to Liverpool on the earl, the girl, or the money."[12] As an example of this sentiment, upon the arrival of the Marquess of Stafford to the United States, the *New York World* asked its readers, "Attention, American heiresses, what will you bid?"[13]

At the same time, first-class American girls advertised themselves in such a way that made it difficult for them later to feel offended by British accusations of buying their way into the British aristocracy. In February 1901, an American heiress placed an advertisement in the *Daily Telegraph:* "Will any dukes, marquesses, earls, or other noblemen desirous of meeting, for the purpose of marriage, young, beautiful *and* rich American heiresses communicate with . . ." It followed with the name and address of a broker in New Orleans.[14] Thus, Americans projected two contradictory messages: American men accused British men of heiress hunting, and American heiresses made themselves more than available for the hunting. As transatlantic marriages became ordinary fare, one candid observer concluded that they "became an opportunity for profitable matrimonial alliances which resulted in a general refurbishing of family coffers."[15]

When the number of Anglo-American unions increased noticeably during the early twentieth century, Americans scrutinized them with mixed emotions. Their love-hate relationship mimics many Americans' dual sentiments of Anglophilia and Anglophobia. In the late nineteenth century, most Americans regarded marriages between American daughters and British sons with excitement along with a latent hostility, similar to their overall disapproval of Anglo-American marriages but great approval of Anglo-American brides. By 1900, however, an increasing number of Americans regarded such weddings with an overt antagonism, though they maintained ideas supporting the superiority of the Anglo-Saxon race. President Theodore Roosevelt, for example, regarded such unions as purely "mammon istic" arrangements that had no moral or emotional backbone to support them. He declared, "The American citizen who deserved the least respect was the man 'whose son is a fool and his daughter a foreign Princess.'"[16] Roosevelt, and likely many others, considered "those who whored after titles abroad 'a might poor lot of shoats,' and traitors to republican principles."[17] At the same time, Roosevelt was one of the leading proponents of assumed Anglo-Saxon racial superiority, believing the race was destined to rule the world, a notion many of the American-born, British-wed women also expressed after their transatlantic marriages. Like the president, Reverend R. S. MacArthur, a pastor in New York City, held a disapproving view of the unions and particularly of British men and described the marriages as "a matter of sale and purchase." He avowed, "American girls have sold their womanhood, their country, their language, and their religion for husbands who are peculiarly contemptible cads." Likewise, U.S. representative Charles McGavin (R-IL) also condemned these marriages, asserting that the brides were guilty of "sacrificing their souls and honor upon the altar of snobbery and vice" and hailing their decision to marry foreigners as an insult to the founders of the United States.

He continued: "While I have engaged in some criticism of those particular women who have made a mockery of the most sacred relations of life—of those not satisfied with any other name than Countess Spaghetti or Macaroni, I want to say one word in tribute to those true American women who spurned the wiles of earls, lords and counts for the love of His Majesty, an American citizen."[18]

One U.S. citizen, who, though well known, was not a public officeholder, espoused strong opinions against transatlantic marriages based on his socialist political views. In 1918, Eugene V. Debs, a four-time presidential candidate for the Social Democratic Party, spoke in Canton, Ohio. While his dialogue focused on his antiwar position regarding World War I, he presented his view on British-American unions.

> To whom do the Wall Street Junkers in our country marry their daughters? After they have wrung their countless millions from your sweat, your agony and your life's blood, in a time of war as in a time of peace, they invest these untold millions in the purchase of titles of broken-down aristocrats, such as princes, dukes, counts and other parasites and no-accounts. [Laughter.] Would they be satisfied to wed their daughters to honest workingmen? [Shouts from the crowd, "No!"] To real democrats? Oh, no! They scour the markets of Europe for vampires who are titled and nothing else. [Laughter.] And they swap their millions for the titles, so that matrimony with them becomes literally a matter of money.[19]

More Than a Symbolic Punishment

While American women gained a great deal socially through Anglo-American marriages, they lost a great deal individually. In 1907, Congress passed the Expatriation Act, which declared that any American woman who married a foreigner would formally assume the nationality of her husband and as a result forfeit her American citizenship. During the 59th Congress, U.S. representative James Breck Perkins (R-NY) introduced the legislation as Public Law 193. It was consistent with immigration restrictions during the period aimed at maintaining the homogenous characteristics of an American nationality based on western and northern European heritage. Under the law, American women who married British aristocrats lost their American citizenship.[20] Of course, as Nancy Cott put it, "placing the woman who married a foreign national outside the American political community entailed more than a symbolic punishment."[21] While an American-born, British-wed wife might gain a great deal socially by virtue of her transatlantic marriage, she now lost her first identity and her American status was officially revoked.

Before the Expatriation Act, the U.S. government had not addressed various questions related to the formation of American nationality and citizenship. Prior to 1855, marriage in the United States did not affect citizenship or nationality. In 1855, the Nationality Act declared, "Any woman who might lawfully be naturalized under existing laws, married, or who shall be married to a citizen of the United States shall be deemed and taken to be a citizen." Thus, marriage between an American man and an alien woman formally provided her with American nationality and citizenship. The law did not address the opposite situation.[22]

Not until the Expatriation Act of 1907 did the U.S. Congress address the issue of marriage between an American woman and an alien man. This law officially codified derivative citizenship—a woman's citizenship being contingent on her husband's.[23] Though the Expatriation Act did not directly terminate her American nationality and citizenship, it stated that an American woman who married a foreigner took her husband's nationality. And since one state cannot force another to grant citizenship to an individual based on the original state's decision to deny citizenship, transatlantic marriages left some transatlantic brides stateless and legally without a national identity. As Candice Bredbenner explains, the "choice of a spouse was the overriding legislative determinant of a married woman's nuptial contract."[24] Not until the British Nationality and Status of Aliens Act of 1914 did British law address the legal question of American wives. Under this act, "the wife of a British subject shall be deemed to be a British subject and the wife of an alien be deemed to be an alien."[25]

Throughout history, nations have enforced expatriation, or the loss of citizenship, as a severe form of punishment, typically in cases of treason. Undoubtedly, the decision to retract an American woman's citizenship following her marriage to a titled foreigner essentially, though unofficially, labeled her a traitor.[26] In discussing the decision to marry an American man or a foreign one, congressional officials posed the question of "whether a woman shall be penalized for marrying a foreigner." While one House member answered that she should, another expressed the perspective of many other Americans: "That is a question for her to decide. She knows that will be the result when she considers marrying a foreigner."[27] During another hearing concerning women's citizenship and marriage, one committee member remarked that the hazards of such marriages were "a good lesson to our American girls to marry American boys." When a woman challenged the committee members on the grounds that men formed such laws from the perspective of a man, safe in his citizenship because of his sex, a congressman declared, "You *have* your citizenship; we *love* ours."[28] Throughout the House hearings on citizenship, the "dukes and counts" argument prevailed. Representative Samuel Dickstein (D-NY) testified, "They brought it about themselves, did they not? . . . The women who married these foreign dukes and counts, these duchesses and countesses and that sort of stuff, when there are enough Americans for them to choose from."[29] From the perspective of the federal government in the early twentieth century, a woman's choice to marry a non-American was wholly un-American.

At a time of "100 percent Americanism," the question of equal and independent citizenship of men and women became secondary to official efforts to restrict American citizenship during a period of rising immigration. Gaining and retaining American citizenship became ever more difficult, and Congress deemed women's decisions to marry foreigners equivalent to "voluntarily forsak[ing] their allegiance to the United States." As Speaker of the House James G. Blaine had explained years earlier, "every woman who leaves the duty and decorum of her native land and prostitutes her American name to the scandals, the vices, the social immoralities and moral impurities of foreign cities not only compasses her own shame, but mars the fair fame of the republic."[30]

American women dealt with their expatriation after marriage to British men in a variety of ways. When President Ulysses S. Grant's daughter, Nellie, married Briton Algernon Sartoris in the White House in 1874, she lost her citizenship. The pair divorced in 1893, and the U.S. Congress reinstated her citizenship by a special act in 1898.[31] Consuelo Vanderbilt's mother became frustrated by what she perceived as her duchess daughter's indifference to having lost her American nationality.[32] On the contrary, Consuelo was quite upset, but given the legal circumstances, she could do little. Many years after divorcing the Duke of Marlborough and leaving Britain, she wrote in her autobiography that she was "back in my native land, having regained a citizenship I would never have resigned had the law of my day permitted me to retain it."[33] In another case, Ethel Mackenzie married Gordon Mackenzie, a British subject, in 1909. As a leader of the women's suffrage movement in California, she tried to register in the San Francisco voter registration drive in 1911, but the Board of Election Commissioners rejected her application, on the grounds that upon her marriage to a Briton she "ceased to be a citizen of the United States." Mackenzie appealed to the U.S. Supreme Court, asserting that her citizenship was a "privilege and immunity which could not be taken away from her except as a punishment for crime or by her voluntary expatriation." The law's implication suggests that any woman who engaged in an Anglo-American marriage had committed a crime. Ultimately, Justice Joseph McKenna rejected her case, arguing that the "marriage of an American woman with a foreigner . . . is as voluntary and distinctive as expatriation and with its consequences must be considered as elected."[34] Finally, Ruth Bryan Owen, the daughter of four-time presidential candidate William Jennings Bryan, married British officer Reginald Altham Owen in 1910. Following the passage of the Cable Act in 1922, she formally regained her citizenship through naturalization in 1925. When she announced her candidacy in 1926 for the U.S. House of Representatives from Florida, she faced major obstacles due to her Anglo-American marriage. She fought once to run for the House—the entity that had terminated her citizenship in the first place—and was successfully elected in 1928 and battled again after she took her seat in the nation's capital. In both cases, her opponents attacked her on the grounds that her marriage to a foreigner disqualified her from running for public office.[35] In her testimony before fellow House members, Owen explained, "The law had taken my citizenship away at the time of my marriage." When Representative Albert Johnson (R-WA), House Immigration and Naturalization Committee chair countered, "You left the country and abandoned your citizenship by marriage to a foreigner," Owen quickly answered, "I did not abandon my citizenship." Johnson replied, "You took on the citizenship of another country," to which Owen retorted, "I did not take it. It was forced upon me by an unjust law, now repealed. A woman who married a foreigner was not considered a loyal citizen, despite her view of the matter."[36] The reflections and comments by many of the American-born, British-wed women examined in this work clearly demonstrate that they all maintained a love and loyalty to their nation of birth. Owen retained her House seat and served as a Florida representative from 1928 to 1932, but she was not reelected in 1932.

With the Expatriation Act, the U.S. Congress sent American women a clear message that marriage to a foreign man was despicable and attempted to influence them formally against such unions through negative reinforcement. Likewise, stories in popular magazines sent American women messages advocating marriage to American men. The *Woman's Journal* published an article titled "Warning to American Heiresses." It begged them to consider the "suicidal folly of abandoning the cheerful freedom and rational simplicity of our democratic social life for such a fate!" And it continued, "Let us hope that the higher education of women may gradually wean the daughters of our millionaires from the worship of titles and aristocracy, and bring them to an intelligent appreciation of the nobility and value of American citizenship."[37] American heiresses now received serious encouragement *not* to marry into the British aristocracy.

The Expatriation Act remained the law and decided the status of American women's citizenship until 1922, when John L. Cable (R-OH) introduced a new piece of legislation. The Married Women's Act, also known as the Cable Act, partially repealed the Expatriation Act by declaring the American woman "subject to the same presumption as a natural citizen."[38] The law finally gave each woman a citizenship in her own right. Since this law, no marriage has granted American citizenship to any alien woman or taken it from any American-born woman who married an alien eligible to naturalize. Under the new law, women became eligible to naturalize on essentially the same grounds as men. The only difference in treatment between men and women was in the handling of the woman whose husband had already been naturalized. If her husband was a citizen, the wife did not need to file a declaration of intention. She could initiate naturalization proceedings with a petition. If her husband remained an alien, she had to start with a declaration of intention. In sum, women who lost their citizenship by marriage regained it under the Cable Act provisions after filing the proper paperwork in any naturalization court, regardless of their residence.[39]

By the time the national government began drafting and imposing laws retracting women's citizenship based on marriages to foreign men, most Americans had already turned against Anglo-American marriages due to a sense of national pride, reflecting the increasing nationalism typical of the period. For many Americans, "a titled American was an affront to American ideals, a blatant repudiation of democratic tradition." As marriage to a British aristocrat required an American woman to leave the United States, her choice often received criticism, as it signified her "indifference toward, if not contempt for, the virtues of democratic society." For these reasons, by the twentieth century even elite Americans strongly condemned transatlantic marriages, and Americans of all classes strongly disapproved of American women who renounced their heritage in favor of the "Old World."[40] As federal legislation now revoked their American citizenship, American-born, British-wed women were without a home and out of place in both countries. If they had no home base from which to mediate, no space that a candid consular could negotiate, their time as the wives of British aristocrats and as drawing-room diplomats was over. They had become envoys without an embassy.

Gilded Prostitution

Just as Americans turned from Anglo-American marriages, so did Britons. They, too, increasingly viewed the transference of money as a key reason to judge such unions with scorn. When aristocratic Tories harassed Irish leader John Redmond for receiving funds from Americans, David Lloyd George came to his defense. "Since when," he boldly demanded of his colleagues, "have the British aristocracy started despising American dollars[?] (Laughter, and a voice, 'Marlborough.') I see you understand me." Thus, Britons considered such financial exchanges as loveless matches. According to contemporary journalist William T. Stead, "it is not too much to say that when there is no love in the matter, it is only gilded prostitution."[41] Such a negative label reflected the widespread sentiment Britons held toward the American heiresses but begs the question of who to identify as the prostitute: the American women, who were paid with a title, or the British aristocrats, paid with riches from the "land of the Almighty dollar"?[42]

The American invasion had diluted the distinction between classes in Britain,

as was arguably the case in the Endicott-Chamberlain marriage, a development
the aristocracy found distasteful. One contemporary journal decried this: "The
main distinction between aristocracy and trade has been founded on money. The
landowning classes inherited their money and did not make it. The commercial
classes earned it by traffic. The recognition of trade at once weakened this distinction, and has practically destroyed it by now."[43] While British aristocrats welcomed American dollars to restore country estates and renovate family palaces,
they did not appreciate that the American plutocracy now served as the backbone
of the British aristocracy.[44]

Even as American heiresses renovated castles and estates across Britain with
their daddies' American dollars, giving rise to a new notion of dollar diplomacy,
one particular group of Britons met their American sisters with a frosty reception:
British women. Titles were few, money was tight, and female members of the British aristocracy considered every American woman in England a potential husband
stealer, as Nancy Langhorne Shaw quickly discovered on one of her first hunting
escapades. British women believed that American heiresses had "an unfair advantage over British girls because of their bank accounts."[45] Many did not hold definite
grudges against American women but simply preferred them to stay on *their* side
of the Atlantic. Lady Dorothy Nevill once explained, "I like the Americans very
well, but there are two things I wish they would keep to themselves—their girls and
their tinned lobster."[46]

In a 1908 magazine article, a British woman expressed the collective view when
she questioned the motivations of American women in pursuing British aristocrats,
specifically their titles. "The American women who are looking for foreign titles
don't stop to weigh whether the marriage will be happy or otherwise, do they—provided they make the title?" From this perspective, American women cared nothing
for their marriages, their spouses, or their positions in Britain as long as they attained an impressive title and proper castle, so they shared the responsibility when
their transatlantic marriages became unhappy or failed entirely. Following that line
of thought, the author asked, "Doesn't it stand to reason that an American girl's best
chance of happiness is in marrying one of her own countrymen?"[47]

After criticizing transatlantic marriages for the transference of money and acquisition of hereditary titles, British women began to disparage Anglo-American
brides as "titled Americans." In 1905, an anonymous author, protectively identifying herself or himself as "Colonial," contended, "The American may become
French, Italian, and even German, but she seldom, if ever, becomes English. Hence
she is in society, but not of it." After further criticizing American women's behavior, education, and training, the author boldly demanded, "take away their millions from Americans and how much would one hear of them in the great world?"
Then she presented her deepest disparagement: the inability of American women

to produce children, specifically boys. "Since 1840 thirty peers or eldest sons of peers have married in the United States. Of these, thirteen have no children at all, five have no sons, and five have an only son. The total number of peers' children with American mothers is thirty-nine, of whom eighteen are sons." She went on to discuss the number, or lack, of children by American mothers in the lower ranks of the aristocracy. She claimed that these numbers "are proof, if any were needed, of the growing sterility of American women, a fact which presents a serious problem." Thus, an American woman either could not or would not produce children for her British husband. Members of the British aristocracy were well aware of the need for children—and specifically male heirs, as Lady Curzon was made acutely aware—to inherit the family estate and carry on the family title. In the absence of children, and sons in particular, no amount of American dollars could sustain the British aristocracy. As "Colonial" concluded, "Anglo-American marriages have no sound basis whatever. Broadly speaking, they are an alliance between title and dollars. . . . American influence is feminine, frivolous, and fleeting."[48] In a climate of such decidedly negative opinions, the once celebrated marital phenomenon, and period of women serving as informal ambassadors, had met a cynical conclusion.

The End of Anglo-American Marriages

For all of these reasons, especially those related to public opinion on both sides of the Atlantic, Anglo-American marriages fell out of favor after 1900. World War I was the final blow to such unions. During the war, safety concerns prevented Americans from traveling to London or Europe for leisure, which cost them the many contacts necessary to enter the highest social circles abroad.[49] By 1919, after the Treaty of Versailles was signed, the war had tied together the economies of the United States and Great Britain but differently from the transatlantic exchange of money prior to 1914. World War I had all but ended the growth of new money in the United States, and the once popular attraction of American women to British titles and of British aristocrats to American dollars no longer existed to the same degree.[50] Thus, the long nineteenth century came to an end when World War I began and consigned Anglo-American marriages to the nineteenth-century ideals of traditional womanhood and likeminded marriages.

In addition to World War I, two specific events resulted in a significant lack of royal support of such unions. On May 6, 1910, King Edward VII died, and his passing seemed "to herald the end of the social sway of American women at the British court."[51] Edward had welcomed American-born, British-wed brides into his circle decades before he ever took the throne. His inclusion of them and his support of Anglo-American marriages gave the unions a regal stamp of approval for approximately forty years. His parents, Victoria and Albert, did not share his views, and Edward's son, George V, favored his grandparents. Thus, in the absence of the Marlborough Set, the royal family no longer greeted American women hospitably upon their arrival in London.

A final factor working against transatlantic marriages in the twentieth century was Edward VIII's 1936 abdication. His choice to marry an American divorcée rather than serve as the King of England showed that he loved an American woman more than his homeland. His resignation left a sour American taste in the mouths of millions of Britons. Ever the liaison, Lady Astor, a good friend of Edward VIII, tried to convince her American friends that the reaction against Wallis Simpson stemmed from the fact that she was a divorcée, not her being American. She convinced few people, but it mattered little. A wealth of factors, financial and otherwise, had already converged to deliver the death knell to Anglo-American marriages and an era in which these women served as nongovernmental but influential attachés of Anglo-American relations.[52] Ladies Churchill, Curzon, and Astor's work in fulfilling a man's job as international emissaries had ended. The utilization of soft power by Mary Endicott Chamberlain and the Duchess of Marlborough was no more.

But historians would be remiss to overlook the fact that not all Britons resented this particular Anglo-American connection. The son of Sir William Harcourt and an American woman declared, "I am not ashamed of the American blood in my veins. I am proud to be the son of the Englishman who led this House, and I am no less proud to be the grandson of the American who wrote the 'Dutch Republic.'" He continued, "There is talk of American dollars. America is not peopled only by those who buy the pictures and the first-born of the British aristocracy at a price somewhat higher than the figure in the Home market." In an era of transatlantic resentment, he eloquently summarized the Anglo-American connection: "America is a sister whose pulse beats with our own."[53] As the son and grandson of Americans, Harcourt had good reason to endorse his Anglo-Saxon blood. But he and other sons of American mothers, such as Winston Churchill, were now in a distinct minority in Parliament and throughout Britain.

Just as a whole host of factors occurred to court transatlantic marriages, numerous developments followed to bring the trend of Anglo-American marriages to an end. Over time, public opinion on both sides of the Atlantic turned against these unions. Americans initially resented bankrupt British dukes stealing away American daughters of democracy from the United States during the nineteenth century, and in the twentieth century, they resented the choice by American women to marry British titles. Likewise, many Britons begrudged the American invasion of Great Britain, London, and Parliament in particular and blamed American heiresses for diluting the British aristocracy's prestige. Specific events—including World War I, the death of Edward VII, and the abdication of Edward VIII—also worked to increase resentment of Anglo-American marriages. Perhaps the 9th Duke of Marlborough, once married to Consuelo Vanderbilt, best summarized the era:

> It was a period when many of the daughters of America elected to marry and identify their lives with Europeans and notably Englishmen—They exchanged the home life of America for that of England, and the new angles of vision with which they perceived the old world enabled them to leave an imprint on the customs of a society which hitherto had grown up sheltered in its insular tradition. This period of social intercourse, this period of international relation is not likely to recur because Europe and its traditions no longer appeal with the same force and vigour to the American feminine mind as they did in the closing years of the Victorian era.[54]

Thus, the age of Anglo-American marriages came to an end, as the "Lord of Position and the Lady of Cash . . . each the price and treasure of a nation, each the center of a thousand hopes, saturated with a sense of distinction, superior by divine right," faded into history.[55]

Conclusion

Ambassadors by Any Name

$\mathcal{D}$uring the late nineteenth and early twentieth centuries, significant numbers of American heiresses married British aristocrats. As a result of these marriages, young women largely left their American families and national identities behind when they took the title of lady or duchess. By virtue of her marriage and position in the British aristocracy, an American woman entered a foreign country and alien cultural experience despite a shared history and language. Consequently, she could crumble beneath the incredible pressure and stress of her position as the wife of Lord Lambert or the Duke of Devonshire, or she could make the most of her lifelong ambassadorial position and mold a new identity and purpose by blending her American past and her British future.

As the wife of Lord Randolph Churchill, Lady Churchill took full advantage of her position in British society. She hosted dinner parties and pursued powerful contacts, just as any diplomat or attaché would do when assigned to a foreign post. She supported her husband's political career and managed his campaigns by using a distinctly American style of politics against a British backdrop. After his early death, she retained her leading poli-social position by founding a journal, working as an international editor, and serving as a literary liaison between her country of birth and country of marriage. She thereby established herself as an Anglo-American advocate through formal philanthropic activities and informal daily interactions with Britons at the highest levels. When her son Winston came of age, she used her contacts and experience to advance his political career. Lady Churchill was called the most powerful Anglo-Saxon woman of her time; her life in Britain demonstrated one woman's ability to serve as a nongovernmental agent, represent two countries at the same time, and work toward one goal: the improvement of Anglo-American relations.

Before Mary Endicott wed Joseph Chamberlain in 1888, the pair kept their engagement secret for fear of its effect on domestic politics; little did either know the tremendous effect the union would have on diplomatic relations. Upon her arrival in England, Mary was greeted with enthusiastic cheers for "our American cousin!" This reception of a drawing-room diplomat proves telling, as twentieth-century wives of official diplomats were given instructional manuals for their new duties that included a chapter titled "Our British Cousins"; this repetitive theme heightens the connection between the two countries. Again, the expectations for elite women of this era and those for wives of official diplomats prove eerily similar, as their work was traditional, unpaid, but absolutely necessary to their respective communities. Like formal ambassadors, Anglo-American brides were dedicated negotiators; savvy international politicians; and masters of soft power over dinner, drinks, and dialogue. Mary certainly did her part—through correspondence, dinner parties, and intimate involvement in her husband's political career—to earn the respect and recognized influence of Britons and Americans alike.

Mary Leiter's marriage to George Curzon in 1895 proved both a love match and an ideal union of beauty and brains. Her fortune and fortitude combined with his breeding and ambition eventually earned them positions as the ruler and consort of the jewel in Britain's imperial crown at the height of the Empire. Upon her approval to serve as vicereine of India, Lady Curzon, the American turned British peeress, represented a world power and acted as international mediator for that power in an imperial land. As her husband's most trusted envoy, she served as his personal emissary to and from Britain—a position of enormous power for an American girl from Chicago. In Mary's every word and deed, her devotion to her homeland and husband was evident.

Consuelo Vanderbilt married the 9th Duke of Marlborough in 1895, only seven months after the Curzon nuptials, a union that symbolized the shift in transatlantic marriages from love match to loveless merger of family fortunes. Upon becoming the Duchess of Marlborough, she fulfilled her mother's dream, not her own. Though her forced marriage exemplified the worst stereotypes of Anglo-American unions, Consuelo's response to her difficult situation was anything but stereotypical. She could have justifiably wallowed in self-pity; instead, she pursued a life of philanthropic works and political ambitions at the national and international level, focusing on the needs of the poor, women, and children. Though her life as an informal ambassador began at the historic nadir of Anglo-American marriages, her life abroad exemplified the very best qualities of American-born, British-wed women as benefactors of Anglo-American relations. Throughout her life in Britain, and particularly after her separation from the duke, as an ideal representative and incredibly elegant envoy of the United States she remained dedicated to improving the lives of those around her. As the "Baby Duchess," she became an American Lady Bountiful to an entire country and in particular to thousands women and children. She constantly negotiated her national identity on both sides of the Atlantic; Britons defined her as the Duchess of Marlborough and American newspapers identified her as the former Miss Vanderbilt. Rather than feel constrained or torn by such labels, Consuelo simply was herself and created a truly Anglo-American identity, which started through philanthropy and ended with a brief career in politics.

Lady Nancy Astor's marriage to William Waldorf Astor II, too, does not fit the "title-hunting American heiress" stereotype. Rather, like Lady Churchill, the Duchess of Marlborough, and other American-born, British-wed women living in Britain, she pursued her life abroad as she believed appropriate. Her marriage to Waldorf later provided her the title of "lady," and her Cliveden estate afforded her the time, servants, and money to become a leading hostess in Britain's poli-social circles in much the same manner as Lady Churchill, as a political peeress, candid consul, and international representative. She eventually pursued a political career, following in her husband's footsteps, and sought to improve the lives of women and children, much like Consuelo Marlborough. Lady Astor, whom her constituents affectionately called "our Nancy," became the first woman to take a seat in the British House of Commons and retained this seat for twenty-five years.

Collectively and individually, the five American women highlighted in this book, and the hundreds of other such Anglo-American brides, left their homes and typically lived the rest of their lives abroad, much like career diplomats. Americans and Britons followed the activities and acquaintances of the American-born, British-wed women and made conclusions about the people on the other side of the Atlantic based on their interactions with the newly titled American women. For better or for worse, through successful or unsuccessful marriages, these women served as informal ambassadors between their country of birth and their country by marriage. They constantly negotiated their own national identities based on the time, place, and circumstances of their surroundings and learned from experience when to emphasize their American or British nationality. Their lives abroad gave them countless diplomatic opportunities to represent the United States to Great Britain as the two nations moved close to a rapprochement and a truly special relationship.

By considering these marriages broadly, and the women presented in this book specifically, historians discover a broad spectrum of endeavors this collective cohort of women pursued. The first significant American-born, British-wed woman, Lady Jennie Churchill skillfully utilized the traditional sector of women's work—as a wife, mother, and internationally celebrated hostess—to make contacts, establish friendships, and manipulate a wealth of poli-social affairs for the betterment of Anglo-American relations. Through her pathbreaking activities and her feminine leadership, she united other American-born, British-wed women as the American Amazons, who served as lifelong ambassadors advocating a collective Anglo-Saxon identity and enhanced Anglo-American relations. As the wife of an imperialist politician and proud advocate of her Anglo-American identity, Mary Endicott Chamberlain continued such womanly duties as a subtle but significant drawing-room diplomat who worked independent of and with Lady Churchill's American Amazons to unite her two countries. The magnitude and reach of her transatlantic correspondence united Anglo-Americans across the Atlantic, as did the letters of Mary Leiter Curzon, eventually an emissary not only to Britain but to India. Their shared interests in correspondence and superb interpersonal skills identify them as masters of soft power. Through Lady Curzon's dedication to her husband and her two countries, she demonstrated her professional skills as an accomplished mediator. By examining their collective and individual efforts, one can evaluate elite women's work as a silhouette of the professional and traditional responsibilities and requirements often charged to (male) diplomats. While she began her life abroad as an envoy abroad behind this shielded classification of women's work, the Duchess of Marlborough, like Lady Churchill before her, demonstrated her most important influences after her marriage had ended. Like Lady Astor after her, she increasingly engaged in political practices to improve the lives of women. Thus, the lives of these women trace a spectrum of increasing independence inside and outside the home and demonstrate the degree to which women could carve their own identity and participate in politics, internationally or otherwise. They influenced Anglo-American perceptions at a critical moment in bilateral relations while also offering a broader image of how a person, and a woman at that, could serve as an informal ambassador.

The existence of marriages between powerful British policymakers and American heiresses raises several questions about the evolution of Anglo-American relations. The disagreement among scholars as to the significance of these marriages makes further research even more intriguing. Whether they influenced diplomatic policy remains debatable, but their significance to Anglo-American relations remains the core issue. The consideration of transatlantic marriages through a lens of cultural diplomacy contributes to the traditional field of diplomatic history by incorporating new ideas and research possibilities. The diplomacy resulting from British-American marriages offers a unique position from which to consider unofficial international relations; despite the importance contemporaries attached to such marriages, historians have not yet studied the connections among foreign policy, gender roles, and transatlantic marriages. Thus, this project ties together race, class, and gender though diplomatic history.

As transatlantic marriages reached their peak at the turn of the twentieth century, American-born, British-wed women seized multiple opportunities to unite their countries by birth and marriage through a variety of Anglo-American ventures; they skillfully negotiated their dual identities as opportunities dictated. Both collectively and individually, these women were seen and saw themselves through a contemporary lens of Anglo-Saxonism, a third identity this transnational cohort manipulated upon demand. Their transnational activities traversed political, economic, and social boundaries outside of traditional historic parameters. Their shared principles regarding class, race, imperialism, and nationalism motivated their efforts in avoiding war in the Venezuelan boundary dispute, in creating an elite Anglo-American literary and philanthropic network, and finally, in being activists during both the Boer War and World War I. By examining the international activities and efforts of women, the study offers historians specifically and scholars broadly an opportunity to reconsider the interaction of countries outside the rigid domain of traditional nation-to-nation dealings, providing a more inclusive, and thus richer, view of historical inquiry. With a delicate readjustment of the historical lens, researchers may bring the full picture into focus and see for the first time the transnational actors, in this case, women, who have been in the background all the while.

Diplomatic representation abroad has thus far been limited to clerks with pens or men with titles such as "the honorable" or "ambassador." In seeking to understand the shaping of foreign relations—not necessarily foreign policy—a whole host of factors must be acknowledged and considered if the most thorough picture possible is to be painted. In assessing the overall gradual rapprochement of the United States and Great Britain, a number of developments must therefore be considered— including Anglo-American marriages. While these unions are not the key to unlocking the mystery of British-American relations, historians omit a serious factor if they overlook them as little more than a passing marital trend. These marriages, these women, these informal ambassadors are critically important if historians are to consider the comprehensive picture of Anglo-American relations.

Appendixes

U.S. Presidents

Name	Party	Dates of service
Abraham Lincoln	Republican	March 4, 1861–April 15, 1865
Andrew Johnson	Democrat	April 15, 1865–March 3, 1869
Ulysses S. Grant	Republican	March 4, 1869–March 3, 1877
Rutherford B. Hayes	Republican	March 4, 1877–March 3, 1881
James Garfield	Republican	March 4, 1881–September 19, 1881
Chester Arthur	Republican	September 19, 1881–March 3, 1885
Grover Cleveland	Democrat	March 4, 1885–March 3, 1889
Benjamin Harrison	Republican	March 4, 1889–March 1893
Grover Cleveland	Democrat	March 4, 1893–March 3, 1897
William McKinley	Republican	March 4, 1897–September 14, 1901
Theodore Roosevelt	Republican	September 14, 1901–March 3, 1909
William Taft	Republican	March 4, 1909–March 3, 1913
Woodrow Wilson	Democrat	March 4, 1913–March 3, 1921
Warren G. Harding	Republican	March 4, 1921–August 2, 1923
Calvin Coolidge	Republican	August 2, 1923–March 3, 1929

U.S. Vice Presidents

Name	President served under	Dates of service
Hannibal Hamlin	Lincoln	March 4, 1861–March 4, 1865
Andrew Johnson	Lincoln	March 4, 1861–April 15, 1865
Vacant	Johnson	April 15, 1865–March 4, 1869
Schuyler Colfax	Grant	March 4, 1869–March 4, 1873
Henry Wilson	Grant	March 4, 1873–November 22, 1875
Vacant	Grant	November 22, 1875–March 4, 1877
William Wheeler	Hayes	March 4, 1877–March 4, 1881
Chester A. Arthur	Garfield	March 4, 1881–September 19, 1881
Vacant	Arthur	September 19, 1881–March 4, 1885

Name	President served under	Dates of service
Thomas Hendricks	Cleveland	March 4, 1885–November 25, 1885
Vacant	Harrison	November 25, 1885–March 4, 1889
Levi Morton	Harrison	March 4, 1889–March 4, 1893
Adlai E. Stevenson I	Cleveland	March 4, 1893–March 4, 1897
Garret Hobart	McKinley	March 4, 1897–November 21, 1899
Vacant	McKinley	November 21, 1899–March 4, 1901
Theodore Roosevelt	McKinley	March 4, 1901–September 14, 1901
Vacant	Roosevelt	September 14, 1901–March 4, 1905
Charles W. Fairbanks	Roosevelt	March 4, 1905–March, 1909
James S. Sherman	Taft	March 4, 1909–October 30, 1912
Vacant	Taft	October 30, 1912–March 4, 1913
Thomas R. Marshall	Wilson	March 4, 1913–March 4, 1921
J. Calvin Coolidge	Harding	March 4, 1921–August 2, 1923
Vacant	Coolidge	August 2, 1923–March 4, 1925
Charles G. Dawes	Coolidge	March 4, 1925–March 4, 1929

U.S. Secretaries of State

Name	President(s) served under	Dates of service
William H. Seward	Lincoln, Johnson	March 5, 1861–March 4, 1869
Elihu B. Washburne	Grant	March 5, 1869–March 16, 1869
Hamilton Fish	Grant	March 17, 1869–March 12, 1877
William M. Evarts	Hayes	March 12, 1877–March 7, 1881
James G. Blaine	Garfield, Arthur	March 7, 1881–December 19, 1881
Frederick T. Frelinghuysen	Arthur	December 19, 1881–March 6, 1885
Thomas F. Bayard Sr.	Cleveland	March 7, 1885–March 6, 1889
James G. Blaine	Harrison	March 7, 1889–June 4, 1892
John W. Foster	Harrison	June 29, 1892–February 23, 1893
Walter Q. Gresham	Cleveland	March 7, 1893–May 28, 1895
Richard Olney	Cleveland	June 10, 1895–March 5, 1897
John Sherman	McKinley	March 6, 1897–April 27, 1898
William R. Day	McKinley	April 28, 1898–September 16, 1898
John Hay	McKinley, Roosevelt	September 30, 1898–July 1, 1905
Elihu Root	Roosevelt	July 19, 1905–January 27, 1909
Robert Bacon	Roosevelt	January 27, 1909–March 5, 1909
Philander C. Knox	Taft	March 6, 1909–March 5, 1913
William Jennings Bryan	Wilson	March 5, 1913–June 9, 1915
Robert Lansing	Wilson	June 24, 1915–February 13, 1920
Bainbridge Colby	Wilson	March 23, 1920–March 4, 1921
Charles Evans Hughes	Harding, Coolidge	March 5, 1921–March 4, 1925
Frank B. Kellogg	Coolidge, Hoover	March 5, 1925–March 28, 1929

U.S. Secretaries of War

Name	President(s) served under	Dates of service
Edwin M. Stanton	Lincoln, Johnson	January 20, 1862–May 28, 1868
John M. Schofield	Johnson	June 1, 1868–March 13, 1869
John Aaron Rawlins	Grant	March 13, 1869–September 6, 1868
William Tecumseh Sherman	Grant	September 9, 1869–October 24, 1869
William W. Belknap	Grant	October 25, 1869–March 2, 1876
Alphonso Taft	Grant	March 8, 1876–May 22, 1876
J. Donald Cameron	Grant	May 22, 1876–March 4, 1877
George W. McCrary	Hayes	March 12, 1877–December 10, 1879
Alexander Ramsey	Hayes	December 10, 1879–March 4, 1881
Robert Todd Lincoln	Garfield, Arthur	March 5, 1881–March 4, 1885
William C. Endicott	Cleveland	March 5, 1885–March 4, 1889
Redifield Proctor	Harrison	March 5, 1889–November 5, 1891
Stephen B. Elkins	Harrison	December 17, 1891–March 4, 1893
Daniel Scott Lamont	Cleveland	March 5, 1893–March 4, 1897
Russell A. Alger	McKinley	March 5, 1897–August 1, 1899
Elihu Root	McKinley, Roosevelt	August 1, 1899–January 31, 1904
William Howard Taft	Roosevelt	February 1, 1904–June 30, 1908
Luke Edward Wright	Roosevelt	July 1, 1908–March 4, 1909
Jacob M. Dickinson	Taft	March 12, 1909–May 21, 1911
Henry L. Stimson	Taft	May 22, 1911–March 4, 1913
Lindley M. Garrison	Wilson	March 5, 1913–February 10, 1916
Newton D. Baker	Wilson	March 9, 1916–March 4, 1921
John W. Weeks	Harding, Coolidge	March 5, 1921–October 13, 1925
Dwight F. Davis	Coolidge	October 14, 1925–March 4, 1929

U.S. Ministers and Ambassadors to the United Kingdom

Name	State of residence	Dates of service
Charles Francis Adams	Massachusetts	1861–68
Reverdy Johnson	Maryland	1868–69
John Lothrop Motley	Massachusetts	1869–70
Robert C. Schenck	Ohio	1871–76
Edwards Pierrepont	New York	1876–77
John Welsh	Pennsylvania	1877–79
James Russell Lowell	Massachusetts	1880–85
Edward J. Phelps	Vermont	1885–89
Robert T. Lincoln	Illinois	1889–93
Thomas F. Bayard Sr.	Delaware	1893–97
John Hay	Washington, D.C.	1897–98
Joseph Choate	New York	1899–1905
Whitelaw Reid	New York	1905–12

Name	State of residence	Dates of service
Walter Hines Page	New York	1913–18
John W. Davis	West Virginia	1918–21
George Harvey	New Jersey	1921–23
Frank B. Kellogg	Minnesota	1924–25
Alanson B. Houghton	New York	1925–29

Between 1815 and 1893, American diplomatic officers to the United Kingdom were termed "Envoys Extraordinary and Ministers Plenipotentiary to the Court of St. James's." From 1893 until the present day, such representatives were called "Ambassadors Extraordinary and Plenipotentiary to the Court of St. James's."

British Monarchs

Name	Dates of rule
Queen Victoria	June 20, 1837–January 22, 1901
King Edward VIII	January 22, 1901–May 6, 1910
King George V	May 6, 1910–January 20, 1936

British Prime Ministers

Name and title	Party	Dates of service
Henry John Temple, 3rd Viscount Palmerston	Tory, Liberal	June 1859–October 1865
John Russell, 1st Earl Russell	Whig, Liberal	October 29, 1865–June 28, 1866
Edward Smith Stanley, 14th Earl of Derby	Conservative	June 28, 1866– February 27, 1868
Benjamin Disraeli, 1st Earl of Beaconsfield	Conservative	February–December 1868
William Ewart Gladstone,	Liberal	December 1868–February 1874
Benjamin Disraeli, 1st Earl of Beaconsfield	Conservative	February 1874–April 1880
William Ewart Gladstone	Liberal	April 1880–June 1885
Robert Gascoyne-Cecil, 3rd Marquess of Salisbury	Conservative	July 1885–February 1886
William Ewart Gladstone	Liberal	February 1886–August 1886
Robert Gascoyne-Cecil, 3rd Marquess of Salisbury	Conservative	August 1886–August 1892
William Ewart Gladstone	Liberal	August 1892–February 1894
Archibald Primrose (Lord Dalmeny), 5th Earl of Rosebury	Liberal	March 1894–June 1895
Robert Gascoyne-Cecil, 3rd Marquess of Salisbury	Conservative	June 1895–July 1902

Name and title	Party	Dates of service
Arthur Balfour	Conservative	July 11, 1902–December 5, 1905
Sir Henry Campbell-Bannerman	Liberal	February 5, 1906–April 3, 1908
Herbert Henry Asquith	Liberal	April 1908–December 1916
David Lloyd George	Liberal (last)	December 1916–October 1922
Andrew Bonar Law	Conservative	October 1922–May 1923
Stanley Baldwin	Conservative	May 1923–January 1924
Ramsay McDonald	Labour	January 22, 1924–November 4, 1924
Stanley Baldwin	Conservative	November 1924–June 1929
Ramsay McDonald	Conservative	June 5, 1929–June 7, 1935
Stanley Baldwin	Conservative	June 1935–May 1937
Neville Chamberlain	Conservative	May 28, 1937– May 20, 1940
Winston Churchill	Conservative	May 10, 1940–July 27, 1945
Clement Atlee	Labour	July 27, 1945–October 26, 1951
Winston Churchill	Conservative	October 26, 1951–April 7, 1955

British Foreign Secretaries
(Secretary of State for Foreign Affairs and Commonwealth Affairs)

Name	Dates of service
John Russell, 1st Earl Russell	June 18, 1859–November 3, 1865
George William Frederick Villiers, 4th Earl of Clarendon	November 3, 1865–July 6, 1866
Edward Henry Stanley, Lord Stanley	July 6, 1866–December 9, 1868
George William Frederick Villiers 4th Earl of Clarendon	December 9, 1868 - July 6, 1870
Granville George Leveson-Gower, 2nd Earl Granville	July 6, 1870–February 21, 1874
Edward Henry Stanley, 15th Earl of Derby	February 21, 1874–April 2, 1878
Robert Arthur Talbot Gascoyne-Cecil, 3rd Marquess of Salisbury	April 2, 1878–April 28, 1880
Granville George Leveson-Gower, 2nd Earl Granville	April 28, 1880–June 24, 1885
Robert Arthur Talbot Gascoyne-Cecil, 3rd Marquess of Salisbury	June 24, 1885–February 6, 1886
Archibald Philip Primrose, 5th Earl of Rosebery	February 6, 1886–August 3, 1886
Stafford Henry Northcote, 1st Earl of Iddesleigh	August 3, 1886–January 12, 1887
Robert Arthur Talbot Gascoyne-Cecil, 3rd Marquess of Salisbury	January 14, 1887–August 11, 1892

Name	Dates of service
Archibald Philip Primrose, 5th Earl of Rosebery	August 18, 1892–March 11, 1894
John Wodehouse, 1st Earl of Kimberley	March 11, 1894–June 21, 1895
Robert Arthur Talbot Gascoyne-Cecil, 3rd Marquess of Salisbury	June 29, 1895–November 12, 1900
Henry Charles Keith Petty-Fitzmaurice, 5th Marquess of Lansdowne	November 12, 1900–December 4, 1905
Sir Edward Grey	December 10, 1905–December 10, 1916
Arthur James Balfour	December 10, 1916–October 23, 1919
George Nathaniel Curzon, 1st Marquess Curzon	October 23, 1919–January 22, 1924
Ramsay MacDonald	January 22, 1924–November 3, 1924
Sir Austen Chamberlain	November 6, 1924–June 4, 1929

British Colonial Secretaries

Name	Dates of service
Edward Cardwell	April 7, 1864–June 26, 1866
Henry Howard Molyneux Herbert, 4th Earl of Carnarvon	July 6, 1866–March 8, 1867
Richard Temple-Nugent-Brydges-Chandos-Grenville, 3rd Duke of Buckingham and Chandos	March 8, 1867–December 1, 1868
Granville George Leveson-Gower, 2nd Earl Granville	December 9, 1868–July 6, 1870
John Wodehouse, 1st Earl of Kimberley	July 6, 1870–February 17, 1874
Henry Howard Molyneux Herbert, 4th Earl of Carnarvon	February 21, 1874–February 4, 1878
Sir Michael Hicks Beach	February 4, 1878–April 21, 1880
John Wodehouse, 1st Earl of Kimberley	April 21, 1880–December 16, 1882
Edward Henry Stanley, 15th Earl of Derby	December 16, 1882–June 9, 1885
Frederick Arthur Stanley	June 24, 1885–January 28, 1886
Granville George Leveson-Gower, 2nd Earl Granville	February 6, 1886–July 20, 1886
Edward Stanhope	August 3, 1886–January 14, 1887
Henry Thurstan Holland, 1st Baron Knutsford	January 14, 1887–August 11, 1892
George Robinson, 1st Marquess of Ripon	August 18, 1892–June 21, 1895
Joseph Chamberlain	June 29, 1895–September 16, 1903

Name	Dates of service
Alfred Lyttelton	October 11, 1903–December 4, 1905
Victor Alexander Bruce, 9th Earl of Elgin	December 10, 1905–April 12, 1908
Robert Crewe-Milnes, 1st Earl of Crewe	April 12, 1908–November 3, 1910
Lewis Vernon Harcourt	November 3, 1910–May 25, 1915
Andrew Bonar Law	May 25, 1915–December 10, 1916
Walter Hume Long	December 10, 1916–January 10, 1919
Alfred Milner, 1st Viscount Milner	January 10, 1919–February 13, 1921
Winston Churchill	February 13, 1921–October 19, 1922
Victor Cavendish, 9th Duke of Devonshire	October 24, 1922–January 22, 1924
James Henry Thomas	January 22, 1924–November 3, 1924
Leo Amery	November 6, 1924–June 4, 1929

British Ministers and Ambassadors to the United States

Name	Dates of service
Richard Bickerton Pemell Lyons, 2nd Baron Lyons of Christchurch	1858–65
Sir Frederick Bruce	1865–67
Sir Edward Thornton	1867–81
Sir Lionel Sackville-West	1881–88
Sir Julian Pauncefote	1889–93
Sir Julian Pauncefote, Baron Pauncefote from 1899	1893–1902
Sir Michael Henry Herbert	1902–03
Sir Henry Mortimer Durand	1903–06
James Bryce	1907–13
Sir Cecil Spring Rice	1913–18
Rufus Isaacs, 1st Earl of Reading, later 1st Marquess of Reading	1918–19
Edward Grey, 1st Viscount Grey of Fallodon	1919–20
Sir Auckland Geddes	1920–24
Sir Esme Howard, later 1st Baron Howard of Penrith	1924–30

In 1893, the British diplomatic mission in Washington was raised from a legation to an embassy, and Sir Julian Pauncefote, minister since 1889, was appointed as the United Kingdom's first ambassador to the United States, with the title "Her Britannic Majesty's Ambassador Extraordinary and Plenipotentiary to the United States." With this, British ministers officially became ambassadors to the United States.

Notes

Introduction

The epigraph is taken from the *Washington Post,* Dec. 4, 2012.

1. *Washington Post,* Jan. 11, 2010.

2. *Washington Post,* Dec. 7, 2012.

3. Katherine Lee Hughes, "Wives of Public Men" (PhD diss., Columbia Univ., 1995), 9.

4. Jewell Fenzi, *Married to the Foreign Service: An Oral History of the American Diplomatic Spouse* (New York: Macmillan, 1994), 25.

5. Hughes, "Wives of Public Men," 22.

6. Joan Wallach Scott, "Gender: A Useful Category of Historical Analysis," *American Historical Review* 91, no. 5 (Dec. 1986): 1056.

7. As the political and social circles of the diplomatic world were so intertwined in this period, I have used the term "poli-social" to further emphasize the overlap of the two arenas.

8. Katie Hickman, *Daughters of Britannia: The Lives and Times of Diplomatic Women* (New York: Perennial, 1999), 53.

9. Catherine Allgor, "'A Republican in a Monarchy': Louisa Catherine Adams in Russia," *Diplomatic History* 21, no. 1 (Winter 1997): 41.

10. Hickman, *Daughters of Britannia,* 184.

11. Molly Wood, "'Commanding Beauty' and 'Gentle Charm': American Women and Gender in the Early Twentieth-Century Foreign Service," *Diplomatic History* 31, no. 3 (June 2007): 507.

12. Linda K. Kerber, "Separate Spheres, Female Worlds, Woman's Place: The Rhetoric of Women's History," *Journal of American History* 75, no. 1 (1988): 9–39; Molly Marie Wood, "A Diplomat's Wife in Mexico: Creating Professional, Political, and National Identities in the Early Twentieth Century," *Frontiers: A Journal of Women's Studies* 25, no. 3 (Winter 2005): 106; Molly Marie Wood, "An American Diplomat's Wife in Mexico: Gender, Politics, and Foreign Affairs Activism, 1907–1927" (PhD diss., Univ. of South Carolina, 1998), 15.

13. Cynthia Enloe, *Bananas, Beaches, and Bases: Making Feminist Sense of International Politics* (Berkeley: Univ. of California Press, 1989), 195.

14. Catherine Allgor, *Parlor Politics: In Which the Ladies of Washington Help Build a City and a Government* (Charlottesville: Univ. of Virginia Press, 2000), 2.

15. Emily S. Rosenberg, "Walking the Borders," *Diplomatic History* 14 (Fall 1990): 568.

16. Hundreds of such marriages united American heiresses with elite European and British men, generally of noble ranking. Unless otherwise specified, the term "transatlantic marriages" refers to Anglo-American marriages between American women and British men.

17. This timeframe differs slightly from that in Maureen E. Montgomery's analysis of Anglo-American marriages, which she bookends with the Franco-Prussian War of 1870 and World War I. See Maureen E. Montgomery, *Gilded Prostitution: Status, Money, and Transatlantic Marriages, 1870–1914* (New York: Routledge, 1989).

18. Howard Temperley, *Britain and America since Independence* (New York: Palgrave, 2002), 82.

19. Charles S. Campbell, *Anglo-American Understanding, 1898–1903* (Baltimore: Johns Hopkins Univ. Press, 1957), 9. Between 1880 and 1910, W. H. Dunlop argues, 817 American women married British and European nobles. See W. H. Dunlop, *Gilded City: Scandal and Sensation in Turn-of-the-Century New York* (New York: Morrow, 2000), 37.

20. Campbell, *Anglo-American Understanding*, 9.

21. Charles S. Campbell, *From Revolution to Rapprochement: The United States and Great Britain, 1783–1900* (New York: Wiley, 1974), 203.

22. Bradford Perkins, *The Great Rapprochement: England and the United States, 1895–1914* (New York: Atheneum, 1968), 153.

23. Kati Marton, *Hidden Power: Presidential Marriages That Shaped Our History* (New York: Anchor Books, 2001), 4.

24. Campbell, *Anglo-American Understanding*, 9.

25. Perkins, *Great Rapprochement*, 153.

26. Richard L. Rapson, *Britons View America: Travel Commentary, 1860–1935* (Seattle: Univ. of Washington Press, 1971), 118.

27. Diana Whitehall Laing, *Mistress of Herself* (Barre, Mass.: Barre Publishers, 1965), 78.

28. Christopher Hitchens, *Blood, Class, and Empire: The Enduring Anglo-American Relationship* (New York: Nation Books, 1990), 120.

29. Kirsty McLeod, *The Wives of Downing Street* (London: Collins, 1976), 14–15.

30. Ibid., 15, 17.

31. Hickman, *Daughters of Britannia*, 65.

32. McLeod, *Wives of Downing Street*, 153.

33. Hickman, *Daughters of Britannia*, 62.

34. *New York Times*, Sept. 14, 1902.

35. Hitchens, *Blood, Class, and Empire*, 121.

36. As an example of such prosperity, a purchasing power of an estimated $1 million in 1880 would be between $130 and $200 million in 2008. Greg King, *A Season of Splendor: The Court of Mrs. Astor in Gilded Age New York* (Hoboken, N.J.: Wiley, 2009), xv–xvi.

37. Ibid., 381.

38. Milton Plesur, "Looking Outward: American Attitudes toward Foreign Affairs in the Years from Hayes to Harrison" (PhD diss., Univ. of Rochester, 1954), 30.

39. Matthew Josephson, *The Robber Barons: The Great American Capitalists, 1861–1901* (New York: Harcourt, Brace & World, 1934), 340.

40. Cornelius A. Van Minner, *Franklin Delano Roosevelt and His Contemporaries: Foreign Perceptions of an American President* (New York: St. Martin's, 1991), 21–22.

41. Thomas W. Zeiler, "The Diplomatic History Bandwagon: A State of the Field," *Journal of American History* 95, no. 4 (Mar. 2009): 1055.

42. Allgor, *Parlor Politics*, 242.

43. Joan Wallach Scott, *Gender and the Politics of History* (New York: Columbia Univ. Press, 1988), 11, 48.

44. Emily S. Rosenberg, "Gender," *Journal of American History* 77 (June 1990): 116, 118.

45. Jessica C. E. Gienow-Hecht, "Introduction: On the Division of Knowledge and the Community of Thought: Culture and International History," in *Culture and International History*, ed. Jessica C. E. Gienow-Hecht and Frank Schumacher (New York: Berghahn Books, 2003), 4, 6. See also Morrell Heald and Lawrence S. Kaplan, *Culture and Diplomacy: The American Experience* (Westport, Conn.: Greenwood, 1977); Emily S. Rosenberg, "Turning to Culture," in *Close Encounters of Empire: Writing the Cultural History of U.S.–Latin American Relations*, ed. Gilbert M. Joseph, Catherine LeGrand, and Ricardo D. Salvatore (Durham, N.C.: Duke Univ. Press, 1998); Jessica C. E. Gienow-Hecht, *Transmission Impossible: American Journalism as Cultural Diplomacy in Postwar Germany, 1945–1955* (Baton Rouge: Louisiana State Univ. Press, 2002); Thomas A. Breslin, *Beyond Pain: The Role of Pleasure and Culture in the Making of Foreign Affairs* (Westport, Conn.: Praeger, 2002).

46. Catherine Forslund, *Anna Chennault: Informal Diplomacy and Asian Relations* (Wilmington, Del.: Scholarly Resources Books, 2002), xiv. Similar to Forslund's description of informal diplomacy is the term "unofficial diplomacy"; see Maureen R. Berman and Joseph E. Johnson, "The Growing Role of Unofficial Diplomacy," in *Unofficial Diplomats*, ed. Maureen R. Berman and Joseph E. Johnson (New York: Columbia Univ. Press, 1977), 1–33.

47. Donna Alvah, *Unofficial Ambassadors: American Military Families Overseas and the Cold War, 1946–1965* (New York: New York Univ. Press, 2007), 40.

48. Thomas W. Zeiler, *Ambassadors in Pinstripes: The Spalding World Baseball Tour and the Birth of the American Empire* (Lanham, Md.: Rowman & Littlefield, 2006), xi–xii.

49. Although a January 22, 1956, *New York Times* article in declared, "Tourists Are Ambassadors," the perception that foreign travel equated foreign policy/relations is faulty. Rather, the duration of time abroad, political and social status of the individual(s), and frequency and notoriety of contacts made while overseas are paramount in weighing the possibility of an individual or group functioning as an informal ambassador.

50. Thomas A. Bailey, *A Diplomatic History of the American People,* 9th ed. (Englewood Cliffs, N.J.: Prentice-Hall, 1974), 1. See also Melvin Small, "Public Opinion," in *Explaining the History of American Foreign Relations*, ed. Michael J. Hogan and Thomas G. Paterson (Cambridge: Cambridge Univ. Press, 1991), 165–76; Robert Beisner, *From the Old Diplomacy to the New, 1865–1900* (Arlington Heights, Ill.: AHM Publishing, 1975), 4.

51. One such work that argues for the power of Anglophobia in this period is Edward Crapol's *America for Americans: Economic Nationalism and Anglophobia* (Westport, Conn.: Greenwood, 1973).

52. Robert J. Moore Jr., "Social Darwinism, Social Imperialism, and the Rapprochement: Theodore Roosevelt and the English-Speaking Peoples, 1886–1901" (PhD diss., Washington Univ., 2003), 4.

53. Thomas G. Paterson, "Defining and Doing the History of American Foreign Relations: A Primer," in Hogan and Paterson, *Explaining the History of American Foreign Relations*, 37.

54. *Washington Post,* Dec. 7, 2012; Joseph S. Nye Jr., *Bound to Lead: The Changing Nature of America Power* (New York: Basic Books, 1990), 188.

55. Nye, *Bound to Lead,* 188; Joseph S. Nye Jr., *Soft Power: The Means to Success in World Politics* (Cambridge: Perseus Books, 2004), x.

56. Enloe, *Bananas, Beaches, and Bases,* 93.

57. Jerrold M. Packard, *Victoria's Daughters* (New York: St. Martin's, 1998).

58. Zeiler, "Diplomatic History Bandwagon," 1057.

59. *New York Times,* Nov. 6, 1896. This quotation reappeared in a book review of Amanda Mackenzie Stuart's *Consuelo and Alva Vanderbilt: The Story of a Daughter and a Mother in the Gilded Age* (2006) as evidence of the continuing interest in these marriages over a century later. Yet the book is a narrative of events rather than an analysis of diplomatic history and international relations. *Vogue,* Dec. 2005, 265.

60. Wood, "American Diplomat's Wife in Mexico," 15; Zeiler, "Diplomatic History Bandwagon," 1064.

61. Emily S. Rosenberg, "Walking the Borders," in Hogan and Paterson, *Explaining the History of American Foreign Relations*, 27.

1. Courting Transatlantic Marriages

Gail MacColl and Carol McD. Wallace, *To Marry an English Lord: Or, How Anglomania Really Got Started* (New York: Workman, 1989), 2.

1. Ibid., 332.

2. Jessica Gienow-Hecht, "The Forgotten Victorians; or, Why Historians Hate American Nineteenth-Century Culture" (paper presented at the German Association for American Studies annual meeting, Wittenberg, Germany, Apr. 5, 2005).

3. E. J. Hobsbawm, *The Age of Empire, 1875–1914* (London: Weidenfeld & Nicolson, 1987), 46.

4. Walter LaFeber, *The New Empire: An Interpretation of American Expansion, 1860–1898* (Ithaca, N.Y.: Cornell Univ. Press, 1963), 7.

5. Walter LaFeber, *The American Search for Opportunity, 1865–1913,* vol. 2 of *The Cambridge History of American Foreign Relations* (New York: Cambridge Univ. Press, 1993), 4.

6. Ibid., 4, 23, 24, 31, 37.

7. David M. Pletcher, "1861–1898: Economic Growth and Diplomatic Adjustment," and William H. Becker, "1899–1920: America Adjusts to World Power," both in *Economics and World Power: An Assessment of American Diplomacy since 1789,* ed. William H. Becker and Samuel F. Wells (New York: Columbia Univ. Press, 1984), 120, 175, 178; LaFeber, *American Search for Opportunity,* 23, 26.

8. LaFeber, *American Search for Opportunity,* 22.

9. LaFeber, *New Empire,* 314.

10. LaFeber, *American Search for Opportunity,* 21, 1, 3.

11. Arthur T. Vanderbilt II, *Fortune's Children: The Fall of the House of Vanderbilt* (New York: Morrow, 1989), 94.

12. Frederick Copel Jaher, "The Gilded Elite: American Multimillionaires, 1865 to the Present," in *Wealth and the Wealthy in the Modern World,* ed. W. D. Rubinstein (London: Croom Helm, 1980), 200.

13. Matthew Josephson, *The Robber Barons: The Great American Capitalists, 1861–1901* (New York: Harcourt, Brace, & World, 1934), 340; Gustavus Myers, *History of the Great American Fortunes,* 3 vols. (Chicago: Charles H. Kerr, 1909), 1:274.

14. David Cannadine, *The Decline and Fall of the British Aristocracy* (New Haven: Yale Univ. Press, 1990), 16.

15. Walter L. Arnstein, "The Survival of the Victorian Aristocracy," in *The Rich, the Wellborn and the Powerful: Elites and Upper Classes in History,* ed. Frederic Copel Jaher (Urbana: Univ. of Illinois Press, 1973), 228.

16. MacColl and Wallace, *To Marry an English Lord,* 125.

17. Christopher Napier, "The British Aristocracy, Capital and Income, and Nineteenth-Century Company Accounting," Univ. of Southampton, Highfield, Southampton, United Kingdom, http://les.man.ac.uk/ipa97/papers/napier75.html, accessed May 29, 2006.

18. Cannadine, *Decline and Fall of the British Aristocracy,* 26.

19. Arnstein, "Survival of the Victorian Aristocracy," 228.

20. Cannadine, *Decline and Fall of the British Aristocracy,* 26–27, 90.

21. Hobsbawm, *Age of Empire,* 171.

22. R. E. Pumphrey, "The Introduction of Industrialists into the British Peerage: A Study in the Adaptation of a Social Institution," *American Historical Review* 65, no. 1 (Oct. 1959): 8.

23. W. L. Guttsman, "The Changing Social Structure of the British Political Elite, 1886–1915," *British Journal of Sociology* 2 (1951): 132.

24. Arnstein, "Survival of the Victorian Aristocracy," 228.

25. Elizabeth Eliot, *Heiresses and Coronets: The Story of Lovely Ladies and Noble Men* (New York: McDowell, Obolensky, 1959), 27. Eliot also published her book in Britain, as *They All Married Well* (London: Cassel, 1960).

26. Eric Homberger, *Mrs. Astor's New York: Money and Power in a Gilded Age* (New Haven: Yale Univ. Press, 2002), 1. See also Mayo Williamson Hazeltine, "Studies of New York Society," *Nineteenth Century,* May 1892, 762–77; Virginia Tatnall Peacock, *Famous American Belles of the Nineteenth Century* (Philadelphia: Lippincott, 1901), chap. 20; Elizabeth Duer, "New York Society a Generation Ago," *Harper's Monthly Magazine,* Nov. 1902, 109–14; Ferdinand Lundberg, *America's Sixty Families* (New York: Citadel, 1946).

27. Homberger, *Mrs. Astor's New York,* 4.

28. MacColl and Wallace, *To Marry An English Lord,* 14.

29. Ward McAllister, *Society As I Have Found It* (New York: Cassell, 1890), 255.

30. Another identifier of elite American society was the *Social Register,* a publication that printed the family names, addresses, birth, marriage, and death announcements of this "American aristocracy." This newsletter served as public recognition of those deemed worthy of social notoriety. Before 1914, the cities covered by the *Social Register* included Atlanta, Augusta, Baltimore, Boston, Buffalo, Charleston, Chicago, Minneapolis, New York, "North Carolina," Oakland, Philadelphia, Pittsburgh, Providence, Richmond, San Francisco, Savannah, St. Louis, St. Paul, and Washington, *Social Register,* http://www.socialregisteronline.com, accessed May, 29, 2006.

31. Vanderbilt, *Fortune's Children,* 120.

32. Dixon Wecter, *The Saga of American Society: A Record of Social Aspiration 1607–1937* (New York: Charles Scribner's Sons, 1937), 216–23. See also Richard Conniff, *The Natural History of the Rich: A Field Guide* (New York: Norton, 2002); Joseph Epstein, *Snobbery: The American Version* (Boston: Houghton Mifflin, 2002).

33. McAllister, *Society as I Have Found It*, 245.

34. Thorstein Veblen, *The Theory of the Leisure Class: An Economic Study of Institutions* (New York: Modern Library, 1934), 35–67, 68–101.

35. Mark Rennella and Whitney Walton, "Planned Serendipity: American Travelers and the Transatlantic Voyage in the Nineteenth and Twentieth Centuries," *Journal of Social History* 38, no. 2 (2004): 367–68. See also Christopher Mulvey, *Transatlantic Manners: Social Patterns in Nineteenth-Century Anglo-American Travel Literature* (Cambridge: Cambridge Univ. Press, 1990).

36. Hon. Maud Paucefote, "Washington DC," *Nineteenth Century and After*, 1903, 175.

37. *London Times*, Nov. 18, 1900.

38. Philippa Pullar, *Gilded Butterflies: The Rise and Fall of the London Season* (London: Hamish Hamilton, 1978), 9, 87, 119, 121, 170.

39. This figure is equivalent to more than $500,000 in 2012 dollars. MacColl and Wallace, *To Marry an English Lord*, 71.

40. Anne De Courcy, *1939: The Last Season* (London: Orion Books, 1989), 25.

41. Pullar, *Gilded Butterflies*, 121, 134. Louis Thomas Stanley, *The London Season* (Boston: Houghton Mifflin, 1956), 75. Gentlemen also participated in a presentation ceremony, called a "levée," which took place at St. James's Palace, but it was considerably smaller and less stressful than the ladies' presentation. Daniel Pool, *What Jane Austen Ate and Charles Dickens Knew: From Fox Hunting to Whist—The Facts of Daily Life in Nineteenth-Century England* (New York: Simon & Schuster, 1993), 71.

42. Michelle Jean Hoppe, "The London Season," *Literary Liaisons*, http://literary-liaisons.com/article024.html, accessed Apr. 24, 2006.

43. MacColl and Wallace, *To Marry an English Lord*, 25; Hoppe, "London Season."

44. Sir Sidney Lee, *King Edward VII: A Biography* (New York: Macmillan, 1927); Helmut E. Gerber, "The Nineties: Beginning, End, or Transition?" in *Edwardians and Late Victorians*, ed. Richard Ellmann (New York: Columbia Univ. Press, 1960).

45. MacColl and Wallace, *To Marry an English Lord*, 82.

46. See also Anita Leslie, *Edwardians in Love* (New York: Arrow Books, 1974). Susan Tweedsmuir, *The Edwardian Lady* (London: Camelot, 1966).

47. MacColl and Wallace, *To Marry an English Lord*, 86. The term "grandes dames" comes from Richard Kenin, *Return to Albion: Americans in England, 1760–1940* (New York: Holt, Rinehart, Winston, 1979), chap. 6.

48. MacColl and Wallace, *To Marry an English Lord*, 64, 67, 138.

49. Jaher, "Gilded Elite," 200.

50. Emily A. Acland, "A Lady's American Notes," *Nineteenth Century*, 1888, 412.

51. C. de Thierry, "American Women from a Colonial Point of View," *Contemporary Review* 70 (1896): 522.

52. Richard Rapson, *Britons View America: Travel Commentary, 1860–1935* (Seattle: Univ. of Washington Press, 1971), 112.

53. Ruth Brandon, *The Dollar Princesses: Sagas of Upward Nobility, 1870–1914* (New York: Knopf, 1980), 47.

54. Rapson, *Britons View America,* 118.

55. *New York Times,* Apr. 30, 1922.

56. William T. Stead, *The Americanization of the World; or, The Trend of the Twentieth Century* (New York: Horace Markley, 1902), 318.

57. *New York Times,* Sept. 3, 1903.

58. Cannadine, *Decline and Fall of the British Aristocracy,* 391.

59. MacColl and Wallace, *To Marry an English Lord,* 26.

60. H. B. Marriott-Watson, "The American Woman: An Analysis," *Nineteenth Century and After,* 1904, 439. See also Charlotte Perkins Stetson, *Women and Economics: A Study of the Economic Relations between Men and Women as a Factor in Social Evolution* (Boston: Small, Maynard, 1898).

61. Jenel Virden, *Good-bye, Piccadilly: British War Brides in America* (Urbana: Univ. of Illinois Press, 1996), 2.

62. Ellen Grant, President Grant's daughter, married Algernon C. F. Sartoris of Rushden and a Member of Parliament, in 1874. Edith Fish, daughter of Hamilton Fish, married Hugh Northcote in 1883. Hamilton Fish served as President Ulysses S. Grant's secretary of state from 1869 to 1877. Fish was Grant's longest serving Cabinet member. Theodore Frelinghuysen, secretary of state under President Chester Arthur, served from 1881 to 1885. His daughter, Alice, married into the baronets in 1885. In 1870 President Grant nominated Frelinghuysen as the United States minister to England to succeed John Lothrop Motley, but he declined the appointment.

63. Mary married Algernon T. B. Sheridan of Frampton Court in 1871, and Susan married Lt. Col. Herbert St. John-Mildmay in 1884.

64. Pauline Whitney married into the British peerage in 1895, as did her stepsister, Adelaide, in 1906.

65. Charles S. Campbell, *From Revolution to Rapprochement: The United States and Great Britain, 1783–1900* (New York: Wiley, 1974), 203.

66. Richard W. Davis, "'We Are All Americans Now!' Anglo-American Marriages in the Later Nineteenth Century," *Proceedings of the American Philosophical Society* 135, no. 2 (June 1991): 142. According to Ruth Brandon, most noble European families had one or more American women as relatives when World War I started. Brandon, *Dollar Princesses,* 1.

67. For more on national identities from a sociological standpoint, see Katharine W. Jones, *Accent on Privilege: English Identities and Anglophilia in the U.S.* (Philadelphia: Temple Univ. Press, 2001).

68. Gyles Brandreth, *Philip and Elizabeth: Portrait of a Marriage* (London: Arrow Books, 2004), 56.

69. Susan K. Harris, *The Cultural Work of the Late Nineteenth-Century Hostess: Annie Adams Fields and Mary Gladstone Drew* (New York: Palgrave Macmillan, 2002), viii, 5.

70. K. D. Reynolds, *Aristocratic Women and Political Society in Victorian Britain* (Oxford: Clarendon, 1998), 220.

71. Kathleen McCarthy, *Lady Bountiful Revisited: Women, Philanthropy, and Power* (New Brunswick, N.J.: Rutgers Univ. Press, 1991), ix, 1.

72. Paul R. Deslandes, *Oxbridge Men: British Masculinity and the Undergraduate Experience, 1850–1920* (Bloomington: Indiana Univ. Press, 2005), 3. Deslandes provides a gendered discussion of undergraduate life at Oxford and Cambridge.

73. Ralph Nevill, *The World of Fashion, 1837–1922* (London: Methuen, 1923), 23.

74. Pool, *What Jane Austen Ate and Charles Dickens Knew,* 90–92.

75. MacColl and Wallace, *To Marry an English Lord,* 38.

76. Margaret S. R. (Mrs. Henry) White Diary, July 28, 1888–Sept. 29, 1889, Jan. 11, 1889, Henry White Manuscript Collection, Rare Book and Manuscript Library, Columbia Univ.

77. Paul A. Kramer, "Empires, Exceptions, and Anglo-Saxons: Race and Rule between the British and United States Empires, 1880–1910," *Journal of American History* 88, no. 4 (Mar. 2002): 1327.

78. Brandon, *Dollar Princesses,* 4.

79. Consuelo Vanderbilt Balsan, *The Glitter and the Gold,* 2d ed. (Maidstone: George Mann, 1973), 59.

80. MacColl and Wallace, *To Marry an English Lord,* 22. See also Pool, *What Jane Austen Ate and Charles Dickens Knew,* 37–38, 46.

81. Richard Jay Hutto, *Crowning Glory: American Wives of Princes and Dukes* (Macon, Ga.: Henchard, 2007), 13.

82. Cannadine, *Decline and Fall of the British Aristocracy,* 397.

83. W. H. Dunlop, *Gilded City: Scandal and Sensation in Turn-of-the-Century New York* (New York: Morrow, 2000), 7. See also Elizabeth L. Banks, *Campaigns of Curiosity: Journalistic Adventures of an American Girl in Late Victorian London* (Madison: Univ. of Wisconsin, 2003).

84. Wecter, *Saga of American Society,* 183.

85. John R. Gillis, *For Better, For Worse: British Marriages, 1600 to the Present* (Oxford: Oxford Univ. Press, 1985), 303, 297.

86. Mary to her father, Nov. 5, 1898, Mary Victoria Curzon Papers, MSS Eur/F306/8, ff48–49, India Office, British Library.

87. Clara Hay to Cecil Spring Rice, no date, Cecil Spring Rice Papers, CASR 1/6/27, Churchill Archives Center, Churchill College, Cambridge.

88. For more on the historical evolution of marriage in the United States and Europe, see Stephanie Coontz, *Marriage, A History: From Obedience to Intimacy; or, How Love Conquered Marriage* (New York: Viking Adult, 2005); Nancy Cott, *Public Vows: A History of Marriage and the Nation* (Cambridge, Mass.: Harvard Univ. Press, 2000); Sonya Ruth Sklar Das, *The American Woman in Modern Marriage* (New York: Philosophical Library, 1948); E. J. Graff, *What Is Marriage For?* (Boston: Beacon, 1999); Hendrik Hartog, *Man and Wife in America: A History* (Cambridge, Mass.: Harvard Univ. Press, 2000); Elizabeth D. Heineman, *What Difference Does a Husband Make? Women and Marital Status in Nazi and Postwar Germany* (Berkeley: Univ. of California Press, 1999); Pat Jalland, *Women, Marriage, and Politics, 1860–1914* (Oxford: Clarendon, 1986); Marilyn Yalom, *A History of the Wife* (New York: Perennial, 2001).

89. George Stocking, "The Turn-of-the-Century Concept of Race," *Modernism/Modernity* 1, no. 1 (1994): 6, 15.

90. Reginald Horsman, *Race and Manifest Destiny: The Origins of American Racial Anglo-Saxonism* (Cambridge, Mass.: Harvard Univ. Press, 1981), 62.

91. Akira Iriye, *The Globalizing of America, 1913–1945,* vol. 3 of *The Cambridge History of American Foreign Relations*(Cambridge: Cambridge Univ. Press, 1993), 9.

92. LaFeber, *American Search for Opportunity,* 41.

93. Rudyard Kipling, "The White Man's Burden," *McClure's Magazine,* Feb. 1899, 290–91.

94. LaFeber, *New Empire, 77*. For other works dealing with ideas about race, whiteness, and the construction of Anglo-Saxonism, see H. C. Allen, *Conflict and Concord: The Anglo-American Relationship since 1783* (New York: St. Martin's, 1959); Stephen J. Heathorn, *For Home, Country, and Race: Constructing Gender, Class, and Englishness in the Elementary School, 1880–1914* (Toronto: Univ. of Toronto Press, 2000); Noel Ignatiev, *How the Irish Became White* (New York: Routledge, 1995); Peter Kolchin, "Whiteness Studies: The New History of Race in America," *Journal of American History* 89, no. 1 (June 2002): 154–73; Eric T. L. Love, *Race over Empire: Racism and U.S. Imperialism, 1865–1900* (Chapel Hill: Univ. of North Carolina Press, 2004); Sue Peabody and Tyler Stovall, eds., *The Color of Liberty: Histories of Race in France* (Durham, N.C.: Duke Univ. Press, 2003); David R. Roediger, *Working toward Whiteness: How America's Immigrants Became White: The Strange Journey from Ellis Island to the Suburbs* (New York: Basic Books, 2005).

95. Kramer, "Empires, Exceptions, and Anglo-Saxons," 1327.

96. Abby G. Baker, "International Marriages," *Independent*, Oct. 1908, 756.

97. Kramer, "Empires, Exception, and Anglo-Saxons," 1323.

98. Davis, "'We Are All Americans Now!'" 140.

99. *Titled Americans: A List of American Ladies Who Have Married Foreigners of Rank* (New York: Street & Smith, 1890), 156, 24.

100. *New York Times*, Apr. 19, 1893.

101. W. B. Brancroft, ed., *Directory of Americans Resident in London and Great Britain, American Firms and Agencies* (London: American Directory Publishing, 1902), 293.

102. Ibid., 296.

103. Stead, *Americanization of the World*, 329.

104. Anglo-American, "American Women in English Society," *Harper's Bazaar*, July 1905, 602.

105. Kramer, "Empires, Exceptions, and Anglo-Saxons," 1327.

106. MacColl and Wallace, *To Marry an English Lord*, 73.

107. Brandreth, *Philip and Elizabeth*, 263.

2. Amazon Attaché

The epigraph is taken from Lady Randolph Churchill (Mrs. G. Cornwallis West), "American Women in Europe," *Nash's Pall Mall Magazine* 29 (1903): 303.

1. Some disagreement exists as to Jennie Jerome's birthplace. In his autobiography, Winston Churchill wrote that his mother was born in Rochester, but other sources, including Jennie's authorized biographer, place her birthplace in Brooklyn. Winston S. Churchill, author's preface to *My Early Life: A Roving Commission* (New York: Charles Scribner's Sons, 1930), n.p.; Ralph G. Martin, *Jennie: The Life of Lady Randolph Churchill*, vol. 1, *The Romantic Years, 1874–1895* (Englewood Cliffs, N.J.: Prentice-Hall, 1969), 6; Charles Higham, *Dark Lady Winston Churchill's Mother and Her World* (New York: Carroll & Graf, 2007), 1. René Kraus wrote a biography of Jennie in 1943, but it contains numerous factual errors; thus, his work is of limited use. René Kraus, *Young Lady Randolph: The Life and Times of Jennie Jerome, American Mother of Winston Churchill* (New York: G. P. Putnam's Sons, 1943). See also Virginia Tatnall Peacock, *Famous American Belles of the Nineteenth Century* (Philadelphia: Lippincott, 1901),

chap. 17; Richard Kenin, *Return to Albion: Americans in England, 1760–1940* (New York: Holt, Rinehart, Winston, 1979), chap. 6.

2. Churchill, author's preface, n. p.

3. Martin, *Jennie*, 1:1, 4, 6; Churchill, author's preface, n. p. The Manhattan Club of New York eventually represented the marriage settlement of Jennie Jerome to Lord Randolph Churchill in 1874. The club's income was paid to Lord and Lady Churchill until his death in 1895, and to her afterward. Upon her death in 1921, the foreclosure of the mortgage benefited her sons, Winston and John, in the amount of £31,000. *New York Times*, Nov. 17, 1921.

4. Martin, *Jennie*, 1:8–15; Anita Leslie, *Mr. Frewen of England: A Victorian Adventurer* (London: Hutchinson, 1966), 117; Elisabeth Kehoe, *The Titled Americans: Three American Sisters and the English Aristocratic World into Which They Married* (New York: Atlantic Monthly Press, 2004); Numerous sets of siblings married across the pond. Several sets of American sisters married into the British aristocracy. Among them were the Bonynges: Louisa *m.* Major General Sir John Maxwell, and stepsister Virginia *m.* Viscount Deerhurst; the Breeses: Eloise *m.* Lord Willoughby de Eresby, later Earl of Ancaster, and Anna *m.* Lord Alastair Innes-Ker; the Carrs: Alys, "the lovely young widow Mrs. Chauncy," *m.* Sir Cecil Bingham, and Grace *m.* Lord Newborough; the Chamberlains: Jeannie *m.* Herbert Naylor-Leyland, later Sir Herbert, and Josephine *m.* T. T. L. Scarisbrick of Lancashire; the Frosts: Jane *m.* Sir Lewis Molesworth, Evelyn *m.* Phillip Beresford-Hope, and Louisa *m.* Hon. William F. C. Vernon; the Graces: Elena *m.* Lord Donoughnore, and Elisa *m.* Hon. Hubert Beaumont; the Jeromes: Jennie *m.* Earl Randolph Churchill, Clara *m.* Moreton Frewen, and Leonie *m.* Sir John Leslie; the Leiters: Mary *m.* George Curzon, later Lord Curzon, Marguerite (Daisy) *m.* Earl of Suffolk, and Nancy *m.* Major Colin Campbell; the Randolph and Whitney stepsisters: Adelaide Randolph *m.* Hon. Lionel Lambart, and Pauline Whitney *m.* Almeric Paget, later Lord Queenborough; the Wadsworths: widow Cornelia Wadsworth Ritchie *m.* John Adair of County Rathdaire, Ireland, and her widowed sister Elizabeth Wadsworth *m.* Arthur Barry, later Lord Barrymore; the Yznagas: Consuelo *m.* Viscount Mandeville, later Duke of Manchester, and Natica *m.* Sir John Lister-Kaye. British brothers who married American heiresses include Hon. Charles Coventry *m.* Lily Whitehouse; Hon. Henry Coventry *m.* Edith Kip McCreery; Alexander Gordon Cumming *m.* Florence Garner; Sir William Gordon-Cumming *m.* Frances Eames; 3d Lord Leigh *m.* Frances Helene Beckwith; Hon. Rowland Leigh *m.* Mabel Gordon; George Spencer-Churchill, the 8th Duke of Marlborough *m.* Lily Hammersley; Lord Randolph Churchill *m.* Jennie Jerome; Hon. Amyas Northcote *m.* Helen Dudley; Hon. Hugh Northcote *m.* Edith Fish; Almeric Paget *m.* Pauline Whitney; Arthur Paget *m.* Minnie Stevens: Sidney Paget *m.* Marie Dolan; 8th Duke of Roxburghe *m.* May Goelet; 7th Baron Vernon *m.* Frances Lawrance; Hon. William Vernon *m.* Louisa Frost. A number of father-son duos and mother-daughter duos also married British aristocrats. Gail MacColl and Carol McD. Wallace, *To Marry an English Lord; or, How Anglo-Mania Really Got Started* (New York: Workman, 1989), 308–9, 332, 343, 347.

5. MacColl and Wallace, *To Marry an English Lord*, 118.

6. Mrs. George Cornwallis-West, *The Reminiscences of Lady Randolph Churchill* (New York: Century, 1908), 3, 4; Martin, *Jennie*, 1:1.

7. Cornwallis-West, *Reminiscences*, 6.

8. Ibid., 6–35.

9. Martin, *Jennie*, 1:48.

10. Anita Leslie, *The Remarkable Mr. Jerome* (New York: Holt, 1954), 162.

11. Martin, *Jennie*, 1:53.

12. Peter De Mendelssohn, *The Age of Churchill: Heritage and Adventure, 1874–1911* (London: Thames & Hudson, 1961), 25.

13. Martin, *Jennie*, 1:98.

14. Cornwallis-West, *Reminiscences*, 45.

15. Catherine Allgor, *Parlor Politics: In Which the Ladies of Washington Help Build a City and a Government* (Charlottesville: Univ. of Virginia Press, 2000), 1.

16. Martin, *Jennie*, 1:74.

17. Cornwallis-West, *Reminiscences*, 45.

18. R. F. Foster, *Lord Randolph Churchill: A Political Life* (Oxford: Clarendon, 1981), 18; MacColl and Wallace, *To Marry an English Lord*, 39.

19. Martin, *Jennie*, 1:89.

20. R. J. Minney, *The Edwardian Age* (Boston: Little, Brown, 1964), 51.

21. Martin, *Jennie*, 1:90.

22. Foster, *Lord Randolph Churchill*, 17; Leslie, *Remarkable Mr. Jerome*, 184; Cornwallis-West, *Reminiscences*, 75.

23. Cornwallis-West, *Reminiscences*, 49.

24. Ibid., 60.

25. Ibid., 60–61.

26. Leslie, *Remarkable Mr. Jerome*, 187, 191.

27. Kehoe, *Titled Americans*, 69.

28. Martin, *Jennie*, 1:104.

29. Ibid., 1:108.

30. Higham, *Dark Lady Winston Churchill's Mother and Her World*, 50.

31. Soames, *Winston and Clementine*, 1; Kehoe, *Titled Americans*, 71; Martin, *Jennie*, 1:108.

32. Martin, *Jennie*, 1:110.

33. Churchill, *My Early Life*, 4, 5.

34. Christopher Hitchens, *Blood, Class, and Empire: The Enduring Anglo-American Relationship* (New York: Nation Books, 1990), 186.

35. Higham, *Dark Lady Winston Churchill's Mother and Her World*, 57.

36. Minney, *Edwardian Age*, 51–53; Foster, *Lord Randolph Churchill*, 31, 46; Shane Leslie, *Men Were Different: Five Studies in Late Victorian Biography* (Freeport, N.Y.: Books for Libraries Press, 1937), 21. Only Consuelo Yznaga, Duchess of Manchester, a fellow American bride, disobeyed Edward's orders, explaining that she held friendship above snobbery. Not until 1885 did Lord James of Hereford make Randolph's peace with Edward, although Lady Churchill attended an event at the request of Queen Victoria in 1883 (53).

37. Martin, *Jennie*, 1:122.

38. Leslie, *Remarkable Mr. Jerome*, 207.

39. Martin, *Jennie*, 1:126.

40. Leslie, *Remarkable Mr. Jerome*, 211; Cornwallis-West, *Reminiscences*, 98.

41. Martin, *Jennie*, 1:129–30; Cornwallis-West, *Reminiscences*, 98–109.

42. Robert Rhodes James, *Lord Randolph Churchill: Winston Churchill's Father* (New York: A. S. Barnes, 1960), 60.

43. Cornwallis-West, *Reminiscences*, 119; Martin, *Jennie*, 1:137.

44. Higham, *Dark Lady Winston Churchill's Mother and Her World,* 73.

45. Leslie, *Remarkable Mr. Jerome,* 224; Cornwallis-West, *Reminiscences,* 119–20.

46. Cornwallis-West, *Reminiscences,* 124.

47. Allgor, *Parlor Politics,* 2.

48. Martin, *Jennie,* 1:31, 145.

49. Anita Leslie, *Lady Randolph Churchill: The Story of Jennie Jerome* (New York: Charles Scribner's Sons, 1969), 100.

50. Cornwallis-West, *Reminiscences,* 135.

51. Leslie, *Lady Randolph Churchill,* 123; Martin, *Jennie,* 1:142.

52. Foster, *Lord Randolph Churchill,* 215.

53. Kehoe, *Titled Americans,* 76–78.

54. Martin, *Jennie,* 1:193.

55. Leslie, *Remarkable Mr. Jerome,* 232.

56. MacColl and Wallace, *To Marry an English Lord,* 203.

57. Peregrine Churchill and Julian Mitchell, *Jennie: Lady Randolph Churchill, A Portrait with Letters* (New York: St. Martin's, 1974), 131–32.

58. Cornwallis-West, *Reminiscences,* 173–74.

59. Ibid., 166.

60. Churchill and Mitchell, *Jennie,* 132–33.

61. Martin, *Jennie,* 1:195.

62. *New York Times,* Jan. 25, 1895.

63. Cornwallis-West, *Reminiscences,* 178; Martin, *Jennie,* 1:104; *New York Times,* Jan. 25, 1901.

64. *New York Times,* Jan. 25, 1901.

65. *London Times,* June 26, 1885; *Alumni Cantabrigienses: A Biographical List of All Known Students, Graduates and Holders of Office at the University of Cambridge, From Earliest Times to 1900,* pt. 2, *From 1752 to 1900,* vol. 2, *Chalmers–Fytche,* comp. J. A. Venn (Cambridge: Cambridge Univ. Press, 1944), 38; Soames, *Winston and Clementine,* 651.

66. Cornwallis-West, *Reminiscences,* 184.

67. MacColl and Wallace, *To Marry an English Lord,* 205.

68. *London Times,* Jan. 25, 1895.

69. Churchill and Mitchell, *Jennie,* 170.

70. Ralph G. Martin, *Jennie: The Life of Lady Randolph Churchill,* vol. 2, *The Dramatic Years, 1895–1921* (Englewood Cliffs, N.J.: Prentice-Hall, 1971), 99.

71. Churchill, *My Early Life,* 62.

72. Kehoe, *Titled Americans,* 176; Foster, *Lord Randolph Churchill,* 378–79; Leslie, *Men Were Different,* 78.

73. Martin, *Jennie,* 2:71–72.

74. Allgor, *Parlor Politics,* 1.

75. Martin, *Jennie,* 2:74. By 1895, many American-born, British-wed women were living in Great Britain. It is difficult for historians today to identify specifically the ten women this particularly newspaper article was referring to, but ten leading American women during this period were Lady Churchill, her sister Clara Frewen, her other sister, Leonie Leslie, Consuelo (the Duchess of Manchester), Consuelo (the Duchess of Marlborough), Mary Chamberlain, Lily Hammersley, Mrs. A. A. Blow, Fanny Reynolds, and Cornelia Adair.

76. Kehoe, *Titled Americans,* 200.

77. Elizabeth Eliot, *Heiresses and Coronets: The Story of Lovely Ladies and Noble Men* (New York: McDowell, Obolensky, 1959), 73.

78. Martin, *Jennie*, 2:74.

79. Cornwallis-West, *Reminiscences*, 361.

80. Churchill and Mitchell, *Jennie*, 172.

81. For more on the nature of editorship and gender, see chapter 3 in Hilary Fraser, Stephanie Green, and Judith Johnston, *Gender and the Victorian Periodical* (Cambridge: Cambridge Univ. Press, 2003).

82. Lady Churchill to John Lane, Jan. 21, Apr. 19, June 2, 1899, John Lane Company Record, folder 9.4, Harry Ransom Humanities Research Center, Univ. of Texas at Austin. In addition to conceding to a name change, Lady Churchill also reluctantly agreed to dropping "Blood is thicker than water" as the journal's motto. Higham, *Dark Lady Winston Churchill's Mother and Her World*, 171.

83. Churchill and Mitchell, *Jennie*, 150.

84. Anne Seba, *American Jennie: The Remarkable Life of Lady Randolph Churchill* (New York: Norton, 2007), 233.

85. Lady Churchill to John Lane, Jan. 21, Apr. 19, June 2, 1899, Correspondence, John Lane Company Record, folder 9.4, Harry Ransom Humanities Research Center. Heated financial discussions began early in their business relationship and continued throughout their correspondence.

86. Kraus, *Young Lady Randolph*, 349.

87. *New York Times*, Apr. 28, 1900.

88. *New York Times*, Mar. 28, 1901.

89. Sebba, *American Jennie*, 235.

90. Lady Randolph Spencer Churchill, "Introductory by the Editor," *Anglo-Saxon Review: A Quarterly Miscellany* 1 (June 1899): 1.

91. *New York Times*, July 2, 12, 1899.

92. Kraus, *Young Lady Randolph*, 350.

93. Lady Churchill to John Lane, Dec. 15, 1900, Jan. 5, Nov. 25, 1901, John Lane Company Records, folder 9.4, Harry Ransom Humanities Research Center.

94. Leslie, *Lady Randolph Churchill*, 262.

95. For more on the U.S.-U.K. imperial connection between the Spanish-American and Boer Wars, see Richard B. Mulanax, *The Boer War in American Politics and Diplomacy* (Lanham, Md.: Univ. Press of America, 1994).

96. Martin, *Jennie*, 2:200.

97. Mrs. A. A. Blow originally suggested the idea for an American-sponsored ship. Kehoe, *Titled Americans*, 209.

98. Sebba, *American Jennie*, xiv.

99. Richard J. Kahn, "Women and Men at Sea: Gender Debate Aboard the Hospital Ship *Maine* during the Boer War, 1899–1900," *Journal of the History of Medicine and Allied Sciences* 56, no. 2 (2001): 116, 115.

100. *New York Times*, Oct. 27, 1899.

101. *New York Times*, Nov. 3, 1899.

102. *Nursing Record and Hospital World*, Nov. 4, 1899; Martin, *Jennie*, 2:202.

103. Leslie, *Lady Randolph Churchill*, 265.

104. Kehoe, *Titled Americans,* 209.

105. *London Times,* Oct. 30, 1899.

106. Kahn, "Women and Men at Sea," 119, 127, 112, 114, 120.

107. Ibid., 117, 120. Lady Churchill also maintained that the American Amazons believed "the committee should be represented by a person of authority without a salary." Leslie, *Lady Randolph Churchill,* 269.

108. Cornwallis-West, *Reminiscences,* 454, 458–60.

109. Kahn, "Women and Men at Sea," 137.

110. *New York Times,* Aug. 4, July 29, 1900.

111. Hesketh Pearson, *The Marrying Americans* (New York: Coward McCann, 1961), 84. The public often noted that Captain Cornwallis-West was born the same year that Lady Churchill married her first husband. George Cornwallis-West, *Edwardian Hey-Days; or, A Little About a Lot of Things* (New York: Putnam, 1930).

112. *New York Times,* May 31, June 2, 1918.

113. Kehoe, *Titled Americans,* 275.

114. *New York Times,* June 12, 30. 1921; *Boston Daily Globe,* June 30, 1921.

115. *New York Times,* July 1, July 2, 1921.

116. *New York Times,* Jan. 24, 1965.

117. *London Times,* Mar. 10, 1952.

118. *London Times,* Mar. 27, 1952, Jan. 8, 1953.

119. *Titled Americans: A List of American Ladies Who Have Married Foreigners of Rank* (New York: Street & Smith, 1890), 156.

120. Churchill and Mitchell, *Jennie,* 221.

121. Richard Jay Hutto, *Crowning Glory: American Wives of Princes and Dukes* (Macon, Ga.: Henchard, 2007), 12

122. *New York Times,* June 30, 1921.

123. Higham, *Dark Lady Winston Churchill's Mother and Her World,* 226.

124. *New York Times,* May 2, 1943.

125. "The Most Influential Anglo-Saxon Society Woman in the World," *Current Literature* 45, no. 6 (1908): 626–29.

126. *New York Times,* Nov. 7, 1908.

127. Martin, *Jennie,* 1:xii.

3. Drawing-Room Diplomat

The epigraph is taken from Mary Endicott Chamberlain to Ellen Peabody Endicott, Dec. 21, 1895, Endicott Family Papers, Massachusetts Historical Society (MHS).

1. Mary Endicott Chamberlain to Miss May, Nov. 11, 1933, Endicott Family Papers, Mary Endicott Family Correspondence, MHS. Hereafter, I shall refer to Mary Endicott Chamberlain Carnegie simply as Mary.

2. Diana Whitehall Laing, *Mistress of Herself* (Barre, Mass.: Barre Publishers, 1965), 78.

3. All of the husbands of the other American brides written of here—Lord Randolph Churchill, George Nathaniel Curzon, the 9th Duke of Marlborough, and William Waldorf Astor—were Conservative Party members.

4. William C. Endicott Sr., Biographical Sketches, Guide to the Collection, Endicott Family Papers, 1612–1958, MHS.

5. *Boston Daily Globe,* Nov. 11, 1888.

6. *London Times,* Aug. 23, 1927.

7. Laing, *Mistress of Herself,* 21, 19.

8. Mary Endicott Scrapbook, 1876, Bound Volumes, Endicott Family Papers, MHS.

9. Laing, *Mistress of Herself,* 23.

10. Ibid., 24.

11. Apr. 27, 1883, Mary Endicott diary, 1882–83, Bound Volumes, Endicott Family Papers, MHS.

12. May 25, 1883, Mary Endicott diary, 1882–83, Bound Volumes, Endicott Family Papers, MHS.

13. Both of Secretary Whitney's daughters married British men. In 1895, his first daughter, Pauline Payne Whitney, married Almeric Hugh Paget, who later became Baron Queenborough. His second daughter, Dorothy Payne Whitney, married Leonard Knight Elmhirst in 1925, some years after the death of her first husband.

14. Laing, *Mistress of Herself,* 33, 34.

15. Apr. 11, 1885, Mary Endicott diary, Bound Volumes, Endicott Family Papers, MHS.

16. Laing, *Mistress of Herself,* 34; Apr. 11, 1885, Mary Endicott diary, Bound Volumes, Endicott Family Papers, MHS.

17. Apr. 1885, Mary Endicott diary, 1885, Bound Volumes, Endicott Family Papers MHS.

18. Laing, *Mistress of Herself,* 14, 36; *London Times,* Mar. 21, 1933.

19. Though dated, an article by D. C. Watt provides a political theory foundation for British political activities and diplomatic relationships overall, and Chamberlain specifically, in the United States during a critical period in Anglo-American relations. D. C. Watt, "America and the British Foreign Policy-Making Elite, from Joseph Chamberlain to Anthony Eden, 1895–1956," *Review of Politics* 25, no. 1 (Jan. 1963): 3–33

20. *Town Topics,* Nov. 15, 1888.

21. Joseph Chamberlain to Beatrice Chamberlain, Dec. 9, 1887, Chamberlain Family Papers, Special Collections, Univ. of Birmingham. Manchester, England (UB).

22. Laing, *Mistress of Herself,* 42.

23. Dec. 1887, Mary Endicott diary, Bound Volumes, Endicott Family Papers, MHS.

24. Sir Haycock Willoughby, *With Mr. Chamberlain in the United States and Canada* (London: Chatto & Windus, 1914), 34.

25. Relatively little is known about Chamberlain's earlier marriages. His 1861 marriage to Harriet Kenrick ended after only two years. In 1862 Harriet gave birth to Beatrice, and in 1863 followed Joseph Austen, who later served as chancellor of the Exchequer and foreign secretary, but she died three days after her son's birth. Chamberlain's second marriage, in 1868, to Florence Kenrick, a cousin of Harriet, lasted seven years and produced five children, though his wife and his last child, also named Florence, died shortly after birth. Upon his third engagement, at Mary's request Chamberlain burned all his correspondence with his second wife. Peter T. Marsh, *Joseph Chamberlain: Entrepreneur in Politics* (New Haven: Yale Univ. Press, 1994), 32.

26. At the time of his engagement to Mary, Chamberlain's six children ranged from ages fifteen to twenty-six. Beatrice and Austen, his children from his first marriage, were older than his fiancée. Laing, *Mistress of Herself,* 14.

27. Ibid., 15; Marsh, *Joseph Chamberlain,* 289.

28. Marsh, *Joseph Chamberlain,* 289.

29. Joseph Chamberlain to Mary Endicott, July 18, 1888, Chamberlain Family Papers, UB.

30. Joseph Chamberlain to Mary Endicott, Apr. 28, 1888, Chamberlain Family Papers, UB.

31. Joseph Chamberlain to Mary Endicott, June 21, 1888, Chamberlain Family Papers, UB.

32. Mary Endicott to Joseph Chamberlain, July 18, 1888, Chamberlain Family Papers, UB.

33. Marsh, *Joseph Chamberlain,* 289.

34. Mary Endicott to Fanny Peabody Mason, Dec. 27, 1887, Mary Endicott Papers, Correspondence, 1887, Endicott Family Papers, MHS.

35. *Boston Daily Globe,* Nov. 15, 1888.

36. Joseph Chamberlain to Mary Endicott, Feb. 11, 1888, Chamberlain Family Papers, UB.

37. Mary Endicott to Joseph Chamberlain, July 18, Sept. 28, 1888, Chamberlain Family Papers, UB.

38. Joseph Chamberlain to Mary Endicott, Feb. 12, 1888, Chamberlain Family Papers, UB.

39. Laing, *Mistress of Herself,* 46.

40. Maycock, *With Mr. Chamberlain,* 192.

41. *London Times,* Aug. 23, 1927, Mar. 29, 1933; Marsh, *Joseph Chamberlain,* 298.

42. Unheaded newspaper clipping, Scrapbook, Endicott Family Papers, MHS.

43. Joseph Chamberlain to Mary Endicott, Mar. 10, 1888, Chamberlain Family Papers, UB.

44. Joseph Chamberlain to Mary Endicott, July 8, 1888, Chamberlain Family Papers, UB.

45. "Relations with the United States and the Colonies," Devonshire Club, Apr. 9, 1888, *Mr. Chamberlain's Speeches,* ed. Charles Boyd (New York: Kraus Reprint, 1970), 318.

46. *New York Times,* Nov. 11, 1913.

47. *London Times,* Mar. 29, 1933, Nov. 7, 1888.

48. *Boston Daily Globe,* Nov. 8, 1888.

49. *Boston Daily Globe,* Nov. 16, 1888; *London Times,* Nov. 15, 1888.

50. Grandma to Mary, Nov. 11, 1888, Mary Endicott Family Correspondence, 1888, Endicott Family Papers, MHS.

51. Austen Chamberlain to Mary, Mar. 11, 1888, Mary Endicott Family Correspondence, 1888, Endicott Family Papers, MHS.

52. Beatrice Chamberlain to Mary, Mar. 12, 1888, Mary Endicott Family Correspondence, 1888, Endicott Family Papers, MHS.

53. Neville Chamberlain to Mary, Apr. 9, 1888, Mary Endicott Family Correspondence, 1888, Endicott Family Papers, MHS.

54. *New York Times,* Nov. 16, 1913.

55. William Endicott to Mary, Dec. 28, 1888, Endicott Family Papers, Mary Endicott Family Correspondence, 1888, MHS.

56. Laing, *Mistress of Herself,* 57; Marsh, *Joseph Chamberlain,* 312.

57. William C. Endicott Jr. to Mary, May 5, June 15, 1890, Mary Endicott Family Correspondence, 1890, Endicott Family Papers, MHS.

58. Laing, *Mistress of Herself,* 66.

59. *New York World,* Jan. 8, 1889; Laing, *Mistress of Herself,* 66, 68.

60. *New York World,* Jan. 8, 1889.

61. Clarissa Endicott Peabody to Mary, Jan. 9, 1889, Mary Endicott, Personal Correspondence, 1889, Endicott Family Papers, MHS.

62. Mrs. George Cornwallis-West, *The Reminiscences of Lady Randolph Churchill* (New York: Century, 1908), 119–20.

63. Sigourney Butler to Mary, Mar. 15, 1889, Mary Endicott, Personal Correspondence, 1885–86, Endicott Family Papers, MHS.

64. Laing, *Mistress of Herself,* 75.

65. Joseph Chamberlain to Ellen Peabody Endicott, Jan. 4, 1889, Endicott Family Papers, MHS; Chamberlain quoted in Laing, *Mistress of Herself,* 64.

66. Austen Chamberlain to Ellen Peabody Endicott, Nov. 6, 1890, Endicott Family Autograph/Special Collection, 1721–1938, MHS.

67. Mary Endicott Chamberlain, Visiting List, 1889, 1891, Miscellaneous, 1876–1902, Endicott Family Papers, MHS.

68. Laing, *Mistress of Herself,* 120.

69. Lars Shoultz, *Beneath the United States: A History of U.S. Policy toward Latin America,* (Cambridge, Mass.: Harvard Univ. Press, 1998), 111.

70. Walter LaFeber, "The Background of Cleveland's Venezuelan Policy: A Reinterpretation," *American Historical Review* 66 (July 1961): 963.

71. Mary to Ellen Peabody Endicott, Dec. 21, 1895, Family Correspondence, 1895, Endicott Family Papers, MHS.

72. Joseph Smith, *Historical Dictionary of United States–Latin American Relations* (Lanham, Md.: Scarecrow, 2007), 222.

73. LaFeber, "Background of Cleveland's Venezuelan Policy," 947.

74. Mary Endicott Chamberlain diary, 1895, Bound Volumes, 1876–1902, Endicott Family Papers, MHS.

75. Ralph G. Martin, *Jennie: The Life of Lady Randolph Churchill,* vol. 2, *The Dramatic Years, 1895–1921* (Englewood Cliffs, N.J.: Prentice-Hall, 1971), 74. By 1895, numerous American-born, British-wed women were living in Great Britain. It is difficult for historians today to identify definitively the ten women this particular newspaper article referred to, but Mary Endicott Chamberlain, Lady Randolph Churchill, her sister Clara Frewen, her youngest sister, Leonie Leslie, Consuelo Yznaga (the Duchess of Manchester), Pauline Payne Whitney Paget, Lily Hammersley, Mrs. A. A. Blow, Fanny Reynolds, and Cornelia Adair were prime candidates.

76. Catherine Allgor, *Parlor Politics: In Which the Ladies of Washington Help Build a City and a Government* (Charlottesville: Univ. of Virginia Press, 2000), 245.

77. Laing, *Mistress of Herself,* 101.

78. For more on the activist efforts of American-born, British-wed women, see Dana Cooper, "Country by Birth, Country by Marriage: American Women's Transnational War Efforts in Great Britain, 1895–1918," *Women and Transnational Activism in Historical Perspective,* ed. Kimberly Jensen and Erika Kuhlman (Dordrecht, Netherlands: Republic of Letters Publishing, 2009).

79. Clara Endicott Sears to Mary Endicott Chamberlain, Family Correspondence, 1898, Endicott Family Papers, MHS.

80. J. L. Garvin, *The Life of Joseph Chamberlain,* vol. 3, *1895–1900: Empire and World Policy* (London: Macmillan, 1934), 302; Joseph Chamberlain, quoted in "For Anglo-Saxon Unity," *New York Times,* May 14, 1898.

81. *Boston Herald,* May 22, 1899.

82. Unheaded newspaper clipping, Family Correspondence, Endicott Family Papers, MHS.

83. *Salem News,* Aug. 23, 1895.

84. *New York Times,* July 4, 1914.

85. *Salem News,* Aug. 23, 1895.

86. *Boston Globe,* Mar. 2, 1904.

87. *Boston Sunday Post,* May 1, 1904.

88. *Boston Daily Globe,* July 5, 1914.

89. Marsh, *Joseph Chamberlain,* 627.

90. Richard Cavendish, "Joseph Chamberlain Resigns as Colonial Secretary," *History Today* 53, no. 9 (2003): 54–66.

91. Marsh, *Joseph Chamberlain,* 647.

92. William Endicott Jr. to Mary Endicott Chamberlain, Aug. 26, 1906, Chamberlain Family Papers, UB.

93. Mary Endicott Chamberlain diary, July 2, 1914, Endicott Family Papers, MHS.

94. Austen Chamberlain to Fanny P. Mason, July 20, 1914, Family Correspondence, 1914, Endicott Family Papers, MHS.

95. Austen Chamberlain to Fanny P. Mason, Nov. 1, 1906, Correspondence, 1914, Endicott Family Papers, MHS.

96. George Augustus Peabody to Mary Endicott Chamberlain, Nov. 23, 1914, Correspondence, 1914, Endicott Family Papers, MHS.

97. J. P. Franks to Mary Endicott Chamberlain, June 3, 1915, Mary Endicott, Personal Correspondence, 1915, Endicott Family Papers, MHS.

98. Endicott Peabody to Mary Endicott Chamberlain, Dec. 14, 1914, Correspondence, 1914, Endicott Family Papers, MHS.

99. *London Times,* Aug. 2, 1915.

100. *Boston Herald,* Aug. 4, 1916.

101. Mary Endicott, Personal Correspondence, 1918, Endicott Family Papers, MHS.

102. *New York Times,* Oct. 20, 1936.

103. Laing, *Mistress of Herself,* 192.

104. Mary Endicott Chamberlain to Fanny P. Mason, July 15, 1917, Family Correspondence, 1917, Endicott Family Papers, MHS.

105. Mary Endicott Chamberlain to Fanny P. Mason, Apr. 18, 1917, Family Correspondence, 1917, Endicott Family Papers, MHS.

106. Mary Endicott Chamberlain to Louise Endicott, Mar. 30, 1937, Family Correspondence, 1937, Endicott Family Papers, MHS.

107. Neville Chamberlain to Fanny P. Mason, Jan. 16, 1938, Family Correspondence, 1938, Endicott Family Papers, MHS.

108. Mary Endicott Chamberlain to Fanny P. Mason, July 22, 1940, Family Correspondence, 1940, Endicott Family Papers, MHS.

109. Mary Endicott Chamberlain to Fanny P. Mason, July 10, 1940, Family Correspondence, 1940, Endicott Family Papers, MHS.

110. Mary Endicott Chamberlain to Fanny P. Mason, Sept. 26, 1940, Family Correspondence, 1941, Endicott Family Papers, MHS.

111. Mary Endicott Chamberlain to Fanny P. Mason, Jan. 2, 1942, Family Correspondence, 1942, Endicott Family Papers, MHS.

112. Mary Endicott Chamberlain to Fanny P. Mason, Dec. 1, 1942, Family Correspondence, 1942, Endicott Family Papers, MHS.

113. Mary Endicott Chamberlain to Fanny P. Mason, Jan. 7, 1943, Family Correspondence, 1943, Endicott Family Papers, MHS.

114. Mary Endicott Chamberlain to Fanny P. Mason, Sept. 28, 1944, Family Correspondence, 1944, Endicott Family Papers, MHS.

115. Laing, *Mistress of Herself,* 219.

116. "A Toast by G. Peabody Gardner to Mary Endicott Carnegie on Her Ninetieth Birthday," Mar. 16, 1954, Endicott Family Papers, MHS.

117. Laing, *Mistress of Herself,* 226.

118. *London Times,* May 25, 1957.

119. *New York Times,* July 13, 1916.

120. *London Times,* May 25, 1957.

121. *London Times,* May 25, 1957.

122. Laing, *Mistress of Herself,* 226.

4. Devoted Mediator

The epigraph is taken from Nigel Nicolson, *Mary Curzon* (New York: Harper & Row, 1977), 92.

1. *St. James's Gazette,* Apr. 2, 1895.

2. Nayana Goradia, *Lord Curzon: The Last of the British Moghuls* (Oxford: Oxford Univ. Press, 1993), 112.

3. John Bradley, introduction to *Lady Curzon's India: Letters of a Vicereine,* ed. John Bradley (New York: Beaufort Books, 1985), 2.

4. Anne De Courcy, *The Viceroy's Daughters: The Lives of the Curzon Sisters* (London: Phoenix, 2002), 4.

5. Bradley, introduction, 2.

6. De Courcy, *Viceroy's Daughters,* 5.

7. Nicolson, *Mary Curzon,* 4.

8. De Courcy, *Viceroy's Daughters,* 5.

9. Goradia, *Lord Curzon,* 112.

10. Ibid.

11. De Courcy, *Viceroy's Daughters,* 5.

12. *Boston Daily Globe,* July 19, 1906.

13. Nicolson, *Mary Curzon,* 38.

14. De Courcy, *Viceroy's Daughters,* 2.

15. Goradia, *Lord Curzon,* 114; Mary to Curzon, July 4, 1894, Mary Victoria Curzon Papers (hereafter MCP), India Office, British Library, London, England.

16. Nicolson, *Mary Curzon,* 41.

17. Goradia, *Lord Curzon,* 111.

18. Ibid., 113, 112.

19. Nicolson, *Mary Curzon,* 55.

20. Goradia, *Lord Curzon,* 55.

21. Nicolson, *Mary Curzon,* 56.

22. Ibid., 58.

23. De Courcy, *Viceroy's Daughters*, 6.

24. Goradia, *Lord Curzon*, 114.

25. Nicolson, *Mary Curzon*, 58.

26. The Right Honorable and Reverend A. N. H. Lord Scarsdale to the Honorable George Nathaniel Curzon, Deed of Covenant for payment of an annuity of £1000 and Settlement of landed estates in consequence of the marriage of Mr. Curzon and Miss Leiter, Apr. 9, 1895, MCP; Levi Z. Leiter Esq. to Miss M. V. Leiter, Deed of Trust and Covenant, Apr. 20, 1895, MCP, British Library; De Courcy, *Viceroy's Daughters*, 6.

27. Goradia, *Lord Curzon*, 114.

28. Nicolson, *Mary Curzon*, 74–75.

29. *New York Times*, Apr. 14, Mar. 4, 1895.

30. Nicolson, *Mary Curzon*, 74, 75.

31. Ibid., 75.

32. *London Times*, Nov. 20, 1890.

33. Earl of Ronaldshay, *The Life of Lord Curzon: Being the Authorized Biography of George Nathaniel Marquess Curzon of Kedleston, K.G.*, 2 vols. (New York: Boni & Liveright, 1928), 1:215.

34. *London Times*, Apr. 23, 1895.

35. *New York Times*, Apr. 23, 1895.

36. Nicolson, *Mary Curzon*, 77.

37. Kedleston tenants to the Honourable George Nathaniel Curzon M.P. and the Honourable Mrs Curzon, May 4, 1895, MCP.

38. Goradia, *Lord Curzon*, 117; Nicolson, *Mary Curzon*, 84.

39. *New York Times*, Aug. 4, 1898.

40. Nicolson, *Mary Curzon*, 85.

41. Nicolson, *Mary Curzon*, 84, 85.

42. Goradia, *Lord Curzon*, 116.

43. Nicolson, *Mary Curzon*, 83, 90, 88–89.

44. De Courcy, *Viceroy's Daughters*, 30.

45. Nicolson, *Mary Curzon*, 83, 86.

46. Ibid., 99.

47. Ibid., 83, 84.

48. Ibid., 88.

49. Ibid., 92.

50. Ibid.

51. Ibid.

52. *New York Times*, Apr. 19, 1893.

53. Nicolson, *Mary Curzon*, 99.

54. *Daily Telegraph*, Aug. 11, 1898.

55. *Boston Daily Globe*, July 31, 1898.

56. *New York Times*, June 19, 1898, Sept. 25, 1904.

57. *New York Times*, Aug. 22, 1898; *Boston Daily Globe*, Apr. 23, 1899; *London Times*, July 19, 1906.

58. *Boston Daily Globe*, Aug. 8, 1898.

59. Nigel Nicolson, foreword to *Lady Curzon's India*, vii.

60. *Boston Daily Globe*, July 31, 1898.

61. *New York Times*, Aug. 21, 1898.

62. Nicolson, *Mary Curzon*, 103–4, 107.

63. *Sketch*, Aug. 17, 1898.

64. De Courcy, *Viceroy's Daughters*, 7–11.

65. Mary Curzon to her father, Dec. 26, 1898, *Lady Curzon's India*, 18.

66. Nicolson, *Mary Curzon*, 111.

67. Penny Beaumont and Roger Beaumont, *Imperial Divas: The Vicereines of India* (London: Haus Publishing, 2010), 10.

68. Hugh Tinker, *Viceroy: Curzon to Mountbatten* (Oxford: Oxford Univ. Press, 1997), 19.

69. Mary to her father, Jan. 12, 1899, Jan. 17, 1899, MCP.

70. St. John Brodrick, *Relations of Lord Curzon as Viceroy of India with the British Government, 1902–05* (London: Privately published, 1926).

71. Nicolson, *Mary Curzon*, 129.

72. Mary to her mother, May 3, 1899, MCP.

73. Goradia, *Lord Curzon*, 189.

74. Ibid., 189–90. Mary's other sister married a Britons as well: In November 1904, Nancy married Colin Campbell, and Daisy's nuptials to the Earl of Suffolk followed in December. *New York Times*, Dec. 12, 1904.

75. *New York Times*, Aug. 12, 1894.

76. *New York Times*, Jan. 5, Mar. 5, 1899.

77. Nicolson, *Mary Curzon*, 120; Joseph S. Nye Jr., *Soft Power: The Means to Success in World Politics* (New York: Perseus Books, 2004), x.

78. *New York Times*, Jan. 5, 1899.

79. Winston Churchill to Lady Randolph Churchill, Mar. 2, 1899, Churchill Archives Centre, Churchill College Cambridge, 28/26/11–12.

80. Earl of Ronaldshay, *The Life of Lord Curzon: Being the Authorized Biography of George Nathaniel Marquess Curzon of Kedleston, K.G.*, 2 vols. (New York: Boni & Liveright, 1928), 2:51.

81. Nicolson, *Mary Curzon*, 120.

82. Ronaldshay, *Life of Lord Curzon*, 2:52.

83. Ibid., 53.

84. Nicolson, *Mary Curzon*, 131, 188.

85. Mary to her mother and sisters Nancy and Daisy, Feb. 27, 1900, *Lady Curzon's India*, 60.

86. Nicolson, *Mary Curzon*, 131.

87. John Bradley, notes on part 1 of *Lady Curzon's India*, 13.

88. Nicolson, *Mary Curzon*, 143, 142.

89. Ibid., 142.

90. Mary to George, Apr. 8 1901, *Lady Curzon's India*, 82.

91. George to Mary, May 1, 1901, *Lady Curzon's India*, 85.

92. Curzon to Mary, Sept. 18, 1901, MCP.

93. Nicolson, *Mary Curzon*, 141, 143, 154.

94. Brodrick to Curzon, Sept. 26, 1901, MCP, vol. 10B.

95. Nicholson, *Mary Curzon*, 144.

96. George to Mary, May 14–15, 1901, *Lady Curzon's India*, 92.

97. Beaumont and Beaumont, *Imperial Divas*, 98.

98. Mary to George, July 14, 1901, *Lady Curzon's India*, 111.

99. Beaumont and Beaumont, *Imperial Divas*, 264.

100. Ibid., 158.

101. Ronaldshay, *Life of Lord Curzon*, 1:359. Lady Curzon had long considered India "a dangerous, if not fatal, venue for women and children, no matter what their status." Beaumont and Beaumont, *Imperial Divas*, 40.

102. Ronaldshay, *Life of Lord Curzon*, 1:359.

103. Nicola Thomas, "Embodying Imperial Spectacle: Dressing Lady Curzon, Vicereine of India, 1899–1905," *Cultural Geographies* 14, no. 3 (2007): 369–400.

104. Nicola Thomas, "Exploring the Boundaries of Biography: The Family and Friendship Networks of Lady Curzon, Vicereine of India 1898–1905," *Journal of Historical Geography* 30, no. 3 (2004): 496–519. Thomas has written much about the intersection of British and Indian lives, focusing specifically on Mary Curzon. See Peter Jackson, Nicola Thomas, and Claire Cwyer, "Consuming Transnational Fashion in London and Mumbai," *Geoforum* 38, no. 5 (2007): 908–24. Nicola J. Thomas, "Mary Curzon: 'American Queen of India,'" in *Colonial Lives across the British Empire: Imperial Careering in the Long Nineteenth Century*, ed. David Lambert and Alan Lester (Cambridge: Cambridge Univ. Press, 2006), 285–308.

105. Beaumont and Beaumont, *Imperial Divas*, 217.

106. De Courcy, *Viceroy's Daughters*, 13.

107. *New York Globe*, Dec. 3, 1899; *New York Times*, Sept. 25, 1904.

108. "Relations of Lord Curzon as Viceroy of India with the British Government, 1902–5," 1, Mss Eur F 111–12, India Office, British Library.

109. Ronaldshay, *Life of Lord Curzon*, 1:237.

110. Nicolson, *Mary Curzon*, 155.

111. *New York Times*, June 17, 1928.

112. Nicolson, *Mary Curzon*, 168.

113. De Courcy, *Viceroy's Daughters*, 13–14.

114. Nicolson, *Mary Curzon*, 171.

115. Producing a male heir would not only have taken pressure off of Mary and George, it would also have further enhanced Mary's position in India, as the mother of a boy. See Nupur Chaudhuri, "Memsahibs and Motherhood in Nineteenth-Century Colonial India," *Victorian Studies* 31, no. 4 (1988): 517–35.

116. *New York Times*, June 10, 1904.

117. Mary to George, Mar. 2, 1904, MCP.

118. Nicolson, *Mary Curzon*, 170, 171.

119. "Relations of Lord Curzon as Viceroy of India with the British Government, 1902–5," 15, Mss Eur F 111–12, India Office, British Library.

120. Nicolson, *Mary Curzon*, 169.

121. Ibid., 180.

122. Ronaldshay, *Life of Lord Curzon*, 1:31, 359.

123. Mary to her mother, Mar. 9, 1905, *Lady Curzon's India*, 157.

124. *Hindu Patriot*, Mar. 7, 1905.

125. Nicolson, *Mary Curzon*, 169.

126. John Bradley, introductory comments to part 3 of *Lady Curzon's India*, 154; Nicolson, *Mary Curzon*, 199.

127. Nicolson, *Mary Curzon*, 199

128. *London Times*, Aug. 21, 1905; *New York Times*, Aug. 21, 1905.

129. *New York Times*, Aug. 21, 1905.

130. *Winning Post*, Sept. 2, 1905.

131. *London Times*, undated, 1905.

132. Beaumont and Beaumont, *Imperial Divas*, 295.

133. De Courcy, *Viceroy's Daughters*, 14.

134. Nicolson, *Mary Curzon*, 207, 208–9.

135. Goradia, *Lord Curzon*, 245.

136. *London Times*, July 19, 1906.

137. *London Times*, July 24, 1906.

138. David Gilmour, *Curzon: Imperial Statesman* (New York: Farrar, Straus & Giroux, 1994), 359.

139. Lord Curzon to Mrs. Leiter, July 19, 1906, *Mary Curzon*, 169–70.

140. Nicolson, *Mary Curzon*, 120.

141. *London Times*, July 19, 1906.

142. *New York Times*, July 21, 1906 (These are selected stanzas from the much longer poem. Emphasis on the word ambassador in the eighth stanza is mine).

143. *New York Times*, Nov. 23, 1906.

144. *New York Times*, Dec. 4, 1906.

145. *London Times*, Dec. 30, 28, 1913. The Curzon and Leiter families bickered over the trustees for the settlement, whether American or British law would be followed, and estate mismanagement as but a few examples of the financial squabbles that arose between Mary's death in 1906 and George's in 1925. *New York Times*, May 9, 1923. The theft of some £75,000 of liquor from her brother's wine cellar only added to the Leiters' financial woes. *London Times*, Oct. 11, 1921.

146. *New York Times*, Dec. 11, 1916.

147. *New York Times*, Mar. 19, 1913, May 9, 1923, Apr. 2, 1924, July 26, 1925, Feb. 4, 1927; Mar. 25, 1931; *Time*, Aug. 3, 1925.

148. *London Times*, Mar. 21, 1925.

149. Nicolson, *Mary Curzon*, 214.

5. Elegant Envoy

Consuelo Balsan, *The Glitter and the Gold*, 2d ed. (Maidstone, England: George Mann Books, 1973), xi.

1. Charles S. Campbell, *Anglo-American Understanding, 1898–1903* (Baltimore: Johns Hopkins Univ. Press, 1957), 9. For more on the Venezuelan boundary dispute, see Robert L. Beisner, *From the Old Diplomacy to the New, 1865–1900* (Arlington Heights, Ill.: AHM Publishing, 1975), 98–125.

2. Louis Auchincloss, *The Vanderbilt Era: Profiles of a Gilded Age* (New York: Charles Scribner's Sons, 1989), 46.

3. James Brough, *Consuelo: Portrait of an American Heiress* (New York: Coward, Mc-Cann & Geoghegan, 1979), 22. See also Margaret Hayden, *Alva, That Vanderbilt-Belmont Woman* (Wickford, R.I.: Dutch Island Press, 1992); Richard Kenin, *Return to Albion: Americans in England, 1760–1940* (New York: Holt, Rinehart, Winston, 1979), chap. 6.

4. Clarice Stasz, *The Vanderbilt Women: Dynasty of Wealth, Glamour, and Tragedy* (New York: St. Martin's, 1991), 83; Arthur T. Vanderbilt II, *Fortune's Children: The Fall of the House of Vanderbilt* (New York: Morrow, 1989), 88. See also Marian Fowler, *In a Gilded Cage: From Heiress to Duchess* (New York: St. Martin's, 1993), 129–99. In an effort to one-up Mrs. Astor, Mrs. Vanderbilt held a massive fancy dress ball in the spring of 1883 and deliberately failed to invite Mrs. Astor's daughter, which forced Mrs. Astor to pay a call to Mrs. Vanderbilt; Mrs. Vanderbilt's acceptance to New York society was hard won. *New York Times,* Mar. 27, 1883.

5. Brough, *Consuelo,* 56.

6. Alva Smith Vanderbilt Belmont Memoir, 98, Matilda Young Papers, Duke Univ. Rare Book, Manuscript & Special Collections Library. The Matilda Young Papers are one of the very few archival collections containing archival information regarding Alva or Consuelo Vanderbilt. Many of Consuelo's own papers were destroyed at the time of her death. When she was clearing out Consuelo's house in Southampton, Long Island, her granddaughter, Lady Sarah Russell, thought Consuelo's papers were of no interest. Two of Lady Sarah's daughters, Mimi and Serena, were rather horrified when they discovered this and thus rescued some cuttings and photograph albums, which they still have. Unfortunately, the Vanderbilt collections at Vanderbilt University in Nashville, Tennessee, hold some photographs and some newspapers articles but little in the way of private papers or a manuscript collection typical of traditional archives.

7. Brough, *Consuelo,* 40.

8. Ibid., 42; Stasz, *Vanderbilt Women,* 99.

9. Winthrop Rutherford has also appeared as Winthrop Rutherfurd. See Brough, *Consuelo,* and Stasz, *Vanderbilt Women.*

10. Amanda Mackenzie Stuart, *Consuelo and Alva Vanderbilt: The Story of a Daughter and a Mother in the Gilded Age* (New York: HarperCollins, 2005), 113.

11. Brough, *Consuelo,* 57–71; Stasz, *Vanderbilt Women,* 116.

12. Brough, *Consuelo,* 74.

13. Alva Smith Vanderbilt Belmont Memoir, 142.

14. G. E. Cokayne, *The Complete Peerage or a History of the House of Lords and All Its Members from the Earliest Times,* vol. 3, *Lindley to Moate* (London: St. Catherine, 1932), 503; *Winston and Clementine: The Personal Letters of the Churchills,* ed. Mary Soames (New York: Houghton Mifflin, 2001), 656.

15. *New York Times,* Aug. 28, 1895.

16. *London Times,* Sept. 23, 1895; Gustavus Myers, *History of the Great American Fortunes,* vol. 1 (Chicago: Charles H. Kerr, 1909), 274.

17. Auchincloss, *Vanderbilt Era,* 49.

18. Stuart, *Consuelo and Alva Vanderbilt,* 154.

19. *London Times,* Oct. 14, 1895.

20. Balsan, *Glitter and the Gold,* 40, 41; Alva Smith Vanderbilt Belmont Memoir, 149.

21. *New York Times,* Oct. 27, 1895.

22. *Punch,* Nov. 16, 1895

23. *New York Times,* Nov. 3, 1895, Oct. 27, 1895.

24. Stuart, *Consuelo and Alva Vanderbilt,* 1.

25. *New York Times,* Nov. 6, 1895.

26. Myers, *History of the Great American Fortunes,* 274; Stasz, *Vanderbilt Women,* 127.

27. Stuart, *Consuelo and Alva Vanderbilt,* 3.

28. *New York Times,* Oct. 20, 1895.

29. *New York Times,* Sept. 22, 1895.

30. *New York Times,* Nov. 2, 1895.

31. *New York Times,* Nov. 3, 1895.

32. *London Times,* Nov. 13, 1895.

33. Balsan, *Glitter and the Gold,* 41.

34. Vanderbilt, *Fortune's Children,* 172.

35. *London Times,* Nov. 7, 1895.

36. Balsan, *Glitter and the Gold,* 42–43.

37. *New York Times,* Nov. 7, 1895.

38. *New York Times,* Oct. 20, 1895.

39. *New York Times,* May 4, 1896.

40. Hendrik Hartog, "Marital Exits and Marital Expectations in Nineteenth Century America," *Georgetown Law Journal* 80 (Oct. 1991): 96.

41. *New York Times,* Nov. 7, 1895.

42. Balsan, *Glitter and the Gold,* 44.

43. Brough, *Consuelo,* 86.

44. Balsan, *Glitter and the Gold,* 45, 46.

45. Ibid., 54.

46. Brough, *Consuelo,* 95.

47. Ibid., 91.

48. Balsan, *Glitter and the Gold,* 55, 56.

49. Ibid., 57.

50. Gail MacColl and Carol McD. Wallace, *To Marry an English Lord; or, How Anglomania Really Got Started* (New York: Workman, 1989), 209.

51. Balsan, *Glitter and the Gold,* 57.

52. Hesketh Pearson, *The Marrying Americans* (New York: Coward McCann, 1961), 97.

53. Stuart, *Consuelo and Alva Vanderbilt,* 202, 240.

54. Balsan, *Glitter and the Gold,* 45.

55. Ibid., xi; Stasz, *Vanderbilt Women,* 131; Brough, *Consuelo,* 136.

56. Stasz, *Vanderbilt Women,* 133, 162, 165; Balsan, *Glitter and the Gold,* 68; Ruth Brandon, *The Dollar Princesses: Sagas of Upward Nobility, 1870–1914* (New York: Knopf, 1980), 109.

57. Elisabeth Kehoe, *The Titled Americans: Three American Sisters and the English Aristocratic World into Which They Married* (New York: Atlantic Monthly Press, 2004), 211.

58. Stuart, *Consuelo and Alva Vanderbilt,* 261.

59. Katharine W. Jones, *Accent on Privilege: English Identities and Anglophilia in the U.S.* (Philadelphia: Temple Univ. Press, 2001).

60. Balsan, *Glitter and the Gold,* 76.

61. Brough, *Consuelo,* 91.

62. *New York Times,* Sept. 19, 1897.

63. *New York Times,* Oct. 15, 1898.

64. *Boston Daily Globe,* July 19, 1914.

65. Richard Jay Hutto, *Crowning Glory: American Wives of Princes and Dukes* (Macon, Ga.: Henchard, 2007), 282.

66. *New York Times,* Aug. 20, 1902.

67. Balsan, *Glitter and the Gold,* 148.

68. Stuart, *Consuelo and Alva Vanderbilt,* 272–73; Stasz, *Vanderbilt Women,* 166.

69. Elizabeth Eliot, *Heiresses and Coronets: The Story of Lovely Ladies and Noble Men* (New York: McDowell, Obolensky, 1959), 192.

70. *New York Times,* Mar. 6, 1907.

71. Catherine Allgor, *Parlor Politics: In Which the Ladies of Washington Help Build a City and Government* (Charlottesville: Univ. of Virginia Press, 2000), 240.

72. Balsan, *Glitter and the Gold,* 149.

73. Stuart, *Consuelo and Alva Vanderbilt,* 285.

74. Stuart, *Consuelo and Alva Vanderbilt,* 285 (emphasis mine). See also Kathleen D. McCarthy, *Lady Bountiful Revisited: Women, Philanthropy, and Power* (New Brunswick, N.J.: Rutgers Univ. Press, 1991); F. K. Prochaska, *Women and Philanthropy in Nineteenth-Century England* (Oxford: Oxford Univ. Press, 1980); Pat Thane, "The Social, Economic and Political Status of Women," in *Twentieth Century Britain: Economic, Social and Cultural Change,* ed. Paul Johnson (London: Longman, 1994), 94–110.

75. Balsan, *Glitter and the Gold,* 151.

76. Brough, *Consuelo,* 174.

77. *New York Times,* June 30, 1916.

78. Stasz, *Vanderbilt Women,* 194.

79. Balsan, *Glitter and the Gold,* 151.

80. Stuart, *Consuelo and Alva Vanderbilt,* 290.

81. Balsan, *Glitter and the Gold,* 152.

82. The Duchess of Marlborough, "The Position of Women," *North American Review,* 189 (Jan. 1909): 11–24, (Feb. 1909): 180–93, (Mar. 1909): 352–59.

83. Stuart, *Consuelo and Alva Vanderbilt,* 293.

84. *New York Times,* Jan. 19, 1914.

85. Brough, *Consuelo,* 188.

86. Balsan, *Glitter and the Gold,* 152.

87. Stasz, *Vanderbilt Women,* 195.

88. Balsan, *Glitter and the Gold,* 168.

89. Brough, *Consuelo,* 188.

90. Balsan, *Glitter and the Gold,* 169.

91. Consuelo Marlborough, "Hostels for Women," *Nineteenth Century and After,* May 1911, 858, 861, 866.

92. Women in many countries have used the connection between philanthropy and politics. For more on the role of upper-class women, philanthropy, and politics in Mexico, for example, see Víctor Manuel Macías-González, "The Mexican Aristocracy and Porfirio Díaz" (PhD diss., Texas Christian Univ., 1999).

93. Stuart, *Consuelo and Alva Vanderbilt,* 329.

94. *New York Times,* June 27, 1914. The article headline read, "American Duchess Here: Former Consuelo Vanderbilt for Suffrage, but not Militants."

95. *New York Daily News,* April 5, 2013; Stuart, *Consuelo and Alva Vanderbilt,* 335.

96. Stuart, *Consuelo and Alva Vanderbilt,* 354.

97. Brough, *Consuelo,* 189.

98. Anglo-American, "American Women in English Society," *Harper's Bazaar,* July 1905, 607.

99. Mary Curzon to her mother, June 22, 1896, MSS Eur F 306/5, ff143, MCP.

100. MacColl and Wallace, *To Marry an English Lord,* 247.

101. *New York Times,* May 30, 1909. Consuelo received some degree of support from the monarchy due to her close friendship with King Edward's wife, Alexandra.

102. Anglo-American, "American Women in English Society," 603.

103. Box 19, Clubs and Organizations, American Women's Club (London), Printed Matter and Miscellaneous. Lou Henry Hoover Papers, Herbert Hoover Presidential Library, West Branch, Iowa (hereafter Lou Henry Hoover Papers).

104. This organization also maintained close ties to the U.S. official diplomatic leaders and regularly hosted dinners for the sitting American ambassador to England. *New York Times,* June 8, 1901, July 9, 1913.

105. Box 19, Clubs and Organizations, Society of American Women in London, 1908–1914, Lou Henry Hoover Papers.

106. Box 19, Clubs and Organizations, Society of American Women in London, 1908–1914, Lou Henry Hoover Papers.

107. *New York Times,* May 8, 1910.

108. Box 19, Clubs and Organizations, Society of American Women in London, 1908–1914, Lou Henry Hoover Papers.

109. In addition to her war efforts, Consuelo Vanderbilt Marlborough also promoted the cause of suffrage in England and worked closely with her mother, Alva (now Belmont), a suffrage leader in the United States, who patronized suffrage groups in the United States as well as in Great Britain. Alva was a member of the National American Women's Suffrage Association, an alternate delegate to the International Women's Suffrage Association, and founded the Political Equality League, which later merged with the Congressional Union for Women's Suffrage. For more on the mother-daughter suffrage efforts, see Stuart, *Consuelo and Alva Vanderbilt.*

110. Nancy Beck Young, *Lou Henry Hoover: Activist First Lady* (Lawrence: Univ. Press of Kansas, 2004), 23.

111. Box 1, American Women's War Relief Fund, Correspondence, 1915, Lou Henry Hoover Papers. Anne Beiser Allen, *An Independent Woman: The Life of Lou Henry Hoover* (Westport, Conn.: Greenwood, 2000), 53, 62–67.

112. Box 2, American Women's War Relief Fund, Philanthropic Committee, Minutes & Agendas, 1916–1918, Lou Henry Hoover Papers.

113. Anne Seba, *American Jennie: The Remarkable Life of Lady Randolph Churchill* (New York: Norton, 2007), 308.

114. Box 2, American Women's War Relief Fund, Executive Committee, 1914–1917, Lou Henry Hoover Papers.

115. *London Times,* Mar. 22, 1917.

116. Box 2, American Women's War Relief Fund, Red Cross, 1914–1917 and undated, Lou Henry Hoover Papers. Box 2, American Women's War Relief Fund, Hospital, 1914–1918 and undated, Lou Henry Hoover Papers.

117. Box 2, American Women's War Relief Fund, Lectures and Classes, Lou Henry Hoover Papers.

118. Box 2, American Women's War Relief Fund, Economic Relief Committee, Reports and Miscellaneous, 1914–1915 and undated, Lou Henry Hoover Papers.

119. Box 2, American Women's War Relief Fund, Reports of Activities and Finances, 1915, Lou Henry Hoover Papers.

120. Box 1, American Women's War Relief Fund, Clothing Committee, 1914–1915 and undated, Lou Henry Hoover Papers.

121. Box 2, American Women's War Relief Fund, Lists of Committees, Lou Henry Hoover Papers.

122. Box 2, American Women's War Relief Fund, Information for Travelers, Lou Henry Hoover Papers.

123. Box 2, American Women's War Relief Fund, Lists of Committees, Lou Henry Hoover Papers; Box 2, American Women's War Relief Fund, Fundraising, 1914–1918, and undated, Lou Henry Hoover Papers.

124. Box 1, American Women's War Relief Fund, American Benevolence Committee, 1915–1917 and undated, Lou Henry Hoover Papers; Box 1, American Women's War Relief Fund, American Citizens Relief Committee, 1914, Lou Henry Hoover Papers; Box 1, American Women's War Relief Fund, American Convalescent Home, 1915–1916, Lou Henry Hoover Papers; Box 1, American Women's War Relief Fund, American Care Committee for Soldiers and Sailors, 1917, Lou Henry Hoover Papers.

125. Stasz, *Vanderbilt Women*, 228; Brough, *Consuelo*, 195.

126. Stuart, *Consuelo and Alva Vanderbilt*, 362.

127. Balsan, *Glitter and the Gold*, 176, 178. Many of Consuelo's efforts in this regard focused on causes and remedies of infant mortality, specifically as they pertained to Anglo-Saxon babies. *New York Times*, June 30, 1916.

128. Stasz, *Vanderbilt Women*, 228.

129. Balsan, *Glitter and the Gold*, 174.

130. *New York Times*, Oct. 1, 1914. A September 13 *Times* article also identified the Duchess as "formerly Consuelo Vanderbilt."

131. Box 3, American Women's War Relief Fund, Resignation of Lou Henry Hoover, 1915–1918, Lou Henry Hoover Papers.

132. Box 19, Club and Organizations, American Women's Club (London), 1919–1933, Lou Henry Hoover Papers; Box 19, Club and Organizations, American Women's Club (London), Printed Matter and Miscellaneous, Lou Henry Hoover Papers.

133. *New York Times*, Sept. 16, 1913.

134. *New York Times*, Aug. 3, 1918.

135. Stasz, *Vanderbilt Women*, 254; Balsan, *Glitter and the Gold*, 180.

136. Stasz, *Vanderbilt Women*, 254.

137. *New York Times*, Oct. 16, 1918.

138. *New York Times*, Nov. 10, 1920.

139. *New York Times*, May 14, 1921; *London Times*, Nov. 16, 1926, Dec. 8, 1926, Nov. 20, 1980; Stuart, *Consuelo and Alva Vanderbilt*, 390.

140. *New York Times*, July 3, 1921; *London Times*, July 5, 1921.

141. Consuelo Vanderbilt Folder, Vanderbilt Family Collection, Special Collections, Univ. Archives, Jean and Alexander Heard Library, Vanderbilt Univ.

142. Consuelo Vanderbilt Folder, Vanderbilt Family Collection, Special Collections, Univ. Archives, Jean and Alexander Heard Library, Vanderbilt Univ.

143. *London Times*, May 11, 1959.

144. *London Times*, Nov. 6, 1956.

145. *London Times*, Dec. 7, 1964.

146. Brough, *Consuelo*, 246.

147. Fowler, *In a Gilded Cage*, 199.

148. Balsan, *Glitter and the Gold*, 212.

149. Ibid., xi.

6. Candid Consul

Mary C. Davidson, London, to Lady Astor, Plymouth, ALS, 1 Dec 1919, MS 1416/1/1/1721, Astor Papers. Archives and Manuscripts, University of Reading Library, Reading, England. "The cry of the children" alludes to Elizabeth Barrett Browning, "The Cry of the Children," reprinted in *The Literature of England*, vol. 2, *Dawn of the Romantic Movement to the Present Day*, ed. George K. Anderson and William E. Buckler, 5th ed. (Chicago: Scott, Foresman, 1966), 710–13.

1. John Halperin, *Eminent Georgians: The Lives of King George V, Elizabeth Bowen, St. John Philby, and Nancy Astor* (New York: St. Martin's, 1995), 173.

2. Christopher Sykes, *Nancy: The Life of Lady Astor* (Chicago: Academy Chicago, 1972), 12.

3. James Fox, *Five Sisters: The Langhornes of Virginia* (New York: Simon & Schuster, 2000), 21. For a concise biography of the Astor family, see Richard Kenin, *Return to Albion: Americans in England, 1760–1940* (New York: Holt, Rinehart, Winston, 1979), 195–219.

4. Halperin, *Eminent Georgians*, 173.

5. Anthony Masters, *Nancy Astor: A Life* (London: Weidenfeld & Nicolson, 1981), 10.

6. Fox, *Five Sisters*, 26.

7. Halperin, *Eminent Georgians*, 174.

8. Fox, *Five Sisters*, 38.

9. Draft of Nancy Astor's autobiography, Nancy Astor Manuscripts, MSS5:1 As885:1, 34; Virginia Historical Society; Draft of Nancy Astor's autobiography, MS 1416/1/6/86, Univ. of Reading.

10. Anthony Masters, *Nancy Astor: A Life* (London: Weidenfeld & Nicolson, 1981), 15.

11. Halperin, *Eminent Georgians*, 175.

12. Ibid., 175.

13. Fox, *Five Sisters*, 65.

14. Ibid., 65.

15. Halperin, *Eminent Georgians*, 176; Michael Astor, *Tribal Feeling* (London: Butler& Tanner, 1963), 28.

16. Draft of Nancy Astor's autobiography, Nancy Astor Manuscripts, MSS5:1 As885:1, 55; Virginia Historical Society; Draft of Nancy Astor's autobiography, MS 1416/1/6/86, Univ. of Reading.

17. Draft of Nancy Astor's autobiography, Nancy Astor Manuscripts, MSS5:1 As885:1, 66; Virginia Historical Society; Draft of Nancy Astor's autobiography, MS 1416/1/6/86, Univ. of Reading.

18. Masters, *Nancy Astor,* 19; Fox, *Five Sisters,* 72–73; Halperin, *Eminent Georgians,* 176.

19. Halperin, *Eminent Georgians,* 176.

20. Fox, *Five Sisters,* 76.

21. Halperin, *Eminent Georgians,* 176.

22. Fox, *Five Sisters,* 79, 80.

23. Astor, *Tribal Feeling,* 35.

24. Fox, *Five Sisters,* 81.

25. Draft of Nancy Astor's autobiography, Nancy Astor Manuscripts, MSS5:1 As885:1, 67; Virginia Historical Society; Draft of Nancy Astor's autobiography, MS 1416/1/6/86, Univ. of Reading.

26. Fox, *Five Sisters,* 81.

27. Draft of Nancy Astor's autobiography, Nancy Astor Manuscripts, MSS5:1 As885:1, 69; Virginia Historical Society; Draft of Nancy Astor's autobiography, MS 1416/1/6/86, Univ. of Reading.

28. Fox, *Five Sisters,* 81.

29. Draft of Nancy Astor's autobiography, Nancy Astor Manuscripts, MSS5:1 As885:1, 74; Virginia Historical Society; Draft of Nancy Astor's autobiography, MS 1416/1/6/86, Univ. of Reading.

30. Halperin, *Eminent Georgians,* 178.

31. Fox, *Five Sisters,* 85, 86.

32. Years after she married Waldorf, Nancy would refer to the Astor family as "those skunk skinnin' Astors" when she was upset with her husband's family. Ibid., 136.

33. Ibid., 86.

34. Axel Madsen, *John Jacob Astor: America's First Multimillionaire* (New York: Wiley, 2001), 6, 283, 284.

35. Fox, *Five Sisters,* 97

36. *New York Times,* Mar. 9, 10, 1906.

37. *New York Times,* May 4, 1906. Both gentlemen were widowers: Mrs. Langhorne died in 1903, Mrs. Astor in 1894.

38. *New York Times,* Mar. 21, 1906.

39. Halperin, *Eminent Georgians,* 180; Fox, *Five Sisters,* 88; Karen J. Musolf, *From Plymouth to Parliament: A Rhetorical History of Nancy Astor's 1919 Campaign* (New York: St. Martin's, 1999), 8.

40. Courtney Wilson, "Our Nancy: The Story of Nancy Astor and Her Gift to the University of Virginia," manuscript, Astor Collection, Univ. of Virginia, Charlottesville.

41. Halperin, *Eminent Georgians,* 182; Wilson, "Our Nancy."

42. Halperin, *Eminent Georgians,* 181.

43. Musolf, *From Plymouth to Parliament,* 9.

44. Wilson, "Our Nancy."

45. Musolf, *From Plymouth to Parliament,* 9.

46. Madsen, *John Jacob Astor,* 284.

47. May Goelet married the 8th Duke of Roxburghe in 1903.

48. Fox, *Five Sisters,* 113.

49. Halperin, *Eminent Georgians,* 182.

50. Fox, *Five Sisters,* 115.

51. Ibid., 105.

52. *New York Times,* Apr. 11, 1916; Sykes, *Nancy,* 205–6.

53. Draft of Nancy Astor's autobiography, Nancy Astor Manuscripts, MSS5:1 As885:1, 114; Virginia Historical Society; Draft of Nancy Astor's autobiography, MS 1416/1/6/86, Univ. of Reading.

54. Musolf, *From Plymouth to Parliament,* 9.

55. Masters, *Nancy Astor,* 59. Sutton was a division of Plymouth.

56. Fox, *Five Sisters,* 138.

57. Halperin, *Eminent Georgians,* 183.

58. Draft of Nancy Astor's autobiography, Nancy Astor Manuscripts, MSS5:1 As885:1, 114; Virginia Historical Society; Draft of Nancy Astor's autobiography, MS 1416/1/6/86, Univ. of Reading.

59. Draft of Nancy Astor's autobiography, Nancy Astor Manuscripts, MSS5:1 As885:1, 132; Virginia Historical Society; Draft of Nancy Astor's autobiography, MS 1416/1/6/86, Univ. of Reading.

60. Halperin, *Eminent Georgians,* 185.

61. Draft of Nancy Astor's autobiography, Nancy Astor Manuscripts, MSS5:1 As885:1, 131; Virginia Historical Society; Draft of Nancy Astor's autobiography, MS 1416/1/6/86, Univ. of Reading.

62. Madsen, *John Jacob Astor,* 289.

63. Ruth Brandon, *The Dollar Princesses: Sagas of Upward Nobility, 1870–1914* (New York: Knopf, 1980), 162–63.

64. *Sunday Evening Telegram,* Oct. 26, 1919, as cited by Musolf, "Angel Sings," 8.

65. Musolf, "Angel Sings," 8.

66. Musolf, *From Plymouth to Parliament,* 10.

67. Fox, *Five Sisters,* 282.

68. Musolf, "Angel Sings," 86.

69. Gail MacColl and Carol McD. Wallace, *To Marry an English Lord; or, How Anglomania Really Got Started* (New York: Workman, 1989), 208.

70. *New York Times,* Nov. 16, 1919.

71. *Daily Chronicle,* Oct. 25, 1919, as cited by Musolf, "Angel Sings," 15.

72. Elizabeth Langhorne, *Nancy Astor and Her Friends* (New York: Praeger, 1974), 89.

73. Musolf, " Angel Sings," 20.

74. Fox, *Five Sisters,* 281.

75. Karen J. Musolf, *From Plymouth to Parliament: A Rhetorical History of Nancy Astor's 1919 Campaign* (New York: St. Martin's, 1999), 103.

76. Ibid., 131.

77. Langhorne, *Nancy Astor and Her Friends,* 87.

78. Lady Astor was not the first woman to be elected to the House of Commons. In 1918 Constance Georgine Gore-Booth, better known Countess Markiewicz, was elected as a Sinn Fein candidate. She refused the oath of allegiance to the king and rejected British jurisdiction over Ireland and was thereby ineligible to take her seat. Fox, *Five Sisters,* 279.

79. Barbara Ann Knoles, "Orphans of the Storm": The Integration of Women in Parliament, 1918–1988" (PhD diss., Northern Arizona Univ., 1988), 26.

80. Langhorne, *Nancy Astor and·Her Friends,* 90.

81. Ibid., 90.

82. Knoles, "Orphans of the Storm," 27.

83. Halperin, *Eminent Georgians,* 184.

84. MacColl and Wallace, *To Marry an English Lord,* 210.

85. *New York Times,* Dec. 3, 1944.

86. Fox, *Five Sisters,* 284.

87. *New York Times,* May 3, 1964.

88. *London Times,* Feb. 25, 1920. Nancy continued to focus on temperance throughout her political career. *London Times,* Apr. 13, July 14, 1923.

89. Fox, *Five Sisters,* 284. She repeated these sentiments again in 1922, saying it was "almost as difficult for some of them as it was for the lady MP herself." *Boston Daily Globe,* Apr. 30, 1922.

90. Musolf, "Angel Sings," 294; Knoles, "Orphans of the Storm," 32.

91. *Boston Daily Globe,* Sept. 10, 1926.

92. Fox, *Five Sisters,* 290.

93. Ibid., 288; *Boston Daily Globe,* Sept. 5, 1923.

94. Viscountess Astor, M.P., "What Women Can Do in Politics That Men Cannot Do," *Woman's Home Companion,* Sept. 1920, 7–8.

95. Musolf, *From Plymouth to Parliament,* 154.

96. *New York Times,* May 5, 1922.

97. Musolf, *From Plymouth to Parliament,* 155.

98. Lady Nancy Astor, *My Two Countries* (New York: Doubleday, Page, 1923), 41, 3, 24, 27, 8, 16.

99. Masters, *Nancy Astor,* 117.

100. Musolf, *From Plymouth to Parliament,* 156.

101. *New York Times,* Apr. 30, 1922.

102. Musolf, *From Plymouth to Parliament,* 158.

103. Ibid.; Masters, *Nancy Astor,* 139.

104. Rachel McMillan was Margaret's sister who died in 1917. Masters, *Nancy Astor,* 140.

105. Nancy Astor Manuscripts, Mss1 As885 a 49–50, Virginia Historical Society.

106. *London Times,* Dec. 13, 1927. Shortly after this speech, Lady Astor sat on the National Council for Prevention of War, which focused on Anglo-American relations. This seat led to the Anglo-American Committee for International Discussion, composed of fifty British and fifty American members who dedicated themselves to "strengthening a good understanding between the two nations." *London Times,* May 29, Dec. 10, 1928.

107. Nancy Astor Manuscripts, Mss1 As885 a 49–50, Virginia Historical Society.

108. Masters, *Nancy Astor,* 149.

109. *New York Times,* May 3, 1931.

110. Hesketh Pearson, *The Marrying Americans* (New York: Coward McCann, 1961), 256.

111. Fox, *Five Sisters,* 368–69.

112. Langhorne, *Nancy Astor and Her Friends,* 117; Fox, *Five Sisters,* 375.

113. Fox, *Five Sisters,* 423.

114. Musolf, *From Plymouth to Parliament,* 161.

115. *London Times,* Apr. 18, 1969.

116. *New York Times,* Mar. 6, 1938.

117. Fox, *Five Sisters,* 423; *London Times,* Feb. 27, 1973.

118. *New York Times,* Apr. 28, May 6, 1938, Nov. 25, 1945; Viscountess Astor, "Lady Astor Interviews Herself," *Saturday Evening Post,* Mar. 4, 1939, 5–6, 76–79.

119. Fox, *Five Sisters,* 444, 446.

120. Ibid., 456.

121. Masters, *Nancy Astor,* 209.

122. Musolf, *From Plymouth to Parliament,* 165.

123. Masters, *Nancy Astor,* 213.

124. Astor, *Tribal Feeling,* 217.

125. Sykes, *Nancy,* 568, 570.

126. *London Times,* May 14, 1964.

127. Langhorne, *Nancy Astor and Her Friends,* 260.

128. *Observer,* May 3, 1964.

129. *New York Times,* Dec. 3, 1944.

7. The American Invasion

The epigraph is taken from Richard W. Davis, "'We Are All Americans Now!' Anglo-American Marriages in the Later Nineteenth Century," *Proceedings of the American Philosophical Society* 135, no. 2 (June 1991): 142. (Davis cites Ralph Nevill, ed., *Leaves from the Notebooks of Lady Dorothy Nevill* [London: Macmillan, 1907], 33.)

1. Bradford Perkins, *The Great Rapprochement: England and the United States, 1895–1914* (New York: Atheneum, 1968), 153

2. Sondra R. Herman, "Loving Courtship or the Marriage Market? The Ideal and Its Critics, 1871–1911," *American Quarterly* 25, no. 2 (May 1973): 237.

3. Christopher Hitchens, *Blood, Class, and Empire: The Enduring Anglo-American Relationship* (New York: Nation Books, 1990), 121.

4. *New York Times,* Sept. 14, 1902. Several authors have used the term "American invasion" in reference to Anglo-American marriages. See Kathleen Burk, "Anglo-American Marital Relations, 1870–1945," paper presented at Barnard's Inn Hall, Holborn, London, England, Feb. 3, 2004; R. H. Heindel, *The American Impact on Great Britain, 1898–1914: A Study of the United States in World History* (New York: Octagon, 1968), 346; David Cannadine, *The Decline and Fall of the British Aristocracy* (New Haven: Yale Univ. Press, 1990), 358; Maureen E. Montgomery, *Gilded Prostitution: Status, Money, and Transatlantic Marriages, 1870–1914* (New York: Routledge, 1989), 32; Hesketh Pearson, *The Marrying Americans* (New York: Coward McCann, 1961), 66; Jane Abdy and Charlotte Gere, *The Souls* (London: Sidgwick & Jackson, 1984), 159. Other scholars, diplomatic historians in particular, have used the same term to refer to the "American invasion" of Europe in terms of American-made goods. See Walter LaFeber, *The American Search for Opportunity, 1865–1913,* vol. 2 of *The Cambridge History of American Foreign Relations* (Cambridge: Cambridge Univ. Press, 1993), 21; David Dimbleby and David Reynolds, *An Ocean Apart: The Relationship between*

Britain and America in the Twentieth Century (New York: Random House, 1988), 39. The combination of American women and products invading Britain was a decisive factor in the movement against such marriages.

5. Anita Leslie, *Mr. Frewen of England: A Victorian Adventurer* (London: Hutchinson, 1966), 61.

6. *New York Times,* Nov. 10, 1892.

7. Leslie, *Mr. Frewen of England,* 114.

8. Elizabeth Cameron to Cecil Spring Rice, Apr. 3, 1893, Cecil Spring Rice Papers, CASR 1/6/91, Churchill Archives Center, Churchill College, Cambridge. Spring Rice served as the British Ambassador to the United States from 1912 to 1918.

9. *New York Times,* Apr. 19, 1893.

10. Elizabeth Eliot, *Heiresses and Coronets: The Story of Lovely Ladies and Noble Men* (New York: McDowell, Obolensky, 1959), 254.

11. Ruth Brandon, *The Dollar Princesses: Sagas of Upward Nobility, 1870–1914* (New York: Knopf, 1980), 49; Gail MacColl and Carol McD. Wallace, *To Marry an English Lord: or, How Anglomania Really Got Started* (New York: Workman, 1989), 316.

12. Albert K. Steigerwalt, "The National Association of Manufacturers: Organization and Policies, 1895–1914," (PhD diss., Univ. of Michigan, 1952), 71–72, as cited by LaFeber in *American Search for Opportunity,* 112.

13. MacColl and Wallace, *To Marry an English Lord,* 126.

14. Hitchens, *Blood, Class, and Empire,* 122.

15. Richard Jay Hutto, *Crowing Glory: American Wives of Princes and Dukes* (Macon, Ga.: Henchard, 2007), 13.

16. Candice Lewis Bredbenner, *A Nationality of Her Own: Women, Marriage, and the Law of Citizenship* (Berkeley: Univ. of California Press, 1998), 62.

17. Perkins, *Great Rapprochement,* 153.

18. Bredbenner, *Nationality of Her Own,* 62–63.

19. "The Canton, Ohio, Speech," *Writings and Speeches of Eugene V. Debs,* ed. Arthur M. Schlesinger (New York: Hermitage, 1948), 422.

20. Montgomery, *Gilded Prostitution,* 27.

21. Nancy Cott, "Marriage and Women's Citizenship in the United States, 1830–1934," *American Historical Review* 103, no. 5 (Dec. 1998): 1461.

22. Waldo Emerson Waltz, *The Nationality of Married Women: A Study of Domestic Policies and International Legislation* (Urbana: Univ. of Illinois Press, 1937), 23.

23. Ann Marie Nicolosi, "'We Do Not Want Our Girls to Marry Foreigners': Gender, Race, and American Citizenship, (PhD diss., Rutgers, The State Univ. of New Jersey, 1999), 12; Ann Marie Nicolosi, "'We Do Not Want Our Girls to Marry Foreigners': Gender, Race, and American Citizenship," *National Women's Studies Association Journal* 13, no. 3 (2001): 14. See also Blanche Crozier, "The Changing Basis of Women's Nationality," *Boston University Law Review* 14 (Jan. 1934): 129–53.

24. Bredbenner, *Nationality of Her Own,* 4; Norma Basch, *In the Eyes of the Law: Women, Marriage, and Property in Nineteenth-Century New York* (Ithaca, N.Y.: Cornell Univ. Press, 1982), 225.

25. Virginia Sapiro, "Women, Citizenship, and Nationality: Immigration and Naturalization Policies in the United States," *Politics and Society* 13 (Mar. 1984): 7.

26. Linda Kerber, *No Constitutional Right to Be Ladies: Women and the Obligation of Citizenship* (New York: Hill & Wang, 1998), 41.

27. National Archives and Records Administration, *Relating to the Expatriation of Citizens, Hearings Before the Committee on Foreign Affairs of the House of Representatives on H.R. 21358* (Washington, D.C.: GPO, 1912), 8.

28. Bredbenner, *Nationality of Her Own*, 73 (emphasis mine).

29. Sapiro, "Women, Citizenship, and Nationality," 17.

30. Bredbenner, *Nationality of Her Own*, 6, 16.

31. Kerber, *No Constitutional Right to Be Ladies*, 41.

32. Memorandum, General Statement, Doris Steven Unprocessed Papers, box 9, folder 290, 1–20. Schlesinger Library, Radcliffe Institute for Advanced Study, Harvard Univ.

33. Consuelo Vanderbilt Balsan, *The Glitter and the Gold*, 2d ed. (Maidstone, England: George Mann Books, 1973), xi.

34. Kerber, *No Constitutional Right to Be Ladies*, 42; Linda Kerber, "The Meanings of Citizenship," *Journal of American History* 84, no. 3 (Dec 1997): 840.

35. Sarah Pauline Vickers, "The Life of Ruth Bryan Owen: Florida's First Congresswoman and America's First Woman Diplomat," (PhD diss., Florida State Univ., 1994).

36. Sapiro, "Women, Citizenship, and Nationality," 17.

37. Bredbenner, *Nationality of Her Own*, 61.

38. Ibid., 98. The law dictated that American men and women would lose American citizenship if they lived in the countries of their spouses, or any foreign territories, for five or more years.

39. Gladys Harrison, "The Nationality of Married Women," *New York University Law Quarterly Review* 9 (1932): 457.

40. Bredbenner, *Nationality of Her Own*, 62.

41. William Thomas Stead, *The Americanization of the World; or, the Trend of the Twentieth Century* (New York: Harce Markley, 1902), 323. Maureen F. Montgomery is quick to point out that this phrase "has never been used other than a figure of speech, and neither suggests that a transatlantic marriage was an act of physical prostitution, nor imputes that any of the transatlantic marriages' partners was a prostitute." Montgomery, *Gilded Prostitution*, ix.

42. *Punch*, Dec. 5, 1906.

43. H. B. Marriott-Watson, "The Deleterious Effect of Americanization upon Women," *Nineteenth Century and After*, 1903, 785.

44. Jaime Camplin, *The Rise of the Plutocrats: Wealth and Power in Edwardian England* (London: Constable, 1978), 180.

45. Perkins, *Great Rapprochement*, 153.

46. Ralph G. Martin, *Jennie: The Life of Lady Randolph Churchill*, vol. 1, *The Romantic Years, 1854–1895* (New York: Prentice Hall, 1969), 261.

47. Abby G. Baker, "International Marriages," *Independent*, Oct. 1908, 750, 758.

48. Colonial, "Titled Colonials v. Titled Americans," *Contemporary Review* 87 (1905): 861, 862, 865, 866, 869.

49. Montgomery, *Gilded Prostitution*, 3.

50. Kathleen Burk, "The House of Morgan in Financial Diplomacy, 1920–1930," in *Anglo-American Relations in the 1920s: The Struggle for Supremacy*, ed. B. J. C. McKercher (Edmonton: Univ. of Alberta Press, 1990), 126, 130.

51. Montgomery, *Gilded Prostitution,* 2.

52. See Francis Donaldson, *Edward VIII* (New York: Lippincott, 1974); Charles Higham, *The Duchess of Windsor: The Secret Life* (New York: McGraw-Hill, 1988).

53. Perkins, *Great Rapprochement,* 151–53.

54. MacColl and Wallace, *To Marry an English Lord,* 320.

55. George Barr Baker, "Dollars vs. Pedigree: The Truth About International Marriages," *Everybody's Magazine* 16, no. 2 (Feb. 1907): 175.

Bibliography

Archives

Draft of Nancy Astor's Autobiography. Nancy Astor Collection. University of Reading, Reading, United Kingdom.

Nancy Astor Manuscripts. Virginia Historical Society, Richmond.

Alva Smith Vanderbilt Belmont Memoir. Matilda Young Papers. Rare Book, Manuscript and Special Collections Library. Duke University, Durham, North Carolina.

Chamberlain Family Papers. Special Collections. University of Birmingham, Manchester, England.

Lady Randolph Spencer Churchill, editor. *Anglo-Saxon Review*. A Quarterly Miscellany. Vols. 1–10. London and New York: John Lane, 1899–1901.

Lady Randolph Churchill Papers. Churchill Archives Centre, Churchill College, Cambridge, England.

Mary Victoria Curzon Papers. India Office. British Library, London, England.

Endicott Family Papers. Massachusetts Historical Society, Boston.

Lou Henry Hoover Papers. Herbert Hoover Presidential Library, West Branch, Iowa.

John Lane Company Record. Harry Ransom Humanities Research Center. The University of Texas at Austin.

Cecil Spring Rice Papers. Churchill Archives Center. Churchill College, Cambridge, England.

Doris Steven Unprocessed Papers. Schlesinger Library. Radcliffe Institute for Advanced Study. Harvard University, Cambridge, Massachusetts.

Consuelo Vanderbilt Folder. Vanderbilt Family Collection. Special Collections. University Archives. Jean and Alexander Heard Library. Vanderbilt University, Nashville, Tennessee.

Margaret S. R. (Mrs. Henry) White Diary. July 28, 1888–September 29, 1889. Henry White Manuscript Collection. Rare Book and Manuscript Library. Columbia University, New York.

Wilson, Courtney. "Our Nancy: The Story of Nancy Astor and Her Gift to the University of Virginia." Online at http://xroads.virginia.edu/~ma04/ranger/astor_collection/our-nancy.html. Astor Collection. University of Virginia, Charlottesville.

Newspapers and Magazines

Boston Daily Globe
Boston Globe
Boston Herald
Boston Sunday Post
Contemporary Review
Current Literature
Daily Chronicle
Daily Telegraph
Everybody's Magazine
Harper's Bazaar
Hindu Patriot
Independent
London Times
McClure's Magazine
New York Globe
New York Times
New York World
Nineteenth Century
Nineteenth Century and After
North American Review
Observer
Punch
Salem News
Saturday Evening Post
Sketch
Sunday Evening Telegram
St. James's Gazette
Winning Post
Town Topics
Vogue
Woman's Home Companion

Reference Materials

Brancroft, W. B., ed. *Directory of Americans Resident in London & Great Britain, Americans Firms and Agencies.* London: American Directory Publishing, 1902.

Cokayne, G. E. *The Complete Peerage; or, A History of the House of Lords and All Its Members from the Earliest Times.* Vol. 3, *Lindley to Moate.* London: St. Catherine Press, 1932.

Gardiner, Juliet, ed. *The History Today: Who's Who in British History* London: Collins & Brown, 2000.

Smith, Joseph. *Historical Dictionary of United States–Latin American Relations.* Lanham, Maryland: Scarecrow, 2007.

Social Register, accessed May, 29, 2006, available at http://www.socialregisteronline.com.

Venn, J. A., comp. *Alumni Cantabrigienses: A Biographical List of All Known Students, Graduates and Holders of Office at the University of Cambridge, From Earliest Times to 1900. Part 2, From 1752 to 1900.* Vol. 2, *Chalmers–Fytche.* Cambridge: Cambridge University Press, 1944.

Books

Abdy, Jane, and Charlotte Gere. *The Souls.* London: Sidgwick & Jackson, 1984.

Allen, Anne Beiser. *An Independent Woman: The Life of Lou Henry Hoover.* Westport, Connecticut: Greenwood, 2000.

Allen, H. C. *Conflict and Concord: The Anglo-American Relationship since 1783.* New York: St. Martin's, 1959.

Allgor, Catherine. *Parlor Politics: In Which the Ladies of Washington Build a City and a Government.* Charlottesville: University of Virginia Press, 2000.

Alvah, Donna. *Unofficial Ambassadors: American Military Families Overseas and the Cold War, 1946–1965.* New York: New York University Press, 2007.

Astor, Lady Nancy. *My Two Countries.* New York: Doubleday, 1923.

Astor, Michael. *Tribal Feeling.* London: Butler & Tanner, 1963.

Auchincloss, Louis. *The Vanderbilt Era: Profiles of a Gilded Age.* New York: Charles Scribner's Sons, 1989.

Bailey, Thomas A. *A Diplomatic History of the American People.* 9th ed. Englewood Cliffs, New Jersey: Prentice-Hall, 1974.

Balsan, Consuelo Vanderbilt. *The Glitter and the Gold.* 2d ed. Maidstone, England: George Mann, 1973.

Banks, Elizabeth L. *Campaigns of Curiosity: Journalistic Adventures of an American Girl in Late Victorian London.* Madison: University of Wisconsin, 2003.

Basch, Norma. *In the Eyes of the Law: Women, Marriage, and Property in Nineteenth-Century New York.* Ithaca, New York: Cornell University Press, 1982.

Beaumont, Penny, and Roger Beaumont. *Imperial Divas: The Vicereines of India.* London: Haus Publishing, 2010.

Becker, William H., and Samuel F. Wells, eds. *Economics and World Power: An Assessment of American Diplomacy since 1789.* New York: Columbia University Press, 1984.

Beisner, Robert. *From the Old Diplomacy to the New, 1865–1900.* Arlington Heights, Illinois: AHM Publishing, 1975.

Berman, Maureen R. and Joseph E. Johnson. *Unofficial Diplomats.* New York: Columbia University Press, 1977.

Brandreth, Gyles. *Philip and Elizabeth: Portrait of a Marriage.* London: Arrow Books, 2004.

Brandon, Ruth. *The Dollar Princesses: Sagas of Upward Nobility, 1870–1914.* New York: Knopf, 1980.

Bredbenner, Candice Lewis. *A Nationality of Her Own: Women, Marriage, and the Law of Citizenship.* Berkeley: University of California Press, 1998.

Breslin, Thomas A. *Beyond Pain: The Role of Pleasure and Culture in the Making of Foreign Affairs.* Westport, Connecticut: Praeger, 2002.

Brodrick, St. John. *Relations of Lord Curzon as Viceroy of India with the British Government, 1902–05.* London: Privately published by the author, 1926.

Brough, James. *Consuelo: Portrait of an American Heiress.* New York: Coward, McCann & Geoghegan, 1979.

Campbell, Charles S. *Anglo-American Understanding, 1898–1903.* Baltimore: Johns Hopkins University Press, 1957.

———. *From Revolution to Rapprochement: The United States and Great Britain, 1783–1900.* New York: Wiley, 1974.

Cannadine, David. *The Decline and Fall of the British Aristocracy.* New Haven: Yale University Press, 1990.

Camplin, Jaime. *The Rise of the Plutocrats: Wealth and Power in Edwardian England.* London: Constable, 1978.

Chamberlain, Joseph. *Mr. Chamberlain's Speeches.* Edited by Charles Boyd. New York: Kraus Reprint, 1970.

Churchill, Peregrine, and Julian Mitchell. *Jennie: Lady Randolph Churchill, A Portrait with Letters.* New York: St. Martin's, 1974.

Churchill, Winston S. *My Early Life: A Roving Commission.* New York: Charles Scribner's Sons, 1930.

Conniff, Richard. *The Natural History of the Rich: A Field Guide.* New York: Norton, 2002.

Coontz, Stephanie. *Marriage, A History: From Obedience to Intimacy; or, How Love Conquered Marriage.* New York: Viking Adult, 2005.

Cornwallis-West, George. *Edwardian Hey-Days; or, A Little About a Lot of Things.* New York: Putnam, 1930.

Cornwallis-West, Mrs. George. *The Reminiscences of Lady Randolph Churchill.* New York: Century, 1908.

Cott, Nancy. *Public Vows: A History of Marriage and the Nation.* Cambridge, Massachusetts: Harvard University Press, 2000.

Crapol, Edward. *America for Americans: Economic Nationalism and Anglophobia.* Westport, Connecticut: Greenwood, 1973.

Curzon, Mary. *Lady Curzon's India: Letters of a Vicereine.* Edited by John Bradley. New York: Beaufort Books, 1985.

Das, Sonya Ruth Sklar. *The American Woman in Modern Marriage.* New York: Philosophical Library, 1948.

De Courcy, Anne. *1939: The Last Season.* London: Orion Books, 1989.

———. *The Viceroy's Daughters: The Lives of the Curzon Sisters.* London: Phoenix, 2002.

Debs, Eugene V. *Writings and Speeches of Eugene V. Debs.* Edited by Arthur M. Schlesinger. New York: Hermitage, 1948.

De Mendelssohn, Peter. *The Age of Churchill: Heritage and Adventure, 1874–1911.* London: Thames & Hudson, 1961.

Deslandes, Paul R. *Oxbridge Men: British Masculinity and the Undergraduate Experience, 1850–1920.* Bloomington: Indiana University Press, 2005.

Dimbleby, David, and David Reynolds. *An Ocean Apart: The Relationship between Britain and America in the Twentieth Century.* New York: Random House, 1988.

Donaldson, Francis. *Edward VIII.* New York: Lippincott, 1974.

Dunlop, W. H. *Gilded City: Scandal and Sensation in Turn-of-the-Century New York.* New York: Morrow, 2000.

Eliot, Elizabeth. *Heiresses and Coronets: The Story of Lovely Ladies and Noble Men*. New York: McDowell, Obolensky, 1959.

Ellmann, Richard, ed. *Edwardians and Late Victorians*. New York: Columbia University Press, 1960.

Enloe, Cynthia. *Bananas, Beaches, and Bases: Making Feminist Sense of International Politics*. Berkeley: University of California Press, 1989.

Epstein, Joseph. *Snobbery: The American Version*. Boston: Houghton Mifflin, 2002.

Fenzi, Jewell. *Married to the Foreign Service: An Oral History of the American Diplomatic Spouse*. New York: Macmillan, 1994.

Forslund, Catherine. *Anna Chennault: Informal Diplomacy and Asian Relations*. Wilmington, Delaware: Scholarly Resources Books, 2002.

Foster, R. F. *Lord Randolph Churchill: A Political Life*. Oxford: Clarendon, 1981.

Fowler, Marian. *In a Gilded Cage: From Heiress to Duchess*. New York: St. Martin's, 1993.

Fox, James. *Five Sisters: The Langhornes of Virginia*. New York: Simon & Schuster, 2000.

Fraser, Hilary, Stephanie Green, and Judith Johnston. *Gender and the Victorian Periodical*. Cambridge: Cambridge University Press, 2003.

Gienow-Hecht, Jessica C. E. *Transmission Impossible: American Journalism as Cultural Diplomacy in Postwar Germany, 1945–1955*. Baton Rouge: Louisiana State University Press, 2002.

Gienow-Hecht, Jessica C. E., and Frank Schumacher, eds. *Culture and International History*. New York: Berghahn Books, 2003.

Gillis, John R. *For Better, For Worse: British Marriages, 1600 to the Present*. Oxford: Oxford University Press, 1985.

Gilmour, David. *Curzon: Imperial Statesman*. New York: Farrar, Straus and Giroux, 1994.

Goradia, Nayana. *Lord Curzon: The Last of the British Moghuls*. Oxford: Oxford University Press, 1993.

Graff, E. J. *What Is Marriage For?* Boston: Beacon, 1999.

Halperin, John. *Eminent Georgians: The Lives of King George V, Elizabeth Bowen, St. John Philby, and Nancy Astor*. New York: St. Martin's, 1995.

Harris, Susan K. *The Cultural Work of the Late Nineteenth-Century Hostess: Annie Adams Fields and Mary Gladstone Drew*. New York: Palgrave Macmillan, 2002.

Hartog, Hendrik. *Man and Wife in America: A History*. Cambridge, Massachusetts: Harvard University Press, 2000.

Hayden, Margaret. *Alva, That Vanderbilt-Belmont Woman*. Wickford, Rhode Island: Dutch Island Press, 1992.

Heald, Morrell, and Lawrence S. Kaplan. *Culture and Diplomacy: The American Experience*. Westport, Connecticut: Greenwood, 1977.

Heathorn, Stephen J. *For Home, Country, and Race: Constructing Gender, Class, and Englishness in the Elementary School, 1880–1914*. Toronto: University of Toronto Press, 2000.

Heindel, R. H. *The American Impact on Great Britain, 1898–1914: A Study of the United States in World History*. New York: Octagon, 1968.

Heineman, Elizabeth D. *What Difference Does a Husband Make? Women and Marital Status in Nazi and Postwar Germany*. Berkeley: University of California Press, 1999.

Hickman, Katie. *Daughters of Britannia: The Lives and Times of Diplomatic Women*. New York: Perennial, 1999.

Higham, Charles. *Dark Lady Winston Churchill's Mother and Her World*. New York: Carroll & Graf, 2007.

————. *The Duchess of Windsor: The Secret Life*. New York: McGraw-Hill, 1988.

Hitchens, Christopher. *Blood, Class, and Empire: The Enduring Anglo-American Relationship*. New York: Nation Books, 1990.

Hobsbawm, E. J. *The Age of Empire, 1875–1914*. London: Weidenfeld & Nicolson, 1987.

Hogan, Michael and Thomas Paterson, eds. *Explaining the History of American Foreign Relations*. Cambridge: Cambridge University Press, 1991.

Homberger, Eric. *Mrs. Astor's New York: Money and Power in a Gilded Age*. New Haven: Yale University Press, 2002.

Horsman, Reginald. *Race and Manifest Destiny: The Origins of American Racial Anglo-Saxonism*. Cambridge, Massachusetts: Harvard University Press, 1981.

Hutto, Richard Jay. *Crowning Glory: American Wives of Princes and Dukes*. Macon, Georgia: Henchard, 2007.

Ignatiev, Noel. *How the Irish Became White*. New York: Routledge, 1995.

Iriye, Akira. *The Globalizing of America, 1913–1945*. Vol. 3 of *The Cambridge History of American Foreign Relations*. Cambridge: Cambridge University Press, 1993.

Jaher, Frederic Cople, ed. *The Rich, the Wellborn and the Powerful: Elites and Upper Classes in History*. Urbana: University of Illinois Press, 1973.

Jalland, Pat. *Women, Marriage and Politics, 1860–1914*. Oxford: Clarendon Press, 1986.

James, Robert Rhodes. *Lord Randolph Churchill: Winston Churchill's Father*. New York: A.S. Barnes, 1960.

Jensen, Kimberly, and Erika Kuhlman, eds. *Women and Transnational Activism in Historical Perspective*. Dordrecht, Netherlands: Republic of Letters Publishing, 2009.

Jones, Katharine W. *Accent on Privilege: English Identities and Anglophilia in the U.S*. Philadelphia: Temple University Press, 2001.

Joseph, *Gilbert M., Catherine LeGrand*, and *Ricardo D. Salvatore*, eds. *Close Encounters of Empire: Writing the Cultural History of U.S.-Latin American Relations*. Durham, North Carolina: Duke University Press, 1998.

Josephson, Matthew. *The Robber Barons: The Great American Capitalists, 1861–1901*. New York: Harcourt, Brace & World, 1934.

Kehoe, Elisabeth. *The Titled Americans: Three American Sisters and the English Aristocratic World into Which They Married*. New York: Atlantic Monthly Press, 2004.

Kenin, Richard. *Return to Albion: Americans in England, 1760–1940*. New York: Holt, Rinehart, Winston, 1979.

Kerber, Linda. *No Constitutional Right to Be Ladies: Women and the Obligation of Citizenship*. New York: Hill & Wang, 1998

King, Greg. *A Season of Splendor: The Court of Mrs. Astor in Gilded Age New York* Hoboken, New Jersey: Wiley, 2009.

Kraus, René. *Young Lady Randolph: The Life and Times of Jennie Jerome, American Mother of Winston Churchill*. New York: G. P. Putnam's Sons, 1943.

LaFeber, Walter. *The American Search for Opportunity, 1865–1913*. Vol. 2 of *The Cambridge History of American Foreign Relations*. Cambridge: Cambridge University Press, 1993.

————. *The New Empire: An Interpretation of American Expansion, 1860–1898*. Ithaca, New York: Cornell University Press, 1963.

Laing, Diana Whitehall. *Mistress of Herself*. Barre, Massachusetts: Barre Publishers, 1965.

Lambert, David, and Alan Lester, eds. *Colonial Lives Across the British Empire: Imperial Careering in the Long Nineteenth Century*. Cambridge: Cambridge University Press, 2006.

Langhorne, Elizabeth. *Nancy Astor and Her Friends.* New York: Praeger, 1974.

Lee, Sir Sidney. *King Edward VII: A Biography.* New York: Macmillan, 1927.

Leslie, Anita. *Edwardians in Love.* New York: Arrow Books, 1974.

———. *Lady Randolph Churchill: The Story of Jennie Jerome.* New York: Charles Scribner's Sons, 1969.

———. *Mr. Frewen of England: A Victorian Adventurer.* London: Hutchinson, 1966.

———. *The Remarkable Mr. Jerome.* New York: Henry Holt and Company, 1954.

Leslie, Shane. *Men Were Different: Five Studies in Late Victorian Biography.* Freeport, New York: Books for Libraries Press, 1937.

Love, Eric T. L. *Race over Empire: Racism and U.S. Imperialism, 1865–1900.* Chapel Hill: University of North Carolina Press, 2004.

Lundberg, Ferdinand. *America's Sixty Families.* New York: Citadel, 1946.

MacColl, Gail, and Carol McD. Wallace. *To Marry an English Lord; Or, How Anglomania Really Got Started.* New York: Workman, 1989.

Madsen, Axel. *John Jacob Astor: America's First Multimillionaire.* New York: Wiley, 2001.

Marsh, Peter T. *Joseph Chamberlain: Entrepreneur in Politics.* New Haven: Yale University Press, 1994.

Martin, Ralph G. *Jennie: The Life of Lady Randolph Churchill.* Vol. 1, *The Romantic Years, 1874–1895.* Englewood Cliffs, New Jersey: Prentice-Hall, 1969.

———. *Jennie: The Life of Lady Randolph Churchill.* Vol. 2, *The Dramatic Years, 1895–1921.* Englewood Cliffs, New Jersey: Prentice-Hall, 1971.

Marton, Kati. *Hidden Power: Presidential Marriages That Shaped Our History.* New York: Anchor Books, 2001.

Masters, Anthony. *Nancy Astor: A Life.* London: Weidenfeld & Nicolson, 1981.

McAllister, Ward. *Society As I Have Found It.* New York: Cassell, 1890.

McCarthy, Kathleen D. *Lady Bountiful Revisited: Women, Philanthropy, and Power.* New Brunswick, New Jersey: Rutgers University Press, 1991.

McKercher, B. J. C., ed. *Anglo-American Relations in the 1920s: The Struggle for Supremacy.* Edmonton: University of Alberta Press, 1990.

McLeod, Kirsty. *The Wives of Downing Street.* London: Collins, 1976.

Minney, R. J. *The Edwardian Age.* Boston: Little, Brown, 1964.

Montgomery, Maureen E. *Gilded Prostitution: Status, Money, and Transatlantic Marriages, 1870–1914.* New York: Routledge, 1989.

Mulanax, Richard B. *The Boer War in American Politics and Diplomacy.* Lanham, Maryland: University Press of America, 1994.

Mulvey, Christopher. *Transatlantic Manners: Social Patterns in Nineteenth-Century Anglo-American Travel Literature.* Cambridge: Cambridge University Press, 1990.

Musolf, Karen J. *From Plymouth to Parliament: A Rhetorical History of Nancy Astor's 1919 Campaign.* New York: St. Martin's, 1999.

Myers, Gustavus. *History of the Great American Fortunes.* Vol. 1 of 3. Chicago: Charles H. Kerr, 1909.

National Archives and Records Administration. *Relating to the Expatriation of Citizens, Hearings Before the Committee on Foreign Affairs of the House of Representatives on H.R. 21358.* Washington, D.C.: GPO, 1912.

Nevill, Ralph. *The World of Fashion, 1837–1922.* London: Methuen, 1923.

Nicolson, Nigel. *Mary Curzon.* New York: Harper & Row, 1977.

Nye, Joseph S. Jr. *Bound to Lead: The Changing Nature of America Power.* New York: Basic Books, 1990.

———. *Soft Power: The Means to Success in World Politics.* Cambridge: Perseus Books, 2004.

Peabody, Sue, and Tyler Stovall, eds. *The Color of Liberty: Histories of Race in France.* Durham, North Carolina: Duke University Press, 2003.

Packard, Jerrold M. *Victoria's Daughters.* New York: St. Martin's, 1998.

Peacock, Virginia Tatnall. *Famous American Belles of the Nineteenth Century.* Philadelphia: Lippincott, 1901.

Pearson, Hesketh. *The Marrying Americans.* New York: Coward McCann, 1961.

———. *The Great Rapprochement: England and the United States, 1895–1914.* New York: Atheneum, 1968.

Pool, Daniel. *What Jane Austen Ate and Charles Dickens Knew: From Fox Hunting to Whist— The Facts of Daily Life in Nineteenth Century England.* New York: Simon & Shuster, 1993.

Prochaska, F. K. *Women and Philanthropy in Nineteenth-Century England.* Oxford: Oxford University Press, 1980.

Pullar, Philippa. *Gilded Butterflies: The Rise and Fall of the London Season.* London: Hamish Hamilton, 1978.

Rapson, Richard L. *Britons View America: Travel Commentary, 1860–1935.* Seattle: University of Washington Press, 1971.

Reynolds, K. E. *Aristocratic Women and Political Society in Victorian Britain.* Oxford: Clarendon, 1998.

Roediger, David R. *Working toward Whiteness: How America's Immigrants Became White: The Strange Journey from Ellis Island to the Suburbs.* New York: Basic Books, 2005.

Ronaldshay, Earl of. *The Life of Lord Curzon: Being the Authorized Biography of George Nathaniel Marquess Curzon of Kedleston, K.G.* Vol. 1. New York: Boni & Liveright, 1928.

——— *The Life of Lord Curzon: Being the Authorized Biography of George Nathaniel Marquess Curzon of Kedleston, K.G.* Vol. 2. New York: Boni & Liveright, 1928.

Rubenstein, W. D., ed. *Wealth and the Wealthy in the Modern World.* London: Croom Helm, 1980.

Shoultz, Lars. *Beneath the United States: A History of U.S. Policy toward Latin America.* Cambridge, Massachusetts: Harvard University Press, 1998.

Scott, Joan Wallach. *Gender and the Politics of History.* New York: Columbia University Press, 1988.

Seba, Anne. *American Jennie: The Remarkable Life of Lady Randolph Churchill.* New York: Norton, 2007.

Soames, Mary, ed. *Winston and Clementine: The Personal Letters of the Churchills.* New York: Houghton Mifflin, 2001.

Stasz, Clarice. *The Vanderbilt Women: Dynasty of Wealth, Glamour, and Tragedy.* New York: St. Martin's, 1991.

Stanley, Louis Thomas. *The London Season.* Boston: Houghton Mifflin, 1956.

Stead, William Thomas. *The Americanization of the World; or, The Trend of the Twentieth Century.* New York: Harce Markley, 1902.

Stetson, Charlotte Perkins. *Women and Economics: A Study of the Economic Relations between Men and Women as a Factor in Social Evolution.* Boston: Small, Maynard, 1898.

Stuart, Amanda Mackenzie. *Consuelo and Alva Vanderbilt: The Story of a Daughter and a Mother in the Gilded Age.* New York: HarperCollins, 2005.

Sykes, Christopher. *Nancy: The Life of Lady Astor.* Chicago: Academy Chicago, 1972.

Temperley, Howard. *Britain and America since Independence.* New York: Palgrave, 2002.

Tinker, Hugh. *Viceroy: Curzon to Mountbatten.* Oxford: Oxford University Press, 1997.

Titled Americans: A List of American Ladies Who Have Married Foreigners of Rank. New York: Street & Smith, 1890.

Tweedsmuir, Susan. *The Edwardian Lady.* London: Camelot, 1966.

Vanderbilt, Arthur T. II. *Fortune's Children: The Fall of the House of Vanderbilt.* New York: Morrow, 1989.

Van Minner, Cornelius A. *Franklin Delano Roosevelt and His Contemporaries: Foreign Perceptions of an American President.* New York: St. Martin's, 1991.

Veblen, Thorstein. *The Theory of the Leisure Class: An Economic Study of Institutions.* New York: Modern Library, 1934.

Virden, Jenel. *Good-bye, Piccadilly: British War Brides in America.* Urbana: University of Illinois Press, 1996.

Waltz, Waldo Emerson. *The Nationality of Married Women: A Study of Domestic Policies and International Legislation.* Urbana: University of Illinois Press, 1937.

Wecter, Dixon. *The Saga of American Society: A Record of Social Aspiration 1607–1937.* New York: Charles Scribner's Sons, 1937.

Willoughby, Sir Maycock, *With Mr. Chamberlain in the United States and Canada.* London: Chatto & Windus, 1914.

Yalom, Marilyn. *A History of the Wife.* New York: Perennial, 2001.

Young, Nancy Beck. *Lou Henry Hoover: Activist First Lady.* Lawrence: University Press of Kansas, 2004.

Zeiler, Thomas W. *Ambassadors in Pinstripe: The Spalding World Baseball Tour and the Birth of the American Empire.* Lanham, Maryland: Rowman & Littlefield, 2006.

Articles

Acland, Emily A. "A Lady's American Notes." *Nineteenth Century,* 1888, 403–13.

Allgor, Catherine. "'A Republican in a Monarchy': Louisa Catherine Adams in Russia." *Diplomatic History* 21, no. 1 (1997): 15–43.

Anglo-American. "American Women in English Society." *Harper's Bazaar,* July 1905, 602–9.

Astor, Viscountess. "Lady Astor Interviews Herself." *Saturday Evening Post,* March 4, 1939, 5–6, 76–79.

Astor, Viscountess, M.P. "What Women Can Do in Politics That Men Cannot Do." *Woman's Home Companion,* September 1920, 7–8.

Baker, Abby G. "International Marriages." *Independent,* October 1908, 750–58.

Baker, George Barr. "Dollars vs. Pedigree: The Truth About International Marriages." *Everybody's Magazine,* February, 1907, 167–76.

Cavendish, Richard. "Joseph Chamberlain Resigns as Colonial Secretary." *History Today* 53, no. 9 (2003): 54–66.

Chaudhuri, Nupur. "Memsahibs and Motherhood in Nineteenth-Century Colonial India." *Victorian Studies* 31, no. 4 (Summer 1988): 517–35.

Colonial. "Titled Colonials v. Titled Americans." *Contemporary Review* 87 (June 1905): 861–69.

Cooper, Dana. "From New England to Old England: The Anglo-American Life of Mary Endicott Chamberlain Carnegie, 1864–1957," *Massachusetts Historical Review* 13 (2011): 97–125.

———. "Country by Birth, Country by Marriage: American Women's Transnational War Efforts in Great Britain, 1895–1918," *Women and Transnational Activism in Historical Perspective,* edited by Kimberly Jensen and Erika Kuhlman (Dordrecht, The Netherlands: Republic of Letters Publishing, 2010), 37–62.

Cott, Nancy. "Marriage and Women's Citizenship in the United States, 1830–1934." *American Historical Review* 103 (December 1998): 1440–74.

Crozier, Blanche. "The Changing Basis of Women's Nationality." *Boston University Law Review* 14 (1934): 129–53.

Davis, Richard W. "'We Are All Americans Now!' Anglo-American Marriages in the Later Nineteenth Century." *Proceedings of the American Philosophical Society* 135, no. 2 (June 1991): 140–99.

Duer, Elizabeth. "New York Society a Generation Ago." *Harper's Monthly Magazine,* November 1902, 109–14.

Guttsman, W. L. "The Changing Social Structure of the British Political Elite, 1886–1915." *British Journal of Sociology* 2 (1951): 122–34.

Harrison, Gladys. "The Nationality of Married Women." *New York University Law Quarterly Review* 9 (June 1932): 445–62.

Hartog, Hendrik. "Marital Exits and Marital Expectations in Nineteenth Century America." *Georgetown Law Journal* 80 (October 1991): 95–129.

Hazeltine, Mayo Williamson. "Studies of New York Society." *Nineteenth Century,* May 1892, 762–77.

Herman, Sondra R. "Loving Courtship or the Marriage Market? The Ideal and Its Critics, 1871–1911." *American Quarterly* 25 (May 1973): 235–53.

Hoppe, Michelle Jean. "The London Season." *Literary Liaisons,* http://literary-liasons.com/article024.html, accessed April 24, 2006.

Jackson, Peter, Nicola Thomas, and Claire Dwyer, "Consuming Transnational Fashion in London and Mumbai." *Geoforum* 38, no. 5 (2007) 908–24.

Kahn, Richard J. "Women and Men at Sea: Gender Debate Aboard the Hospital Ship *Maine* during the Boer War, 1899–1900." *Journal of the History of Medicine & Allied Sciences* 56, no. 2 (April 2001): 111–39.

Kipling, Rudyard. "The White Man's Burden." *McClure's Magazine,* February 1899, 290–91.

Kolchin, Peter. "Whiteness Studies: The New History of Race in America." *Journal of America History* 89, no 1 (June 2002): 154–73.

Kramer, Paul A. "Empires, Exceptions, and Anglo-Saxons: Race and Rule between the British and United States Empires, 1880–1910." *Journal of American History* 88 (March 2002): 1315–53.

Kerber, Linda K. "Separate Spheres, Female Worlds, Woman's Place: The Rhetoric of Women's History." *Journal of American History* 75, no. 1 (1988): 9–39.

LaFeber, Walter. "The Background of Cleveland's Venezuelan Policy: A Reinterpretation." *American Historical Review* 66 (July 1961): 947–67.

Marlborough, Consuelo. "Hostels for Women." *Nineteenth Century and After,* May 1911, 858–66.

Marlborough, The Duchess of. "The Position of Woman." *North American Review* 189 (January–March 1909): 11–24, 180–93, 352–59.

Marriott-Watson, H. B. "The Deleterious Effect of Americanization upon Women." *Nineteenth Century and After*, 1903, 782–93.

"The Most Influential Anglo-Saxon Society Woman in the World." *Current Literature* 45, no. 6 (1908): 626–29.

Nicolosi, Ann Marie. "'We Do Not Want Our Girls to Marry Foreigners': Gender, Race, and American Citizenship." *National Women's Studies Association Journal* 13, no. 3 (2001): 1–21.

Pauncefote, Hon. Maud. "Washington DC." *Nineteenth Century and After*, 1903, 275–83.

Pumphrey, R. E. "The Introduction of Industrialists into the British Peerage: A Study in the Adaptation of a Social Institution." *American Historical Review* 65, no. 1 (1959): 1–16.

Rennella, Mark, and Whitney Walton. "Planned Serendipity: American Travelers and the Transatlantic Voyage in the Nineteenth and Twentieth Centuries." *Journal of Social History* 38, no 2 (2004): 365–83.

Rosenberg, Emily S. "Gender." *Journal of American History* 77 (June 1990): 116–24.

———. "Walking the Borders." *Diplomatic History* 14 (Fall 1990): 565–74.

Sapiro, Virginia. "Women, Citizenship, and Nationality: Immigration and Naturalization Policies in the United States." *Politics and Society* 13 (March 1984): 1–26.

Scott, Joan W. "Gender: A Useful Category of Historical Analysis." *American Historical Review* 91, no. 5 (December 1986): 1043–75.

Stocking, George. "The Turn-of-the-Century Concept of Race." *Modernism/Modernity* 1, no 1 (January 1994): 4–16.

de Thierry, C. "American Women from a Colonial Point of View." *Contemporary Review* 70 (July–December 1896): 516–28.

Thomas, Nicola. "Embodying Imperial Spectacle: Dressing Lady Curzon, Vicereine of India, 1899–1905." *Cultural Geographies* 14, no. 3 (2007): 369–400.

———. "Exploring the Boundaries of Biography: The Family and Friendship Networks of Lady Curzon, Vicereine of India 1898–1905." *Journal of Historical Geography* 30, no. 3 (2004): 496–519.

Watt, D. C. "America and the British Foreign Policy-Making Elite, from Joseph Chamberlain to Anthony Eden, 1895–1956." *Review of Politics* 25, no. 1 (January 1963): 3–33.

Wood, Molly M. "'Commanding Beauty' and 'Gentle Charm': American Women and Gender in the Early Twentieth Century Foreign Service." *Diplomatic History* 31, no. 3 (June 2007): 505–30.

———. "A Diplomat's Wife in Mexico: Creating Professional, Political, and National Identities in the Early Twentieth Century." *Frontiers: A Journal of Women's Studies* 25, no. 3 (2004): 104–33.

Zeiler, Thomas W. "The Diplomatic History Bandwagon: A State of the Field." *Journal of American History* 95, no. 4 (March 2009): 1053–73

Dissertations and Unpublished Papers

Burk, Kathleen. "Anglo-American Marital Relations, 1870–1945." Paper presented at Barnard's Inn. Gresham College Lectures. Holborn, London, England. February 3, 2004.

Gienow-Hecht, Jessica. "The Forgotten Victorians; or, Why Historians Hate American Nineteenth Century Culture." Paper presented at the German Association for American Studies annual meeting, Wittenberg, Germany, April 5, 2005.

Hughes, Katherine Lee. "Wives of Public Men." PhD diss., Columbia University, 1995.

Knoles, Barbara Ann. "Orphans of the Storm": The Integration of Women in Parliament, 1918–1988." PhD diss., Northern Arizona University, 1988.

Macías-González, Víctor Manuel. "The Mexican Aristocracy and Porfirio Díaz." PhD diss., Texas Christian University, 1999.

Moore, Robert J. Jr. "Social Darwinism, Social Imperialism, and the Rapprochement: Theodore Roosevelt and the English-Speaking Peoples, 1886–1901." PhD diss., Washington University, 2003.

Musolf, Karen Joy. "The Angel Sings: The Rhetorical Quest of Lady Nancy Astor, November 1919." PhD diss., University of Minnesota, 1994.

Napier, Christopher. "The British Aristocracy, Capital and Income, and Nineteenth-Century Company Accounting." Paper presented at the Ninth Accounting, Business, and Financial Conference, Cardiff, Wales. September 17–18, 1997.

Nicolosi, Ann Marie. "We Do Not Want Our Girls to Marry Foreigners": Gender, Race, and American Citizenship." PhD diss., Rutgers, The State University of New Jersey, 1999.

Plesur, Milton. "Looking Outward: American Attitudes toward Foreign Affairs in the Years from Hayes to Harrison." PhD diss., University of Rochester, 1954.

Steigerwalt, Albert K. "The National Association of Manufacturers: Organization and Policies, 1895–1914." PhD diss., University of Michigan, 1952.

Vickers, Sarah Pauline. "The Life of Ruth Bryan Owen: Florida's First Congresswoman and America's First Woman Diplomat." PhD diss., Florida State University, 1994.

Wood, Molly Marie. "An American Diplomat's Wife in Mexico: Gender, Politics, and Foreign Affairs Activism, 1907–1927." PhD diss., University of South Carolina, 1998.

Index

256   INDEX

Jerome, Leonard: adultery of, 42–43; daughters of, 41–42, 45, 53
Jerome, Leonie, 35, 42
Johnson, Albert, 185

Kahn, Richard, 64
Kedleston estate, 99; Curzon's love for, 94, 103, 122
Kennedy, Joseph and Rose, 88
Kerber, Linda, 3
King, Greg, 9
Kipling, Caroline Starr Balestier, 31
Kipling, Rudyard, 30, 31, 120–21
Kitchener, Horatio Herbert, 115, 117–18

LaFeber, Walter, 18, 38
land, as wealth, 20–21
Lane, John, 59–61
Langhorne, Chiswell Dabney, 151–56, 159
Langhorne, Harry, 153
Langhorne, Irene, 153, 155–56
Langhorne, Keene, 153
Langhorne, Lizzie, 153
Langhorne, Nancy Witcher Keene, 151–52, 155–56
Langhorne, Nora, 153, 167
Langhorne, Phyllis, 153–54, 156, 159, 167
Langhorne, William ("Buck"), 153
Lansdowne, Lady, 116
League of Nations, Nancy Astor promoting U.S. membership in, 169–71
Lee, Julia, 153
leisure destinations, of American elite, 23–24
Leiter, Joseph, 93, 105
Leiter, Levi Zeigler, 37, 91–93, 99, 106, 116
Leiter, Marguerite ("Daisy"), 93, 108
Leiter, Mary Teresa Carver, 91–93
Leiter, Mary Victoria. See Curzon, Mary Victoria Leiter
Leiter, Nancy ("Nannie"), 93, 108
Leiter family, 105, 121–22
Lind, Jenny, 42
Lloyd George, David, 162–63, 167, 186
Lodge, Senator and Mrs. Henry Cabot, 81
London, 97. See also England; American community in, 39, 87, 142–43; as Americans' top destination, 25, 43; Mary Curzon in, 100–101, 111; Mary Endicott Chamberlain's first impression of, 71–72; Mary Leiter's social acceptance in, 93–94; Women's Municipal Party in, 147–48
London County Council, Consuelo Vanderbilt elected to, 148
London Season, 44, 128; Churchills' success in, 47–48; exodus following, 26–27; leading to marriages, 25, 27, 46; Mary Curzon missing,

100, 110; wives expecting continuation of, 37, 100
Lorne, Marquess of, 39
love, 35; role in transatlantic marriages, 17, 74, 98, 161; transatlantic marriage in spite of others', 123–24; transatlantic marriage not focused on, 37, 186; Vanderbilt/Marlborough marriage not based on, 131–32

MacArthur, R. S., 181
Mackenzie, Ethel, 184
Mackenzie, Gordon, 184
Macmillan, Margaret, 172
Mandeville, Kim, 126
Marker, Raymond, 108
Marlborough, Consuelo Vanderbilt. See Balsan, Consuelo Vanderbilt Marlborough
Marlborough, Duchess, 50, 52–53
Marlborough, 8th Duke of, 49
Marlborough, 9th Duke of (Charles Spencer-Churchill), 190; divorce of, 136, 148–50; reluctant marriage of, 103–4, 123–24
Marlborough family, Consuelo Vanderbilt and, 132–33, 142, 149
marriages. See also transatlantic marriages: desire for, 75, 159; effects on U.S. citizenship, 185–86; expectations of, 37, 45–46; gender roles in, 96, 98, 100, 107, 154; importance of choice in, 2, 95; London Season as market for, 25, 27; Nancy Langhorne's to Robert Shaw, 154–55; in oldest methods of diplomacy, 14; pressure for intra-American, 180, 183–85; required for heiresses, 30–31; sexuality in and outside of, 37, 48
Married Women's Act (Cable Act, 1922), 184–86
Martin, Cornelia Sherman, 36–37
Mary, Queen, 87
Mary Curzon Lodging House for Poor Women, 140
McAllister, Sarah Gibbons, 22
McAllister, Ward, 20, 22–24, 28
McCormick, Cyrus, 19
McGavin, Charles, 181–82
McKenna, Joseph, 184
mediation: Mary Curzon's between husband and Kitchener, 115, 117–18; Mary Curzon's skills at, 91, 105, 110, 194
military, as unofficial ambassadors, 12
Milner, Alfred, 111
Monroe Doctrine, 56–57, 82
Morgan, J. P., 19
Motley, John Lothrop, 31
Musolf, Karen, 166
Myers, Gustavus, 20